ANTI-AMERICANISM

ANTI-AMERICANISM

Edited by

ANDREW ROSS and KRISTIN ROSS

New York University Press • *New York and London*

NEW YORK UNIVERSITY PRESS
New York and London
www.nyupress.org

© 2004 by New York University
All rights reserved

Library of Congress Cataloging-in-Publication Data
Anti-Americanism / edited by Andrew Ross and Kristin Ross.
p. cm.
Includes bibliographical references and index.
ISBN 0–8147–7566–7 (cloth : alk. paper) —
ISBN 0–8147–7567–5 (pbk. : alk. paper)
1. Anti-Americanism.   2. United States—Relations—
Foreign countries.   I. Ross, Andrew, 1956–   II. Ross, Kristin.
E840.A675   2004
327.73—dc22   2004007955

New York University Press books are printed on acid-free paper,
and their binding materials are chosen for strength and durability.

Manufactured in the United States of America

c 10 9 8 7 6 5 4 3 2 1
p 10 9 8 7 6 5 4 3 2 1

Contents

Introduction

Andrew Ross and Kristin Ross

ANY TREATMENT OF THE TOPIC OF THIS BOOK has to begin by acknowledging that caricature is intrinsic to the standpoint known as anti-Americanism. After all, taking Americanism seriously in the first place means accepting vastly exaggerated versions of ideals, traits, and postures that are believed to be quite distinct from those of other cultures and countries. "Only in America" is the phrase commonly used to typify this belief in U.S. exceptionalism, and it is a simple, but effective, wand for waving away the complexity of social life in the United States. Repugnance or hostility toward this overstated profile of Americanism is no less useful. It can make the antagonist feel morally superior, or it can validate his or her own native culture; it can help to trigger and organize dissent, or it can dramatize a grievance against imperious conduct. Just as important, anti-Americanism conveys benefits to the accused that cannot be underestimated. A nation bent on gathering power for itself needs threats and foes (concocted ones if necessary) more than it needs allies.

Anti-Americanism is as old as political modernity and could be said to be one of its founding discourses. After all, the establishment of the U.S. republic and its Constitution was intended to be an idealization of how a free citizenry would live according to the Rights of Man. Naturally, all of those who stood to benefit from pre-Enlightenment traditions could be expected to object to the result. Consequently, Americaphobia was a habitual attitude among the ruling classes and the traditional intelligentsia of Europe from 1776 on. The more modernization came to be identified with Yankee enterprise, the sharper the antipathy became. Perennial targets for rancor at the American Way included its moralistic work ethic, its appetites for novelty in commerce and its simplicity in taste and manners, its hectic pursuit of materialism, its enthusiasm for a demotic culture, and its embrace, however ambiguous, of multiracialism.[1] Foreign aversion to these and other qualities was predominantly genteel and was emulated to some degree by the upper class in the United States itself. This pattern of contempt was tempered by more populist responses when the foreign experience of Americanization became massified in the course of the twentieth century, but its elitist instincts have proven resilient to this day. Indeed, the patrician sentiment behind this disposition has been consistent enough that it can be loosely categorized as anti-Americanism from above.

Anti-Americanism from below was another matter. It took root in organic responses to the brutal record of native genocide and plantation slavery and was nurtured by opposition to the territorial expansion that sparked the Mexican-American War (1846–1848). Increasingly, dissent against Washington drew on neighbors' fears about the imperial ambitions of the "giant with the seven-league boots," as José Martí famously described the Yankee state stepping beyond its borders. The declaration of the Monroe Doctrine (1823), ostensibly to protect the new Latin American republics from European colonization, established what would prove to be a durable formula for foreign intervention. Washington would pursue its own imperial interests overseas in the name, or under the guise, of defending other countries from imperialist threats. Thus was struck the template for the Spanish-American War and the subsequent conquest of former Spanish possessions. By the time of Theodore Roosevelt's openly colonial adventures, the credo of Manifest Destiny not only served the expansionist needs of U.S. capital but also wrapped its missionary ideals in doctrines of racial supremacy.

The ensuing century of U.S. dominion over Central and Latin America was typified by Washington's repression of most of the region's efforts at democratic reform and economic self-determination. The profits from this policy flowed into Wall Street. Looking back on his illustrious career in the U.S. Marine Corps (in which he was twice awarded the Medal of Honor), the legendary Major-General Smedley Butler summarized the role he had played in what he called "war as a racket":

> I helped make Honduras "right" for American fruit companies in 1903. I helped make Mexico, especially Tampico, safe for American oil interests in 1914. I helped make Haiti and Cuba a decent place for the National City Bank boys to collect revenues in. I helped in the raping

of half a dozen Central American republics for the benefits of Wall Street. The record of racketeering is long. I helped purify Nicaragua for the international banking house of Brown Brothers in 1909–12. I brought light to the Dominican Republic for American safeguard interests in 1916. In China, I helped to see to it that Standard Oil went its way unmolested.[2]

In China and other parts of Asia, Butler's paymasters at least had to contend with stiff competition from the great European powers. Virtually uncontested in its hemispheric sphere of influence, the United States established throughout the Americas a record of exploitation so systematic that opposition to Washington assumed its purest anti-imperialist expression in Latin America. After the brief hiatus of the united front against fascism, this tradition of dissent was reborn with the advent of the cold war. Fortified by a revitalized sense of mission, the Truman Doctrine extended the hemispheric purview of the Monroe Doctrine to every corner of the globe. Some foreign states escaped the fierce pressure to align themselves with the free world, but there were few political movements anywhere, whether socialist, nationalist, or regionalist, that did not feel the heat if they deviated from the gospel of capitalist modernization. As a result, tens of millions died in regions—Asia, Latin America, and Africa—where the cold war turned out to be red-hot. Wherever the combination of right-wing death squads and psychotic dictators proved untenable, the Communist threat was wielded as a restraint on the most extreme expressions of anti-Americanism. The empire of the dollar provided additional economic controls. An extensive arrangement of trade incentives and rewards effectively put a check on insurgencies and ensured that client states remained within the orbit of the capitalist system. Even so, the worldwide revulsion unleashed by the high-profile U.S. intervention in Vietnam broke through the floodgates that had been designed to contain anti-American sentiment. The Reagan administration's revival of the cold war, implemented through a series of counterinsurgency campaigns in Central America and elsewhere, provoked a similar response.

When the United States emerged from the cold war, it confronted a unipolar world where its dominance was neither challenged nor defined by threats and enemies. Its power could be expressed primarily in economic terms through the Washington Consensus, an accord by which U.S. financial elites promoted and managed free-trade policies around the world on behalf of the national capital pools of the G-8 industrial powers and the major banks. In line with structural adjustment policies pioneered by the International Monetary Fund (IMF) and the World Bank, trade and investment liberalization continued to be imposed on poor countries in nonnegotiable terms. While the intimidation of U.S. trade representatives, and even the U.S. military, was never far away, the official face of neoliberalism was that of a multilateral rule-based system, enforced by institutions like the World Trade Organization. Opposition to neoliberalism took many forms—from the IMF food riots to the Zapatista uprising—before it crystallized as a loosely organized mass movement in protests in Seattle, Genoa, Quebec, and elsewhere and took a more formal turn in the initiatives for alternative globalization discussed at the World Social Forums in Porto Alegre. Because the movement's main targets were global corporations and the free-trade rules written to benefit them, the role of nation-states was bracketed, in part for strategic reasons. With the most righteous anger reserved for the likes of Monsanto, Nike, Philip Morris, Pfizer, Disney, General Electric, Shell, Chevron, Wal Mart, and McDonald's, the ancient sport of nation-bashing was perceived by some in the movement as a distraction, almost an anachronism. Yet the fact that it was these American-led multinationals, and not Toyota, Unilever, or Vivendi, that became the movement's prime targets revealed an acknowledgment of sorts of the leadership role the United States played in managing and organizing the world capitalist system. Even in these circles, any assumptions about the death of anti-Americanism, or the withering away of the nation-state in the era of globalization, proved premature. A view of inexorable international economic forces subsuming and subordinating national processes had to give way to a more nuanced perspective: one in which a major role continued to be played by national-level policies and actors and in which a dominant role was played by the United States.

The launching of the so-called war on terror in 2001 (this time around, "a war without end") confirmed that it had taken little more than a decade since the collapse of the Communist menace for Washington hawks to cultivate an enemy fully adequate to their ambitions. Although the Bush administration had pursued unilateralism in policy making from its first day in office, the events of September 11 presented themselves almost as a tailor-made opportunity to justify the new policy of going it alone. Bush and his cohorts steadily withdrew the United

States from international agreements, promoted regional and bilateral trade treaties, and resorted to military adventurism in a punitive campaign against "rogue states" of its own choosing. The legacy of Wilsonian internationalism, including its intricate postwar architecture of diplomacy, was brusquely tossed aside. In Washington, the customary posture of denying American imperial ambitions quickly gave way to a more open acknowledgment that the United States was assuming the burden of what Michael Ignatieff calls an "empire lite": a global hegemony whose "grace notes are free markets, human rights and democracy, enforced by the most awesome military power the world has ever known."[3]

Initially, and especially among U.S. allies, the September 11 attacks generated their share of sympathy. Gestures of solidarity came from unlikely quarters. Most eloquently, Le Monde's editorial page declared, "Nous sommes tous américains," the editorialist explicitly echoing JFK's "Ich bin ein Berliner" statement in 1962. But even this gesture met with widespread popular outcry in France from citizens who presumably would have preferred their sympathy for the victims to be expressed with a "Nous sommes tous des New-Yorkais," and not via an identification with the country at large. Outside the core precincts of Atlanticism, much of the world surfed along on a wave of schadenfreude, openly savoring the uncommon spectacle of the United States as victim. Within a year, the gunslinger chauvinism displayed by the Bush administration (exacerbated by its crackdown on immigrants and its illegal treatment of detainees) had cost the United States most of the goodwill, along with the ambiguous political capital that accrues to victims. Its bullying campaign to wage war in Iraq, and the slipshod reconstruction effort that accompanied the Anglo-American occupation, frittered away any of the remnants. European leaders (Blair, Aznar, Berlusconi) who sided with Washington were isolated and humiliated at home. France was restored to its time-honored place in the anti-American firmament. Global public opinion (identified by the New York Times as the "second superpower" after tens of millions of antiwar protesters took to the streets on February 15, 2003) appeared to be united as never before in fierce opposition to the conduct of American policy.

Was there any evidence that Bush officials agonized about this eruption of anti-Americanism? Shortly after September 11, Charlotte Beers (former chairwoman of Ogilvy & Mather and J. Walter Thompson) was appointed as Under Secretary of State for Public Affairs and

Public Diplomacy in an effort to improve the image of the United States abroad. Though she had no experience in international diplomacy, it was assumed that her expertise in the Madison Avenue art of brand management would be more than adequate to the mission at hand. Secretary of State Colin Powell brushed aside the obvious criticisms: "We are selling a product. We need someone who can re-brand diplomacy." After all, he added, "she got me to buy Uncle Ben's rice." Aside from the crude propaganda leaflets and psy-ops warfare in Afghanistan and Iraq, most of Beer's efforts were concentrated on promoting Brand USA among Muslim populations in the Middle East. Videos, booklets, PSAs, and broadcasts on Arab-language radio propagated the view that the United States was a multicultural society that tolerated all religious faiths.[4] Yet, none of the materials addressed, or sought to explain, the most salient reason for hostility in the region: Washington's unswerving pro-Israeli policy.

Beers resigned after less than a year, ostensibly for health reasons, though many sources allege that she and her staff found that the mile-high obstacles encountered early on in the effort to win over the natives suggested the campaign would prove unwinnable. (A similar, covert effort launched by the Department of Defense, under the name of Office of Strategic Influence, was even more short-lived when the Pentagon's plan—to push news items and, almost undoubtedly, disinformation on foreign journalists—was ditched after its public disclosure caused a media outcry.) Even if Beers did not see the writing on the wall, she was right to throw in the towel. The administration's self-righteous zeal guaranteed that the U.S. propaganda war abroad would be a lost cause. In the subsequent Iraqi campaign, Al-Jazeera and a hundred other foreign media sources trumped Washington's efforts to control information and define international opinion about the war. Nowhere else in the world was the public force-fed the kind of high-calorie militarism cooked up by the U.S. networks. Even CNN International regularly ran a split screen in its broadcasts, to accommodate the coverage of civilian casualties that was demanded by non-U.S. audiences in the two hundred countries reached by the network.

In September 2002, the State Department's Bureau of Intelligence and Research revealed that it had been conducting research on worldwide anti-Americanism and that it was convening a conference, in conjunction with the CIA's National Intelligence Council, "to explore its various manifestations and roots." According to Richard Boucher, the department's spokesman, U.S. officials needed to understand "the sources and causes and reasons that people don't like us in some places, if we're going to counteract that." A group of scholars and writers was invited to brief officials, with the overall goal of "improving the quality of the product" of U.S. intelligence on the topic. Conference panel titles included "Regional Attitudes toward the United States," "Has the American Model Become a Lightning Rod for Global Discourse?" and "New Players in the Anti-American Coalition—Has Soft Power Hurt or Helped America's Image?" Though the proceedings were not publicized, it is unlikely that the handpicked participants did anything but affirm the customary U.S. view that dissenters are irrationally driven by resentment and envy at the power and material affluence of the United States or that at best they are indulging in the bad side of a love-hate relationship with American idealism. If the title of the third panel was any indication, the organizers also intended to gather opinion on whether hard power might be a better way to deal with America's image problem.

By the summer of 2003, public commentary was no longer preoccupied with how the Bush administration understood, or intended to combat, anti-Americanism. Rather, opinion elites, tempted by the juicy topic of "American empire," had begun to wonder whether the United States was now so powerful that it no longer needed to do anything about the problem. The first serious airing of the concept of the "new imperialism" in the mainstream media came in April 2002 from Robert Cooper, senior adviser to Tony Blair. In a much-discussed essay, he called for a "liberal imperialism" that would be "acceptable to a world of human rights and cosmopolitan values." With so many states incapable of safeguarding their own security, "all the conditions for imperialism are there," he argued, "but both the supply and demand for imperialism have dried up. And yet the weak still need the strong and the strong still need an orderly world." Cooper's value-added imperialism ("an imperialism which, like all imperialism, aims to bring order and organisation but which rests today on the voluntary principle") was what the newly cooperative syndicate of Old Europe had to offer its former dominions.[5]

Across the Atlantic, the hawks in the Bush circle had an even less collegial idea of what the new imperialism meant. Drawing on a common agenda hashed out during their prior discussions as members of the Project for a New American Century, they argued that U.S. hegemony should be perceived as a "duty" on the part of a "preeminent power" that cannot "shirk its responsibilities" to the rest of the world.[6] These views were embodied in the Pentagon's new National Security Strategy (September 2001), which declared the U.S. intention "to exercise our right of self-defense by acting preemptively" to eliminate all potential rivals. The formulation of this belligerent policy rested solely on an assessment of U.S. interests and made no provision at all for the kind of "cooperative empire" proposed by Cooper. Nor was there much to suggest otherwise in the record of U.S. conduct since September 11. The Bush administration's fierce passion for flexing the nation's military might appeared to run directly against the grain of diplomatic culture, even among the Pentagon command. It suggested a mentality that was oblivious even to the kind of criticism traditionally labeled as anti-Americanism and that Washington was accustomed to rely on to affirm the righteousness of its policy making. Either the hostility was much too intense and widespread to manage, or else it no longer mattered.

In any event, the vision of a new imperium traveled well beyond the hawks. Human rights ideologues like Ignatieff, cited earlier, and some "second thoughts" liberals, persuaded by the concept of the "just war," began to speak out loud about the need for Americans to accept, however reluctantly, the imperial mantle.[7] It would somehow be unhealthy, proposed several "limps" (as the liberal imperialists have been nicknamed), to continue in the vein of denial about the hegemonic role that the United States already played in geopolitics. National psychology would be better served by open acknowledgment of the existence of the American empire. To prepare public consciousness for what was deemed unavoidable, comparisons with previous world empires were laid out in great detail.[8] Within this orbit of opinion, it was rare to hear imperialism condemned outright. Far more prevalent was a nostalgic return to counting up the glories and benefits, the roads and the hospitals, bequeathed to the less fortunate by hard-working imperialists of the past. The tenor of the debate was governed by the assumption that the United States might turn out to be an inept imperialist, a bad manager, lacking in the dedication and the rigor that were required for successful colonial administration. The implication was that, for the benign sake of world order, any anti-imperialism that had traditionally operated at the popular level in the United States ought to be put to rest.

Leftists have been quick to point out that the Bush administration's recent season of militarism is not qualitatively different from Washington's long record of foreign interventions, dating, in the postbellum era, from the 1893 coup that led to the annexation of Hawaii. The Marines have never needed provocation to launch preemptive strikes in other countries, nor has the record of territorial dispossession been any less dependent on nostrums about "peace through strength." Left responses to the new American imperium draw on the traditions of neo-Marxist analysis that see imperialism as an intrinsic aspect of capitalist accumulation. The mechanisms of global accumulation that systematically favor the United States and other core nations occasionally require extraordinary measures to bring "rogue states" into conformity. For some on the left, imperial wars like the U.S. invasion of Iraq are viewed as the disarming and refashioning of wayward states; once "reshaped," these can then meet the needs of the countries at the center. For others, the new blatant militarism the United States proposes as a response to global terrorism derives from economic weakness and masks a somewhat desperate attempt to sustain a threatened hegemony within the global system.[9]

In addition, it has long been argued (and not only on the left) that it is precisely because of popular belief in one form of American exceptionalism—that we are an anti-imperial, anti-colonial power by birthright—that Washington has been able to throw its weight around so often and with such impunity, overthrowing democratic governments, tossing aside international law, sponsoring one brutal dictatorship after another, and commandeering commercial markets and monopolies on behalf of U.S. corporations. It is not at all clear, then, what benefits are to be drawn from jettisoning a conventional wisdom that has proven so serviceable for so long. Nor is it a given that the outcome will be good for business—an axiomatic rule of American life.

Throughout the world, the repercussions of these policies and beliefs—whether imperial or anti-imperial—are a very serious matter. Yet, public discussion, especially in the United States, has been limited to a relatively narrow band of political opinion, dominated all too often by fast talk with scant basis in historical evidence. Alternately, evidence is offered in a statistical form through data collected by opinion polling. A case in point is the rolling survey of worldwide public opinion about the United States conducted by the Pew Research Center since the summer of 2001, under the direction of Madeleine Albright. (These surveys followed a long-established practice of polling for anti-American views in Europe, first adopted by the Unites States Information Agency in the 1950s.) The periodic publication of the Pew survey results charted a precipitous slide in the image of the United States. A summary of the June 2003 survey report concluded that the war on Iraq "had widened the rift between Americans and Western Europeans, further inflamed the Muslim world, softened support for the war on terrorism, and significantly weakened global public support for the pillars of the post–World War II era—the UN and the North Atlantic alliance."[10]

Not surprisingly, these results, pronounced to be the largest survey of global opinion ever conducted, attracted a good deal of attention from media organs accustomed to acknowledging the primacy of polling in modern politics. From month to month, the public could play the spectator sport of estimating why the United States had won a few percentage points in Uzbekistan or Nigeria, both of which appeared to host a majority pro-American sentiment, or lost considerably more support, as was the case in Turkey, Russia, Argentina, Jordan, and almost every other country in the world, for that matter. The result was a crude, if popular, way of suggesting that the essence of a complex spectrum of political views and attitudes was easily knowable and that its temperamental dimensions could be reduced to numbers on a graph. The surveys also promoted the more ominous view that global public opinion might, one day, be researched, spin-doctored, and managed in virtually the same way as an electoral, or a market product, campaign.

This volume of essays was conceived, in part, to meet the need for a much broader and more historically informed range of debate. It originated in a public conference organized by the editors and held, in February 2003, at New York University. Scholarly experts from NYU's area studies programs were asked to lend substance and depth to the recent spate of commentary about anti-Americanism by analyzing its history and currency in select regions: Latin America, the Middle East, Europe, East Asia, and the United States. These regions were chosen for their strategic importance in current affairs (the Middle East and Europe), as well as for a proven consistency of anti-American sentiment over a long history of past and—probably—future antagonism toward the United States (Latin America, East Asia). A panel on domestic anti-Americanism addressed the differences between organic protest and exterior critiques of the United States. Since the organization of the volume reflects that of the conference, all of the contributors are, or were, NYU faculty members. Individual essays focus on the distinct histories of the different regions in their fraught relations with (and perceptions of) the United States. Taken as a whole, the volume lays the groundwork for possible comparisons of the experience now shared almost universally: that of a world order stamped with American characteristics and enforced by American military power.

Anti-Americanism has a long and venerable history as an object of study in Europe, and particularly in France, where several recent books on the topic have been best-sellers.[11] The political standpoint of their authors ranges quite widely. For example, Jean-François Revel's *L'Obsession anti-américaine* is actually a fiercely *pro*-American book disguised as an anti-American one. Philippe Roger's *L'Ennemi américain,* the most serious and comprehensive of the recent French studies, represents a massive and erudite attempt to write a complete history of French anti-Americanism, a sentiment whose vicissitudes he relates to the French perception of their own national decline. Unlike the contributors to this volume, Roger treats anti-Americanism largely as an effect of discourse, a set of tropes and representations that ultimately transcend ideological differences. His extensive use of belletristic evidence—the fantasies and myths that inhabit narratives of Chateaubriand's or Stendhal's trips to the United States, for example—supports a discursive history unanchored in economic unevenness, governmental policies, wars, or other significant political events.

In this country, anti-Americanism has received a great deal of recent attention from journalists, from policy makers, and from government sponsored think tanks, but there has been surprisingly little systematic attention from scholars.[12] Individual volumes have been published in the past twenty years on Chinese, German, Canadian, Greek, and Spanish anti-Americanism, respectively; their titles appear in the bibliographic note at the end of the volume. The only study that attempts a more global comprehension of the problem is Paul Hollander's *Anti-Americanism: Rational and Irrational.*[13] Yet only three of his book's ten chapters are devoted to anti-Americanism abroad, and these omit virtually any mention of the Middle East or Asia. Most of its pages focus on domestic anti-Americanism and read largely as a diatribe against what Hollander variously calls "political correctness," "multiculturalism," "victim culture," or "whining." For Hollander, American self-criticism, or opposition by Americans to U.S. foreign or domestic policy, can be understood only as a betrayal of an exemplary birthright. The "rational" anti-Americanism of his subtitle refers to protest against modernization, while "irrational" anti-Americanism holds capitalism to blame—and Hollander is unduly confident that he can distinguish between the two. In the end, though, as he states in his preface, he believes that the vast majority of anti-American sentiment is almost entirely irrational and misdirected.

In assuming that he speaks for the rest of the world, Hollander employs a scholarly approach and tone that sadly reflect the arrogance and overreaching qualities that many recent critics have come to associate with U.S. conduct, both in policy making and in cultural outlook. In preparing this volume, we have tried to counteract this tendency. Though our book does not profess to be a comprehensive global survey, its coverage of several regions is aimed at deep analysis of the various dimensions of anti-American opinion and sentiment in different cultures, the tropes and the targets, why these have changed over time, and how they might be compared with each other. To do this, we have drawn on the regional expertise of both humanists and social scientists (history, cultural analysis, literature, sociology, political science) in order to ensure wide-ranging commentary on a phenomenon that demands it.

NOTES

1. Simon Schama offers a summary profile of this history in "The Unloved American," *New Yorker* (March 10, 2003), pp. 34–39.

2. Smedley Butler, *War Is a Racket* (New York: Round Table Press, 1935).

3. Michael Ignatieff, "America's Empire Is an Empire Lite," *New York Times,* January 10, 2003.

4. Naomi Klein's analysis of Beer's re-branding campaign, "America Is Not a Hamburger," is included in *Fences and Windows: Dispatches from the Front Lines of the Globalization Debate* (New York: PicadorUSA, 2002).

5. Robert Cooper, "The Postmodern State," *The Observer* (April 7, 2002). See his longer paper, "Re-Ordering the World: The Long-term Implications of September 11th," Foreign Policy Center, London.

6. Bush officials identified with these views include Paul Wolfowitz, Dick Cheney, Eliot Cohen, Lewis Libby, Donald Rumsfeld, Zalmay Khalilzad, Douglas Feith, John Bolton, Dov Zakheim, Richard Perle, and Stephen Cambone. They shared membership ranks in the Project for the New American Century (PNAC) with Jeb Bush, William Kristol, William Bennett, Midge Decter, Steve Forbes, Francis Fukuyama, Fred Ikle, Donald Kagan, Norman Podhoretz, Dan Quayle, and Stephen Rosen. A blueprint of the Bush Doctrine is contained in the 2000 PNAC report titled "Rebuilding America's Defense: Strategies, Forces and Resources for a New Century."

Of all the commentators who have argued for the America First version of the new imperium, perhaps the most influential has been Robert Kagan, a PNAC co-chair. His opinions on the topic were previewed in "The Benevolent Empire," *Foreign Policy* (summer 1998); his book *Of Paradise and Power: America and Europe in the New World Order* (New York: Knopf, 2003) expanded on a much-discussed 2002 article, "Power and Weakness: Why Europe and the U.S. See the World Differently," *Policy Review* 113 (June–July 2002). The article, which begins "Americans are from Mars and Europeans are from Venus," was a key text in the campaign to justify the break with Western Europe. Other opinion makers aligned with the neoconservative network (Charles Krauthammer, Max Boot, Irving Kristol, Dinesh D'Souza, Thomas Donnelly) have normalized the journalistic use of the term "American empire" in the pages of the *Wall Street Journal*, the *Washington Times*, the *National Review*, the *New York Post*, the *New Republic*, and the *Weekly Standard*.

7. For a survey of the journalistic contributions to the debate about a new U.S. imperium, see the bibliographic notes at the end of the volume.

8. Analogies with Rome have been persistent throughout U.S. political history. Roman metaphors were habitually used as caveats against the corruptions of power. When the cold war ended, direct comparisons with the extensive power of the Roman Empire become rote, even in foreign policy analysis. Yet, when it came to advocating explicit imperial policies, the analogy was too remote. More persuasive to those mindful of the vestigial Anglo-American alliance was the commentary from historians like Niall Ferguson, author of *Empire: The Rise and Demise of the British World Order and the Lessons for Global Power*. In a series of articles and appearances in the U.S. and British media, he openly advised Washington to learn lessons from the British imperial experience as the U.S. adopts its own frankly imperial policy for managing the world.

9. References to left responses to "the new U.S. imperium" are included in the bibliographical notes at the end of the volume.

10. The June 2003 report on the survey, titled "Views of a Changing World," can be found on the Pew Research Center website at http://people-press.org/reports/display.php3?ReportID=185.

11. These include Noel Mamère, *Non merci, Oncle Sam* (Paris: Ramsay, 1999); Philippe Roger, *L'Ennemi américain: généaologie de l'antiaméricanisme français* (Paris: Seuil, 2002); Jean-François Revel, *L'Obsession anti-américaine* (Paris: Plon, 2002); and Emmanuel Todd, *Après l'empire: essai sur la décomposition du système américain* (Paris: Gallimard, 2002).

12. Legislation pending in the Congress, for example, would rewrite the Title VI legislation that funds "area studies" programs (Latin American, African, Asian, and Middle East programs) and the teaching of foreign languages to implement a federal advisory "oversight" board. Created in consultation with the homeland security agencies, the board would advise Congress

on matters of international education. During a House subcommittee hearing in June 2003 on the matter, one witness argued in favor of such a board in light of what he called the strong "anti-American" bias in many college and university international departments—a bias that he claimed could undermine American foreign policy. See the American Council of Education's newsletter at http://www.acenet.edu/hena.

A good example of the think tank genre is Stephen Haseler, *The Varieties of Anti-Americanism: Reflex and Response* (Washington: Ethics and Public Policy Center, 1985).

13. Paul Hollander, *Anti-Americanism: Rational and Irrational* (New York: Transaction Books, 1995), originally published as *Anti-Americanism: Critiques at Home and Abroad, 1965–1990* (Oxford University Press, 1992).

PART I

LATIN AMERICA

I

The Narcissism of Violent Differences

Greg Grandin

I don't mean to sound brutal and cruel here—but we needed to go into the very heart of their world with American boys and girls and show them that we're not just ready to kill but we are ready to die to defend our open society. We need to go into the heart of their world and beat their brains out, frankly. . . . At the same time, though . . . we [have to] partner with them now to build a decent and different Iraq. . . . We did Iraq for one reason: because we could, period, paragraph ended.
—Thomas Friedman, September 2003[1]

IN SEPTEMBER 2002, the State Department's Bureau of Intelligence and Research held a two-day conference on anti-Americanism, bringing together twenty scholars and opinion makers from the United States and abroad to ponder the question "Why do they hate us?" The event grew out of a larger investigation by the Bureau into rising antagonism toward the United States in Europe, Russia, and the Middle East.[2] While the conference was closed and invitees secretly sequestered, one participant, the sociologist Paul Hollander, summed up to the press three different types of anti-Americanism: the first an antipathy toward capitalism, the second a form of nationalism, and the third a rage against modernity. Despite their different expressions, all forms of "anti-Americanism," Hollander believes, share a psychological "sense of grievance and the compelling need to find some clear-cut and morally satisfying explanation for a wide range of unwelcome circumstances associated with either actual states or feelings of backwardness, inferiority, weakness, diminished competitiveness or a loss of coherence and stability in the life of a nation, a group or individual."[3]

The Foggy Bottom conference, curiously, did not include a discussion of Latin America. None of the participants, as best can be told, were from Latin America or worked on Latin American issues. In one sense, this omission reflects the region's current position in the geopolitical visions of foreign policy officials and intellectuals. If Asia is seen as an area of potential economic and military competition, Africa as a basket case, a place that tests our resolve to do moral good in the world, and the Middle East as the staging ground for an epic clash of civilizations, Latin America is portrayed, until recently at least, as a success story: confronted in the post–World War II period with insurgent states, ideologies, and political movements, the United States responded with an effective mix of hard and soft power, neutralized the opposition, and helped transform most of the continent's nations into free-market allies and their populations into willing consumers of U.S. goods and technology. Compared with the "uncertainty of the rest of the world," said Barry McCaffrey, then commander of U.S. armed forces in Latin America, in 1995, Latin America was a model of stability.[4] "We have a lot to be proud [of]," said Secretary of Defense William Cohen two years later, "and I believe the Western Hemisphere has a lot to teach the world as the world reaches for the kind of progress we have made."[5]

So why was Latin America not included in the conference? The Argentine writer and critic Jorge Luis Borges once remarked that the absence of camels in the Koran confirms their importance to Middle Eastern culture, and surely the same can be said of Latin America in accounts of the ascent of the United States as a world power. It has served as both the literal and the ideological site of U.S. imperial expansion, but rarely is the experience of the United States in Latin America figured into discussions of the former's global hegemony. Much like the camel omitted from the Koran, that experience has been central in shaping the instincts that guide U.S. responses to global threats and crises. Many of the popular, scholarly, and policy definitions of "anti-Americanism" currently in circulation, for instance, were composed within the long history of inter-American relations. "Anti-Americanism," as laid out by Hollander, assumes a harmonization of the United States with capitalist modernity, a harmonization that is at its most resonant when it is uncontested by either detractors and defenders of the United States. Yet, before the universalism embedded in such an understanding could be exported to the rest of the world, it had to be defined in opposition to the world, or at least to the old European world. At least since the early nineteenth century, the idea "America"—both in the United States and in Latin America—conveyed a dual and ambiguous meaning: it increasingly referred to a unique U.S. national identity *and* to a larger hemisphere-wide democratic imaginary. At its most benign, the second meaning suggested an association of equal and sovereign republics with shared interests and values, an association led but not dominated by the United States. This universal pretense was more than just an armed narcissism. The idea of a distinct progressive, entrepreneurial American "spirit" resonated, however ambivalently, among Latin America's political elite, who were among the first to celebrate the dynamic moderation of the American Revolution against the excesses of the French and Haitian Revolutions.[6] At its most predatory, "America" implied an inevitable destiny of U.S. expansion and conquest. Through the course of nearly two centuries, but especially after World War II, Latin American critics of U.S. imperial actions and economic policies challenged the ecumenical values the United States claimed to embody. That they did so largely from the standpoint of those values created a serious crisis of legitimacy for U.S. authority. In response, U.S. foreign policy officials, pundits, and intellectuals mobilized the concept of "anti-Americanism," a malleable interpretive lens that both rendered diverse expressions of opposition as pathological deviations from the model of society and economy embodied by the United States and justified, when needed, a sure and brutal remedy.

Two broad arcs of antagonism define U.S.–Latin American relations. The first began in the early nineteenth century and paralleled the initial phase of U.S. territorial and economic expansion. Latin American intellectuals, politicians, and nationalists reacted with increasing hostility not only toward the growing influence of U.S. capital—which both displaced European economic interests and subordinated aspiring domestic elites—but also toward ever more frequent and threatening military interventions: the Mexican-American War, the Spanish-American War, the creation of Panama, the occupations of Haiti and the Dominican Republic, and the Marine campaign against Augusto Sandino in Nicaragua. Between 1869 and 1897, the U.S. Navy engaged in 5,980 operations in Latin American territories to protect U.S. shipping.[7] By the beginning of the twentieth century, such actions inflamed a generation of political and literary critics of U.S. power—Manuel Ugarte, of Argentina; José Martí, of Cuba; Rubén Darío, of Nicaragua; José Enrique

Rodó, of Uruguay; Eduardo Prado, of Brazil; Isidro Fabela, of Mexico; and José María Vargas Vila, of Colombia. While they often focused on specific outrages, using the words "imperialism" and "intervention" interchangeably, they also drew from a more diffuse Spanish Catholic antipathy toward Anglo-Protestant "individualism" and "materialism." This form of criticism was most prominent among elite conservatives hostile toward the social liberalization that the United States represented, yet it was also notably present in the writings of modernist radical democrats such as Martí and the Peruvian José Mariátegui. In the 1920s, these critiques were sharpened by Marxist theory and gained political momentum with the growth of communist, socialist, and nationalist political parties. The early twentieth century also saw a rise in instances of peasant and working-class demonstrations aimed at U.S. companies throughout the hemisphere, as well as the pillaging and destruction of U.S.-owned plantations, factories, and mines, especially in Colombia, Mexico, and Nicaragua.[8] This first cycle came to a close in the 1930s with Franklin Roosevelt's Good Neighbor Policy and the Popular Front, which aligned Latin America's communist and socialist parties with the United States against fascism and dampened the anti-imperialist rhetoric of the Left.

The second round of opposition to U.S. ambitions coincided with the advent of the cold war and intensified with Eisenhower's overthrow of Guatemala's democratically elected government in 1954. It continued with the triumph of the 1959 Cuban revolution, the spread of insurgencies, and the promulgation of dependency theory, which lent conceptual support for the growing opinion that the United States represented not a model for but an obstacle to the attainment of development and democracy. As in earlier periods, the tectonics of interimperial rivalry sparked enmity against the United States, as both Moscow and Beijing provided important theoretical and political reference points for dissent from Washington's lead (the first Spanish-language translations of Mao's writings, such as his "U.S. Imperialism Is a Paper Tiger," began to circulate in Latin America just a few months after the CIA's Guatemalan intervention).[9] In the 1980s, the military defeat of insurgencies and the violent repression of political movements paved the way for a return to constitutional rule and neoliberal restructuring, bringing this period of antagonism to an end and leading to the success story celebrated during the Clinton years.

Throughout both these periods, critics, reflecting the tension inherent in the concept "America," repeatedly complained that the United States was not living up to the best of its ideals. As early as 1856, the Chilean writer Francisco Bilbao celebrated the "genius" of the American Revolution for unleashing the spirit of liberty and enterprise upon the world while at the same time condemning the corruption of that spirit in its birthplace: "beholding themselves so great," the "sons of Penn and Washington" fell to the "temptation of the Titans. They believed they were the arbiters of the earth, and even rivals of Olympus. . . . They would concentrate the universe in themselves. The American is replaced with the Yankee; Philosophy with Roman patriotism . . . ; Justice with self-interest. . . . They hurl themselves upon the South, and the nation that should have been our star, our model, our strength, daily becomes a greater threat to the independence of South America."[10] During the second cycle of antagonism, Castro's 1953 "History Will Absolve Me" speech captured the inspiration the progressive currents of U.S. history, particularly the New Deal as a development model, continued to hold for Latin American intellectuals and politicians well into the cold war.

Yet the United States's increasingly heavy hand in hemispheric and world affairs reawakened anti-imperialist resentment. Many Latin American nationalists and democrats saw the dawning cold war as heralding the defeat of the democratic potential of the popular front and World War II and directly related the global chill to domestic politics within the United States. An impressive letter-writing campaign organized by Left unions and parties throughout Latin America, for instance, pleaded for the lives of Julius and Ethel Rosenberg and condemned their executions in harsh terms. "Your consent to the assassination of the Rosenbergs," Guatemala's national labor federation telegrammed Eisenhower in 1953, "makes clear the brutal imperialist policy of the United States. American democracy has been buried."[11] Many of Latin America's politicized literati seized on Walt Whitman as a symbol of the United States' betrayal of its progressive promise. In 1952, for instance, the Dominican poet Pedro Mir lamented the conscription of Walt Whitman's radical exuberance into a more martial campaign: "The ones who defiled his luminous beard and put a gun on his shoulders . . . Those of you who do not want Walt Whitman, the democrat, but another Whitman, atomic and savage" (a decade later,

Mir's poetics would prove prophetic when Walt Whitman Rostow, an advocate of military escalation in Vietnam, became a key adviser to presidents Kennedy and Johnson).[12]

Prior to the Spanish-American War, in 1898, accusations of "anti-Americanism" were mostly the froth that lay atop imperial rivalry and high politics. The press infrequently deployed the term, which was used more often than not as a descriptive category to refer to European tariffs placed on U.S. agricultural and manufacturing products.[13] As the United States began to displace British, French, and German economic interests in Latin America, the U.S. press occasionally complained of those powers' "anti-American propaganda" in the hemisphere.[14]

After 1898—when the United States took military possession of Cuba, Puerto Rico, and the Philippines and consolidated its control over Hawaii—the term begins to take on two new dimensions. First, "anti-Americanism" increasingly referred to popular anger at and destruction of U.S. interests and installations. At first, this usage focused on the Philippines and Cuba, but it then spread to cover the U.S. occupation of Haiti, the Mexican Revolution, and Sandino's insurgency (as well as the Chinese nationalist revolution).[15] Second, as U.S. politicians from Theodore Roosevelt to Woodrow Wilson increasingly justified foreign policy in idealistic terms, "anti-Americanism" took on a normative meaning of an innate hostility toward or an incompatibility with those ideals. Starting in 1920s, scholarly journals published a number of articles that presented Latin America "yankee-phobia" in similar terms.[16]

After World War, this reorientation of the concept "anti-Americanism" both repeated and accelerated. During the early cold war years, "anti-Americanism" referred primarily to official Soviet propaganda. Yet, as superpower conflict overlapped with decolonization movements, the term was once more used to explain grassroot opposition to U.S. concerns and values. Even before the Cuban Revolution, worsening hemispheric relations quickened this reconfiguration. The stones and spit that rained on Vice President Richard Nixon during his disastrous 1958 visit to Latin America, followed by the Panama Canal Zone riots, in 1964, created the impression among policy elites that such eruptions of "anti-Americanism" sprang from deep reserves of mass anger. Throughout the 1960s, State Department officials frequently used the phrase "anti-Americanism" to link Latin America's anti-imperialist insurgencies to a general perception that the "third world" was in revolt.

From the beginning of the cold war, and intensifying as super-power conflict spread outside Europe, sociologists, psychologists, and political scientists, particularly those tied to the national security apparatus, helped translate the concept "anti-American" into a psychological idiom. In elaborating unified theories of human behavior, including behavior understood as hostile to the United States, they tended to discount ideas, ideology, values, and history as factors motivating dissent. Instead, they explained behavior in terms of repression or trauma. Belief systems were interpreted not as cognitive frameworks but as rationalizations of behavioral routines. The more foreign and "inscrutable" the object of analysis, the more "intimate" and knowable it appeared, as "distinct people and events were translated into measurable ideal types," with their behavior reduced to a common set of psychological tropes.[17]

In other words, against a global field of increasingly militant nationalist challenges, charges of "anti-Americanism" served both to deny historical and cultural diversity and to dismiss communist, anti-imperialist, social democratic, and nationalist dissent as pathological reactions to the contemporary world, thus reaffirming the United States as both the embodiment and the defender of a universal model of modernity. "Criticisms of or complaints about America," wrote the *Saturday Review* in 1951, "are criticisms of the modern world."[18] A year later, the *New York Times* described Mexican "anti-Americanism" in terms of "fear," "envy," "pride," and a stubborn refusal to let go of past grievances, particularly the indignities suffered in the Mexican-American War (charges of anti-Americanism against the French and the Germans today focus on their failure to remember history, particularly the United States's role in delivering them from totalitarianism).[19] Foreign policy officials increasingly blamed opposition on psychological resentments, on a "belief that the U.S. does not pay attention to Latin American problems," or on an "irrational and unjustified" nationalism.[20] Along with this propensity to pathologize and psychologize politics came a tendency to insist that the United States must be more sensitive to, as Eisenhower put it in 1958, the "injured feelings" of "other American Republics."[21] George Allen, while director of the U.S. Information Agency (USIA), urged the United States to "grow up psychologically" and to stop its "boast[ing] about our richness, our bigness, and our strength."[22]

But the real nature of North American reaction would be much less considerate. Following the Cuban Revolution, the United States responded with decided determination. As JFK's "Cuban Study Group," headed by Maxwell Taylor, Robert Kennedy, and Allen Dulles, put it, in 1961, Castro's "continued presence within the hemispheric community as a dangerously effective exponent of Communism and Anti-Americanism constitutes a real menace capable of eventually overthrowing the elected governments in any one or more of weak Latin American republics. There are only two ways to view this threat: either to hope that time and internal discontent will eventually end it, or to take active measures to force its removal. . . . [T]here is little reason to place reliance on the first course of action."[23] The White House launched a continental counterinsurgency campaign, which included covert operations (Guatemala, 1954; Cuba, 1961; and Chile, 1973, for just a few examples) and wars (Dominican Republic, 1965; Grenada, 1983; Nicaragua, in the 1980s; and Panama, 1991). Yet, the backbone of the U.S. response was the provision of constant and steady material and financial aid that helped create centralized intelligence agencies— which coordinated the work of death squads, paramilitaries, and tor- turers—able and resolved to destroy all communist—and, by extension, all democratic and socialist—opposition.

The certainty with which the U.S. responded, notwithstanding oc- casional moments of doubt, to the Latin American Left was driven by another current of cold war social science, namely the influence of ra- tional choice in counterinsurgency theory and practice beginning in the mid-1960s. As in Vietnam, Rand Corporation experts in internal war and insurgencies such as Charles Wolf, Nathan Leites, and Leon Goure proposed defeating revolutions not by "constructive counterinsur- gency," that is, by winning hearts and minds and by promoting reforms to improve economic standards. Rather, they advocated "coercive counterinsurgency," which sought to increase the "price" of supporting political movements.[24] Such an inflation could be brought about by, as Thomas Schelling put it in his *Arms and Influence* (1966), inflicting "sheer pain and damage." The United States had a capacity to mete out "pure, unconstructive, unacquisitive pain and damage," making oppo- sition "terrible beyond endurance."[25] Confronted with an overwhelm- ing show of force, the social base of the enemy would "seek evasive ac- tion, ranging from defection to capitulation."[26] On one level, the elabo- ration of repressive rational-choice theory contradicted many of the assumptions of previous psychological interpretations of human be- havior; yet, both models concocted universal prescriptions that reduced the complexity of political commitment and action to easily treatable symptoms.

Leavening this hardheadedness remained the self-flattery that other countries not only really did love us but also wanted what we had to offer—a conceit that the realist Dean Acheson dubbed "Narcissus psychosis."[27] A number of post–World War II polls carried out by UN-ESCO, the USIA, and other groups reinforced this opinion, providing statistical confirmation that U.S. values and lifestyles held great appeal for much of the world's population.[28] Such affirmations of national self-esteem folded nicely with rational-choice counterinsurgency doctrine: an overwhelming preponderance of power, often in the form of terror, would separate ordinary citizens from their ideologically fired leadership, erode irrational revolutionary solidarity and nationalism, and force an acceptance of the modern world as defined and policed by the United States—which, it goes without saying, was what such citizens wanted all along. As a National Intelligence Estimate put it, in 1958, "Latin American attitudes toward the U.S. were 'ambivalent.'" They expressed "envy by disparaging U.S. materialism," yet wanted our consumer goods and capital; they espoused pan-Americanism but engaged in petty nationalism; they chafed at our military power but wanted our protection.

Alternations between coercive and consensual power were not merely instrumental switchbacks but reflected the essence of U.S. influence. As the hemisphere's unrivaled military power, principle source of capital, dominant supplier of manufactured goods, and primary importer of raw material, U.S. private interests and government institutions exercised considerable persuasion in defining the permissible limits of political and cultural debate. Broadly speaking, throughout its two centuries of hemispheric ascendance, the United States responded to "anti-Americanism" in Latin America with a mix of hard and soft power. Gunboat interventions of the nineteenth and early twentieth centuries yielded to the commercial, cultural, and military treaties, alliances, and intercontinental organizations of the World War II period. When the cold war ended this period of good will, the United States continued to temper military power with government-funded efforts to disseminate U.S. cultural and intellectual influence and the rhetoric of developmentalism, as expressed in Point Four Aid, the Alliance for Progress, and the work of private agencies, such as the Rockefeller Foundation.

Nor should manifestations of hard and soft power be thought of as distinct instruments, for they functioned concurrently, with one reinforcing the other. In Nicaragua, the Reagan administration successfully combined the coercion of the Contra War with genuine popular support, particularly among the Anglo-identified Miskitu Indians of the Atlantic Coast region. During moments of crisis, overlapping fields of economic, repressive, and cultural power collapsed together, such as in Argentina during the 1970s, when the Ford Motor Company reportedly not only supplied death squads with vehicles but established a detention and torture center in its manufacturing plant outside Buenos Aires.[29] In Guatemala, Coca-Cola took similar actions.[30] "Pure, unconstructive, unacquisitive pain"—to return to Schelling's phrase—remained thinly cloaked behind the unsteady privileges of a weekly wage and the allure of "American" brands.

Many of the simplifying tropes used to rhetorically contain and respond to Latin American dissent continue to circulate. The sociologist Paul Hollander advises the State Department that hostility toward the United States is a psychological reaction to capitalist modernity, while Michael Mandelbaum, a professor at Johns Hopkins and the author of *Ideas That Conquered the World: Peace, Democracy, and Free Markets*, argued that an invasion of Iraq would not increase Islamic "anti-Americanism" because such sentiments stem not from specific U.S. policies but from the region's failure to modernize.[31] The same contradictory assumptions that underwrote cold war counterinsurgency doctrine animate justifications of current U.S. bellicosity. On the one hand, Kenneth M. Pollack, former CIA analyst and author of *The Threatening Storm: The Case for Invading Iraq,* argued that a U.S. occupation of Iraq would be successful because Iraq, like the United States, has a middle-class urban society. On the other hand, Orientalists and terrorism scholars are rehashing repressive rational-choice principles to justify swiftness and surety of action. After September 11, Princeton's Bernard Lewis, an intellectual mentor to many of Bush's Middle East counselors, briefed the White House foreign policy staff, brushing aside concerns that too harsh a retaliation would provoke the Arab street: "In that part of the world," he said, "nothing matters more than resolute will and force"[32]—or, as the House Republican majority leader Tom DeLay now puts it, maintaining strong resolve in the face of apparently escalating resistance in Iraq: "In the Arab world before 9/11, they thought the U.S.

was a paper tiger. We had a president [Bill Clinton] whose retaliation to terrorism was throwing a few bombs in the desert. They laughed at that. And now they see this real stuff, and real power. And they respect power."[33]

For their part, Latin American–U.S. relations appear to be on the cusp of a new period of antagonism, as opposition to neoliberal economic policies begins to take political form, as it has in Bolivia, Argentina, Venezuela, Ecuador, and Brazil. A new Pew Global Attitudes poll charts hostility toward the United States, particularly in Bolivia and Argentina, at an all-time high. To make matters worse, the United States has once again stepped up military aid and training. On a recent trip to Chile, Secretary of Defense Donald Rumsfeld urged Latin American armies to take a more active role in national and regional policing. Such advice is particularly worrisome since so much effort on the part of civilian reformers and human rights activists over the past ten years has been directed at pushing soldiers back into their barracks. In contrast to the optimism that marked the Clinton years, Major General Gary Speer, in charge of the Southern Command, told Congress, in April 2002, that Latin American nations "appear" to be peaceful and stable, yet "underlying this perception . . . are the multiple transnational threats of terrorism, drug and arms trafficking, illegal migration, and organized crime. . . . Transnational threats in the region are increasingly linked as they share common infrastructure, transit patterns, corrupting means, and illicit mechanisms. These threats transcend borders and seriously affect the security interests of the United States."[34] The war on terrorism now provides an articulating framework that allows us to treat social and political problems as part of a larger martial conflict.

The fundamental harshness of free-market restructuring propels this hemispheric militarization. While the inter-American economic system that held sway between the 1940s and the 1970s held up, at least rhetorically, a redistributive welfare state as the endpoint of modernization, Washington's current free-market fundamentalism posits not social security but rivalry as the foundation of society. Presented as nonnegotiable, such a regime mutes whatever universal resonance the idea "America" may have held during the cold war. Brazil will accept a free-trade treaty, the U.S. foreign trade representative said matter-of-factly, or it can try selling its products to "Antarctica."[35] As the current global political crisis intensifies, such coarse and threatening language will continue. In response to Mexico's hesitancy in supporting the U.S.-led war on Iraq, George Bush threatened "discipline," while a U.S. diplomat intimated that Mexicans living in the United States could face internment, as did Japanese-Americans during World War II.[36] Even during its best moments, U.S. enterprise rests on military power, or, as the free-market optimist turned warrior Thomas Friedman puts it, "McDonald's cannot flourish without McDonnell Douglas."[37] Yet, today, in Latin America, not only has McDonald's shut down its operations in Bolivia due to declining revenues, it has been kicked out of Oaxaca, Mexico, in a spasm of culinary nationalism. At the same time, the United States has recommenced high-tech arms sales to Latin America after a twenty-year ban, threatening to kick off a regional arms race.[38] As McDonald's recedes, McDonnell Douglas proceeds.

NOTES

1. *Tim Russert Show,* CNBC, September 13, 2003.

2. U.S. Department of State, daily press briefing, Richard Boucher, spokesman, August 28, 2002. Available at http://usinfo.state.gov/regional/nea/sasia/afghan/text/0828state.htm.

3. Quoted in *Courier Mail,* September 7, 2002.

4. See his testimony before the House National Security Committee, March 8, 1995, in *Defense Issues* 10 (50).

5. See his speech to the Western Hemisphere Symposium, published in U.S. Department of Defense, *Defense Issues* 12 (24). Similarly, the Project for the New American Century, the neocon lobby group pushing the United States's new imperial foreign policy, pays little attention to Latin America except to note that, under Ronald Reagan, democracy bloomed in the region. See http://www.newamericancentury.org.

6. Charles A. Hale, "Political Ideas and Ideologies in Latin America, 1870–1930," in Leslie Bethell, ed., *Ideas and Ideologies in Twentieth-Century Latin America* (Cambridge: Cambridge University Press, 1996), pp. 135–138.

7. From a report commissioned by the U.S. Navy and titled, "An Indicator of Informal Empire: Patterns of U.S. Navy Cruising on Overseas Stations, 1869–97." Cited in William Appleman Williams, *Empire as a Way of Life* (New York: Oxford University Press, 1980), p. 122.

8. See Thomas O'Brien, *The Revolutionary Mission: American Enterprise in Latin America, 1900–1945* (Cambridge: Cambridge University Press, 1996), and John Mason Hart, *Empire and Revolution: The Americans in Mexico since the Civil War* (Berkeley: University of California Press, 2002).

9. See William E. Ratliff, "Chinese Communist Cultural Diplomacy toward Latin America, 1949–1960," *Hispanic American Historical Review* 49 (1) (February 1969): 53–79.

10. Francisco Bilbao, *América en peligro* (Santiago: Ediciones Ercilla, 1941 [1856]), pp. 144–154.

11. Library of Congress, Guatemalan Transcripts, Reel 5, Frame 8004-P, June 23, 1953.

12. Pedro Mir, *"Countersong to Walt Whitman" and Other Poems,* trans. Jonathan Cohen and Donald D. Walsh (Washington, DC: Azul Editions, 1993), p. 97. See also the Guatemalan literary critic and Communist Party member Huberto Alvarado's "Walt Whitman: poeta nacional, democrático, y realista," in *Cuadernos del Guayas,* vol. 6 (1955), published a year after he was driven into exile following a U.S.-orchestrated coup.

13. Apparently, the first use of the term "anti-American" occurred in 1773 in reference to British policy. See Alan McPherson, "Latin American Anti-Americanism and U.S. Responses: Venezuela 1958," paper presented at the 2002 Symposium on Latin America hosted by the Driskell Center at the University of Maryland, College Park. See also McPherson's *Yankee No: Anti-Americanism in U.S.-Latin American Relations* (Cambridge, MA: Harvard University Press, 2003).

14. In 1899, for example, the U.S. press accused the London *Saturday Review* of trying to forge an "anti–North American alliance" between Brazil and Argentina. See, for examples, the *New York Times,* "Foreign Feeling in Brazil," February 4, 1894, and "Warned of the United States," August 13, 1899.

15. See for examples, *New York Times,* "Anti-American Manifesto," February 20, 1899, p. 1, and "Filipinos Unfit to Rule Themselves," November 3, 1899, p. 6.

16. See, for examples, Edward Perry, "Anti-American Propaganda in Hispanic America," *Hispanic American Historical Review* 3 (1) (1920): 17–40; Anna Powell, "Relations between the United States and Nicaragua, 1898–1916," *Hispanic American Historical Review* 8 (1) (1928): 43–64; and J. Fred Rippy, "Literary Yankee-Phobia in Latin America," *Journal of International Relations* 12 (1921–1922): 350–371.

17. Ron Robin, *The Making of the Cold War Enemy: Culture and Politics in the Military-Intellectual Complex* (Princeton: Princeton University Press, 2001), p. 7. See chapters 1 and 3, where Robin identifies the research associated with the publication of *The American Soldier* (1949), as well as the work of Daniel Lerner, Bernard Berelson, James Charlesworth, David McClelland, Paul Lazarsfeld, and Harold Lasswell, as emblematic of "behavioralist" approaches that downplayed ideology, politics, and history as motivating factors in human action. Lasswell in particular viewed politics as a "a natural arena for 'displacement,' partly because of the great visibility of public affairs and partly due to the am-

biguity of most political symbols." See also chapter 1 of Arno J. Mayer, *Dynamics of Counterrevolution in Europe, 1870–1956: An Analytical Framework* (New York: Harper and Row, 1971), for the relationship of behavioralism to cold war conflict.

18. "America through British Eyes," *Saturday Review,* October 13, 1951, p. 19, in McPherson, "Latin American Anti-Americanism," p. 8.

19. See, for one example of this analysis, Flora Lewis, "Why There Is Anti-Americanism in Mexico," *New York Times Magazine,* July 6, 1952. See also National Intelligence Estimate 80/90-58, "Latin American Attitudes toward the U.S.," *Foreign Relations of the United States 1958–1960,* quoted in McPherson, "Latin American Anti-Americanism."

20. Joseph Silberstein to Terry Sanders, May 14, 1958, National Archives, folder Vice President Nixon's Trip, box 24, lot 62D31, RG 59, cited in McPherson, "Latin American Anti-Americanism," p. 21.

21. McPherson, "Latin American Anti-Americanism."

22. Ibid.

23. Maxwell Taylor, Robert F. Kennedy, Allen Dulles, Allen Welsh, and Arleigh Burke, "Recommendations of the Cuban Study Group," June 13, 1961, folder Cuba—Bay of Pigs, box 2, John F. Kennedy Library. Available online at http://cisweb.lexis-nexis.com/histuniv/.

24. The phrases "constructive" and "coercive" counterinsurgency come from Robin, *The Making of the Cold War Enemy,* pp. 189–199, who analyzes the transition from one to the other. For the classics of repressive counterinsurgency doctrine, see Nathan Leites and Charles Wolf Jr., *Rebellion and Authority: Myths and Realities Reconsidered* (Arlington, VA: Rand Corporation, 1966), and Leites and Wolf, *Rebellion and Authority: An Analytical Essay on Insurgent Conflicts* (Chicago: University of Chicago Press, 1970); and Samuel Huntington, "The Bases of Accommodation," *Foreign Affairs* 46 (July 1968): pp. 642–656. See the discussions of these works in Robin, *The Making of the Cold War Enemy.*

25. Thomas Schelling, *Arms and Influence* (New Haven: Yale University Press, 1966), pp. 2–3.

26. Robin, *The Making of the Cold War Enemy,* p. 195.

27. In Lloyd Free and Hadley Cantril, *The Political Beliefs of Americans: A Study of Public Opinion* (New York: Simon and Schuster, 1968), p. 78.

28. McPherson, "Latin American Anti-Americanism," p. 8; see also Alan Girard and Raul Samuel, *Situación y perspectives de Chile en septiembre de 1957* (Santiago: Instituto de Sociología, Universidad de Chile, 1958), which confirmed that the United States enjoyed more support among the working class than did the Soviet Union.

29. "Ford Motor Is Linked to Argentina's 'Dirty War,'" *New York Times,* November 27, 2002.

30. See Deborah Levenson-Estrada, *Trade Unionists against Terror: Guatemala City 1954–1985* (Chapel Hill: University of North Carolina Press, 1994).

31. *The Brian Lehrer Show,* New York Public Radio, February 18, 2003.

32. For Lewis, as well as the influence of other prominent Orientalists on Bush's foreign policy, see Nicholas Lemann, "The Next World Order," *New Yorker,* April 1, 2002. For the resurrection of repressive rational-choice counterinsurgency doctrine in relation to the war on terrorism, see Nicholas Lemann, "What Terrorists Want," *New Yorker,* October 29, 2001. Likewise, a number of the Bush administration's hawks—Elliot Abrams, for example, who infamously helped design the Contra War, is now the National Security Council's Mideast expert, while John Negroponte, who as ambassador to Honduras was accused of covering up human rights violations committed by Honduran security forces, is the U.S. envoy to the United Nations—earned their stripes in the Latin American cold war. See "Contra-era Envoy Nominated to Be U.N. Ambassador," *Baltimore Sun,* March 7, 2001; "Knowing Negroponte's Role," *Los Angeles Times,* May 8, 2001; "Bush Formally Nominates Envoy to UN: Diplomat Negroponte Dogged by Questions on Honduran Human Rights Abuses," *Baltimore Sun,* May 15, 2001.

33. *International Herald Tribune,* Paris, July 26–27, 2003.

34. Written statement of Major General Gary D. Speer, U.S. Army Acting Commander in Chief, United States Southern Command, before the 107th Congress House Appropriations Committee Subcommittee on Foreign Operations, April 10, 2002, pp. 2–3.

35. "A Leftist Takes Over in Brazil and Pledges a 'New Path,'" *New York Times,* January 2, 2003.

36. Paul Krugman, "Let Them Hate as Long as They Fear," *New York Times,* March 6, 2003.

37. Thomas Friedman, *The Lexus and the Olive Tree* (New York: Anchor Books, 2000), p. 464.

38. "In Unusual Deal, Chile Will Buy Advanced U.S. Fighter Jets," *New York Times,* January 31, 2002. See also Arms Control Association, http://www.armscontrol.org/act/1997_08/latamer.asp.

2

Back Yard with Views

Mary Louise Pratt

THE UNITED STATES'S RECENT FORAY INTO IRAQ was not the first time it has sent thousands of troops into a desert land in pursuit of an ally turned enemy. It happened in 1916, and the object of the hunt was the Mexican military virtuoso and popular revolutionary leader Pancho Villa. The story tellingly echoes contemporary events and at the same time evokes the multivalent and entangled relationships that frame anti-Americanism south of the border.

Pancho Villa is remembered as a bandit, romantic and ruthless, but at one time, like many others, from Noriega to Bin Laden to Saddam Hussein, he enjoyed the support of the United States. The ardent democrat Woodrow Wilson for a time saw Villa as Mexico's future president and the best hope for just government in Mexico. In early 1914, he suspended a U.S. arms embargo against Mexico to help the forces of the revolution. Villa returned the good will. Heading the popular revolutionary movement from the north (while Emiliano Zapata mobilized the south), he was careful to maintain good relations with the United States, guaranteeing the security of U.S. property and interests at the border and counting on U.S. cooperation in acquiring arms, equipment, and supplies. The coziness depended, however, on respect for the border. The wholesale opening up of Mexico to U.S. business interests had been one of the chief causes joining Mexicans of all classes in a mass uprising against the dictator Porfirio Diaz (1872–1910). In the years of civil strife that followed Diaz's removal, Villa and the United States were friends and allies, and his Division del Norte became famous for its snazzy uniforms, its abundant weaponry and food, its huge train complete with hospital car, and its moving city of soldiers, horses, women, and children. A Robin Hood figure, Villa displayed daring and charisma that made sensational drama for the U.S. media—William

Randolph Hearst sold papers denouncing him as an outlaw and a savage; an admiring D. W. Griffith sent a film crew to make the revolution into a screen epic.[1]

Before long, Wilson transferred his sympathies to another, more orthodox presidential contender, the wealthy rancher and nationalist oligarch Venustiano Carranza. Like Villa, Carranza had been part of the general uprising of Mexicans against Porfirio Diaz, and as a businessman he ardently opposed the U.S. economic domination in Mexico. Wilson's betrayal of Villa became complete when he allowed the Mexican army to cross U.S. soil to ambush Villa at a border town, where he suffered a crushing defeat. Villa reciprocated, attacking the border town of Columbus, New Mexico, killing seventeen U.S. citizens. Historians are still debating why he deliberately provoked the wrath of the United States. Perhaps, some say, he aimed to arouse nationalism in Mexico by inciting a U.S. intervention, then mobilizing a nationalist backlash that would return public support to his cause.[2] The very plausibility of such a scenario suggests the intricate tangle of nationalism, democratic ideology, and pro- and anti-Americanism in play in the situation. If this was Villa's plan, it worked like a charm. Within days, General John "Black Jack" Pershing was dispatched to the border with an army of ten thousand troops and the fanciest new military machinery in existence. (His assistant was a young lieutenant colonel with a future, a man named George Patton.) The mandate of the Punitive Expedition, as it was called, was clear: find Pancho Villa (and, if possible, kill him). By June 1916, 150,000 troops, mainly national guard units, were on active duty along the border.

Both the scale and the significance of the Pershing expedition are little known to Americans. Its echoes in today's Middle East adventures are more than coincidental. It was the first war to be accompanied by movie crews; Villa even had his own embedded reporter, the brilliant American socialist and former Harvard *Lampoon* editor John Reed.[3] It was the first time airplanes were used in combat (the pilots had never landed at night). It marked the debut of the armored vehicle, destined to evolve into today's Humvees and tanks. It was a dress rehearsal for the machine warfare of World War I, and the last major deployment of mounted cavalry in American history.

And it was a disaster. As if in rehearsal for Afghanistan and Iraq, the army combed the arid mountains of northern Mexico for months and never managed to lay eyes on Villa. Its huge military apparatus was a liability in the mountainous desert. The locals, to be liberated from the rule of a ruthless outlaw, were uncooperative and prone even to attacking their liberators. And who could find water for thousands of horses—big, pampered cavalry horses with swollen appetites—let alone the men? Gasoline for five hundred vehicles?[4] Supplies for thousands of soldiers who, like those today, expected three square meals a day? Who knew where to look if there were no maps and every canyon (and every Mexican) looked the same? If the locals didn't speak English and were as likely to lie as to tell the truth? And the heat! Few of the Americans had ever experienced it, nor did they know how to live in it. They wrote letters about having to choose between drinking the water in their canteens and wetting handkerchiefs on their burning heads. The villistas, meanwhile, were at home. In the early 1990s the Los Angeles–based filmmaker Paul Espinosa made a documentary on the hunt for Pancho Villa and interviewed the handful of surviving Villa soldiers. "We rode parallel to the Americans," said Enrique Alférez, "but we always rode on the side where the sun was shining, so they couldn't see us." "I can't figure out how they figured they could catch a man in this kind of terrain with the kind of outfit they had," said the border rancher Rey Whetten. "Villa's army, they were country people. They were used to starving."[5]

However they felt about Pancho Villa or the United States, Mexicans across the board did not welcome the American intrusion. For the most part, they hated it. Even Villa's arch-rival, President Carranza, withheld his support. General Pershing found himself surrounded by a populace with little interest in helping him resolve its affairs. Nobody wanted to be America's back yard.

After eleven months, Wilson got smart. He called Pershing home. Publicly, the general declared victory, while privately admitting he had been "outwitted and outbluffed at every turn." "When the true history of this expedition is written," Pershing recorded in a letter, "it will not be a very inspiring chapter for school children or even grownups to contemplate."[6] He was right. The lessons of the Pershing expedition did not make their way into the national wisdom. As of this writing, the tanks are still in the deserts and streets of Iraq, and marines patrol the mountains of Afghanistan; the locals still mistrust, the leaders still elude.

EL PATIO DE ATRÁS

Geography and history mean that the United States and Latin America have been entwined and entangled in a way that other places have not. In fact, it is hard to talk about Latin America as a block because history and geography work together: the closer a country is to the United States, the more entangled it has been. Porfirio Diaz himself summed it up memorably in 1900: "Pobre México," he said, "tan lejos de Dios y tan cerca de los Estados Unidos" [Poor Mexico, so far from God and so near the United States]. In Latin America over the past 150 years, the most conspicuous coordinates defining anti-Americanism have been anti-capitalism, anti-imperialism, nationalism, and anti-materialism. An equally important and less obvious reference point, however, is a positively defined *americanismo*, a hemispheric New World identity marked above all by a commitment to democracy and liberty and a rejection of what a poet in the 1830s called *la caduca Europa*, "worn-out Europe."[7] Readers will no doubt hear an echo of his line in the allusions to "old Europe" that Donald Rumsfeld used to insult the United Nations in 2003—New Worldism is an ideology that can still be mobilized, with or without its democratic trappings.

The Pershing expedition evokes one of the most common images of U.S. dominance in Latin America: Latin America as the United States's back yard, *el patio de atrás*.[8] It's actually a pretty interesting and apt metaphor with a lot of resonance, especially for Mexico, the Caribbean, and Central America. What is your back yard? It's where you keep the stuff that you don't want anymore. It's where you sit in the sun, drink beer, and scratch yourself, where you send your dog to do his business. It's the space you can turn your back on, close the door, and not worry about for six months if something else distracts your attention. It's where you grow fruit trees and maybe keep a garden. At the affective level, that metaphor captures what many Latin Americans perceive as the lack of mutuality and respect in their relations with the United States. This is the dimension that people often find most infuriating and wounding, devastating and enraging. In Mexico, a common stereotype of the *pinche gringo* is *el gordo obeso en la camisa hawaiiana*—the fat guy in the Hawaiian shirt, ill spoken, ill mannered, excessively informal, oblivious to the way he is seen by others. ("Who was his mother?" people ask.) In their relations with the United States, Latin Americans continually encounter a refusal or an inability to recognize them as equals or even as players in the same game. This translates into a denial of accountability for hemispheric conditions, from the corporate empires that produced the banana republics of the 1930s, to the U.S.-created and U.S.-trained militaries that became the dictatorships of the 1970s, to the neoliberal restructuring that imposed devastating immiseration in the 1980s and 1990s. Latin America has been the most economically unequal region on the planet for decades, and the combination of back yard status and internal colonialism has had everything to do with it.

The back yard relationship is performed every day in U.S.–Latin American public relations. In Mexico, the democratic election of the opposition candidate Vicente Fox in 2000 after seventy-one years of one-party rule represented a tremendous new hope for Mexico, inaugurating a new period in its history. Although Fox aligned himself with the party of the right, the fact that the monopoly of the Partido Revolucionario Institucional (PRI) was broken was felt to be a major breakthrough. Initially, Fox's relation with Bush had the look of mutual recognition as equals, even cultural cousins: they visited each other at their respective ranches, posed as cowboys, exchanged boots, rode horses and trucks together. Their apparent personal connection raised great hopes in Mexico for a possibility of renegotiating some of the more ruthless dimensions of the North American Free Trade Agreement (NAFTA) and reaching some kind of sane agreement about immigrant labor. But on September 11, 2001, Mexico disappeared again into the back yard. Bush closed the screen door and forgot all about it. Fox's political career fell into ruins, and it quickly became likely that the PRI would be returned to power in Mexico.

Insult followed injury two years later when, as a voting member of the Security Council, Mexico was put under enormous pressure by the United States to support its invasion of Iraq. After visiting Bush in Texas, Spain's prime minister, José María Aznar, was sent south to persuade Fox to support the war despite rock-solid public opposition in Mexico (as Aznar also faced in Spain). After all the other disappointments at the hands of Bush, Fox was asked to commit political suicide to support him. This is the back yard syndrome in action. Chile was the other Latin American country that had a seat on the UN Security Council during the Iraq war deliberations. In hopes of securing Chile's vote for a resolution supporting invasion, Colin Powell had a fit of decency and announced that he considered the United States's participation in the coup of 1973 to be a chapter in its history that the nation could not be proud of. Imagine being on the receiving end of that remark in Chile. On the one hand, how significant for the United States to acknowledge its role and recognize it was wrong; on the other hand, how painful to have that happen because the administration is cynically seeking your vote to support another intervention against another country whose president they dislike.

AMERICANISMO AND ANTI-AMERICANISM

Historically, the United States acquired the status of Latin America's other at the end of the nineteenth century when it emerged as a full-fledged imperial power. The war of 1898 drove Spain out of its remaining colonies, and the United States, through the Monroe Doctrine, declared itself proprietor of the region. It had all started much earlier, of course—the United States had snatched its southwest from Mexico in 1848, after all, and invaded Canada in 1812. But the Spanish-American War is seen as beginning the long list of military interventions, invasions, and occupations that have been the continuously renewed backbone for both American policy and anti-Americanism in the hemisphere. At the end of World War II, a new cold war approach was added. Through the newly established Organization of American States, the United States created strong national militaries in Latin American countries designed to make war on their own people in the name of fighting communism.[9] The result was the counterinsurgency state and eventually the dictatorships of the 1970s and 1980s. All of this seems more than enough to account for just about any kind or degree of anti-Americanism. It is the variegations, particularities, and counter-currents that we are called on to examine here. These include a sometimes grudging admiration and, at times, a sense of a shared hemispheric chronotope.

At the end of the nineteenth century, intellectual discourse in Latin America defined the United States as other primarily in cultural terms. In the weighty debate about identity that runs through nineteenth- and early-twentieth-century writing in Latin America, the United States supplies several kinds of otherness. In many canonical documents of the period, a Latin American cultural identity and historical destiny emerge in the backlight of the rapidly emerging industrial modernity of the United States. "I admire them but I don't esteem them," said the

Brazilian José Veríssimo, in 1890. "Los admiro pero no los amo" [I admire them but I don't love them], echoed Uruguayan essayist José Enrique Rodó a few years later. "Nuestra América" [Our America, 1891], a
classic essay by the Cuban hero José Martí, juxtaposes "our" America
with an implicit "their" (North) America, whose imperial potential, already apparent, requires a vigorous response from the south:

> Since strong nations, self-made by law and shotgun, love strong na-
> tions, and them alone . . . the pressing need of Our America is to show
> itself as it is, one in spirit and intent, swift conqueror of a suffocating
> past. . . . The scorn of our formidable neighbor who does not know us
> is Our America's greatest danger.[10]

By the 1920s, starker contours had emerged. The Peruvian José Carlos
Mariátegui, widely seen as the founder of socialism in Latin America,
drew the lines prophetically: "It is for Anglo-Saxon North America to
consummate and draw to a close capitalist civilization. The future of the
Latin America is socialist."[11] For subsequent writers, including Pablo
Neruda, anti-capitalism was far more important than anti-Americanism, in part because it implied a critique at home as well as abroad.

Simultaneously, in the nineteenth and early twentieth centuries, the
United States was evoked as a model of modernity and liberal democracy, as Latin American countries sought to establish secular, republican
institutions and as liberals sought ascendancy over colonial oligarchies.
Veríssimo's remark quoted earlier, for instance, was made in a treatise
on national education systems, for which the United States was widely
seen as the model. The fledgling Latin American states regularly sent
their men of letters north to examine U.S. institutions. Argentina dispatched its future president Domingo Faustino Sarmiento to Philadelphia in 1847 to study public education. He formed a lasting relationship
with Horace Mann.[12] Around the same time, Mexico sent the writer
Manuel Payno to study penitentiary systems in New York, Philadelphia, and Florida. He came back horrified at racial segregation but admiring the concept of rehabilitation.[13] In the 1850s, a remarkable group
of Mexican liberals, including the future president Benito Juárez, assembled in New Orleans in exile from Payno's employer, the autocrat
general Santa Anna.[14] The profile of Mexican liberalism coalesced, to a
significant degree, there, culminating in Juárez's presidency
(1861–1863, 1867–1872). Cuba's Martí spent fifteen years in exile in New

York and published a series of fascinating, insightful essays on American culture in the age of runaway capitalism: Coney Island, the Brooklyn Bridge, the New York cattle fair, a land grab in Oklahoma, a trial of anarchists in Chicago.[15] Martí was repulsed by the abjectness of the immigrant multitudes and by the social fabric constructed around money making. He decried the monopoly capitalism and business oligarchy that he saw taking shape before him. At the same time, his enthusiasm for the energy, the crowds, the inventiveness and openness of U.S. society saturates the essays.

For Martí and many others of his generation, the United States's positive qualities coalesced in a single larger-than-life and hypermasculine figure—Walt Whitman.[16] "Only the sacred books of antiquity," Martí wrote in 1887, "offer a comparable doctrine, with the prophetic language and robust poetry . . . that this old poet emits, like mouthfuls of light." Martí makes a soaring tribute, energized in particular by Whitman's naturalness, egalitarianism, and (homo)eroticism: "If not the poet of best taste, he is the most intrepid, all-embracing and uninhibited voice of his time."[17] The Nicaraguan Rubén Darío, seen as the founder of Latin American modernism, was another. His Whitman is a benevolent imperial figure, a "patriarch serene and holy" with "the proud face of an emperor."[18] (Darío also wrote a poem to Teddy Roosevelt, criticizing his "big stick.") Testosterone-driven, the fascination lasted. Neruda called Whitman "my necessary brother"; Octavio Paz pointed to his imperial, predatory tendency.[19] In 1969, Borges translated *Leaves of Grass* and dedicated it to Richard Nixon.[20] The fact that one can ask whether Borges's gesture was sincere or tongue-in-cheek exemplifies the ambiguities of the North-South relationship, as well as of Whitman.

But there is a third term in all these ideological schemas: Europe. For the century following their independence from Spain, the Latin American republics were also renegotiating their relations, imaginary and material, with Europe. Sarmiento got to the United States via Europe and North Africa, and his pro-American attitudes were conditioned by that experience. The United States was often included in a binary vision that celebrated the youth and energy of the New World against the fatigue and violence of the old. For instance, when the Cuban Gertrúdis Gómez de Avellaneda composed an ode to George Washington in the 1840s, she identified his greatness as American virtue over and against a war-torn Europe:

> *He watched Europe bloody its soil*
> *in the spirit of war and victory*
> *But to America fell the glory*
> *of housing the spirit of good*[21]

American nature was a privileged signifier for such hemispheric sentiments. Niagara Falls, for example, was one of a series of obligatory stops for Latin American travelers in the United States and generated a sizable corpus of writings throughout the century.[22]

Independence from Spain opened the door to a wave of British and French investment and to a neocolonial economic order that renewed Latin America's economically dependent status. This neocoloniality both collided and squared with European cultural loyalties among the elites and with the imperative to develop independent cultural identities. In the domain of the imaginary, the triangulation staged itself repeatedly through another literary referent: Shakespeare's *The Tempest.* Prospero was read as Europe, Caliban as indigenous, black, and mestizo America, and Ariel as white or *criollo* Euro-America. The mutations of the schema are as numerous as the cultural prescriptions for the new American republics. In 1900, the Uruguayan José Enrique Rodó wrote a classic cultural manifesto called *Ariel* in which Caliban embodies the negative qualities of the United States, while Ariel represents the noble force of a Euro-American high culture true to its *criollo* (white) roots. Here democracy is the enemy, the rule of Caliban. The anti-U.S. argument serves to relegitimate oligarchic structures of privilege rooted in the colonial era. The racial text is unmistakable and predominates especially in the countries of the Southern Cone, which built themselves around explicit policies of white supremacy. Sarmiento modeled his racial policies on the United States's own policy of segregation and on its eradication of the country's indigenous peoples. Responding to the war of 1898, the Franco-Argentine Paul Groussac saw the United States as having shed its "formless and Calibanesque body" to become "the newest civilization that intends to supplant our own, declared to be in decay." The prospect provoked "disquiet and terror."[23] Martí assigned the same terms opposite valences: *mestizaje* and racial democracy were what distinguished America positively from Europe. Ariel had to choose between serving Prospero and serving Caliban, and the right choice was Caliban: "The American intelligence is an indigenous plumage. Is it not evident that America itself was paralyzed by the same blow that paralyzed the Indian? And until the Indian is caused to walk, America itself will not begin to walk well."[24] To exclude the United States from this schema, Martí misreads U.S. society as segregated and as lacking in racial admixture.

And Miranda? No one mentions her. But Latin American women intellectuals and activists were certainly confirming Rodó's fears of the uncivilized north and its barbarian influence. They found allies and models in U.S. women's movements (as well as in European anarchism). They founded pan-American organizations, teachers' unions, and labor movements. Through Horace and Mary Mann, strong relations developed between Columbia Teachers College and women's movements in Latin America.[25] Pan-American congresses laid out hemispheric feminist and anti-war platforms. From midcentury on, the United States's emancipated women were a touchstone for what might be called anti-anti-Americanism among Latin American women activists and intellectuals. Today, gay writers make the same point in their dialogues with the Left.[26]

Despite the Calibanian pressures of democratic movements, the sociocultural model Rodó was defending—white oligarchies ruling barbarous masses—in effect, won. That is, it became the dominant, continuously challenged structure of power in most countries in Latin America, and it remains so in many today. It predominates, of course, in deep collaboration with the "colossus of the north."[27] Carlos Fuentes, in his fine novel *La Muerte de Artemio Cruz* [The Death of Artemio Cruz, 1962], was among the few novelists of the Latin American boom to take on the intricacies of the love-hate relations between the United States and Latin American capitalist classes. I end with a couple of passages from this novel, in which Fuentes stages this relationship in an insightful way, dramatizing both the corrupt power game and the workings of mutual contempt. Though written in 1962, the text resonates deeply today. The protagonist of the novel is a Mexican businessman, Artemio Cruz, who, out of the upheaval of the Mexican Revolution, has risen from nothing to become extremely wealthy after World War II, in the wake of development fever. The first quotation is from a scene in which he is negotiating with American investors who want him to be the front man for their investment in sulphur domes:

> He [the American] explained the system again and the other Americans said that they were very pleased with their findings, and sliced

the air several times with his hand, shaking it quite close to his leath-
ery red face and repeating in Spanish, "Domes good, pyrites bad,
domes good, pyrites bad." He [Cruz, the Mexican protagonist]
drummed his fingers on the glass top of the table and nodded, accustomed to the fact that whenever they spoke to him in Spanish they
thought he didn't understand. Not because they spoke Spanish badly,
but because he didn't understand anything well.[28]

The Americans appear to be merely inviting him to invest in their project, but Cruz decides to win this game and demands a payment of two
million dollars up front for his collaboration:

The geologist cleaned his glasses with a small piece of chamois that he
kept in his shirt pocket, while the other American began to walk from
the table to the window, from the window to the table. Until he [Cruz]
repeated that those were his conditions. The two million dollars was
not an advance or credit, or anything like that. This was how much
they owed him for getting the concessions for them. Without him,
without the front man, as he said in English, apologizing for his frank-
ness, they would never get the concessions to work those deposits. He
pushed a button to call his secretary, and the secretary rapidly read a
sheet of figures, and the Americans said "OK" several times, "OK, OK,
OK" and he smiled, and offered them whiskey and told them they
could exploit those sulphur deposits until well into the next century,
but they weren't going to exploit him for one minute in this one. And
they all toasted, and the two Americans smiled as they muttered just
once under their breath "son of a bitch."[29]

Notice here that Cruz's anti-Americanism does not involve feeling victimized or inferior. On the contrary. As a Mexican friend once said, "No
es que pensemos que los gringos sean malévolos, sino pendejos" [It's
not that we think the gringos are evil, we just think they're jerks]. (Pen-
dejo means stupid, ignorant or just dumb.) The sense is that gringos have
more money and power than they deserve; at the same time their consumer culture, as Fuentes explores through Cruz, inspires envy, fascination, and emulation.

Later in the novel the author goes back over the same scene in a
stream-of-consciousness mode that explores the structure of desire that
shapes the interaction:

You must feel proud that you could impose your will on them. Confess it—you imposed yourself so that they would let you in, as your equal. . . . You admire their efficiency, their comforts, their hygiene, their power, their will, and you look around you at the incompetence, the misery, the filth, the langour, the nakedness of this poor country that has nothing. All seems intolerable to you. And what pains you even more is knowing that no matter how much you try, you cannot be like them. You can only be a copy, an approximation, because after all, say it now, was your vision of things in your worst or your best moments, ever as simplistic as theirs? Never. Never have you been able to think in black and white, good guys versus bad guys, God or the devil. Admit that always, even when it seemed just the opposite, you have found the germ, the reflection, of the white in the black. You know that all extremes contain their opposites, cruelty and tenderness, power and slavery, life and death. In some way, almost unconsciously, because of who you are, because of what you have lived through, you know this. And for that reason you can never resemble them, who don't know these things. Does that bother you? Of course it does. It's uncomfortable, annoying. It's much easier to say, "this is good and that is good." And that is evil. Evil. You could never say "that is evil." Perhaps because we are more forsaken we do not want to lose that intermediate, ambiguous zone between light and shadow. The zone where we can find forgiveness.[30]

Today this contrast between an unforgiving black-and-white American moralism and a forgiving Latin American ambiguity is a cliché. It remains one of the most widespread formulations of the "our America/their America" cultural polarity. The paradox must be noted: if the contrast is accurate, the Latin American preference for ambiguity should dissolve the polarity itself. But it comes back, helped in recent times by dogmatic right-wing power in the United States, whose words and deeds daily confirm the cliché. The paradox is as good an index as any of the depths of our *américan* dilemmas.

NOTES

1. In September 2003, an HBO extravaganza recalled, fairly accurately, Villa's dealings with Griffith. After Wilson withdrew his support, Villa made a

second contract with Griffith, this time for a scripted feature film in which he becomes president of Mexico. Villa acted in scenes and was even willing, at the cost of lives, to transfer attacks from night to day for the cameras. HBO surely intended its viewers to make the connections with today's spectacle wars, where media and military objectives are scarcely distinguished.

2. This at least is the hypothesis of the contemporary authority on Villa, the historian Friedrich Katz. See his *Life and Times of Pancho Villa*, 2 vols. (Palo Alto: Stanford University Press, 1998).

3. Reed wrote a famous account of his adventures with the villistas, *Insurgent Mexico* (New York: Appleton, 1914). He went on to cover the Russian Revolution in his famous *Ten Days That Shook the* World (New York: Boris and Liveright, 1919) and became himself the hero of Warren Beatty's movie *Reds* (1991).

4. They brought it in by mule. In photos from Baghdad, at the time of this writing, boys deliver gasoline by bicycle.

5. Paul Espinosa, film, "The Hunt for Pancho Villa" (San Diego: San Diego State University, 1992).

6. Ibid.

7. José Mármol, *Obras Poéticas* (Buenos Aires: Maucci, 1889).

8. The image is potent. Mexico's high-profile ambassador to the UN, Adolfo Aguilar Zinser, was fired in November 2003 after asserting, in a speech in Mexico City, that "the United States sees us as its back yard," wanting a "relationship of convenience and subordination." "It was the wrong thing to say," opined President Vicente Fox, rejecting the statement. ("Mexico Dismisses Its UN Envoy for Critical Remark about U.S.," *New York Times*, November 19, 2003).

9. The School of the Americas in Panama, for instance, was founded in 1946. For a discussion of accompanying U.S. cultural policies, see Jean Franco, *The Rise and Fall of the Lettered City: Culture and the Cold War in Latin America* (Cambridge, MA: Harvard University Press, 2002).

10. José Martí, cited in Roberto Fernández Retamar's classic reconsideration of the *Tempest* trope, *"Caliban" and Other Essays*, trans. Edward Baker (Minneapolis: University of Minnesota Press, 1989), pp. 10–11. Spanish original, *Calibán: Apuntes sobre la cultura en nuestra América* (Mexico City: Díogenes, 1972). For discussion of Martí, see also José Saldívar, *The Dialectics of Our America* (Durham: Duke University Press, 1991).

11. José Carlos Mariátequi, cited in Retamar, *"Caliban" and Other Essays*, p. 11.

12. Sarmiento returned to the United States as a diplomat in 1865–1868 before becoming president of Argentina (1869–1874).

13. I thank Karina Hodoyan for this information. See her forthcoming doctoral thesis on Payno, Department of Spanish and Portuguese, Stanford University.

14. Others included Melchor Ocampo, José María Mata, Ponciano Arriaga, Manuel Cepeda, and Juan Bautista Ceballos. See Gustavo Baz, *Vida de Benito Juárez* (Puebla: José M. Cajica, 1972).

15. José Martí, *Crónicas*, ed. Susana Rothker (Madrid: Alianza, 1993).

16. See Doris Sommer, "The Bard of Both Americas," in Donald D. Kummings, ed., *Approaches to Teaching Whitman's* Leaves of Grass (New York: Modern Language Association, 1990), pp. 159–167, and Fernando Alegría, *Walt Whitman en Hispanoamérica* (México: Studium, 1954).

17. José Martí, "El Poeta Walt Whitman," in *Crónicas*, p. 113.

18. Rubén Darío, "Walt Whitman," in his 1888 volume *Azul*, included in *Obras completas* (Madrid: Aguilar, 1968), p. 583.

19. Sommer, "The Bard of Both Americas," p. 260.

20. Retamar, *"Caliban" and Other Essays*, p. 26.

21. "A Washington," in Gertrúdis Gómez de Avellaneda, *Obras literarias*, vol. 1 (Madrid: M. Rivadeneyra, 1869), p. 76. Translation mine. The original lines are: "Miró la Europea ensangrentar su suelo / Al genio de la guerra y al victoria . . . / Pero le cupo a América la gloria / De que al genio del bien le diera el cielo."

22. See, for instance, the now classic ode to Niagara by the Cuban José María Heredia in the 1820s, and Gómez de Avellaneda's "Niagara," from the 1860s.

23. Quoted in Retamar, *"Caliban" and Other Essays*, p. 10. The Spanish original first appeared in Havana in 1971. See Retamar's book for a review of the *Tempest* trope in Latin American letters. For a more recent review, see the special issue of *Nuevo Texto Crítico* 9–10 (1992), Stanford University, on Caliban.

24. Quoted in Retamar, *"Caliban" and Other Essays*, p. 20. The original text was an 1884 essay on indigenous American writers.

25. Seminar on Feminism and Culture in Latin America (Bergmann et al.), *Women, Culture and Politics in Latin America* (Berkeley: University of California Press, 1990).

26. See for example the Chilean gay activist and intellectual Pedro Lemebel's 1996 "Manifesto: I Speak from My Difference," addressed to defenders of Marxism "that so many times rejected me." Don't talk to me about the injustices of capitalism, he says; "in New York the gays are kissing in the street." Pedro Lemebel, *Loco afán: Crónicas del sidario* (Santiago de Chile: LOM, 1997), p. 89. Translation mine. Lemebel's position is to be distinguished from the straightforwardly U.S.-identified posture of the group of contemporary writers led by the Chilean Alberto Fuguet, which adopted the name McOndo. These writers embrace U.S. mass culture and in a parricidal gesture reject magic realism. Their manifesto is strongly masculinist and heterosexist. Alberto Fuguet and Sergio Gómez eds., *McOndo* (Barcelona: Grijalbo, 1996).

27. That is why recent political developments in Bolivia, Ecuador,

Venezuela, Brazil, and Argentina are so important. They suggest that neoliberalism finally seems to have produced a political response with the capacity to take over governments. It will be very interesting to see what happens in those countries in the immediate future.

28. Carlos Fuentes, *The Death of Artemio Cruz,* trans. Alfred MacAdam (New York: Farrar, Straus and Giroux, 1991), p. 18. Spanish original, *La Muerte de Artemio Cruz* (Mexico City: Fonde de Cultural Económica, 1962).

29. Ibid., p. 19.

30. Ibid., p. 27.

3

The 3:10 to Yuma

Ana María Dopico

WRITING THE DAY BEFORE HIS DEATH on April 8, 1895, and finally in the field of the Cuban War of Independence, Cuba's revolutionary hero and national poet, José Martí, declared to his friends:

> I am everyday in danger of giving my life for my country and in the duty . . . of impeding, with the independence of Cuba, the United States from extending into the Antilles, and then falling, with still greater strength, upon the rest of our American lands. Everything I have done until now and everything I will do is for that. I have had to labor for this in silence and indirectly because there are things that must be hidden to be achieved, and proclaiming them for what they are would have raised difficulties too stringent to surmount in reaching our end. . . . With our blood we are blocking the path leading to the annexation of the peoples of our America to that chaotic and brutal north which so despises them.
>
> I lived in the monster and I know its entrails—and my way is that of David's. Only days ago . . . fresh from the sense of victory with which Cubans saluted our expedition's free emergence from the Sierras, I was dragged from my hammock, on my ranch, by the correspondent of the *Herald*, talking of annexation.[1]

José Martí, who himself lived most of his adult life in New York, tried to wrest the word *América* away from its U.S. owners and restore it as a hemispheric denotation, a transnational binding identity capable of serving as a proud alternative to U.S. culture. Martí lived through and reported on the violent dispossessions and seizures that marked U.S. expansion to its west; he chronicled the bottomless greed for land and resources and the spectacles of progress and capital that showcased and legitimized U.S. power at the end of the century.[2] In his journalism, speeches, and essays, Martí warned Latin Americans and Cubans of annexationist designs and imperial futures that were funded, promoted, and debated privately and publicly in Washington and New York. Even as he raised funds for a revolutionary party and an insurgent movement, Martí contemplated with horror the possibilities of U.S. expansion in Latin America and was constantly preoccupied with public plans and designs on Cuba in particular, whose political and military vulnerability and whose geographical proximity to the United States might doom its independence and lead to the island's transfer from one imperial order to another. Martí's articulation of the American danger, written in the last days of his life, is heroic and oracular, and his desire for an autonomous and uncompromised Cuban state is, in a certain sense, still incomplete.

Cuban anti-Americanism represents a deep knowledge shared across Latin America in the twentieth century. As anti-imperialism, it is inextricable from the drive for Cuban national autonomy. Growing out of Cuba and its exiles within the past 130 years, anti-Americanism as critique and ideology has hemispheric, international, and domestic dimensions. The hemispheric dimensions were decisive in the nineteenth-century articulation of a geopolitical critique of U.S. expansionism from the Americas, expressed as profound alarm by Cuban revolutionaries who feared annexation. Thus, anti-Americanism was a founding, although covert, critical attitude for the Cuban republic. The international dimensions multiplied and intensified after the 1959 revolution, as Cuba led and promoted third-worldist and nonaligned movements. For Cubans at home and in exile, the domestic dimensions of anti-Americanism affect everyday life and often define the limits between public and private. After 1959, anti-Americanism evolved as both the defining ideology of state discourse and a problematic doublebind of national identity.

Cuban anti-Americanism is profoundly and intimately connected to the idea of revolution, both as insurgent movement against imperialism and as an ideology institutionalized by the state, in what can be called socialism or *castrismo*, depending on one's perspective, since 1959. Cuban anti-Americanism today can be read both as part of a continuum of Latin American sentiments and ideology and as an exceptional result of revolution and cold war. Since the revolution of 1959, anti-Americanism has functioned as a major but mobile fixture of state discourse that helped to define Cuba's socialist aims through opposi-tion to the island's powerful enemy and former master. Anti-Ameri-canism has consistently identified the United States as a doubly offen-sive and threatening enemy that embodies both the evils of imperialism and the corruptions of capitalism. As it became subsumed into state rhetoric over the past forty years, the critical and strategic force of anti-Americanism became so fluid in its conjugations and so totalizing in its coverage that, I suggest, it lost its urgent critical force. Participation in that rhetoric of anti-Americanism became, from 1961 on, a litmus test for participation in and solidarity with *la revolución* and with the na-tion—the mark of solid citizen and militant patriot. The enforcement of that rhetoric as official ideology robbed it of spontaneity and displaced it from its popular origins and articulations, freezing it into the political liturgy of the state and the gestural ritual of Fidel Castro.

GENEALOGIES OF ANTI-AMERICANISM

Cuban anti-Americanism was born in national memory as resentment and frustration at the U.S. hijacking of the War of Independence of 1895: known as the *Guerra de Independencia* among Cubans, it was renamed in the United States, erasing Cuba itself, the Spanish-American War. Dur-ing that struggle, Cubans watched as their hard-fought victory against Spain, a result of more than fifty years of struggle and thirty-four years of sporadic war, was wrested from their hands by their American "pro-tectors." For the United States, the Cuban national cause was the thresh-old for their belated entry into imperial power, and the Cuban theater of operations served as a proving ground for military and political strategies and methods similarly applied in Puerto Rico and the Philip-pines. As Cuban revolutionary victory turned into American occupa-tion, the anger and frustration of at least three generations were both in-ternalized and institutionalized: internalized as national shame and re-sentment and institutionalized in the form of cynicism and corruption.

With the end of occupation and the inauguration of the Cuban state in 1902, national independence was hopelessly compromised. Self-de-termination and sovereignty were hamstrung by the imposition of the Platt Amendment, which legally inscribed the prerogatives of empire into both the U.S. and the Cuban constitutions. The Platt Amendment's extraordinary provisions excluded black Cubans from enfranchisement, submitted Cuban electoral process and election results to U.S. supervision and approval, subordinated Cuban state sovereignty to U.S. interests, and guaranteed the reserved right of intervention as remedy to any offensive act of Cuban autonomy.[3] Although the Platt Amendment was officially repealed in 1934, its aims and functions had by then become part of the permanent infrastructure of the Cuban economy and the republic. Its interventionist prerogatives shifted from military occupation and occasional invasion to a more systemic dissemination of American authority, defended by Cuban puppets, clients, and subordinates. Its aims were exercised more effectively through complete economic penetration, its policing functions delegated to corrupt civil and military subalterns, and its control over self-determination and sovereignty guaranteed by the large-scale corruption, patronage, and coercion that had been integrated into the electoral system.

From the birth of the Cuban republic, therefore, we can trace generational continuities of anti-Americanism that organize national structures of feeling and that functioned beyond political alignments and exigencies: feelings that correspond to resentment, to intervention, to encroachment, to negation of agency, and to a general sense of violation and shame. The anti-Americanism of those who lived through successive failed republics and dictatorships led directly to social resistance, to attempted rebellions, and, eventually, to the revolution of 1959. Articulations of anti-Americanism emerged from internationalist and socialist movements and from labor and student struggles. In many cases, those feelings and their expression (bound within the social relations of a neoimperial colony) were not necessarily connected to collective or communal ties but lived individually and privately as outrage over corruption, abuse, patronage. Anti-Americanism then, emerged from the individual and collective sense of paralysis experienced by Cubans for whom the state was a spectacle of power, controlled beyond their reach.

By the 1950s, with Cuba under Batista's second dictatorial term in office, anti-Americanism in Cuba could be described as divided along race, class, and territorial lines. Anti-Americanism as an attitude and a structure of feeling was distributed among and defined by metropolitan middle classes, urban and agricultural workers, and rural populations, from landholders to the impoverished agricultural proletariat. A vocal and educated metropolitan middle class, of various income levels, racial origins, social aspirations, and political affiliations, articulated anti-Americanism as an indignant resentment of U.S. economic interests and patronage, which blocked professional and social mobility. Anti-Americanism was a dominant, although sometimes camouflaged, theme in political critiques, and it was registered as disgust at Cuban corruption and shame at Cuba's national impotence. Campaign slogans like "*Vergüenza contra dinero*"[4] ["Shame against money"] articulated the negative dialectics of corruption, humiliation, shame, and outrage constructed and fueled by American power in Cuba. Such appeals tapped into a popular critique leveled against successive thieving politicians and elected officials, revealing open anger and widespread cynicism at Cuba's systematic corruption. This unofficial and perpetual campaign served more as a palliative than as a solution, increasing the sense of impotence and failed autonomy and confirming for many Cubans the absurdity of an electoral democracy controlled by American interests.

Middle-class Cubans also articulated a moral anti-Americanism in critiques of American tourists—their manners, their loudness, their sexual mores, and their sense of entitlement. This was one form of anti-Americanism that would survive the trip into exile. Such indignation was localized, and critiques of the United States could be deflected from domestic politics and social conflicts and turned into critiques of macroeconomics or foreign policy and alliances, heavily tempered and compromised by those who could afford and admired U.S. products and the reified charms of "standard of living" and "American know-how." Thus, Cubans resentful of U.S. power nevertheless aspired to consume the comforts of U.S. exports and commodity cultures and were increasingly interpellated by an expanding "American" consumer imaginary and by an infrastructure for advertising, public relations, and popular media that served as threshold for selling the United States to the rest of Latin America.

For rural populations that lived in a privatized state on the plantations of United Fruit and other U.S. corporations (which owned vast percentages of the island and its resources), anti-Americanism evolved differently. This sphere is the world that Fidel Castro grew up in; the son of a prosperous family exempted from the direct discipline of neocolonialism, he nevertheless grew up in close proximity to a United Fruit plantation. A Cuban legend about Fidel as a child offers an ironic prehistory for his strategic appraisal of U.S. power. According to the tale, the young Fidel, hearing about the Good Neighbor Policy that the United States promoted in Latin America, decided to write to President

Franklin D. Roosevelt in the White House. Taking the American president at his word about good neighbors, Fidel wrote asking the president for ten dollars. The juvenile humor and shrewdness implicit in the tale affirm the *comandante*'s understanding of the double-edged realities of U.S. power and his ability to manipulate the ideological seductions of "American" hemispheric strategy. This trajectory of anti-Americanism, marked by realism, wiles, irony, and gamesmanship, is important in the Cuban context and is worth considering, even as legend, since it continues to mark the ambivalences and the contradictions, the opportunism and the strategic calculus implicit in every official Cuban policy regarding the United States.

For the Cuban working classes, anti-Americanism was similarly variegated, but less mitigated by access to the rewards of U.S. commodities, gold standards, and high prices. For many involved in unions and labor activism, U.S. intervention was not an old chimera but a very threatening and present specter, outsourced to U.S. puppets who undermined, outlawed, and repressed labor organizations and movements, first through outright military or police violence and then through corruption, graft, and coercion. In the historical memory of working-class Cubans, and in particular black Cubans, for whom mobility was limited, anti-Americanism was not a sentiment or a mere resentment but a daily critical response to their private and collective experience. That historical memory and the lived experience of exclusion would bear important fruit after 1959, when the socialist revolution triumphed among the black population and cemented its mass popular base by making racial justice and equal opportunity an ideological priority and an institutional reform.

It is worth noting that the critique of racism in the United States has been perhaps the most important critical stream of anti-Americanism that came out of the revolution of 1959. That critique, and with it the compromised progress in racial equality in Cuba over the past forty years, has secured loyalty to the revolution inside Cuba. The rhetoric of anti-racism and racial justice has also helped to sustain alliances and support for Cuba abroad throughout the life of the revolution. From the moment of Castro's decision to stay in Harlem in his 1960 visit to New York,[5] he traced a clear a line of demarcation between his anti-Americanism and his American alliances. In a sense, he made clear the battle over who claims America and who is excluded from that claim. By visiting Harlem as neutral zone, liberated territory, or privileged site of

asylum, Fidel took sides and asked black Americans to do the same, offering Cuba as a corresponding and national ideal state for blacks in the
Americas and a defender of Africa, its autonomies, and its diasporas
worldwide. The loyalties inspired then, and across decades of oppositional and sometimes violent resistance in the United States, when
Cuba offered asylum to Black Panthers and other enemies of the
"American" state, have been part of a long dialectic of opposition, and
perhaps the most positive and least corrupted rhetoric of the Cuban
revolution.

Fidel echoed and reaffirmed his solidarity with black Americans in
the autumn of 2000, when, during a six-hour speech at Riverside
Church, he announced an official offer of free medical education and
training for African American and low-income minority students from
the United States. That offer reflects Cuba's strategic use of anti-Americanism as a critique of capitalism and its racial exclusions, offering condemnation of power and solidarity with the disenfranchised abroad
and reaffirming Cuba's identity as a defender or haven for black America. Castro's offer also reaffirmed José Martí's distinction between a
"good," popular, democratic, and revolutionary America, properly belonging to the miscegenated masses, and a "bad," imperial, racist
"America," whose name had been kidnapped by the greedy and powerful. That symbolic representation is not necessarily translated into political power in governing councils in Fidel's dictatorship of the proletariat; indeed, it seems to function as a discursive ideology detached
from the tourist economy, the economic apartheids, and the racialized
markets for exoticism that many black Cubans are presently negotiating. There is no denying, however, the significance of Cuba's symbolic
status as vanguard and haven for struggles for black liberation, black
culture, and black causes—its forty years of sustained critique and social experiment in racial justice have been extraordinary and perhaps
unprecedented in the Americas since Haiti's revolution of 1802. Remarkably, Cuba's status as a black world nation is a phenomenon that
has been underestimated and undertheorized until quite recently,
among two generations of largely white Cubanologists who watched
the state from successive waves of exile. The powerful critique of racism
is part of the continued bite of Cuba's anti-Americanism and a potent
reminder to black Cubans well educated in U.S. racial politics. This
strand of revolutionary critical ideology holds up an uncomfortable
and defamiliarizing x-ray of U.S. culture for white critiques. It must also

be used as an unsettling measure for the Cuban state as it weighs its ideals against the socioeconomic realities of the Special Period: compromised realities that exploit "blackness" as mass revolutionary identity and as marketable commodity, while deferring and constricting the access of black Cubans to real political agency and self-representation.

THE REVOLUTION:
ANTI-AMERICANISM AS IDEOLOGY AND INSTITUTION

The defining moment of anti-Americanism in the early days of the Revolution came in the week of April 16–23, 1961. Radically altering the path of what until then had been an ideologically variegated popular movement and insurrection, Fidel Castro declared, on April 16, 1961, "This is a socialist revolution." By later that same day, John F. Kennedy had given permission to run and fund an interventionist force to go into Playa Girón, or the Bay of Pigs. This armed intervention, guided by the CIA, manned by exiled Cubans of different political stripe but ultimately abandoned by the United States in terms of official military support, was met by a massive and popular Cuban mobilization. Fidel called the people to arms against the common enemy of the newly autonomous national revolution and consolidated the popular victory of resistance with a season of mass-media political theater. With the revolution and its popular heroes as protagonists, the televised events aimed to teach the population in exhaustive and even theoretical detail the connection that linked neoimperial power, the capital it deployed in the form of armed intervention, and the corrupt and "parasitical" native class that was willing to cooperate as clients or carriers of U.S. power. The intervention and its televised aftermath, complete with excruciating but compelling show trials, served as a potent object lesson: a domestic and international master class in U.S. imperialism and in the vile weakness of Cuban complicity as revealed by the exiled invaders. Creating a typology of villains and violations in the televised trials, the state at once revealed U.S. designs, exposed the fatal consequences of American arrogance and Cuban treachery, and decisively defined anti-Americanism as a requisite quality of a true revolutionary.

Anti-Americanism translated in revolutionary Cuban into the important phrase *"imperialismo yanqui"* and in the outraged demand of

"*¡Fuera imperialistas yanquis!*" ["Yankee go home!"]—phrases employed throughout Latin America and worldwide and that evoke an ironic laughter of recognition here in the United States, a laughter that indicated just how much the phrase had become a political cliché in which we warmly recognized outmoded forms, futile struggles, or enduring and revitalized world outrage at U.S. power and intervention. The phrase evoked a series of contested and graduated meanings among nations where it served as a historical graffiti marking the circuits of empire and the struggles against it. Within the revolution as institution and state, anti-Americanism became synonymous with anti-imperialism, and the eternal signifier "*imperialismo yanqui*" became the Cuban way to triangulate and redevelop an "Americas" version of a socialist critique of capitalism.

In Cuba, since the revolution, those who side with or express sympathy for Americans or who articulate skepticism regarding the official state rhetoric of anti-Americanism have been called *gusanos,* or worms, a phrase that became a verb in the 1980s, particularly following the Mariel exodus, when to *gusanear* meant to express or embody counterrevolutionary sentiments, tendencies, or intentions. Beyond denoting a spineless and base form of life, *gusano* and its morphing forms serve to connote cowardly and subterranean movements, annoying and pusillanimous pests, a natural and recurring life form that interferes with progress and provokes disgust. And, although the insult is meant to dismiss Castro's opposition, it also signals cooperation and collusion among the enemies of Cuba at home and abroad. As a symptom of a frozen official nomenclature, the word and its variations continue to circulate and hold prominence in official rhetoric, where *gusaneo* evokes a dirty writhing movement and where *gusanera,* or wormlike cohort, is applied again and again to a Miami exile community perceived as a constantly conspiratorial and cowardly eternal enemy.

To monitor and battle *gusanos* and *gusanería,* as well as acts of sabotage, the Cuban state has had recourse to a number of institutions and resources, with the *Comités de Defensa de la Revolución,* or Committees for the Defense of the Revolution (CDRs), serving as its most penetrating and omnipresent instrument of surveillance and social control. The CDRs predate the invasion of Playa Girón: they were founded on November 28, 1960, to respond to acts of urban terrorism, in particular an attack on the presidential palace. The *Comités* offer a provocative example for the United States today, since they serve as the "popular" institutionalization of surveillance, and their founding mission condenses local pride and participation (however coerced), patriotic voluntarism, and a daily vigilance in a war against dissent and domestic terrorism. In 1961, and following Fidel's clarification of the revolution's "socialist" identity, anti-Americanism as ideology was further solidified, required, and monitored as a key function of the *Comités de Defensa de la Revolución*.

Anti-Americanism as enforced by the CDRs has been monitored across their extraordinary horizontal organization, which at one point claimed the participation and loyalty of 90 percent of the Cuban population. Within that network of belonging, potential affiliation, and coercion, anti-Americanism became a speech-act test of loyalty to the revolution that must be practiced publicly and uttered to colleagues, neighbors, friends, and family. It served as a performative compulsory utterance continuously woven into the fabric of everyday life. Sympathy for or mention or praise of American culture or actions became a heretical utterance for Cubans. That ideological heresy was tracked vertically through party censorship and surveillance but more potently through the low-level policing of the CDRs and their compulsory social networks. The policing of the formidable *Comités* was more intimate and therefore more frightening in its reach: it was accomplished in conversations that were actually interrogations, carried by rumor, monitored through a paranoia of detail. Loyalty was confirmed or denied by the degree to which citizens participated at the local level in expanding that web of information or in contributing their work to collective projects and labor. Sympathy for the United States was permanently identified with counterrevolution in this highly sensitive system of vigilance, where one weakness of thought, inconsistency of critique, or inadvertent comment or reluctant action was weighed on a constantly accumulating and overcalibrated scale setting loyalty against treachery, the new man against the *gusano*.

SPECTERS OF ANTI-AMERICANISM:
CUBA AS IDEAL AND SOCIALIST MIRAGE

Moving to the Special Period and its anti-Americanisms, we might consider a couple of significant inconsistencies between Cuba's anti-American rhetoric and its economic strategies. The Special Period represents a threshold moment analogous to the pronouncement of the "socialist revolution" in 1961: it ushered in a new political and economic reality. In October 1990, Fidel Castro, acknowledging the devastating effects of the withdrawal of Soviet aid and subsidies, declared that Cuba had entered "a special period in time of peace" and that the economy would operate under wartime conditions and provisions for the foreseeable future. The Special Period and its urgencies not only revealed the insufficiencies of a socialist state capitalism subsidized by the Soviet Union but also exposed a bifurcation implicit to anti-Americanism, a bifurcation between critiques of capitalism and critiques of dominance and imperialism that continues to divide both America's friends and its enemies. Shifts and experiments in Cuban alignments, economic policy, and mixed economies revealed variations between a "geopolitical" branch of anti-Americanism that denounced U.S. hegemony, domination, and neoimperialism and an anti-embargo and antiglobalization branch that simultaneously denounced and invited international capital and foreign investment.

Special Period Cuba may be anti-imperial in its rhetoric, but it is no longer anti-capitalist. In the past ten years, Cuba's economic survival has depended on its ability to court and attract multinational capital. In 1995, Cuba's Foreign Investment Act revised socialist economic policy and invited foreign investment on a massive scale. The Foreign Investment Act licensed the embattled and impoverished Cuban state and its bureaucracy to serve as agents and partners in joint venture projects with foreign and multinational companies from Europe, Japan, and elsewhere that trade in everything from hotels to communications to commodities and transportation. By shifting the terms of the anti-American critique from capitalism to geopolitics, official Cuban discourse distinguished between U.S. hegemony and its new free-market investors. Defined chiefly by critiques of the U.S. embargo and the Helms-Burton Bill, this new anti-Americanism was conveniently severed from potentially dangerous critiques of Cuba's traffic with and dependence on other sources of capital and cultural hegemony. The legacy of the anti-American position produced a slightly surreal or ironic effect, as Fidel greeted every luminary and celebrity who visited the island like a hotel owner hosting an open house but also took the time, whenever necessary, to rehearse the old oppositional routine at the level of public spectacle.

For the American Left, which has been belatedly loyal to the idea of Cuba's moribund socialism and to Fidel Castro as a charismatic oppositional world leader, Cuba's anti-American critiques serve as the familiar liturgy of a posthumous revolutionary age. Fidel Castro serves as the embodiment of revolution, condensing patriarchal tradition and messianic appeal, a strong man alone, who symbolizes the heroic status of the revolution and its compromises during the Special Period. Fidel's authority continues to be justified within the logic of the dictatorship of the proletariat: his seemingly eternal power ascends, constant and unyielding, from the will of the people channeled through that of the party, the Congress, and the Council of Ministers. Representing a despotic and interminable exercise of popular will, seeking no apparent alternative or successor, and ruling with increasingly terrible waves of repression, Fidel himself, as a singular personality, seems to have earned the right to a pop star's double life. He survives politically in an exceptional (although disappearing) state of dispensation from condemnation by many who profess to love the Cuban nation and its people. Needing Cuba as an exceptional voice, a spectral conscience, for domestic anti-imperialism, Cuba's allies have for too long ignored the nation's problems and slow decay; such solidarity has often been blind to the slow erosion, if not the complete disappearance, of the ideals and social experiment that onlookers still imagine present. Fidel's anti-imperial, anti-globalization rhetoric has seemed valuable enough as special commemorative currency for many in the American Left, no matter how devalued that currency became for Cubans who live the real collapse and repressive afterlife of his revolutionary society.

In one outrageous instance of that sympathetic blindness, Cubans, their government, and even its allies were curiously silent about anti-imperial incursion when the naval base at Guantánamo was redeployed as Camp Delta and used to house prisoners of the Afghan war, serving as a bizarre gulag for prisoners of the global "war on terror." There was not a word of condemnation from Fidel Castro, or the Cuban government, which seemed strangely pliant and supportive of the rhetorical major keys of the war on terror, a war Cuba claimed it had been fighting for forty years. The events surrounding that astonishing development point to the complicated limits and traffic of anti-Americanism, and Cuba's silence on the matter was strangely eloquent, especially since it was followed by months of visits, encounters, and special conversations between Fidel or his deputies and important American

citizens who traveled to Cuba. In that same year, the United States allowed significant and strategic exceptions to the blockade, particularly
in the form of agricultural sales to the island; this move was celebrated
by grain-state legislators and governors, who subsequently traveled to
Cuba to seal the covert symbiosis of that *realpolitik* exchange. The Special Period delivered another variation of incongruity when Fidel continued to denounce globalization and American hegemony worldwide
in his *comandante supremo* fatigues and then slipped into a deep blue be-
spoke suit and guided guests like Jesse Ventura around the American
exhibit of agricultural products in Havana in October 2002.

The U.S. agricultural lobby, which had long campaigned for an easing of the export ban, achieved a significant victory when Washington
authorized "humanitarian" exports to Cuba in 2001; grain-state representatives pushed in November 2003 for an easing of travel restrictions.
The Special Period thus seems to be holding for embargos, as well: in a
stunning report that belies the ideological posturing of both sides regarding the Cuban embargo, the Spanish daily *El País* reported, in October 2003, that U.S. businesses now make more than $500 million a
year as the principal suppliers of comestibles and agricultural products
to Cuba.[6] Since 2001, such American agricultural exports to Cuba have
grown to represent the largest market share of comestibles, outstrip-
ping their competitors from Spain, France, and Italy and making an officially sanctioned end run around the economic sanctions of the embargo and the Helms-Burton Bill.

One continuous theme connecting old anti-Americanism vigilance
to the surveillances of the present war on terror did crop up in official
Cuban rhetoric in the year following the Afghan War. Cuban attention
to this new American hegemonic fixation suffered a perverse inversion
in official communiques of the embattled but still ubiquitous *Comités de
Defensa de la Revolución.* Apparently reinvigorated by a new ideological
front in the war on terror, the CDRs reflected on the necessity for domestic surveillance: after September 11, 2001, their website reiterated
their founding mission against terrorism, claiming Cuban originality
and forward-thinking. The CDR discourse underlines this new permu-
tation of Cuba's status as a model state and reinforces its significance in
the historical trajectory of the present conflict and its obsessions.[7] The
implications are bizarre, since such Cuban official discourse plays
poker with American strategic interests and anti-terror domestic policies and, by condemning the present "acts of terror," simultaneously

distances itself from a mutation of Arab anti-Americanism that it does not wish to recognize. The CDR website highlights analogies and continuities between its own mission and the necessity for vigilance presently forced upon the United States. As of March 2004, the website continues to run "In the Kingdom of Terrorism," a piece that covers an appeal by John Ashcroft to Americans, presenting local surveillance as a popular responsibility and asking Americans to revive neighborhood watch committees in order to guard against terrorism.[8] The CDR report is written in remarkably neutral language and displays a strange noncritique of the "American" dimension, suggesting instead an insidious appraisal of how useful such organizations can be. The piece issues a "we got there first" claim, relating the CDR's founding mission as a domestic struggle against terrorism. The page offers a disturbing web of associations, implied analogy, and mutual interests in domestic surveillance: disastrously, cynically, or innocently, the writer highlights the echo of Cuba's important invention in the pronouncements of the Opus Dei colossus to the North. Nowhere is anti-imperialism part of the discourse; official rhetoric has clearly moved to another strategic field of engagement.

In closing, I want to suggest two other ideological conjunctures that further complicate the tangled and compromised spectacles, postures, and rhetorics of Cuban anti-Americanism. The first concerns anti-Americanism and un-Americanism among exiled Cubans in the States, particularly as exposed by the Elián González case. My last meditation concerns what it means to like or love America for a generation raised within the Cuban revolution.

EXILE ANTI-AMERICANISMS

The case of Elián González, the exile dramas, the contests over custody and best interests, and the ensuing media circus that occupied Miami for months upended the notion that a Cuban national discourse of anti-Americanism was articulated in and emanated exclusively from the island. The case disrupted the illusion that exile Cubans were exultant and exemplary adoptive citizens of the United States, monolithically loyal to their powerful cold war rescuers and consistently supportive of American policy. In the wake of Elián's seizure and return, the captured images contradicted the image of a long-quiescent Miami as an insular "little Cuba": photos and video footage offered unprecedented scenes of exiles protesting to the edge of riot, flags being desecrated or turned upside down, tires burning, and even inflammatory calls to revolt being issued by elected officials eager to exploit bad-faith solidarity and to test their virtual autonomy as a semi-independent Latin state of South Florida. An attempt to burn a flag apparently failed: whether by accident or by an act of discretion or self-censorship by participating protesters we cannot tell. These events provoked a crisis of self-consciousness among several generations of exiles and a crisis of resentment and outrage among other Latin Americans and anglo Miamians, who for a few days saw the city riven and deformed by spectacles of negative patriotism and reactionary subnationalism. This extraordinary moment, however, was not merely a defensive and moblike primal reaction by exiles who had been vilified as unthinking reactionaries by the Left press for decades. More important, I believe, it reawakened old resentments and shame dating back to the Bay of Pigs, feelings leveled at a new betrayal by the U.S. government and inflamed by its disregard of the exiles' opinions and right to self-determination in the face of an international scandal. The "Elián event" revealed an old anger at the contemptuous disregard (what Martí in his writing calls the *desprecio*) of the United States for the rights, the integrity, and the autonomy of Latin American subjects and citizens, "rights" of affect and identity that Cubans implicitly claim as bicultural subjects. For the media, it seemed the cold war white gloves were off with respect to Cuban exiles, and Miami was represented and interpreted as un-American: a banana republic floating away from the Florida peninsula and back to the Caribbean. In that mass media frame, Miami was screened as just another rebellious and retrograde Latin American city, its citizens recoded as aliens who had severed themselves from their own assimilation and from the reasonable limits of U.S. civil society. Finally, a small armed invasion in the middle of the night recouped U.S. interests and brought things to a head.

I suggest that, as they became outlaws before the cameras and were vilified by both friends and strangers, Miami Cubans sensed that they had lost their bicultural status by not surrendering their Cuban "parental" rights to Elián; they realized also that they had lost their white exile status[9] and were being condemned as criminal urban Latinos, potentially banal agents of urban terror. This moment caused an incredible breakdown in the Cuban community and provoked a number of obvious and latent splits. One strategy was denial: the people who had attempted the flag burning were identified as agents of Castro who were seeking to besmirch the Cubans' reputations. Another reaction was horror at being compared to other "un-American" or insurgent U.S. populations such as blacks, Chicanos, and Native Americans. The crisis revealed the prospect that perhaps Cubans were not different at all, and this loss of exceptionalism provoked disorientation. A third response to such a recognition was shame and disassociation from the extreme displays of retrograde or backward ethnic Cubanism. This third response revealed a rip in the seams of assimilation.

The Elián crisis provoked an important generational break among those born within exile or raised under the exceptional pressures of simultaneous assimilation and separatism: this Cuban generation was bound to both exemplary achievement and status as Americans and exceptional memory and loyalty to the imprisoned motherland and its exile. Part of what Elián revealed was that, for Cubans who have faced assimilation, their hyphenated Americanization has gone hand in hand with a private or latent anti-Americanism that requires them to be perfect but set apart, close to home and safe from potential diffusion in mainstream culture. Even as it thrived within the U.S. economies of achievement, finance, professionalism, and consumerism, the Cuban exile community developed its integrity through identification with and segregation from U.S. culture; up to a point, exile national character has depended on familial and communitarian anti-American suspicion and critique. This critique has a moral dimension that extends to both private values and cultural decadence, and its focus has shifted over the years as assimilation has required either accommodation or resistance.

Cuban anti-Americanism that is contemptuous of American earnestness, identity politics, and unstable values is somewhat selective: such critiques are exercised most potently at the level of racial and gender politics, when the progressive pragmatism of assimilation and advancement push against patriarchy, tradition, and deep-seated historical prejudice. Such anti-Americanism continues to haunt private relations, curtails alliances, integration, and solidarities, and drives public critiques of U.S. policy. The anti-Americanism leveled at U.S. policy is self-righteous and moralistic as well, holding up the last crusading banner of the forgotten cold war, where Cubans see the United States as guilty of strategic treachery, abandonment of mission, or failure of nerve where Cuba is concerned. This critique has targeted successive Democratic administrations, which (inheriting the stain of Kennedy's abandonment of the Cuban invaders at the Bay of Pigs) have been perceived as appeasers of Cuba and as successive saboteurs of the possibility of a true Cuban state. This strain of anti-Americanism has shaped the generation now in power in Miami, those brought up in the late 1960s and into the 1980s in a Miami keenly attentive to the hemispheric cold war. Those forty-somethings have gone on to occupy political office and to shape a civil society in Miami that is deeply but selectively patriotic, negotiating beyond the "enclave" to balance old geopolitical critiques, pragmatic affiliations, and local alliances but reserving always a distancing skepticism about the good faith and idealistic spectacles of American political life.

The Elián event opened a moment of schism when assimilated Cubans from the upper and middle classes suddenly confronted a mirror image of themselves that they could not recognize; that moment, and the disavowals that it forced, created deep confusions in terms of communal and "naturalized" solidarities, disrupting their identities as either Cubans or Americans. It brought Cubans out of the cold war closet and into a wider Latino struggle where the dialectic between anti-Americanism and Americanization shapes the process of assimilation. The Elián crisis served as a sort of psychotic episode for the Cuban community, bringing alienation but also a certain bitter clarity: it revealed the high price of enclave identity and exposed discourses of distrust and paranoia that had long been a latent element of exile affect and cognition. These lessons in disillusion and suspicion connected the Miami exile community in the strangest of ways to other discourses of surveillance and mistrust, discourses circulating both from and against the U.S. government to which they had sworn their naturalized allegiance and which, in a new intervention, had made aliens of them once more.

CUBAN YOUTH CULTURE AND THE 3:10 TO YUMA

I want to conclude by reflecting on the situation of Cubans in Cuba during the long Special Period, those who grew up within the revolution and who continue to live and think through the fluctuations and dynamic of anti-Americanism both there and here. For Cubans of my generation, who grew up within the revolution, and for the generations beyond, anti-Americanism, as I have noted, was official doctrine and official religion. The effects on the Cuban economy of the collapse of the Soviet Union and the end of Soviet subsidies were so extreme that the state's cold war discourse of anti-Americanism began to be hollowed out. As the United States colluded in extending the structure of the old standoff, anti-American rhetoric was reinvigorated in Cuba. Nevertheless, an avidity for American consumer products and cultural artifacts increased, perhaps representing the shifting expectations of access and entitlements of the new mixed economy. Cuba's unstable new order brought new unevenness, scarcity, and unrest, and social control was exercised by a new policing of counterrevolutionary thought. With European capital and wealthy tourists invading the island, the oppositional content of anti-Americanism became more focused on the United States as a pernicious, unjust enemy. Intellectual or ideological Americanisms or Americanization took on new and dangerous contours. Carefully monitoring this phenomenon, the regime sought to preserve what was perhaps the last solid ideological currency of the state.

This control was directed in part at youth culture, and it affected a generation that discovered (with generations of youth internationally) a transgressive or emancipatory individualism, an alternative subculture, and a certain utopian discourse in American literature, cinema, and rock culture. Under this policing regime, youths waving an American flag at a rock concert were sentenced to thirty days in prison. These are perhaps clichéd instances, but they reveal a complicated and risky relationship to the United States among a generation trained and compelled to occupy the official "always already" of anti-Americanism. For that generation, the United States was a forbidden word in the long Special Period, when successive waves of repression censored potential transformations in civil society. In order to avoid saying "*América*" or "*Estados Unidos,*" or to indicate a thought, desire, intention, or plan to leave, Cubans had to speak under the official radar. According to the memories of the exiled Cuban Enrique del Risco, young Cubans during the Special Period developed a code to signal their thoughts and intentions about the United States. To inquire whether someone was considering leaving, they asked, "*¿Te vas para Yuma?*" ["Are you leaving for Yuma?"][10]

Young Cubans took the word "Yuma" from an American film, Delmer Daves's 1957 western, *The 3:10 to Yuma,* to designate what could not be named, ironically invoking a destination in a work of fiction that is never quite arrived at in order to signify a word that cannot be spoken. The film revolves around the plight of a desperate farmer in need of money who agrees for a fee to transport an outlaw on the 3:10 train to Yuma, Arizona. The outlaw offers the hero ten thousand dollars to let him go. The film's moral question revolves around whether the trip to Yuma will ever take place, whether Yuma is a principle or a destination, deferred by the necessities and corrupt compromises of the present. Young people used this film as a signifying metaphor for the problems of naming, departure, and compromised choice.

For those brought up within revolutionary critique, called the *generación de hierba mala* [the weed generation] of the revolution, a generation simultaneously wary and curious about the United States as a demonized and forbidden object, the beginning of the Special Period brought hopes that Cuban society and socialist bureaucracy would change. As the domestic potential for critique and substantial change or movement evaporated in successive cycles of experimentation and repression, the possibility or forced necessity of leaving began to grow, and the final decision to exile oneself to "Yuma" within an uncertain political world order became a very problematic choice. Those who have come to the United States in the past ten years, through various channels and routes of exile, are both satisfied and dissatisfied with their forced choices: selective about their Americanization and both critical of and pragmatically loyal to the United States.

Among the *exilio de hierba mala,* now testing their U.S. "naturalization," the war against Iraq represents a vexing test of alliance and judgment. For these Cuban exiles, the American invasion and occupation once more illuminates the potential possibilities and disasters of the old American routine of intervention and its recycled strategy of selective democratization. The exiles' experience of watching American power from within mobilizes a new, nuanced anti-Americanism that must now be channeled into their Cuban residency, becoming one of many preoccupations that circumscribe and haunt their new lives. Such reflections, I suggest, recall U.S. Cubans to their nationhood, and to a kind of *pena*—at once shame, pain, mourning, and sentence—about old and new homelands now bound together by forced abandonments of ideals and loyalties. This *pena* is worth reflecting on, since it connects Cuba and its exiles to other nations and exiles around the world, whose experience of repression, frustration, and anger about "home" is always superceded by the way in which their *patria* is doubly humiliated by both its own failure and its potential American rescuers.

The backstory for the easy dramas of anti-Americanism, the context for the isolated images, is rarely explored beyond facile interpretations of motivating resentments and envy. Exile anti-Americanism, I suggest, is forged in a double-bind of two bad choices for the nation: in the knowledge that the United States is not necessarily the lesser but the more powerful of the two evils, and that neither at home nor abroad can the promise of its ideal of justice or its liberty be redeemed. For Cubans, anti-Americanism is the symptom of the forced choice. For the *hierba mala* of the revolution, as their time in the U.S. lengthens and the absurdity of U.S. foreign policy steps out of history books and into their lived present as new Americans, the ideological conflicts deepen but do not necessarily broaden as social critique: instead, the private crises of conscience may become more extreme. Cubans' appreciation for their American exile is haunted by the anti-Americanism of their youth, but it also echoes with their hopeful projections onto a Hollywood film. Having arrived in the United States—the evaded, the desired, and the costly destination—Cubans raised with anti-Americanism who have fled to their American dream must critically revisit the political mirages and polarities created within that overdetermined nationalist ideology. They carry on by embracing the pragmatism of millions of exiles and immigrants who live on the soil of their former homelands' enemy. Like their compatriots before them, Cubans here both maintain their Cuban-ness and affirm that they are real "Americans" by concluding that "Yuma no es tan Yuma," admitting from their station of arrival that "Yuma is not so Yuma after all."

NOTES

1. My abbreviated translation, from José Martí, "Carta a Manuel Mercado, Campamento Dos Ríos, 18 de mayo 1895" (José Martí, Letter to Manuel Mercado, Dos Ríos Camp, May 18, 1895), in Martí, *Obras Completas,* vol. 4 (Habana: Casa de las Américas, 1963), pp. 167–168.

2. See, for example, pieces like "Oklahoma Land Rush," in which Martí chronicled the ruthless competition and mad fervor for territory that made the United States a nation. "Oklahoma Land Rush" is the translated title for an excerpt from "Cómo se crea un pueblo nuevo en los Estados Unidos," in Martí, *Obras Completas,* vol. 12, p. 203.

3. The Platt Amendment, incorporated into the articles of the Cuban constitution of 1902, was originally a rider appended to an U.S. Army appropriations bill in March 1901, following the Treaty of Paris, which granted Cuban independence. The amendment detailed terms of withdrawal of U.S. troops and authorized unprecedented subordination of Cuban autonomy to U.S. interests. It prohibited Cuba from transferring land to any power other than the United States and curtailed Cuba's international sovereignty by limiting its right to negotiate treaties. It established U.S. rights to Guantánamo Bay and legitimated U.S. intervention in Cuba. Under President Roosevelt's Good Neighbor policy, the amendment was abrogated, although the United States reserved its rights to the Guantánamo naval base. By 1934, however, U.S. economic interests were so firmly in control of Cuban land, infrastructure, and capital that the amendment was in a sense translated into the interstices of the national economy, compromising local and state autonomy and guaranteeing Cuba's status as a privatized "national" subsidiary of the United States.

4. A campaign slogan for Edgardo Chibás against his opponent Carlos Prío Socarrás, long known among Cubans as a profoundly corrupt politician deeply indebted to the service of American interests.

5. Fidel Castro chose to stay in Harlem at the Hotel Theresa during his visit to the United Nations. He used the opportunity to establish ties of sympathy and solidarity with black leaders and oppositional groups. In his last visit to the United States, Castro returned to his oppositional Harlem constituency, delivering a six-hour speech at Riverside Church and speaking out against globalization, economic unevenness, and social injustice. During that speech, Castro pointed out conditions of economic injustice in the United States and offered low-income "American" minority students six free years of medical education and training in Cuba.

6. Mauricio Vincent, "EEUU se convierte en el mayor abastecedor de Cuba pese al embargo: Empresas españolas se quejan de que el doble rasero de Washington les hace perder mercado," El País, October 6, 2003. Leading with "incredible but true," the El País report cites the Cuban state agency Alimport as reporting a nine-month market share of $238 million dollars for U.S. agricultural products imported to Cuba. The article highlights Spanish irritation at Washington's "double-edged" policy, which had resulted in a loss of market share for Spanish and European exporters. The report details the special conditions of this commercial arrangement and cites instances of Cuba's growing relationships with U.S. exporters, among them a $450,000 sale of livestock by cattle ranchers from Florida, the "home state" of exiles who were presumed to be the strongest supporters for the embargo.

7. The official website of the Comités de Defensa de la Revolución is found at http://www.lacalle.cubaweb.cu. The address does not bear the official title but indicates instead that one has reached "the street" at Cubaweb.

8. In his article "El reino del terrorismo," Víctor Joaquín Ortega opens by citing John Ashcroft's admonition to Americans to join together to protect their neighborhoods. Available at http://www.lacalle.cubaweb.cu/latitudes/cdr_usa.html.

9. It is important to note that this crisis of self-perception was preceded only by the Mariel exodus and its waves of black Cubans, along with other disenfranchised, marginal, and "criminal" Cubans. In 1980, the Cuban community, having worked for "exceptional" status within the racial coding of Latino and immigrant populations, sought to distance itself from this new "polluted" national identity.

10. The reflections in this section evolved in part from a conversation with Enrique del Risco, a fellow Cuban and a friend who is an important interlocutor regarding Cuban culture. In responding to my thoughts regarding this article, he recounted personal memories of anti-American ideological education and of the nature and consequences of pro-American sentiments in Cuban youth culture during the 1980s and early 1990s. I am deeply grateful to him for sharing anecdotes about "Yuma" that I found richly provocative. Del Risco is an exiled Cuban writer and the author of two books of stories and satirical prose; he is currently completing a promising doctoral thesis on Cuban national identity and historiography at New York University.

4

U.S. *Prepotencia*

Latin Americans Respond

George Yúdice

LATIN AMERICANS ARE DISPARATE PEOPLES, but there are few things that unite them more than their shared resentment at the persistent record of U.S. high-handedness in the region as a whole. Historically, and especially after Washington stepped up its regional interventions after the Spanish-Cuban-American War (1895–1898), many political figures and writers developed a continental Hispanic or Latin Americanist position that reprised a historical counterpoint between Iberian and Anglo-Saxon peoples. The advocates of this Latin Americanism emphasized the region's cultural and aesthetic identity over the overweening utilitarianism of the North. Equating the United States with the thin culture of nineteenth-century positivism, they associated Latin America with a new classicism based in part on its modern interpretation of the "Latin" legacy and its connections to Greek civilization. Primary among these values was an appreciation of *mestizaje*, which was seen to contrast markedly with white racial suprematism in the United States.

For the Cuban José Martí, for example, U.S. imperialism was the outward manifestation of a utilitarian mentality that underpinned the political and economic expedience of civic life within the United States. Such views were echoed in the observations of other political and intellectual figures of the early twentieth century. In his famous essay *Ariel* (1900), the Uruguayan writer José Enrique Rodó urged Latin American youth to cultivate their aesthetic sensibilities over and above the utilitarian preferences of North Americans. Only in this way, he argued, would disinterest guide their capacity to govern more justly. The Argentine diplomat and writer Manuel Ugarte upheld Latin Americanism as the cultural antidote to U.S. imperialism in *The Destiny of a Continent* (1923). In *The Cosmic Race,* the Mexican intellectual and politician José Vasconcelos contrasted the U.S. penchant for apartheid with the Latin American proclivity to mix racially. These and other critics embraced regional nationalism, continental Latin Americanism, and a renewed Hispanism as bulwarks with which to stave off the predatory actions of the United States. Today, with some exceptions, the pointed nationalism and the fervent Latin Americanism of the early twentieth century have not survived well. Nor has the culturalism of these earlier critics, largely because of the pervasive influence of U.S. commercial culture, particularly in Central America, the Caribbean, and the northernmost countries of South America.

Nonetheless, there has been a noticeable move toward Latin American economic and cultural integration in recent years, not least because of widespread dissatisfaction with twenty years of neoliberal policies, structural adjustment programs, and unequal terms of trade that resulted in ever greater income gaps. Regional integration is seen as an alternative to incorporation into a U.S.-led Free Trade Area of the Americas. In his recent book, *Latinoamericanos buscando lugar en este siglo* [Latin Americans Seeking a Place in This Century] (2002), Néstor García Canclini advocates policies for promoting Latin American cultural integration in the new global landscape so that "our identity will not be read in quotation marks." Integration for him does not translate into a continentwide version of nationalism but rather is a means to acknowledge the diasporas that have served to redefine Latin America. In particular, integration means regaining sufficient control over the means of production and distribution so that Latin American cultures are not Rickymartinized or choked off by global conglomerates. García Canclini argues that these dreaded outcomes should not be conceived of as "Americanization"—they are, instead, a corporatization of culture—and he cautions against a knee-jerk anti-Americanism, especially when "American" is also Latin American. Indeed, he calls for establishing strong connections with the Latin American diaspora in the United States in the interest of staking out a place for a truly different society.

The increasing hybridization of Latin Americanness has not rendered redundant the premises of the Bolivarian tradition, which, for the past two centuries, has been a repository of hope for Latin American integration. While clearly aimed at diminishing the ability of the United States to meddle in the affairs of the nations of the south, the new integration initiatives are also proactive and seek to define nonreactive terms for collaboration and cooperation. This affirmative character is most clearly discernible in the negotiations among the countries of the Common Market of the South (Mercosur), especially now that Brazil and Argentina are under the progressive leadership, respectively, of Luiz Inácio "Lula" da Silva and Néstor Kirchner. Trade and economic policy are counterbalanced by serious social justice concerns that reflect two decades of democratization movements in both countries. Both of these leaders have given Latin American politics the kind of hope that hasn't been seen since the euphoria of (re)democratization in the 1980s.

Placing all his hopes in a Latin American confederation that never materialized, Bolívar fretted over the role of the United States in the hemisphere, predicting that "in the name of freedom the U.S. seems destined by Providence to bring the plague of misery on [Latin] America" (Bolívar 2001).[1] Accordingly, Bolívar sought an integration that excluded the United States. Given the need for trade ties with the United States, this exclusion was unworkable, both then and now. Yet Bolivar's suspicion has only heightened over time as the United States has used trade and economic policies regarding Latin America as political intervention in the region by other means. U.S. domestic subsidies to large-scale industrial farming, for example, have devastated the production of corn—the most important Mexican staple. U.S. economic policy makers are also in a position to push for tough-love decisions at the IMF, as they opted to do in December 2001 by lobbying for the denial of further loans to Argentina, which led to default and political chaos. As the *New York Times* columnist Paul Krugman (2002) saw it, IMF officials took their cue directly from the Bush administration and acted "like medieval doctors who insisted on bleeding their patients, and repeated the procedure when the bleeding made them sicker—prescribing austerity and still more austerity, right to the end." Nor, he added, did Latin Americans regard the United States as an innocent in this instance and others. In general, *estadounidenses* have a hard time understanding this perception, largely because they are unaware of Washington's long history of interventions, all too resonant for Latin Americans, beginning with the expropriation of Mexican lands in 1846–1848 and continuing unabated until the present day.[2]

With this history of two centuries of self-serving intervention in mind, it is impossible to argue that anti-Americanism should simply be dismissed as a misplaced animus. Yet, some prominent critics have advocated laying aside the animus as the most beneficial path for Latin America to adopt. The former Mexican minister of foreign relations Jorge Castañeda recently (2003) cautioned that venting against *pinches gringos* [fucking gringos] is not a viable political option; it doesn't win any points in trade agreements, border negotiations, immigrant guest-worker arrangements, and amnesty legislation. Yet, as Castañeda would surely concede, Mexican overtures and concessions did not establish a strong enough relationship to withstand the Bush administration's abandonment of negotiations with its southern neighbor in the wake of the September 11 attacks and its subsequent, exclusive turn of attention to the Middle East and South and Central Asia.

As Enrique Krauze noted, Latin America went entirely unmentioned in Bush's State of the Union speech in January 2003, and its citizens are now "aware that the United States has returned to an essentially reactive diplomacy that seems to come to life only when there are missiles pointing at its shores, Marxist guerrillas in the jungles, or revolutionary governments in the old banana republics" (Krauze 2003). Not even when the United States needed Mexican and Chilean votes on the UN Security Council did its representatives take a friendlier stance. Instead, Mexico was warned that there could be reprisals against Mexicans and Mexican Americans similar to those taken against the Japanese during World War II, if Mexico did not cast its vote for war. Bush himself stated that countries opposed to the U.S. war on Iraq would face "discipline" (quoted in Krugman 2003).

Shame at the policies of the Bush administration is no doubt more widespread in the United States than is reported in its mainstream media. To the degree that there is, among *estadounidenses,* this difference of opinion and sentiment regarding the United States's intervention in Iraq and other countries, some degree of anti-Americanism is partly misplaced. Indeed, many *estadounidenses* agree with the vast majority of people throughout the world who see the United States as a rogue state. Be that as it may, it is disingenuous, in my view, to ignore the overwhelming anti-American sentiment of the majority of Latin Americans. Even those who sympathized with the friends and relatives of victims of the September 11 attacks felt these sentiments give way to a more complex mix of emotions as the Bush administration adopted a unilateral stance for which other countries have already paid dearly. The dramatic decline of interest in the economies of the region has been difficult to ignore. Yet, again, Latin Americans were made to feel that they just don't matter.

To sample some of the complexity of these emotions, I decided to conduct an informal survey of a number of Latin American colleagues and acquaintances in the spring of 2003. In what follows, I draw liberally upon the results, alongside reports gleaned from the Latin American press before and after that date. In general, the results have led me to conclude that we are closer than ever to the early 1960s "Yankee go home" sentiment south of the Rio Bravo. And this despite the fact that Latin Americans both resemble *estadounidenses* in many external cultural trappings (e.g., consumerism), as mentioned by several respondents to my survey, and need the United States more than ever as a trading partner.

In drawing on this survey, I do not pretend to provide hard and fast scientific evidence.[3] Instead, I am trying to focus on the rather unmeasurable phenomenon of "international feeling." To be sure, indicators of animus can be devised, but I am less interested in such instruments than in the dramatic and performative aspects of the frustration, resentment, and exasperation that so many Latin Americans feel over the bullying arrogance or *prepotencia* of U.S. actions. This *prepotencia*—a word that conveys so much more than arrogance and that conveys high-handedness and abuse of power—was mentioned by *all* of my respondents and can be found in the historical record going as far back as Bolívar. According to Goodwin, Jasper, and Polletta (2001), emotions help channel action. They dredge up those "uncomfortable memories" mentioned by Rohter (2003) in connection with Latin American anti-Americanism, which are sedimented in history; they (re)activate "forms of defiance patterned by historical and structural forces" (Eckstein 2001: xv).

If the United States is not to find itself a perennial target of worldwide opposition, *estadounidenses* will have to work hard to reverse the animus. But this cannot be done by insulting people's intelligence and feelings by recourse to Hollywood-style publicity. In the wake of September 11, the U.S. government enlisted the entertainment industries. Muhammad Ali and other celebrities were sought out for propaganda films shown in Islamic countries (Associated Press 2001). According to a *New York Times* report, the State Department planned "a television and advertising campaign to try to influence Islamic opinion; one segment could feature American celebrities, including sports stars, and a more emotional message" (Gordon 2001). Latin Americans, along with critics elsewhere, wondered whether the Bush administration was in touch with reality in assuming that Ali or some other celebrity could sell the U.S. invasion as if it were Coca-Cola. In any event, such crude PR could only backfire: in general, the military-industrial-media-entertainment complex under Bush has only exacerbated global anti-Americanism.

During the war in Iraq, viewers throughout Latin America were subjected to coverage that had been edited in a way that "violated CNN's own style manuals . . . and the norm of providing equal access to alternative opinions. In all of these respects, CNN broke its own codes, compelled by jingoism and blood-thirsty vengeance" (Piscitelli 2001). Significantly, no one suggested a Hollywood campaign aimed at improving the U.S. image among Latin Americans, no doubt because the region is perceived to be quite unimportant to the "war on terrorism." It may not be important at this juncture for Latin Americans to feel better disposed to *estadounidenses*—there is no other option, according to some analysts, than for the countries of the region to fall in line with the United States, since they have lost all capacity for resistance (Binder 2002: 100)—but they may be important allies in a not too distant future. Accordingly, Washington ought to be making some concessions in pursuit of its self-interest, whether or not its politicians take seriously their own rhetoric about reducing poverty and democratizing the world.

Critics of anti-Americanism like Jean-François Revel argue that "U.S.-bashers" are either reacting out of timidity in taking action on behalf of national security (Europe) or irrationally putting on blinders regarding the desire of developing countries to have greater access to rich markets and corporate investment. Critics to the left of Revel argue that anti-Americanists are overshooting the targets of their animus by indicting all *estadounidenses,* thereby ignoring the diversity of viewpoints in the United States. This was the critique that Adolfo Gilly, a distinguished visiting Latin American historian, leveled at an early version of this paper, presented at NYU in February 2003. In his view, I had exaggerated the extent of anti-American sentiment among Latin Americans. The cases of acute anti-Americanism that I cited were exceptional, he argued, and the vast majority of Latin Americans could easily distinguish between the "American" people and the U.S. government as the object of their protest. While there is some truth to this observation, in the ensuing year, I have gotten a greater sense that the repudiation of the U.S.

government's actions in international affairs extends increasingly to what many Latin Americans imagine the majority of *estadounidenses* to be like. Most of the respondents to my survey report an increase in a generalized anti-Americanism that extends to all *estadounidenses.* No doubt, this tendency to imagine all *estadounidenses* as complicit with the Bush agenda is largely a result of the paucity of reporting on domestic opposition to the wars in Afghanistan and Iraq. After all, major media venues in the United States "narrate the nation to itself," as García Canclini (2003) notes, and because of their global reach, their framing of the news has an international impact. By contrast with the most popular media outlets among *estadounidenses,* Latin American newspapers and newscasters are not inhibited in their reporting on war casualties and the like. Nor have more recent political developments in the United States helped alter this perception. The election of Arnold Schwarzenegger as governor of California in October 2003 hardly mitigated the feeling among many Latin Americans that *estadounidenses* have bought into a noxious populism, strengthening the conditions for postmodern-style fascism.

On the evidence of my survey, the reactions to the attacks on the World Trade Center and the Pentagon on September 11, 2001, were like a release of pent-up rage at the long history of U.S. interventions in the region's affairs. Some prominent Latin American intellectuals felt vindicated, as if the attacks were also a retaliatory strike on their behalf. Perhaps the most extreme response was that of Hebe Pastor de Bonafini, a founder of the Mothers of the Plaza de Mayo, the group most identified with protest against the disappearances of dissenters carried out by the authoritarian military dictators of Argentina in the late 1970s and early 1980s. Bonafini declared her admiration for the men who piloted the planes that struck the World Trade Center and the Pentagon. She opined that they "declared war with their bodies, driving a plane that smashed and knocked the shit out of the greatest power on earth. It made me happy. Some may think that is wrong. Each will have to evaluate it and think about it. I will not be false. I will make a toast to my children, for so many who have died, for the end to the [Cuban] blockade." She also saw the deaths as a payback for the thousands of disappeared Argentines. "Now [North Americans live] the same fear that they produced in us, with persecution, disappearances and torture. . . . The [North American] people remained silent and even applauded the wars." Bonafini uttered these words during a class session on "imperialist war" [*Sobre la guerra imperialista*] at the People's Universidad Popular de las Madres de la Plaza de Mayo. While there were conflicting opinions expressed in this forum (Natalichio et al. 2001; Iramain 2001), important intellectuals, like David Viñas, Sergio Schoklender, and Vicente Zito Lema, expressed views quite similar to Bonafini's.

Viñas characterized the attacks as an expression of class struggle, a retaliation from below against the "institutional violence of empire" and the "violence encysted above." He compared these actions of the "subjected and humiliated of the world" to those of Robespierre and Castelli.[4] Zito Lema agreed with this "class analysis" and characterized Osama bin Laden as a revolutionary comparable to San Martín, Belgrano, Artigas, Che Guevara, and his "comrades fallen in battle" during the cold war. Shoklender did not see these as terrorist acts but, using the rhetoric of the U.S. government, as "surgical operations against specific power centers" of the "enemy that is destroying us." He added that he was happy to see that the United States was not invulnerable and that "we have the possibility to resist it and confront it."

While Latin American intellectuals are entitled to begrudge and to resist U.S. interventions in their countries, the idea that the death of three thousand people from eighty countries, many of them workers and an inestimable number of them undocumented, can be regarded as retribution shows an egregious lack of judgment and a lapse in the human rights activism for which Bonafini and some of these other activists and intellectuals are known. What I am trying to emphasize here, however, is the intensity of their feelings, which led many to conclude that the United States had finally got a taste of its own medicine. As the Puerto Rican intellectual and academic Ramón Grosfoguel put it: "One can't expect that the North American state can bomb Iraq for an entire decade, finance the Israeli state's daily massacre of Palestinians, invade Panama with a death toll of thousands, train military executioners in the arts of terrorism in the School of the Americas, and subsidize military dictatorships throughout the world for decades on end without someone someday getting it dished back" (2002: 132).

There was also a sense of retribution expressed in a performance by the Mexican performer Jesusa Rodríguez and the Argentine actress Liliana Felipe that I witnessed in Mexico City in early October 2001. It was the most unmerciful treatment of the event that I have seen or read about; any notion of tragedy, a term used in many newspaper reports, was rejected. The actresses vented much spleen, including jokes about the rain of bodies falling from the Twin Towers. It appeared to be cathartic to them to publicly indulge their anger at the *estadounidenses* who had gotten a taste of their own medicine. Several of the Mexican friends who took me to the performance were deeply embarrassed. I myself was torn between commiseration with the aggrieved relatives whom I had seen in New York in the aftermath of the attacks and understanding that we *estadounidenses* could no longer shield ourselves from the many reasons why "they hate us so much."

Similarly, one of the Brazilian respondents reported that "a significant number of people identified with the attackers. In the artistic sphere, there was an episode that generated much debate and commotion. CEP 2000, a well-known group of young poets, performers, and artists, quite influential in Rio de Janeiro, sponsored a commemoration in which they installed numerous television screens of different sizes showing images of the exploding towers and groups of people applauding and shouting 'Hosanna bin Laden,' as they genuflected in religious ritual. Many in the audience did the same." Another respondent, from Cuba, wrote that he witnessed many of his countrymen "applauding, some openly and others more discreetly, and celebrating that *estadounidenses* were getting a taste of their own infliction of war, in their flesh and not only in Hollywood films." Academics who had either studied or worked at U.S. institutions for many years made quite brazen statements: "Anti-Americanism will exist so long as the actions that provoke that anti-Americanism continue"; "anti-Americanism is vengeance for the treatment of our immigrants"; "the reason for anti-Americanism is that *estadounidenses* are egotistic and supremacists, they disdain the rest of the world and define themselves in opposition to the rest of the world"; "violence is not justifiable, but allowing so many children to die, not doing anything about the millions who starve worldwide as *estadounidenses* generate huge agricultural surpluses, among other things, are also forms of violence that the U.S. tolerates."

The premise that sharing U.S.-style values would make others more sympathetic to the United States is belied by another respondent's analysis of the contradictory situation in Brazil. From the cultural point of view, he wrote, Brazil more and more resembles the United States, "as in the Workers' Party's democratic pageantry or the establishment of quotas for Afro-Brazilian minorities in the university and in public service. Pop culture has a massive presence in all sectors of the culture industries: I can't remember the Oscars ever having such importance as now. [This is a reference to the extensive Internet campaign among Brazilians to canvass votes for *Central Station* and *City of God* in the Oscar competition.] And then there is the complex issue of gay identity—should one assume it or not? This is a very American thing. Even in areas that used to be dominated completely by European models, such as literary and cultural criticism, one sees the influential presence of North Americans or those who work in the U.S. In sum, U.S. cultural influence might be pervasive but never before has regard for the U.S. been so low."

In response to my query on the perception of U.S. culture now and five or ten years ago, respondents agreed that even though the United States might be influential in their own society and in their own daily life, their views of U.S. culture had altered. "My perceptions have changed significantly," wrote one participant. "I am extremely concerned about U.S. culture's provincialism, derived in good measure from an information-communication system that binds them to a very restricted view of the world. Never did I have to go out of my way to make an effort to 'feel that I was in the world' as when I was a visiting scholar at Stanford. . . . The world seemed so distant, even evanescent, and the effort to [be in the world] so exhausting that I almost gave up and nearly accepted that CNN or Fox view of the world with which I was bombarded. . . . Gringoness [*la gringuidad*] is such a challenging and complicated object of reflexion. Its individualism, puritanism, belief in predestination, etc. preoccupy me. I guess I believe that anti-Americanism is less a reaction to an overwhelming and deafening power than a reaction to the spectacularization of a power that fails to establish contact with, learn from and gain the respect of other cultures and nations."

Others pointed out that the Bush administration and the media elites had taken advantage of September 11 to launch a vast attack at the level of civilization itself, "drawing others into the conflict, by any means necessary. Other countries, many of them European—Italy and Germany in the 1970s, Ireland and Spain for decades—have suffered all kinds of terrorist attacks but the international community never considered these as an attack on Western civilization as it is now being endlessly imaged and sold to us, and never suspended the revered rule of law so shamelessly. This, together with the numerous interventions, sponsorship of coups d'etat and wars, and support for dictatorships, is what makes it hard to decide whether or not the U.S. deserves the punishment that one would otherwise believe that no nation deserves. Said otherwise and using the terms of the German guerrillas of the 1970s, it's a matter of 'socializing the pain' (one of the first actions of the Baader-Meinhoff was to bomb a supermarket so that Germans would experience the suffering of the Vietnamese)."

Almost all of my respondents characterized the U.S. campaign against terrorism as hypocritical, a view that echoes throughout the Latin American media. Efforts on the part of U.S. officials to show concern for the devastation in Iraq did not help matters. For example, at a September 2003 meeting of the Organization of American States, held in Mexico City, the U.S. representatives from the State Department's Bureau of Educational and Cultural Affairs offended their peers from the other member states by presenting an Iraq heritage protection initiative that was little more than a blatant fund-raising pitch. The relevant communiqué—"How to Donate Money to the Reconstruction of Iraqi Cultural Heritage"—explained that the United States had spearheaded the implementation of the Convention on Cultural Property Implementation Act and boasted about its track record in protecting cultural heritage. Nowhere was there any mention of the destruction of cultural sites during the war on Iraq in March 2003. This blatant omission, added to the generally inept propaganda efforts undertaken by the State Department, only reinforced the disbelief and anger felt by other representatives.

A similar reaction was elicited by the impression that the Bush administration's business cronies are reaping war profits. As one respondent noted, Washington is "making billions of dollars available to U.S. companies for reconstruction in Afghanistan and Iraq. The U.S. government bailed out the airline *industry* but not the 100,000 airline *employees.* The U.S. government will spend billions on Iraq and the `attack on terrorism' while social spending in the U.S. is cut and aid to Latin America and developing countries eliminated." When the United States does provide aid, such as the $30 billion bailout of Brazil in early August 2002, it does not reflect any genuine concern for Latin Americans. On the contrary, as a *New York Times* reporter suggested, the bailout safeguards the vast interests of American banks like Citigroup, Fleet Boston, and J. P. Morgan Chase and their many industrial investments in Brazil (Andrews 2002).

The phrase "forgotten friends" captures quite well the recent state of U.S–Latin American relations: the lack of response to the Argentine economic crisis, the closing of the U.S.-Mexico border, and the abandonment of an amnesty for Mexican and Latin American undocumented workers. The one area in which the United States has not forgotten its friends—the drug war—is hardly uncontroversial. Washington has cast its antiterrorist net ever wider by assimilating drug traffic and guerrilla movements into an integrated antiterrorism policy aimed at military buildup rather than at resolving the economic crisis for farmers and the unemployed. Even the piracy of media and software products—of strategic interest to the U.S. culture industries—has been included under the rubric of this antiterrorism policy, thereby safeguarding corporate interests in this sector. One respondent was aghast that Latin American militaries, "which had lost their legitimacy in the dictatorship years, are now being given a spurious place in the security business." Latin American reporters like Miguel Bonasso (2001) see the inclusion of Latin American militaries in Operation Centaur as a way of increasing their budgets. According to Fuentes and Rojas Aravena (2003), this is the only way for them to increase their funding.

The reach of such security and surveillance schemes is not limited to terrorism and piracy suspects but extends to millions of Latin Americans who have voiced outrage when the schemes were uncovered. As Rohter reports, "the United States has been quietly buying up computerized data banks that contain the names, addresses, telephone listings and identity card numbers of hundreds of millions of people in 10 Latin American countries [drawing] broad criticism and expressions of alarm throughout the region" (2003). The Nobel Peace Prize winner Oscar Arias denounced this increase in militarization and securitization, arguing that a mere 5 percent of defense expenditures, rerouted to humanitarian defense, could allay hunger, eliminate disease, increase education, and safeguard the environment (Hulshizer 2002).

In conclusion, it is important, first of all, to acknowledge the intensity of Latin American emotion on the topic of anti-Americanism. However, we must also see beyond the expressions of vindication or glee of the sort offered by some of my survey participants in their responses to the September 11 attacks. These emotions are surface symptoms, but they make sense when viewed against the cumulative backdrop of the *prepotencia* of deleterious U.S. policies and actions in the region, and they are actively feeding the new sense of regional solidarity. This continental identity is further bolstered by a shared antipathy to the current U.S. positions on neoliberal trade, the death penalty, global warming, preemptive force, and global consumerism (Fresnada 2000). Latin Americans also tend to share, along with western Europeans, the belief that U.S.-style globalization is further eroding sovereignty and traditional cultures (Pew Research Center 2003). Finally, there is the fear that the United States has entered a proto-fascist phase of its political development, but that topic warrants an entirely new survey.

NOTES

1. There were 517 hits on Google for this statement by Bolívar, many of them invoking it in the context of the U.S. war on Iraq.

2. Like many others, including my respondents, I object to the use of the term "American" to refer to U.S. citizens and hence use the Spanish term *estadounidenses*, or Unitedstatesians, which, although awkward in English, sounds perfectly normal in Spanish. However, at times I use the term—in quotes—to reflect the way that most U.S. citizens, the press, and the media refer to themselves.

3. In February 2003, in preparation for writing the first version of this essay, I sent a request to about fifty Latin American friends and acquaintances for them to answer seven questions. I received twenty responses. I asked the following questions:

Have you observed an increase in anti-Americanism in the past few years? If so, exactly when would you date this increase? Also, if there was an increase, what are the reasons for it? (2) Do you think that the events on September 11, 2001, contributed to anti-Americanism? Was there sympathy toward the victims of the World Trade Center? (3) Some have argued that *estadounidenses* deserved such an attack. Do you find such an argument justified? Why or why not? (4) Do you think the war in Afghanistan or the impending war in Iraq are justified? Do they contribute to anti-American sentiment? Among whom? (5) Do you believe that anti-American sentiments extend to all *estadounidenses*? Are they limited? (6) How do you see U.S. culture today? Has there been a change in your view over the past five years? (7) What else can you add about anti-Americanism?

Not everyone who responded wanted to be cited, so for the sake of consistency I do not divulge respondents' names, with one exception. Octavio Getino and Susana Velleggia published their response to me in the online journal *Pimienta Negra*. Like them, several respondents gave very long and detailed answers, which went beyond the scope of this essay.

My survey has no scientific pretensions. In order to broach the topic, however, I did feel that I could rely on the wisdom of people whom I have known to be reliable social and cultural analysts. By "reliable" I mean that they do not simply vent their partisan allegiances but take a range of arguments seriously in their analyses. They do not, of course, make any pretense of objective neutrality, since they, like myself, do not believe that such a position exists.

4. All of the quotations from the discourses of Viñas, Bonafini, Shoklender, and Lema can be found in Verbitsky (October 11, 2001). The complete text of Bonafini's discourse can be found in Bonafini (2001).

BIBLIOGRAPHY

Andrews, Edmund L. 2002. "I.M.F. Loan to Brazil Also Shields U.S. Interests." *New York Times,* August 9. Available at http://www.nytimes.com/2002/08/09/business/worldbusiness/09FUND.html.
Associated Press. 2001. "Ali Asked to Film Public Announcement." *New York Times,* December 23. Available at http://www.nytimes.com/aponline/national/AP-Attacks-Hollywood.html.
Binder, Alberto M. 2002. "Viejas y nuevas razones de la razón gestiva (viejas y nuevas luchas de la emancipación solidaria)." *Nueva sociedad* 177 (January–February): 99–103.
Bolívar, Simón. 2001. "Frases de Simón Bolívar sobre los Estados Unidos." *IV Congreso Anfictionico Bolivariano de América Latina y el Caribe.* Buenos Aires, November 22–25. Available at http://www.geocities.com/juntabolivariana/boli28.htm.
Bonafini, Hebe Pastor de. 2001. "El 11 de septiembre sentí que la sangre de tantos caídos era vengada." *Revista Pretextos.* Available at http://www.nodo50.org/pretextos/bonafini1.htm.
Bonasso, Miguel. 2001. "La CIA traslada a su agente local por una revelacion de Página 12." *Página 12,* January 14. Available at http://www.pagina12.com.ar/2001/01-01/01-01-14/pag03.htm.
Bruni, Frank. 2002. "El mundo sigue apoyando a E.U." Available at http://mensual.prensa.com/mensual/contenido/2002/09/14/hoy/mundo/704812.html.
Castañeda, Jorge. 2003. "The Dilemmas of Latin America." Lecture. New York University, October 10.
Eckstein, Susan, ed. 2001. *Power and Popular Protest: Latin American Social Movements.* Berkeley: University of California Press.
Fresnada, Carlos. 2000. "El antiamericanismo que viene." *El mundo,* December 27. Available at http://www.el-mundo.es/especiales/2001/01/internacional/clintonbush/anti.html.
Fuentes, Claudio, and Francisco Rojas Aravena. 2003. "El patio trasero: Estados Unidos y América latina pos-Irak." *Nueva Sociedad* 185 (May–June): 64–82.

García Canclini, Néstor. 2002. *Latinoamericanos buscando lugar en este siglo*. Buenos Aires: Paidós.

———. 2003. "Conquista militar y fracasos culturales: cruzada de sonámbulos." *Clarín*, April 5. Available at http://old.clarin.com/suplementos/cultura/2003/04/05/u-00611.htm.

Getino, Octavio, and Susana Velleggia. 2003. "Respuesta a un cuestionario sobre 'antiamericanismo.'" *Pimienta Negra*, February 13. Available at http://www.nodo50.org/pimientanegra/Getino_cuestionario.htm.

Goodwin, Jeff, James M. Jasper, and Francesca Polletta, eds. 2001. *Passionate Politics: Emotions and Social Movements*. Chicago: University of Chicago Press.

Gordon, Michael R. 2001. "U.S. Tries to Rally Public Support Overseas." *New York Times*, November 6. Available at http://www.nytimes.com/2001/11/06/international/06MESS.html.

Grosfoguel, Ramón. 2002. "Colonialidad global y terrorismo anti-terrorista." *Nueva Sociedad* 177 (January–February): 132–137.

Hulshizer, Daniel. 2002. "El Porqué del Antiamericanismo." September 10. Available at http://www.aunmas.com/lectores/lector_001.htm.

Iramain, Demetrio. 2001. "Otra campaña contra las Madres de Plaza   de Mayo." *Rebelión*, October 12. Available at http://www.eurosur.org/rebelion/internacional/debate2121001.htm.

Krauze, Enrique. 2003. "Forgotten Friends." *New York Times*, January 30. Available at http://www.nytimes.com/2003/01/30/opinion/opinion/30KRAUZ.html.

Krugman, Paul. 2002. "Crying with Argentina." *New York Times*, January 1. Available   at http://www.nytimes.com/2002/01/01/opinion/01KRUG.html.

———. 2003. "Let Them Hate as Long as They Fear." *New York Times*, March 8. Available at http://www.iht.com/articles/89012.html.

Martí, José. 1968. "Our America" (1891). In *The America of José Martí: Selected Writings*. Trans. Juan de Onís. Introd. Federico de Onís. New York: Funk and Wagnalls.

———. 1975. "Two Views of Coney Island." In *Inside the Monster: Writings on the United States and American Imperialism*, pp. 165–175. Ed. Philip S. Foner. Trans. Elinor Randall et al. New York: Monthly Review Press.

Natalichio, Oscar F., Marcelo Freyre, and Jaime Fuchs. 2001. "La alegría de la vida." *Página 12*, October 11. Available at http://www.pagina12.com.ar/2001/01-10/01-10-11/PAG22.htm.

Pew Research Center for the People and the Press. 2003. "Views of a Changing World: War with Iraq Further Divides Global Publics." Available at http://people-press.org/reports/display.php3?ReportID=185.

Piscitelli, Alejandro. 2001. Editorial. Interlink Headline News, No. 2416. September 11. Available at http://www.ilhn.com/ediciones/2416.html.

Revel, Jean François. 2002. *L'Obsession anti-américaine: son fonctionnement, ses causes, ses inconséquences*. Paris: Plon.

Rohter, Larry. 2003. "The Faraway War Set Latin America on Edge." *New York Times*, April 20. Available at http://www.nytimes.com/2003/04/20/weekinreview/20ROHT.html.

Shifter, Michael. 2003. "EEUU después de Irak: Las papas fritas no son las de antes." *Ideele*, May. Available at http://www.redinter.org/docs/Shifter%20(Ideele,%2005-03).doc.

Verbitsky, Horacio. 2001. "Refutacion a Viñas, Schoklender, Zito Lema y Pastor de Bonafini." *Página 12*, October 11.

PART II

THE MIDDLE EAST

5

American Power and
Anti-Americanism in the Middle East

Timothy Mitchell

THE MOST SURPRISING THING about anti-Americanism in the Middle East is that there is so little of it. On February 15, 2003, opponents of the impending U.S. invasion of Iraq organized anti-war marches in large cities around the world, including one in Cairo. More than one million people marched in London and Rome, hundreds of thousands in New York and Berlin, and thousands more in Tokyo, Seoul, and Jakarta. In Cairo, the number of demonstrators was six hundred.[1] Experts on anti-Americanism had been warning that the invasion of Iraq would cause an explosion of popular anger in the streets of the Arab world, which would threaten to bring down U.S.-supported governments in Egypt, Saudi Arabia, and other countries. For those who thought that this might be one of the more positive consequences of an attack on Iraq, the turnout at the demonstration in Cairo was not an encouraging sign.

In the United States, the threat of anti-Americanism was something on which both supporters and opponents of the war could agree. For many opponents, the war was wrong in part because of the encouragement it would give to anti-Americanism and the damage that would follow to American influence and the stability of friendly Arab states. For the war's proponents, the problem of anti-Americanism provided the war's justification. To persuade Congress and the public that the attack on Baghdad and the overthrow of its government were necessary, the U.S. administration presented the Iraqi regime as an agent motivated not by particular strategic concerns or political goals but by an innate hostility toward America. Labeling Iraq as a "rogue state" and part of an "axis of evil" invoked this essential anti-Americanism. "Rogue states," according to the U.S. government's *National Security Strategy,* are countries that "hate the United States and everything for which it stands."[2] The evil of Iraq lay not simply in the tyranny with which the regime ruled but in the threat this hatred represented to the United States and its allies. There was no need to associate the alleged hatred with a specific motive or cause. Searching for a motive might reveal that Iraq was not a threat to the United States or, worse, that it had a genuine grievance—that it had complied with the requirement to disarm almost a decade earlier yet continued to be subject to sanctions and aerial bombardments. In the absence of a legitimate reason for war, the United States relied upon the widely accepted view that Arabs hated America, portraying Iraq as the extreme form of a latent Arab desire to harm the United States.

The view that the Arab world harbored a general antipathy toward the United States had wide support. One index of its currency was the sudden popularity of the writings of Bernard Lewis, who had been warning of a clash of civilizations between the Arab world and the West since the 1950s. In an essay published in *The Atlantic Monthly* in September 1990, just after Iraq invaded Kuwait, Lewis repeated his views about the dangers of Arab anti-Americanism. His opinions became instantly popular and were reproduced in Samuel Huntington's influential call for a renewed American militarism, *The Clash of Civilizations.* A decade later, Lewis reiterated the same argument about the Arabs in *What Went Wrong?* which became an American best-seller in the months before the U.S. invasion of Iraq.[3]

The arguments of writers like Lewis operate in a curious way. They present anti-Americanism as something elusive and yet ubiquitous. It appears elusive because we are given no concrete evidence of it. In his 1990 essay, Lewis argued that there is a widespread "mood of hatred and violence" in the Arab world, much of which "is directed against us."[4] Yet, he provided no sociological evidence for this mood, nor any examples from contemporary Arab literature, music, film, popular culture, or even political debate. A serious study of literature, television, or other cultural forms in the Arab world would reveal that America and Americans are not a topic of much concern. Elias Khoury remarks on the absence of the figure of the American in modern Arab fiction writing, and the same is true of the region's highly popular television serials.[5] But experts on anti-Americanism tend to be people who have never visited the Arab world and are unfamiliar with its culture and popular life.

The mood of hatred appears ubiquitous because it can be given no specific location in place or time. A specific location would endow the mood with a local context and therefore with the possibility of a particular cause. Arab attitudes toward America, whether among governments, intellectuals, militant groups, or ordinary people, cannot have specific contexts and causes, in this kind of writing, for then they would no longer operate as a pretext for militarism and war. Specific criticisms of the West, we are told, are not really reactions to the things they criticize. "In reality," as Lewis had been arguing for fifty years, "all of them are symptoms or aspects of a fundamental and universal revulsion from all that is Western."[6]

Lewis's 1990 essay, published as the United States prepared for its first war against Iraq, contains not a word of analysis of the Iraq-Kuwait relationship, of U.S. efforts over the previous decade to build an alliance with the Iraqi government, of the complications that ensued, of Washington's role in delaying a resolution to the Iran-Iraq war, or of the place of these events in the U.S. policy of maintaining itself as the dominant military and political power in the Gulf. In place of such an analysis, Lewis presents anti-Americanism as a widespread attitude, caused by the religion and culture of Islam. Periodically, he says, Islam, like other world religions, inspires a mood of violence in some of its followers, and "it is our misfortune" that part of the Muslim world is currently going through such a period. Why is it happening now? "The Muslim," Lewis suggests, has suffered three successive experiences of defeat. First, beginning several centuries ago, he endured the decline of Islamic civilization. Then came the loss of power and autonomy to European expansion and colonization. The final humiliation, "the last straw—was the challenge to his mastery in his own house, from emancipated women and rebellious children. It was too much to endure, and the outbreak of rage . . . was inevitable." Anti-Americanism is the inchoate response of the adult male Muslim to this ubiquitous psychological trauma.

Why should a traumatic experience with rebellious wives and children, assuming this had occurred, express itself as hatred of America and the West? The answer lies in the very historical nature of Muslims. Just as the trauma was inevitable, "it was also natural that this rage should be directed primarily against the millennial enemy and should draw its strength from ancient beliefs and loyalties." Once again, there is no evidence for this claim and no explanation. We are simply assured that "it was natural."

Lewis is aware that there is an alternative explanation for the alleged anti-Americanism of the Arabs. For opponents of the war against Iraq, American policies toward the Arab world were an important cause of negative attitudes toward the United States. Lewis dismisses this view with a couple of historical anecdotes. To refute the argument that Washington's unfavorable policy toward the Palestinians could be relevant, for example, he mentions the Suez crisis of 1956. When Israel, France, and Britain invaded Egypt, the Eisenhower government forced them to withdraw. Yet, this act of support for the Arabs, Lewis says, produced no goodwill toward the United States. Presented without its historical context, the episode may appear to support his argument. As soon as the context is given, the absurdity of the argument appears. The Suez crisis had been triggered by an American attempt to punish Egypt for its policy of nonalignment and to undermine its economic development by blocking international funds to build the Aswan Dam. Washington resumed its hostility toward Cairo soon after the war.[7] But there is another problem with this use of historical anecdotes to support the ahistorical argument that Arab attitudes toward the West are inspired by a general cultural antipathy rather than by criticism of specific American policies. In going back almost half a century to find an instance of U.S. policy apparently favorable toward the Arabs, Lewis tacitly acknowledges that no more recent evidence is available. Even if Washington's action in the Suez crisis had been positive, by what logic could its significance outweigh the effect of all the instances of less favorable U.S. policies in the following decades? It is to these policies I now turn.

Part of the difficulty in examining the question of anti-Americanism in the Middle East is that the grounds for criticism of U.S. policy are not well understood. Most discussions of the subject refer to the fact that Washington tries to maintain its hegemony in the region by supporting unpopular regimes and has occasionally helped bring down more popular governments in order to place its clients in power. But the significance of these events is not straightforward. Washington's support for many of the ruling dynasties across the Middle East and for the military apparatuses that keep them in power is certainly a factor that affects opinions of the United States. More significant, however, is the fact that interventions to create friendly governments became less and less feasible as the region's military-based regimes secured their power, and those that were carried out seldom produced the desired outcome in the longer term. In many parts of the Middle East, the United States became unable to exercise its hegemony by maintaining client regimes in power. The increasingly violent policies the United States pursued in response to these failures are a more important consideration.

America's decision to organize a coup against the nationalist government of Iran in 1953 and to establish the military dictatorship of Muhammad Reza Shah is the best-known instance of direct intervention prior to the invasion of Iraq in 2003.[8] There were several others, however. Five years later, the United States intervened in Lebanon to prevent the defeat of the ruling Lebanese oligarchs by reformist politicians.[9] The following year, in 1959, Washington attempted to kill the president of Iraq, Abd al-Karim Qasim, the nationalist leader who had overthrown the British-installed monarchy the previous summer.[10] The assassination failed, but in 1963 Washington helped a group of army officers seize power, establishing the rule of the military regime and the Baath party through which Saddam Hussein rose to power.[11] In 1967, the United States supported Israel's invasion of Egypt, designed to bring about the collapse of the government of Gamal Abdel Nasser and the political defeat of Arab nationalism and at the same time to eliminate the post-1948 Palestinian resistance movement and to seize East Jerusalem, the West Bank, and the Gaza Strip, the parts of Palestine it had been unable to incorporate when the state of Israel was created in 1948. Although the United States had opposed similar efforts by Israel to acquire territory in 1956, it was now keen to see the removal of Nasser and lent its support.[12]

The significance of these interventions is that in the longer term they were failures. The Shah lost his throne in the Islamic revolution of 1979. The Lebanese oligarchy, propped up by the U.S. intervention of 1958, collapsed in 1975, leading the country into eighteen years of civil war. In Iraq, Saddam Hussein and his allies, who took power from rival military officers in 1968, nationalized the country's foreign-controlled oil and rejected the regional hegemony of the United States. The West Bank and Gaza Strip, rather than submitting to Israeli rule, gave birth to a more vigorous Palestinian nationalism.

It was these failures that came to shape U.S. policy in the later decades of the twentieth century. The policy adopted with increasing frequency was to prolong, intensify, and prevent the resolution of armed conflict. There were three major instances of this policy, in Iran and Iraq, Afghanistan, and Israel and Palestine.

The Iranian revolution left the United States with no ally among either of the two major powers in the Gulf, Iran and Iraq. In September 1980, Iraq invaded Iran, with no objection from Washington and possibly with its encouragement.[13] The United States then seized the opportunity to weaken both countries, by working to prevent a resolution to the war. Washington gave Iraq enough financial and military support to avoid defeat but no way to extricate itself from the conflict. At the same time, U.S. weapons were supplied to Iran, mostly by Israel, while Washington rejected Soviet attempts to organize peace talks.[14] In 1983–1984, Iraq attempted to end the war by escalating it to new levels, first by introducing chemical weapons against Iran, then by attacking oil facilities and shipping in the Gulf. When the U.S. envoy Donald Rumsfeld discussed this escalation with Saddam Hussein in December 1983, the Iraqi president explained that "what was needed was to stop the war, or put the Gulf in a balanced situation for both belligerents." The United States chose the latter course, increasing its support for Iraq.[15] Washington also worked to prevent any UN resolution that would penalize Iraq for launching the war or make it liable for reparations, the conditions Iran demanded for ending the fighting. The United States helped to keep the war going for eight years, at a cost of more then a million people killed and wounded in the two countries.

After the war, the United States hoped to turn Iraq's wartime dependence on its support into a long-term economic and political relationship. However, Iraq's invasion of Kuwait in August 1990, intended to end the financial crisis the earlier war had caused, put an end to that possibility. Instead, it provided Washington with a further opportunity to weaken Iraq through a protracted conflict. After driving the Iraqi forces from Kuwait, the United States and Britain established the UN sanctions regime, officially to disarm Iraq but in practice used to keep the country financially crippled and to prevent its economic recovery. Washington justified this policy by claiming that Iraq had failed to disarm, although it produced no evidence for the claim. The available evidence indicated that Iraq was known to have eliminated its proscribed weapons and weapons programs by 1995. The United States and Britain kept this knowledge secret in order to delay the removal of the sanctions.[16] In March 1997, Washington declared that sanctions would remain in place indefinitely, even if Iraq were found to have complied with its obligations regarding proscribed weapons.[17] A bombing campaign to enforce no-fly zones, which had no UN authorization, was escalated periodically to further harass the Iraqi regime, and information gathered in the UN weapons inspections was used in a series of unsuccessful American efforts to assassinate the Iraqi leadership.

By 1998, Washington's policy of protracted violence in the Gulf had been in place for two decades. But it was proving difficult to sustain. Grassroots campaigns against the sanctions publicized the fact that they had contributed to as many a half a million infant deaths in Iraq and that the United States was continuing to use them to block the supply of medicines, water purification equipment, and food-processing machinery. France and Russia, which were owed billions of dollars by Iraq, wanted to pursue economic opportunities in the country. In response, in December 1998, Washington withdrew the UN inspectors and escalated the bombing. By halting the inspections, the United States delayed the risk of their completion and thus an end to the sanctions, buying more time for its efforts to bring down the Iraqi regime. However, it was not until the attacks on the United States of September 11, 2001, which were unrelated to Iraq, that a domestic climate was created to support the invasion and occupation of Iraq, accomplished eighteen months later.

On Iran's other flank, in Afghanistan, Washington helped exacerbate a second conflict and transform it into a protracted war. U.S. involvement in Afghanistan is usually seen as a response to the Soviet military intervention of 1979. In fact, it began earlier, and its goal was to provoke the invasion by Soviet troops and to prevent their withdrawal. In 1973, army officers had overthrown the Afghan monarchy and, in alliance with the Left, had promised a program of land reform and social transformation. The Shah's Iran, encouraged by the United States, launched a program of aid and intervention to weaken the leftist elements in Kabul and to draw the country away from its long-standing reliance on Soviet support and into the orbit of U.S.-Iranian power. Like other U.S.-backed interventions, this one ended in failure. In April 1978, the Afghan Left seized power, introduced a radical program of land reform in an attempt to overthrow the old social order by force, and turned to the Soviet Union for increased support. As political unrest spread across the country, the United States began to underwrite Pakistan's efforts to destabilize the government, and in March 1979 it started discussing plans for "sucking the Soviets into a Vietnamese quagmire" in Afghanistan.[18] In July, Washington began a secret program to arm the Pakistan-supported counterrevolutionary forces—the Islamic political parties known as the mujahideen—attempting to overthrow the Afghan government. The conflict was funded jointly by the United States and by Saudi Arabia, equipped with Soviet-style weapons purchased from Egypt, China, and Israel, and supplied with additional recruits from the Islamic movements of Egypt, Saudi Arabia, Yemen, and other countries.[19] U.S. support for the Islamic forces based in Pakistan began almost six months before the Soviet invasion, and its aim was not to oppose the invasion but provoke it.[20]

The UN secretary general appointed a mediator, Diego Cordovez, to negotiate an end to the conflict. In 1983, the new Andropov government in Moscow began efforts to reach agreement on a Soviet withdrawal. As Cordovez later reported, Washington rejected this initiative in favor of prolonging the war. The prowar party within the U.S. government, led by Richard Perle, arranged to more than double the supply of arms to the mujahideen, in a successful attempt to prevent the Soviet departure.[21] Negotiations eventually resumed five years later, and the last Soviet troops left in 1989.

The third major conflict that the United States helped prolong was that between Israel and the Palestinians. Like the other two, it is a conflict in which the U.S. role is widely misunderstood. Following the June 1967 war, the Israeli government adopted the Allon plan, a program for the gradual colonization of the newly occupied Palestinian lands and their incorporation into Israel, while reserving pockets of territory for the occupied population, to be administered by Jordan or a quisling Palestinian authority. In opposition to this program, the United Nations, the European Union, and the Arab states presented a series of proposals, based on an end to the occupation and the creation of a Palestinian state alongside Israel, to resolve the conflict.[22] These proposals were ignored or rejected by the United States, which vetoed all calls for an international peace conference.[23] Instead, Washington helped Israel implement the Allon plan. As an alternative to an internationally imposed settlement, which would require an immediate end to the Israeli occupation, Washington promoted a series of agreements between the occupying power and the people whose land it occupied—the 1979 Camp David accords, the 1993 Oslo accords, and the 2003 Road Map—all of which left the occupation in place.[24] This policy, for which there was no precedent in any other modern conflict, enabled Israel to proceed with the colonization, accelerating the seizure of land and the planting of Jewish settlements with each successive "peace plan," while the United States gave Israel the financial and military support necessary to maintain the occupation and suppress Palestinian resistance to it.

None of the three conflicts discussed here was initiated by the United States. In each case, there was an existing conflict or international dispute in which local parties were willing to resort to force. Other outside powers were involved, either indirectly though the supply of arms to the protagonists or directly, for example in the Soviet intervention in Afghanistan. Most governments in the region used military or police violence as a normal instrument of politics, either against specific groups (Turkey against its Kurdish population, for example, the Sudanese government against its rural populations, or Israel against the Palestinians) or as a general instrument of repression. In the case of Iraq, the regime's violence was extraordinary in its scope and degree. In Iraq, too, the role of the United States was different. It was distinguished by the breadth of its involvement in the use of violence across the Middle East, the scale of its financial commitment to providing the means for carrying it out, and its increasing reliance on long-running conflict as a normal instrument of politics. These policies contributed to making the last quarter of the twentieth century perhaps the most violent period in the region's recorded history.

The perpetuation of conflict was a symptom of the relative weakness of the United States, given its imperial ambitions. Unable to establish its hegemony over many parts of the region, or even to control it by force, it fell back upon protracted warfare as the next best means of weakening those local powers that refused to accept its authority.

The argument that anti-Americanism might arise in the Middle East because of the role of the United States in sustaining unpopular governments misunderstands the main character of U.S. power in the region. What shaped that power was its relative weakness, its frequent inability to place client regimes in control, and the long-term failure of many of its efforts to do so.

There is another reason why this view of anti-Americanism is misleading. There are, of course, cases where unpopular Arab regimes are supported and sustained by the United States. The two most important instances are those of Saudi Arabia and Egypt, Washington's leading allies in the Arab world. These are countries with powerful Islamic political movements, often seen as among the most influential sources of popular anti-Americanism in the region. The leaders of al-Qaida, the group held responsible by the United States for the September 11 attacks, and large numbers of the group's recruits, came from Egypt and Saudi Arabia. In the U.S. debate on whether to invade Iraq, warnings about the threat of increasing anti-Americanism referred largely to these two countries. Yet, this anti-Americanism cannot be seen as simply a reaction to America's role in supporting unpopular regimes. In fact, anti-Americanism has played an important role in keeping these American clients in power. It is another facet of the strategies the United States followed in its regional politics, and another symptom of the relative weakness of its regional power.

The United States helped create the Saudi state between the 1930s and 1950s, to control the Arabian peninsula and to secure the profits from its petroleum resources for the U.S. oil industry. The agent of America's involvement was the Arabian American Oil Company (Aramco), originally a department of Standard Oil of California but later a consortium of the leading U.S. oil corporations, formed as an alternative to government proposals for a state-owned U.S. overseas oil corporation modeled on the old British East India Company.[25] America's "Arabia company" built the roads, railways, and airports of the new state on behalf of its first ruler, Abd al-Aziz Ibn Sa`ud, and helped organize its financial and administrative structure. Washington also armed and trained the country's security forces. However, the United States lacked the local resources to unify the country politically or to establish the authority of the Sa`ud dynasty. For this Al Sa`ud made use of another source of support, the powerful movement of Islamic religious reform known as Wahhabism. During the first three decades of the twentieth century, before the Americans' arrival, the movement provided the military recruits to help Abd al-Aziz win control of the peninsula. The new state then transformed the movement into the instrument for enforcing an authoritarian moral order, employed to suppress political dissent and to prevent the organization of oil workers, those who demanded a political constitution, and other challenges to the regime.[26]

The twentieth-century political order in Arabia was the product of two forces working together, the American oil industry and a radical form of political Islam. Popular accounts of contemporary global politics such as Benjamin Barber's *Jihad vs. McWorld* portray these forces as opposites—"narrowly conceived" tribal and religious movements on the one hand and the global power of capitalism on the other.[27] This view makes it difficult to understand how the two forces worked together in cases such as Saudi Arabia, where "jihad"—the Islamic reform movement—made up for the local weaknesses of American corporate capital and helped secure its control of the profits of oil. Instead, we should take seriously the interactions of these different political projects, an interaction that might be labeled "McJihad."[28]

The collaboration between U.S. power and political Islam was not limited to the internal political development of Saudi Arabia and the control of its oil resources. From the late 1950s, the United States began to seek a much wider alliance with the powers of Islamic revivalism. Bernard Lewis and other policy advisers hostile to Arab nationalism had been urging Britain and the United States to see the benefits of encouraging the growth of Islamist politics—a politics based not on constitutional rule but on Muslims "restoring, perhaps in a modified form, their own tradition." This Islamic political tradition was "authoritarian and perhaps even autocratic," Lewis suggested, but was less likely to be anti-Western.[29] Britain had been unwilling to follow this advice, preferring to base its regional power on the strength of the autocratic monarchy it had created in Iraq. But, in 1958, when the secular Iraqi monarchy was overthrown, the United States turned to Saudi Arabia as an alternative agent of Western influence in the region. Washington encouraged the Saudis to assume a regional role, based on the promotion of Islamist politics among the populations of the Arab world.[30] The funding of religious schools, newspapers, organizations, and political parties was intended to undermine secular, nationalist governments and political movements, which Washington saw as a threat to its ambitions in the region. As Lewis and others had advised, building U.S. power in the Middle East came to depend upon the growth of Islamist political forces.

The main target of this Saudi-U.S. policy was Egypt. In the 1970s, Nasser's successor, Anwar Sadat, was drawn into an alliance with Washington and Riyadh. He encouraged the growth of a domestic Islamic movement as a rival to the nationalists and the Left, allowing the Muslim Brotherhood, which Nasser had suppressed, to reorganize. Although refusing to legalize the Brotherhood as a political party, the regime used it to weaken secular opposition and to channel political dissent.

Secular opponents of the regime represented a threat that might contest the structure of power in the country. They challenged the reversal of Nasser's redistributive policies, a reversal that was concentrating wealth in the hands of a small elite close to the regime, and criticized the government's refusal to oppose the regional agenda of the United States, on which it now depended for financial and military support.[31] The Islamist opposition helped contain this kind of threat to the ruling elite and its relationship with the United States. The movement's leadership was drawn from the lesser ranks of the professional and business classes, and it drew popular support by promoting programs of social welfare while defending a conservative moral order and the nation's cultural homogeneity. Its moral conservatism sometimes took the form of a popular anti-Americanism, since immorality could be portrayed as the product of the West. This kind of cultural politics threatened neither the regime nor its relationship with the United States and could be contained and even encouraged with periodic acts of increased moral censorship by the state.

The working of this pro-American politics of anti-Americanism can be illustrated by returning to the event with which this essay began, the anti-war demonstration in Egypt in February 2003, at which only six hundred people showed up. That story is incomplete, for there was in fact a second anti-war demonstration in Cairo later that month. The difference between them is instructive. The first demonstration, on February 14, was organized by the Egyptian Left. It was held in the center of the city, and the plan was to form a human chain around the United States embassy, which occupies a triangular block several acres in size just off the city's main square. The government could not tolerate this symbolic challenge to the position of the United States in the country. Government security forces overwhelmed and broke up the demonstration. The leaders were arrested, joining the tens of thousands of political prisoners held, mostly without trial, under emergency laws, in the country's prisons.

Two weeks later, another demonstration was organized. This was held in the Cairo International Stadium, located in an outlying section of the city several miles from the center, well away from the U.S. embassy. At least 120,000 protesters filled the stadium, and thousands more were turned away at the gates.[32] The rally was organized by the Muslim Brotherhood, with the consent of the regime, as a means of accommodating and containing popular opposition to the war in a manner that did not draw attention to the regime's relationship with the United States.

The two demonstrations illustrate the limits of oppositional politics in Egypt and its relation to anti-Americanism. The largely secular left opposition is allowed almost no room to organize, and its criticisms of neoliberal economic policy, U.S. imperialism, and the corruption of the regime that accommodates these agendas is given no space. The Muslim Brotherhood also opposes the regime, but with a far milder critique in defense of moral and cultural conservatism. Its moral conservatism often takes the form of popular anti-Americanism, which operates as a means to circumscribe and weaken the Left. It offers no real threat to the regime.[33]

The anti-Americanism of Islamist groups in countries like Egypt and Saudi Arabia was not a response to America's overbearing power but another product of the relative weakness of American power. Since the late 1950s, the United States had allied itself with Islamist politics as a means to counteract the more powerful secular threats to its influence.

This weakness had a price. The United States had chosen an alliance with a movement with its own ambitions. While Islamist groups could help defeat more progressive threats to American interests, they could also produce demands of their own. In Egypt, small militant Islamist groups split from the Muslim Brotherhood in the 1970s and began to carry out violent attacks intended to challenge the regime, culminating in the assassination of President Sadat in October 1981. In Saudi Arabia, militant Islamist groups reemerged at the same time. In November 1979, armed rebels seized control of significant territory around the holy cities of Mecca and Medina. The following month, one thousand militants seized the Grand Mosque in Mecca, calling for the liberation of the country from the rule of the Sa`ud dynasty. They denounced the hypocrisy of the government for paying outward respect to religion while engaging in "oppression, corruption, and bribery." They criticized the Sa`ud family for seizing people's land and squandering the state's money, while living "a dissolute life in luxurious palaces." Government troops took a week to regain control of the mosque, killing hundreds of the rebels. Their leader and sixty-three other survivors were later executed.[34] The U.S. response to these events was not to confront Islamist militancy but to try and divert it to its own ends. Militants from Egypt and Saudi Arabia were recruited to join the U.S.-Pakistan organized jihad against the government of Afghanistan and the Soviet troops keeping it in power. A crusade against a Soviet-supported government would revive and refocus the claims of the U.S.-Saudi-Egyptian alliance to be the true defenders of the faith. However, like the policy of protracted warfare in the Gulf, this only postponed and exaccrbated the problem. Following the Soviet withdrawal in 1989 and the subsequent collapse of the Afghan government, the Saudi and Egyptian combatants returned home, not to attack the United States but to bring the Islamist revolution to their own countries. Serious opposition reemerged in Saudi Arabia in 1990s, and militant groups launched a campaign of violence in Egypt. In both cases, the opponents of the regime were defeated, with thousands of them captured and imprisoned or executed. Some of the survivors regrouped back in Afghanistan, under the umbrella of al-Qaida, and began calling for and carrying out attacks on the United States as the only practical way to bring about regime change in Egypt or Saudi Arabia.

Anti-Americanism in the Middle East, I have been arguing, should be understood in relation not to the strength of American power in the region but to its relative weaknesses. Since World War II, the United States has attempted to make itself the dominant political and military force in the area, allowing no other outside power or local state to challenge its position. However, although it succeeded in preventing the emergence of substantial rivals, it was never able to establish its hegemony, or even to dominate the region by force. This relative weakness manifested itself in two common forms. The first was America's resort to the prolongation and intensification of regional conflicts as a means of weakening countries that refused to accept its hegemony. The second was its alliance with forms of Islamist politics as a means of undermining local political forces that represented more serious challenges to its regional political agenda.

By the end of the 1990s, the architects of these U.S. policies began to confront the extent of their failure. The failure was measured not in the millions of casualties of the wars in the Gulf and Afghanistan, nor the tens of thousands of political prisoners in Egypt and Saudi Arabia, nor the escalating violence required to maintain Israel's control of the occupied territories. It was measured in the impasse felt in Washington's attempts to impose its will on countries like Iraq, Iran, and Afghanistan, on Palestine, and increasingly even on Egypt and Saudi Arabia. Discussions of "Muslim rage" and the "clash of civilizations" reduced the causes of this impasse to a problem of anti-Americanism.

The response to this accumulation of failures was the invasion of Iraq in March 2003. The U.S. occupation of Baghdad inaugurated a new era in the Middle East. It was heralded as signaling the end to the weaknesses of American power in the region. It was more likely that it would expose that power to new forms of failure.

NOTES

1. "People Power Takes to the World's Streets," *The Observer* (London), February 16, 2003; Amira Howeidy, "Where Did All the Anger Go?" *Al-Ahram Weekly*, February 20–26, 2003, available at http://weekly.ahram.org.eg/2003/626/sc2.htm.

2. *The National Security Strategy of the United States of America*, September 2002, 14. Available at http://www.whitehouse.gov/nsc/nss.html.

3. Bernard Lewis, "Communism and Islam," *International Affairs* 30, no. 1 (January 1954): 1–12; Lewis, "The Roots of Muslim Rage," *Atlantic Monthly* 266 (September 1990), 47–60, available at http://www.theatlantic.com/issues; and Lewis, *What Went Wrong? Western Impact and Middle Eastern Response* (New York: Oxford University Press, 2001). Samuel Huntington, "The Clash of Civilizations," *Foreign Affairs* 72, no. 3 (1993); and Huntington, *The Clash of Civilizations and the Remaking of World Order* (New York: Simon and Schuster, 1996).

4. Lewis, "Roots of Muslim Rage."

5. Elias Khoury, presentation at the conference "Anti-Americanism: Its History and Currency," New York University, February 28, 2003. A ten-year study of hundreds of hours of Egyptian television drama serials, which deal in a forthright way with a great variety of contemporary social, moral, political, and historical issues and are popular throughout the Arab world, produced almost no instances of the portrayal of Americans. The only notable American character, a woman who married an Egyptian, had both positive and negative qualities— hard working and ambitious, but also acquisitive and materialistic. Lila Abu-Lughod, personal communication. For the study, see Lila Abu-Lughod, *Melodramas of Nationhood* (Chicago: University of Chicago Press, forthcoming).

6. Lewis, "Communism and Islam," p. 3. The article was the text of an address to the Royal Institute of International Affairs in London on October 6, 1953.

7. Lewis himself in those years was helping to orchestrate the antipathy toward Nasser, lecturing policy makers about the benefits of supporting conser-

vative Islamic autocracies such as Saudi Arabia in order to undermine the secular nationalism of Nasser's Egypt. "Communism and Islam," pp. 2–3.

8. Mark Gasiorowski, "The 1953 Coup d'Etat in Iran," *International Journal of Middle East Studies* 19, no. 3 (1987): 261–286; National Security Archive, "The Secret CIA History of the Iran Coup, 1953," National Security Archive Electronic Briefing Book No. 28, available at http://www.gwu.edu/~nsarchiv/ NSAEBB/NSAEBB28/.

9. Irene Gendzier, *Notes from the Minefield: United States Intervention in Lebanon and the Middle East, 1945–1958* (New York: Columbia University Press, 1997).

10. Timothy Mitchell, *Rule of Experts* (Berkeley: University of California Press, 2002), pp. 148–149.

11. Said K. Aburish, *Saddam Hussein: The Politics of Revenge* (New York: Bloomsbury, 1999).

12. Israel's plans to seize East Jerusalem and the West Bank in 1956, in addition to the Gaza Strip, were dropped in the face of British objections, after Britain joined the Israeli-French plan to invade Egypt.

13. Iraq planned a short war, modeled on Israel's six-day war of 1967, to seize the Shatt al-Arab waterway and a section of adjoining territory. Achieving this on the fifth day of the war, September 28, Iraq halted its advance and announced that it was willing to cease fighting and negotiate a settlement. The United States delayed action at the Security Council until this point, then passed a resolution that called for a ceasefire but made no mention of Iraq's aggression or a return of forces to the international border. Efraim Karsh, "Military Power and Foreign Policy Goals: The Iran-Iraq War Revisited," *International Affairs* 64, no. 1 (winter 1987–1988): 83–95, at 92; Said K. Aburish, *Saddam Hussein: The Politics of Revenge* (New York: Bloomsbury, 1999), 186–189, gives evidence of closer U.S.-Iraqi ties on the eve of the war.

14. M. S. El Azhary, "The Attitudes of the Superpowers Towards the Gulf War," *International Affairs* 59, no. 4 (autumn 1983): 609–620, at 614, 616.

15. Rumsfeld had been warned by U.S. diplomats before the talks that, "Given its desperation to end the war, Iraq may again use lethal or incapacitating CW [chemical weapons]." Jonathan T. Howe and Richard W. Murphy, "Iraqi Use of Chemical Weapons," November 21, 1983, p. 8. Rumsfeld told Saddam Hussein that "it was not in interest of region or the West for conflict to create instability or for outcome to be one which weakened Iraq's role or enhanced interests and ambitions of Iran." American Embassy London to Secretary of State, "Rumsfeld Mission: December 20 meeting with Iraq," December 21, 1983, pp. 11–12, 15. Both documents published in "Shaking Hands with Saddam Hussein: The U.S. Tilts toward Iraq, 1980–1984," National Security Archive Electronic Briefing Book No. 82, February 25, 2003, available at http://www.gwu .edu~nsarchiv/nsaebb/nsaebb82/index.htm, documents 25 and 31.

16. The evidence available before the 2003 war, and confirmed after it, indicated that Iraq's nuclear weapons program and its chemical weapons stocks and production facilities were destroyed under UN supervision soon after the 1991 war. Iraq also destroyed its biological weapons stocks then, but without informing the UN. The existence of the pre-1991 biological weapons program was not revealed until 1995, when two senior Iraqi officials defected; the biological weapons facility was destroyed by UNSCOM in 1996. The defectors also revealed that the program had been disbanded, but this part of their information was kept secret by Washington, as it would remove the argument for retaining sanctions. The United States and Britain also claimed that it was technically feasible for Iraq to have produced more chemical weapons in the 1980s than the quantities it declared and destroyed after 1991. They had no evidence to support this hypothesis, despite exhaustive UN inspections. The effectiveness of the hypothesis as an argument for sanctions (and, later, war) lay not in any supporting evidence but in the fact that there was no way Iraq could disprove it. This inability to disprove allegations was presented by the U.S. government and media as a sign of Iraq's duplicity. "We said Saddam Hussein was a master of denial and deception," a senior U.S. member of the UN inspection team later said. "Then when we couldn't find anything, we said that proved it, instead of questioning our own assumptions." Quoted in Bob Drogin, "U.S. Suspects It Received False Iraq Arms Tips," *Los Angeles Times,* August 28, 2003. See Sarah Graham-Brown, *Sanctioning Saddam: The Politics of Intervention in Iraq* (London: I. B. Tauris, 1999); and Glen Rangwala, "Claims and Evaluations of Iraq's Proscribed Weapons," March 18, 2003, available at http://traprockpeace.org/iraqweapons.html. On the failure of a CIA mission to find any evidence of proscribed weapons or weapons programs after the 2003 war, see "Statement by David Kay on the Interim Progress Report on the Activities of the Iraq Survey Group (ISG) before the House Permanent Select Committee on Intelligence, the House Committee on Appropriations, Subcommittee on Defense, and the Senate Select Committee on Intelligence, October 2, 2003," available at http://www.cia.gov/cia/public_affairs/speeches/2003/david_kay_10022003.html.

17. Secretary of State Madeleine Albright explained: "We do not agree with the nations who argue that if Iraq complies with its obligations concerning weapons of mass destruction, sanctions should be lifted." Speech at George Washington University, March 26 1997, available at http://www.globalsecurity.org/wmd/library/news/iraq/1997/bmd970327b.htm.

18. Robert Gates, *From the Shadows: The Ultimate Insider's Story of Five Presidents and How They Won the Cold War* (New York: Touchstone, 1997), pp. 131–149. The quotation, the words of Walt Slocombe of the Department of Defense, is from p. 145. On the political unrest that spread in response to the attempt to break the old social order through land reform, see Barnett R. Rubin,

The Fragmentation of Afghanistan, 2nd ed. (New Haven, Conn.: Yale University Press, 2002), pp. 111–121.

19. John K. Cooley, *Unholy Wars: Afghanistan, America, and International Terrorism,* 2nd ed. (London: Pluto, 2000); Rubin, *Fragmentation of Afghanistan,* p. 197.

20. Zbigniew Brzezinski, U.S. national security adviser, later confirmed that the United States had hoped to instigate a war that would embroil the Soviet Union in "its own Vietnam." "How Jimmy Carter and I Started the Mujahideen: Interview with Zbigniew Brzezinski," *Le Nouvel Observateur,* January 15–21, 1998, p. 76.

21. Diego Cordovez and Selig S. Harrison, *Out of Afghanistan: The Inside Story of the Soviet Withdrawal* (London: Oxford University Press, 1995). U.S. aid to the mujahideen increased from $120 million in fiscal year 1984 to $250 million in 1985 and almost doubled again in the later 1980s, when combined U.S. and Saudi aid reached $1 billion per year (Rubin, *Fragmentation of Afghanistan,* pp. 180–181).

22. The United States refused to support the 1971 Sadat peace proposal, the UN Security Council proposal of January 1976, the PLO proposals of 1977, the 1980 Venice Declaration, the 1981 Fahd peace plan, the 1982 Rabat initiative, the 1983 UN peace conference proposal, and numerous other efforts to end the occupation on the basis of a two-state solution.

23. The partial exceptions to this U.S. veto were the Geneva talks planned for 1977 and the Madrid talks of 1991–1993, although at Israel's request the United States prevented the participation of the Palestinian leadership in both cases. When the talks still threatened to put pressure on Israel to end the occupation, Israel undermined them by opening secret talks outside the conference, offering a concession to a single party—with the Egyptians in 1977, offering them the return of the Sinai, and with the PLO in 1993, offering them a role in administering Palestinian enclaves in the occupied territories and future talks about their status.

24. On June 24, 2002, the United States appeared to end its policy of refusing to support the principle of creating a Palestinian state when President George W. Bush mentioned that "My vision is two states, living side by side in peace and security" ("President Bush Calls for New Palestinian Leadership," available at http://www.whitehouse.gov/news/releases/2002/06/20020624-3.html). By that point, however, Israel had started constructing a twenty-five-foot-high wall around Palestinian enclaves inside the West Bank (the Gaza Strip had been fenced in a decade earlier), unopposed by Washington. The wall made it clear that the Palestinian "state" was to be a series of Israeli-controlled enclosures, as envisioned in the Allon plan, rather than a sovereign political territory. U.S. and Israeli policy proposals since the Oslo Accords can be compared with

the Allon plan by consulting the maps available at http://www.passia.org/palestine_facts/MAPS/0_pal_facts_MAPS.htm.

25. Standard Oil of California (Socal) established Aramco in 1933 as the California Arabian Standard Oil Company, adding Texaco as co-owner in 1936. In 1943, Socal persuaded the U.S. government to take over the company's and Great Britain's funding of the Saudi government. The U.S. government then decided to nationalize the company. Socal managed to limit the proposed state ownership to one-third, but then Exxon and Mobil defeated the plan. In response to these threats, in 1944 Socal renamed the company the Arabian American Oil Company and in 1946 agreed to add Exxon and Mobil as co-owners. Irvine H. Anderson, *Aramco, the United States, and Saudi Arabia: A Study of the Dynamics of Foreign Oil Policy, 1933–1950* (Princeton, N.J.: Princeton University Press, 1981). The reference to the East India Company as a model is from Robert Vitalis (personal communication, February 2000).

26. Alexei Vassiliev, *The History of Saudi Arabia* (New York: New York University Press, 2000), pp. 270–271, 337.

27. Benjamin Barber, *Jihad vs. McWorld: How Globalism and Tribalism Are Reshaping the World* (New York: Times Books, 1995).

28. See Timothy Mitchell, "McJihad: Islam in the U.S. Global Order," *Social Text* 73 (winter 2003),:1–18.

29. Lewis, "Communism and Islam," pp. 2–3, 7, 12.

30. Nathan J. Citino, *From Arab Nationalism to OPEC: Eisenhower, King Sa`ud, and the Making of U.S.-Saudi Relations* (Bloomington: Indiana University Press, 2002), pp. 95–96, 125–133.

31. Mitchell, *Rule of Experts*, pp. 272–303.

32. Gihan Shahine, "A Harmonious Protest," *Al-Ahram Weekly*, no. 628 (March 6–12, 2003), available at http://weekly.ahram.org.eg/2003/626/eg1.htm.

33. On March 20 and 21, 2003, as the U.S. invasion of Iraq began, the Left organized further demonstrations in the center of Cairo. From ten thousand to twenty thousand protestors gathered, some of whom attempted to break through a police cordon and march on the U.S. and British embassies. Further government repression of political opponents followed these events. Paul Schemm, "Egypt Struggles to Control Anti-War Protests," *Middle East Report Online*, March 31, 2003, available at http://www.merip.org.

34. Vassiliev, *History of Saudi Arabia*.

6

A Conversation with Rashid Khalidi

Ella Shohat

Shohat: As a way of beginning our conversation, I'd like to cite Samir Amin's article published in the Egyptian paper *Al-Ahram Weekly* [in spring 2003], entitled "The American Ideology." Amin makes important criticisms of U.S. foreign policy, mostly in the mould of materialist analysis of economic and political interests. But he also offers an ahistorical account of American history, cast in culturalist and essentialist terms. For example, Amin describes U.S. neoimperialism as rooted in the biblical, Judaic foundations of Protestantism that "facilitated the conquest of new continents by grounding its legitimacy in scriptures" and, later, extended this God-given mission "to encompass the entire globe with its predilection for apocalyptic fantasies." Consequently, he argues, "Americans have come to regard themselves as the 'chosen people,' in practice a synonym for the Nazi term *Herrenvolk*." American imperialism, Amin concludes, is even more brutal than its predecessors, since "most imperialists, after all, do not claim to have been invested with a divine mission."

Amin offers an exclusivist argument for U.S. behavior, rather than seeing it as part of a broader colonialist pattern in the Americas as a whole. As for his culturalist version of U.S. history, it is a reductionist and, at times, uninformed account, oblivious to the complexity of the many contradictory forces, movements, and ideologies that have shaped the U.S. state. Even the title, "The American Ideology," suggests that there is one kind of an essence to the Anglo-American spirit, and one kind of ideology.

Khalidi: I would be very wary of talking about Protestantism, even, as if it were a monolith. There are apocalyptic and eschatological aspects to some strands of Protestantism, and then there are universalist, charitable, humanistic, and anti-imperialist strands in American Protestantism. The fact that the present administration happens to have as its political base the former trend doesn't mean that it is Protestantism any more than the liberal Protestantism represented by the Council of Churches is Protestantism.

Shohat: Even Bush's own denomination of the Methodist Church did not line up behind him on the war! My point here is not to defend any religion but to caution that an essentialist anti-Americanism is as problematic, or as irresponsible, as essentialist Americanism. When leftist critics of U.S. foreign policy, like Amin, trace a direct line from the Salem witch trials to John Ashcroft and to the war on Iraq, they deny the U.S. its own diverse and conflicted religious history. The Quakers, after all, were the first to call for the abolition of slavery at the time of the American Revolution, and the black Protestant churches have long played a progressive role. Most of the Protestant denominations condemned Bush's war, and their leaders were frequent speakers at anti-war demonstrations. Ultimately, the problem with this univocal account is that the extreme religious right comes to stand for the quintessence of "America."

Khalidi: Exactly. There is something to this sense of America's manifest destiny as having been blessed by God, but that's not all of America. It doesn't represent the pioneering era when the Native American population was destroyed, anymore than it represents the first American imperial thrust across the seas into Hawaii, the Caribbean, and the Philippines. All along, there were, and still are, countervailing forces in American history, with alternative ideologies and very real political influence. Amin's analysis typifies, in a particularly sophisticated form, one older strand of what might legitimately be called anti-Americanism. It is grounded in a Marxist critique of imperialist power and, I think you are right, tended to essentialize all policy, rather than assessing specific American policies as either imperialist or not. This view, which was once very prevalent in some parts of the Arab world, tended to look on the United States as evil because of an essentializing, totalizing vision of America, its essence, and its ideologies.

This viewpoint has grown much less influential over the last few decades, ironically enough, as the U.S. has become more powerful in the Middle East. Today, it represents a minuscule proportion of public opinion, even intellectual, academic, and leftist public opinion. Those who hold the strongest anti-Americanism sentiments in the Arab world are a particular strand of Islamists. Not all Muslims, not all Islamists, not even many or most Islamists, but the people who are the inheritors of a specific historical strand of Muslim program and thought.

Shohat: But it's not necessarily just anti-American. Due to the colonization of the region that had begun with Napoleon, it was as much anti-French, or anti-British. France and Britain had far more consequences for the daily realities of Arabs, and for the formation of their nation-states. In the Middle East, "America" was still a distant geography.

Khalidi: It was anti-Western, but it saw the United States increasingly as the preeminent Western power. Take the example of Sayyid Qotb, who developed the thinking of Hassan al-Banna, founder of the Muslim Brotherhood in Egypt. He was a thinker of the '60s, even of the 1950s, when America had already become a preeminent power. He also had some firsthand experience of the U.S., which I think affected him. So he and his followers—he was executed by the Egyptian regime—are one strand.

Another strand has its origins in a particularly virulent form of the old Wahabbist xenophobia. Xenophobia was an element in Wahabbist thought going way back to the late 1800s, when the movement first allied itself with the Saudi dynasty. It persisted there, but to see that strand as indicative of the whole of Wahabbism, and to see Wahabbism as all of Islam, is an extreme perversion of fact, though an increasingly common one on the part of opinion makers. There were other variants of Wahabbist thought. The fact that the xenophobes were constantly curbed by the regime indicates that there were all kinds of countervailing forces. This tendency was nowhere near as sophisticated as, say, Sayyid Qotb's followers. It was just generic xenophobia, which was then interpreted in Islamic terms when other elements of Islamic doctrine were picked up to justify it. Out of these two (and probably other) strands has grown an anti-Americanism specifically cast in Islamic terms.

These, I think, are tiny minority trends, and so I would not start any discussion of anti-Americanism in the Middle East there. Rather, I would begin by asking, What has been the primary orientation of the elites, or the major political parties, in the Arab world, over the past century and a half? For most of the region, for most of this period, these elites have been characterized by an orientation towards some form of representative government, constitutionalism, and liberal democracy. Yes, there were authoritarian trends, powerful militarist tendencies, and there was the very strong influence of a one-party system, mainly as the result of Third International communist parties. They all had a big influence on elites. But from the 1850s, some form of limitation on autocracy, some goal of representative government, and some version of liberalism were all extremely attractive ideologies for elites in the largely Arab parts of the Middle East. The Ottoman constitutional revolution, the Iranian constitutional revolution, and efforts in Tunisia and in Egypt in the late nineteenth century all sought to limit the power of the law. The elites themselves were not always democratic, in some cases were oligarchic, and in others were extremely monopolistic in how they controlled power, but they absorbed and wielded these ideologies, which grew enormously in strength with the expansion of education in the late nineteenth and early twentieth centuries. Consequently, by the early or mid-twentieth century, those liberal ideologies were very powerful throughout the Arab world.

Among the countervalent forces were the autocracies, in many cases supported externally, like the monarchy in Egypt, which was supported and operated by the British, who chose and even named the king. The colonial system, which prevented the most popular political party from controlling Egypt's politics from independence in 1922 until the revolution in 1952, was entirely dominated and controlled by the British. Democracy was foiled in Egypt not by anti-democratic Egyptian forces, nor by Islam, but by imperialism.

Shohat: This is the kind of paradoxical situation that populations in the Middle East, as in many countries throughout Africa and Latin America, have found themselves tangled up in. There is a bitter irony expressed in attitudes toward the discourse of democracy, when the very forces struggling to democratize have been suppressed by regimes imposed and managed by colonial or ex-colonial powers. All the talk about "bringing democracy to the Middle East" comes from powers that have stood in the way of democratizing. In fact, you can argue that this dissonance prepared the ground for the contemporary skepticism about the U.S. role in the region.

Khalidi: The same was true in Iran, in the Ottoman Empire, and, to a lesser extent, in a number of other countries like Syria, Lebanon, Iraq. But when we look for the roots of attitudes towards the West, what's usually missing is a sense of how these elites have always been open to democratic ideas and constitutionalism.

Shohat: The struggle for democratization in the Middle East has often been complicated, though, by ideologies of modernization. Along with the battle for liberation from colonialism, nationalism also offered a legitimate vehicle for expressing the desire for modernity, which was identified with the "West."

Khalidi: Precisely, and what's also missing from the general perception of the Middle East as intrinsically anti-American is the fact that for the first half of the twentieth century, the Middle East was overwhelmingly pro-American.

Shohat: Absolutely. "America" was in many ways perceived to be somehow "outside" the violent dynamic of British and French colonialisms. Of course, this perception ignored the U.S.'s own colonial history, and also its imperial policies in places like Latin America, carried out partly under the guise of the Monroe Doctrine. But I think that, at least within the popular imagination, the distance of the U.S.—and I don't mean only geographical but also political—allowed it to remain untainted by the anti-colonial sentiment throughout the first half of the twentieth century.

Khalidi: In World War I, the United States was seen as a possible savior from the imperial powers. From Korea and India to Morocco, and indeed all over the third world, the U.S. was, at the time, regarded with rapture. It's no coincidence that there were national uprisings against national oppressors in Korea, India, and Egypt immediately after the peace conference in 1919.

Shohat: Even later, during the Suez Canal crisis, the U.S. managed its geopolitical influence in a way that was perceived relatively favorably. Washington, via the United Nations, actually intervened to head off a war that was declared on Egypt by the Franco-Anglo-Israeli alliance.

Khalidi: Exactly, and this continues somewhat into the second half of the twentieth century. I would argue that there was a deep reservoir of pro-Americanism, a profound sympathy with American ideals, and a hope that American policy would live up to those ideals, well into the 1950s and 1960s, and partly, as you suggest, because of Suez. This wasn't simply a matter of policy; it had to do with the fact that the great colonial powers engaged in educational, missionary, and other efforts as part of an imperialist strategy for control and domination. Until the second half of the twentieth century, this was not the case for the United States.

Shohat: At least not to the same degree, since you could find American-based missionary activities in East Asia, sub-Saharan Africa, or Latin America, and, from the 1830s onwards, in China.

Khalidi: Yes, but in the Middle East this was certainly not the case. U.S. ideals, it was hoped, might be actuated in a way that would balance the rapaciousness of the European great powers. Of course, none of this happened. The hopes for the Fourteen Points, and Wilson's peace conference, were disappointed, and nothing much followed that would have borne out these expectations.

However, after World War II, there were specific instances where American policy did help in the removal of foreign military forces, from Libya and Iran, for example, immediately after World War I and World War II, and, in the case of the former, right up to 1950, it appeared that the United States was helping to block the ambitions of the traditional colonial powers. Equally in Algeria, where Washington offered support, albeit tepid, to the national liberation movement.

Things begin to change in the 1960s and '70s, largely because of the Palestine issue. The United States became a much more important Middle East power and began to behave more like the other great powers. So, too, there were changes in ideology. The Baath party became much more of a radical party, the Communist party assumed importance in some Arab countries, and other, more radical, nationalist parties took on explicitly anti-imperialist rhetoric. But, even in this period, I think, there was not a deep anti-Americanism in the sense of a rejection of Americans. Until the 1980s, there was very little personal or group violence against Americans in the Middle East, and American institutions were generally not attacked as such.

Shohat: That's true. Even during the 1967 demonstrations in front of American embassies, it was clear that the hostility was directed toward support for Israel rather than toward some American essence. Americans who traveled during this period in Tunisia or Morocco customarily spoke of people making a distinction between Washington's policies and Americans in general. Members of the U.S. Peace Corps enjoyed warm social relations with Tunisians, for example. It is important to bring up this little-written-about history, because it offers quite a contrast to the way that U.S. media today draw on traditional Orientalist narratives to explain "why they hate us." The media tend to represent anti-Americanism as some kind of deep animosity that is wholly irrational, dating back to a clash of civilizations from time immemorial. But testimonies of Americans traveling in the region offer a different picture.

Khalidi: I think you're right, and I think you do see the change in the 1980s when the rhetoric associated with critiques of America begins to take on a religious flavor. This is partly a function of the Iranian revolution. A new strand of bitterness with American policy emerged in Iran that became quite poisonous. There was a move away from criticism of this or that American policy—from saying "the United States is fine but it did a bad thing in supporting the Shah"—to saying, "The United States is bad." Not just American policy, but the United States as a whole.

So now we had three essentialist critiques: the Sayyid Qotb critique, which says there's nothing the United States can do to change its basic nature. Then the specific trend of xenophobia in Wahabbi thought, which essentially says, "Americans are bad because they are poisoning our country." And now you have a third strand, which comes with the Iranian revolution. These three merge in a new form of anti-Americanism, which is quite different from the Marxist form that is represented by the recent example of Samir Amin's article.

Yet, I still believe you can readily distinguish between that kind of visceral anti-Americanism (mainly found in minority Islamist circles growing out of these three trends) and a much broader, majority sentiment that is extremely critical of specific aspects of American policy, while at the same time having a respect, and in some cases even a love, for American values—whether these be American materialism, free-market ideology, American consumer culture, or American representative democracy and constitutionalism. For this majority, there is no intrinsic dislike of the United States, or at least there is an appreciation of certain aspects of what America is seen as standing for.

Shohat: Certainly there has also been a fascinating dialogue with American popular culture. Egyptian musicals from the '30s throughout the '60s alluded to Hollywood musicals. In belly-dance sequences with Samya Gamal or Tahiya Carioca moving to the quarter tones of Arabic music, you can find insertions of the dance forms and music rhythms of jazz, rhumba, and tango, typical of the mélange of the Hollywood musical numbers. By the time of Youssef Chahine's semiautobiographical 1979 film *Iskandariya Leh?* [Alexandria Why?], about an aspiring young Egyptian filmmaker who entertains Hollywood dreams during World War II, you can see the shift away from that incredible fantasy that was America in an era when the Axis-Allies war took place on a land that was Egyptian. In that film, the desire for the space of hope called "America" ends with a disappointing welcome by a Statue of Liberty, pictured as a decadent, toothless woman laughing in a vulgar fashion. This highly gendered national allegory of the love-hate relationship with America reflects its context—the turbulent moment of Sadat's visit to Jerusalem, followed by the normalization of Egypt-Israeli relations and the Camp David accords, all of which were viewed as coming at the expense of Palestine and signified deep shame for the majority of Egyptians.

Khalidi: Yes, the cultural attraction is always combined with a harsh critique of specific policies, especially those regarding Palestine. So, too, there is always mention of U.S. support for structurally oppressive regimes, and now, of course, the policy on Iraq, both the imposition of sanctions after the Kuwait war and the policy since the recent invasion.

Shohat: Your point is very important, because the imaginary construct of anti-Americanism in the U.S. media and in this administration's pronouncements almost entirely glosses over the U.S. historical record of supporting undemocratic regimes throughout the world. After all, it was father Bush, during the Reagan administration, that sustained Saddam Hussein during his war with Iran, and the atrocious crimes he committed against his people were performed with the knowledge of the many functionaries who fill high offices in the current administration. U.S. media tend to underplay that famous handshake between

Hussein and Rumsfeld, and when they do show this image, it is unaccompanied by any narrative that would suggest our complicity in the atrocities.

Khalidi: In fact, as I show in my next book [called *Resurrecting Empire*], American support for the Baath party started soon after the revolution of 1958 and continued almost without interruption through the 1970s, when the United States shifted its support to the Shah. Right after the Iranian revolution, Washington reverted to support of the Baath. So for the thirty-two years between 1958 and the invasion of Kuwait in 1990, with the exception of a few years when the United States supported the Shah, the United States was one of the foremost supporters of the Baath party and its governments. . . .

Shohat: . . . and of their persecution and massacre not only of Kurds and Shiites but also of Communists. We cannot forget that Iraq had the largest Communist party in the Arab world, and many of its members were tortured, killed, or forced into exile. The profile of Saddam as the bad boy who refused to listen to Washington raises serious questions not only about U.S. policy but also about how the Iraqis are represented. In spite of all the talk about making us safer by bringing democracy, many Iraqis have not forgotten that their "savior" supported, and partially funded, the expulsions and massacres.

Khalidi: Another example was the cynical exploitation of the Kurds as a weapon against Saddam so long as it pleased the Shah. As soon as he negotiated what he wanted from the Algiers agreement, the Kurds were dropped and left to their miserable fate at the hands of the Iraqis. Admittedly, the Shah took a lead on this, but the United States was a disgraceful party to it.

Shohat: Nor should we forget that the Shah only came to power in the first place at the behest of the U.S., which engineered the coup.

Khalidi: Finally, there is the murkiest chapter of all, which is American support for Islamist extremist (and, in some cases, Islamist terrorist) movements against secular political parties in the Arab world. This includes the CIA station in Munich, which financed and supported the Muslim Brotherhood in its war against the Baath regime in Syria, and

Gamal Abdel Nasser's regime in Egypt, continuing through the Sadat era and Washington's use of Islamists to fight the secular, leftist tendencies. Then you have the recent history in Afghanistan. Just because Americans don't generally know about these things doesn't mean that people in the Middle East are going to forget them. When they talk about the United States and its policies, they're not referring to the ideal vision of the democracy-loving United States; they are usually talking about these backstreet, dirty, undercover operations.

Shohat: It's very important to speak here about popular memory as a counternarrative to the way U.S. official discourses tend to represent anti-Americanism. These memories are clearly registered and passed on in the communities of the region, but their oral history never shows up in media reports from the region. Nonetheless, this countermemory is crucial to the current discrepancy between what anti-Americanism means in places like the Middle East or Latin America and what it means here. I think that this discrepancy in knowledge nurtures the feeling of innocence and promotes the state of anxiety (and I am here reminded of a common Israeli trope) that the whole world is against us.

Khalidi: We can be even blunter. In order to cover up the fact that there are reactions to specific American policies, it's necessary for the advocates of these policies to claim purity and innocence and insist that we are hated because we are what we are. That's because they cannot ever admit to those policies, which have to be hidden or screened from the American public. The tragedy of U.S.–Middle East policy is that the United States has not been celebrated for its selfless devotion to democracy but rather that it has been bitterly criticized for not showing the slightest commitment to democracy, whether in Turkey, Iran, or country after country in the Arab and non-Arab Middle East, with the sole exception of Israel. And least of all in the occupied territories.

Shohat: Well, here we have a formal democracy, though, as we know, our president was selected in 2000. As for Israel proper—and here we are leaving aside the West Bank and Gaza—what does democracy mean for Palestinian citizens of Israel when in fact they have limited access to power and to self-representation? After all, they are systematically racialized and marginalized in a land that used to be theirs—and within the unresolved paradox of a formal democracy that is also defined as a Jewish state.

Khalidi: There are whole issues there for non-Jewish citizens. . . .

Shohat: And Arab Jews who are also discriminated against.

Khalidi: Nobody ever claimed that discrimination is foreign to democracy! In the U.S., we are living in a country where 50 percent of the population were disenfranchised until the second quarter of this century and where all people of certain racial origins were disenfranchised until the Civil War and then officially discriminated against until the 1950s.

Shohat: Yes, there is a strain of anti-Americanism which forgets that many Americans are also disenfranchised by a certain idea of Americanism. Supremacist thought is more or less foundational to colonial settler states that dispossessed indigenous populations. But it's taboo to mention this when we are supposed to be talking about the "spread of democracy." Pragmatic amnesia is encouraged.

Khalidi: With almost no exceptions, Washington has not exerted any effort to actually bring about constitutionalism and democracy, or respect for human rights, in most of the countries where it has influence. Perhaps you can't blame the United States for Iraq in a certain period, though you can say that the United States actively supported the Baaths against the Communists. But you can blame the United States for countries where the United States has had paramount influence for most of the last few decades: Saudi Arabia, Egypt, and many others.

Shohat: Israel, Turkey—

Khalidi: Morocco, Tunisia, Lebanon, Jordan, and so on and so forth. Where, for example, was the United States when King Hussein in 1957 abrogated the only real functioning democracy in Jordanian history?

Shohat: We've talked about the legitimate critique of U.S. foreign policies in the region, as well as the mythification that tends to expunge from the record the U.S. interventions in the region against forces of democracy. And we've also talked about the essentialism of leftist anti-

American discourses. But we also have to elaborate on the culturalist tendencies of some religious discourses, tendencies that are not uncommon in certain strands of Islam and which characterize many religions, certainly monotheist religions. To a large degree, anti-Americanism in the region now feeds off the perception of American cultural products as corrupting, even on the part of those who might otherwise espouse capitalism.

In addition, much of the tension revolves around gender questions. The veil, for example, functions as an allegory for the nation: "what kind of image or identity do we want for our country, our community?" Consequently, the veil becomes a potent symbol of the conflict between essentialized West and East alike, and in much the same way that colonialist discourse itself was grounded in an East/West binarist framework. Within this framework, a very problematic anti-Westernist discourse comes into existence where the West (as well as the East) is reduced to a monolithic entity and where the Manichean vision of good and evil is invoked on both sides of the Atlantic. Could you comment on this notion of the "corrupting influence of the West," with Israel and the U.S. as the leading bearers of that presumed corrupting influence?

Khalidi: I think you are absolutely right; it is mainly expressed over gender. Among the extreme trends that I described earlier, with the three different strands, all adopt some variant of this culturalist critique because it resonates with deeply rooted revulsions that they have, especially around issues of gender.

But I think there's also a cynical and opportunistic aspect to it. You can see this in Saudi Arabia, where I think that the passion of the Saudi middle and upper classes for Western culture is something which their opponents in these Islamic trends clearly oppose, not directly, but by using it as a rhetoric with which to support their political opposition, people who want to repress public activity by women, such as driving, or the mixing of sexes. Instead of saying, "We're going to force you to do what we say" or "Our interpretation of Islam is stronger than yours," they use what they perceive to be the trump card, by saying, "These are foreign, Western things that you are trying to do. We're authentic, and you are inauthentic."

You can see the same kind of culturalist critique in Gaza and other parts of the occupied territories. Hamas is attacking its secular rivals, and the middle classes, not by saying, "This is the right Islam; here is the wrong Islam," or not only by saying that, but also by declaring, "These are perverse Israeli cultural things introduced to cause the degeneracy of our society." They are using the national banner, rather than the purely religious, to discredit their political rivals and to weaken the opposition from people of the middle classes, who are attracted to Western culture—as are, to be frank, most classes of society in most Arab countries—witness the success of Western cinema.

Shohat: I agree. *Rambo* was popular even among those who espoused anti-U.S. slogans during the Lebanese civil war. But I think that precisely because Islam is equated with fundamentalism, it's important to look at certain strands within Christianity and Judaism that are equally fundamentalist. Take the case of the evangelical TV station in Lebanon; it is not viewed as innocent preaching, and not just because of the historical rivalry between Christianity and Islam. Rather, its message is automatically seen as allied with U.S. regional hegemony. To what extent can we speak about opposition to these evangelical provinces in certain parts of the Middle East as tantamount to a kind of anti-colonial opposition? And to what extent can such opposition be understood in religious terms?

Khalidi: Well, it depends. In the case of Palestine, Israel, and Lebanon, it's clear that a certain evangelical trend has allied itself with Israeli expansionism, and with a right-wing view of Lebanon. This is posited in starkly biblical terms: "We are allied with Israel, because of what we read in the Book of Revelations." It's also considered necessary that Israel should do this, that, and the other, in order for the end of days to come. At its core, that may be a profoundly anti-Semitic vision, by the way, but it doesn't stop these people from supporting Israel as it is today, or some cynical, right-wing Israeli politicians from welcoming the support.

These trends, in Lebanon, Israel, and Palestine, are very much alive, and, as a result, the opposition to them is really at the core of opposition to a certain vision of what Lebanon or Israel are. But the situation in other countries is different. For example, I do not believe that the assassination of missionaries in Yemen (or in South Lebanon, for that matter) is part of any specific resistance to American policy, or Israeli policy, or indeed to a vision of Lebanon. Rather, these actions draw on much more virulent and xenophobic forms of anti-Americanism, or anti-Western-ism in general, which you see in both the Sunni and the Shiite tradi-tions, and they transcend differences in the Islamic worlds. While this may well be a minority trend, it is nevertheless important, certainly worth studying, and, I think, extremely dangerous. After all, we are talking about a politically shrewd minority. These are not unsophisti-cated people, and their manipulation of such themes is very seductive for many young people in the Arab and Islamic world.

Shohat: Parallel to that, here in the U.S., an extreme right wing, which is in fact a minority, is disproportionately powerful. Christian zealotry, corporate greed, and Likkudnik neoconservatives form an unholy al-liance that has somehow come to dominate U.S. policies toward the re-gion.

At this point, however, I'd like us to touch on the critique of the U.S. which you find in the anti-globalization movement. Before 9/11, we were all conscious of the extraordinary activism of the "globalizers from below," who managed to coordinate an impressive opposition to the opening of the borders to global capital, and to the "closing off" of these borders to the rights of workers, immigrants, and the environ-ment. After the attacks, the visibility of this movement suffered an im-mense setback, in part due to heavy filtering by media outlets. Any crit-icism of Bush, who stood in for the wounded America, ran the risk of being perceived as endorsing the horrific attacks. In different parts of the world, many expressed sympathy and were quick to denounce bin Laden's terrorism. But there were also others who used the occasion to rebuke "American arrogance" and who saw the attacks as "payback" for Hiroshima, Vietnam, Chile, and so on. I visited Brazil after 9/11, and, alongside the sympathy and empathy, it was not uncommon to hear the opinion that "this will teach them a lesson." Some even talked about bin Laden as if he were a kind of Che Guevara. This was a par-ticularly disturbing equation, in my view, because it projected the kind of anti-imperialism once characterized as Third Worldist onto a reli-gious leader who espouses terrorism and whose anti-Americanism has very little in common with secular revolutionaries like Guevara. It is hard to imagine what an anti-globalizer from Rio would have in com-mon with a regime that would take great pleasure in banning tangos and sambas. Just imagine burkas and beards on the beaches of Copaca-bana and Ipanema!

Khalidi: Well, we don't know. Maybe that's where he's hiding.

Shohat: Actually, popular culture was quick to invoke such surrealistic images. During the annual carnival procession in Rio, one of the samba schools performed a dance number called "Bin Laden's Harem" in a hilarious combination of Orientalist clichés and Afro-Brazilian popular culture.

All of these sentiments I heard, whether expressed in humor or anger, were pervaded by an ambivalence toward the U.S., and you could still find in them traces of a long-gone third world solidarity. But there is something askew, to my mind, with a view that confounds the utopian hopes and goals of the tricontinental movement with the Islamic fundamentalist cause. They may both host a universalist vision, but they share little in terms of the organization of economic, social, and political life—and least of all when it comes to gender and sexuality.

But of course the anti-globalization movement is not uniform. In gatherings around the world, there are usually always demonstrators who wave the Palestinian flag because they are trying to make the link between that struggle and other forms of justice. But the Middle East is itself no less entangled in globalization policies that profit U.S.-based corporations as well as those from countries like France and Germany, which opposed the war.

Khalidi: For a majority of people in the Middle East, the problem with the United States is not its ideals; it's that the United States is not true to them, as far as democracy, representative government, constitutionalism, and human rights are concerned. I actually think that those are very widespread values and would even argue that the resistance to free-market capitalism and enterprise is pretty much gone among very large segments of the population. With the discrediting of the state-run economies of many of the Arab states, for instance in Egypt and Iraq, along with the parties that implemented them, the resistance—even the legitimate critiques of aspects of free-market commerce and liberalism—has diminished considerably in the Arab world. The overwhelming passion of people for certain aspects of American consumerism and material society makes me conclude that there's no profound critique of these ideas, on either the economic, the political, or the cultural level.

So, too, along with the decline of the Left, a political economy critique has diminished in the Arab world. You can still find elements of it in Turkey and Iran, but it suffered in tandem with the collapse of the Baath and the Communist parties, the dissolution of the Soviet Union, the destruction of left movements and the decline of their intellectual vigor. Of all the regions in the world, anti-globalization probably has the shallowest roots in the Arab world, though I wonder if the looting and free-marketization of Iraq, which is being extensively reported in the Arab world by the ubiquitous satellite TV stations and by the press, might not rekindle that critique. After all, what is being done in Iraq is taking place on a number of levels. There's obviously military occupation, there's resistance, and there's suppression of resistance. There's also an attempt to align Iraq politically with the United States, and it would appear also with Israel in the long run. But something more radical is happening to the Iraqi oil industry, to the health care system, to education, and to the economy generally, in the form of privatization. I was astonished to hear from someone, a friend of mine who works for the International Committee of the Red Cross, that they are actually trying to install the humongously thieving HMO system—by far the most useless element of the U.S. health care system—in Iraq.

Shohat: This is another false linkage that the Bush administration has made. In the push for free marketization, the nationalized economy, education, and health care of Saddam Hussein's dictatorship has been associated with the dependent personality of the Iraqi citizen who doesn't know what freedom is! It's reminiscent of what we used to hear about the colonized Algerian, or about the automaton Soviet citizen, just as any kind of movement in the U.S. for universal health care was once automatically labeled as communist. Iraqis, for the most part, make a healthy distinction between getting rid of their dictator and the social reorganization of the country's resources. They do not generally share the Bush-Cheney vision of a reconstructed Iraq, which entails the complete privatization of national resources.

Khalidi: We are now going to see, among many other things, a struggle over how these two visions play out in Iraq. I believe that the Iraqi division of the state, and the division of the state in the larger Arab world, was a profoundly flawed one. I don't want to go as far as to endorse the Arab Development Report or anything like that, but to see the tragic waste of the resources that could have been invested properly over the course of three decades from the oil movement in the 1970s is to see a system where the power of the state has been without limits and where the corresponding power of civil society, the individual, and other collectives within society was diminished in the Arab world generally.

Etatism was not a good thing from that perspective, but it may now offer a basis from which to resist American free-market liberalism. Indeed, we may see it service a revived political economy critique, especially in light of the most nefarious aspects of U.S. policy in Iraq. It is clearly a violation of international law for an occupying power to give away, either to itself or to its citizens, pieces of the property of the Iraqi people. Currently, these include the oil industry and the private sector, which is going to be sold off, if they have their way, for nothing, to foreign investors. It looks like these foreign investors are going to be American, and ideally supporters of the Republican party, like Halliburton, who contribute to President Bush's campaigns. These are the people who are in a position to inherit the Iraqi people's patrimony, either by stealing it or getting it for a steal. We already saw in Russia what it all means.

PART III

EUROPE

7

Anti-Americanization in Germany

Mary Nolan

DEBATES ABOUT THE PROMISE AND PERILS of Americanization have been a constant feature in European economic, cultural, and social life since World War II. For both proponents and opponents of Americanism, Germany—or the Western part thereof—has been regarded as a model of economic, social, and cultural Americanization that promoted both political democratization and close cooperation with the American global hegemon. This seemed particularly true in the 1990s. In Germany, as in the rest of Europe, capitalism had become the only game in town, and democracy was firmly embedded in Western Europe and accepted rhetorically, if hardly practiced persuasively, in the East. American mass culture and mass consumption, those objects of ambivalent desire and anxious acquisition in the pre– and post–World War II decades, were integral to everyday life and identity, embraced with national accents but embraced all the same.

Fast forward to 2003. Despite or because of or alongside Americanization, there is resurgent anti-Americanism—or what is labeled as such by the American government and media. It is rampant not only in the Middle East and across the global south but also in Europe. And within Europe not just in France, long noted for its vitriolic cultural anti-Americanism[1] but in Britain, Tony Blair excepted, and even more in Germany. What kind of anti-Americanism has emerged in Germany, that seemingly most Americanized of European countries, and why is it so visible now?

Dan Diner insists that America is resented now, as in the past, for what it is and not for what it does.[2] Stanley Hoffmann, Tony Judt, and Claus Leggewie, among other scholars, view German and European anti-Americanism as a new response to the altered post–cold war world and America's claimed place within it.[3] The current escalation of anti-Americanism, I argue, is not déjà vu all over again, for both the tropes and the targets of German anti-Americanism have changed substantially over the course of the cold war and in the wake of its demise. The new German anti-Americanism is political, rather than cultural; its economic critique, which is shaped by social and ecological concerns, occurs on the terrain of capitalism, rather than being anti-capitalist or anti-modern. The discursive mutations and ruptures traced in this chapter are responses to what America has done and is doing. They also reflect shifting German perceptions of what America is. Both reactions to America and reassessments of that capacious and contradictory category Americanism have, in turn, been shaped by the ways in which the Americanization of Germany created a capitalist modernity that both is and is not like that of America.

My purpose is not to offer a rigorous definition of anti-Americanism and to judge particular statements and stances accordingly, for anti-Americanism is a polemical, elastic, and contradictory concept. It refers in some cases to a resentment and a fear of modernity that is informed by anti-capitalism and anti-Semitism, in others to a jealousy of American lifestyles, prosperity, freedom, and power, and in still others to a criticism of the actions of America and the costs of modernity American-style. My aim is to contextualize purported manifestations of anti-Americanism, track their shifting tropes and targets, and explore the intentions of German critics and the responses of Americans.

In 2002, the once special German-American relationship deteriorated markedly. For whatever complex combination of electoral opportunism and principle, Chancellor Gerhard Schröder opposed the U.S. war on Iraq, and his criticism of American unilateralism and interventionism found widespread support among workers, businessmen, students, religious leaders, and politicians. Germans, like other Europeans, took to the streets by the hundreds of thousands. Disaffection predated the war. According to a 2002 Pew public opinion survey, "critical assessments of the U.S. in countries such as Canada, Germany and France are much more widespread than in the developing nations of Africa and Asia."[4] A March 18, 2003, Pew survey concluded that Europeans blamed Bush rather than America in general for U.S. policy; in Germany, 68 percent held this view.[5] Anti-Bushism is certainly very pronounced, but "anti-Americanism" goes beyond the man and the moment. To understand why, we need to look at America's foreign policy and global vision under Bush.

America once had, to borrow Geir Lundestad's phrase, an "empire by invitation." It was "a self-consciously liberal hegemon, operated through multilateral institutions that disguised, legitimized, and moderated its dominance and provided a narrative (or rationale) of common values shared by the 'free world,' which were declared to be universal in their application."[6] Germany was assigned a subordinate role in America's postwar order. Under the American occupation, Germany was viewed and encouraged itself to be viewed as a feminized, passive, dependent nation, victimized by the misbehavior of a few and needing help and guidance.[7] Throughout the 1950s and 1960s the Federal Republic, in whose creation the United States was instrumental, remained closer to and much more dependent on the United States than were other European countries. Despite its growing economic power and political prestige, West Germany was viewed by America as an immature adolescent, liable to severe parental discipline if it acted out or talked back.[8] The pervasive military, political, and ideological presence of the cold war in Germany encouraged West Germans to accept their subordinate position, stress America's commitment to internationalism—and the U.S. commitment was greater then—and ignore such interventions as Guatemala and Iran. Vietnam aroused anger on the part of the younger generation of students, who criticized American imperialism, the Federal Republic, and the National Socialism of their parents' generation in similar terms. (Recall the ubiquitous chant "USA-SA-SS.")[9] The political anti-Americanism of the '68ers found little resonance, however, and when some leftists adopted violent tactics and the government resorted to severe repression, terrorism displaced America as the dominant concern.[10] From the late 1970s on, there were chronic disagreements over détente, disarmament, and the stationing of American Cruise and Pershing II missiles in Germany, over the oil crisis and *Ostpolitik,* and over the proper response to the Soviet Union's invasion of Afghanistan. In the cold war context, however, heated debates on particular issues did not develop into a fundamental critique of U.S. policies.

Now the cold war and the Soviet Union are gone, and America is the world's only superpower. According to William Wallace, "the rhetorical justification for this dominant position is more often couched in realist than in liberal terms; with reference to American national interests rather than to shared global values and concerns."[11] What is at issue, argues Charles Kupchan, is "not America's culture, but its power." It is "competing values, not competing interests."[12] These shifts are neatly captured in the government's 2002 *National Security Strategy*, which declared emphatically that the United States would pursue "an American internationalism that reflects the union of our values and our national interests."[13] Europeans understandably had difficulty finding the international in that formulation. In the *National Security Strategy*, in several Bush speeches, and in the war against Iraq, America reiterated its new commitment to unilateralism, preventive war, an extreme variant of neoliberal capitalism, and a Pax Americana to which the rest of the world was told to accommodate itself or suffer irrelevance if not worse.[14] Iraq was the proclaimed opening of a war, undertaken with messianic zeal, against "evildoers" who are potentially everywhere. Empire is implicitly and increasingly explicitly advocated not only by such right-wing groups as the Project for the New American Century but also by such liberal human rights advocates as Michael Ignatieff.[15]

Germans and most Europeans oppose the theory and practice of preemptive war, the circumvention of the United Nations, and the violation of international law. They are deeply disturbed by American unilateralism on multiple fronts. The United States withdrew from the Kyoto Accord on global warming, the Anti-Ballistic Missile Treaty, and the test ban treaty. It signed neither the land mine treaty nor the Convention on the Elimination of All Forms of Discrimination against Women. It refuses to join the International Criminal Court. It abandoned the agreement to sell anti-HIV drugs at prices the global south can afford. On the question of Palestine, it has ignored the pleas of Germany and much of Europe for rapid movement toward a fair two-state solution.

Like many European countries, Germany has developed a political culture different from America's.[16] As Anatol Lieven persuasively argues, Europe is postnational and frightened by American nationalism; it is postimperial and believes that America's new and explicitly stated imperial ambitions are unrealizable. Europe is worried by America's hubris, confused priorities, and refusal to compromise on any issue, large or small. The Bush administration claims to be realist, but to Europe it seems surrealist.[17]

Differing European and American views on nationalism, unilateralism, power, and law lie at the heart of American anti-Europeanism. Unprecedentedly vitriolic attacks on European values, politics, and culture have issued from conservative think thanks, the mainstream media, and average Americans. According to Robert Kagan and participants in an American Enterprise symposium, Europeans have an aversion to power, reject healthy and necessary competition, and lack virility—literal and metaphorical.[18] The American media are replete with references to Euroweenies, wimps, and EU-nuchs, suggesting that homosexualization rather than feminization has become the preferred rhetoric of insult.[19] The *New York Post* labeled France and Germany the "Axis of Weasel."[20] Charges of cowardice and utopian internationalism alternate with accusations of crass materialism and self-interest. According to William Safire, "the old Berlin imperiousness" has reemerged, and Germany is collaborating with France to dominate the small democracies of the European Union.[21] While Secretary of Defense Rumsfeld dismissively lumps all critics together as the "old" Europe, others angrily single out the French, those "cheese-eating surrender monkeys." The House of Representatives has mandated that its cafeteria henceforth sell only "freedom fries" in place of the now unmentionable other sort, and restaurants try to drum up business by dumping their merlot. (This has led some Germans to boycott Heinz Ketchup, Coca-Cola, and Esso gas stations.)[22] On a more serious note, Secretary of State Powell has promised that France will be punished for its refusal to support the U.S. war.[23]

Germany has been threatened with economic retaliation, troop withdrawals, and political marginalization. But the American government and media view Germany less with furious anger than with a sort of hurt bewilderment. The feminized postwar nation and the adolescent state of the middle cold war decades imagined by America are gone, but the language of hurt paternalism survives in the many references to all we have done to liberate and rebuild Germany and to the Germans' unexpected disloyalty and ungratefulness. America's disappointment goes deeper than the current crisis, however. What Josef Joffe, editor of *Die Zeit,* wrote about the drifting apart of Germany and America in the 1980s, as the Greens critiqued American weapons and energy policy and the United States leveled charges of Euro cowardice, is equally applicable today. American accusations of German anti-Americanism "reflect the disappointment with an ally that, more faithful than the rest, embodied America's fondest myths about itself."[24]

American anti-Europeanism reflects a dramatic shift in how Americans see themselves and the world. In the 1950s, Americans presented themselves as pragmatic, optimistic, and rational and as possessing technological cures for every imaginable problem, while Europeans were pessimistic and suspicious and preferred philosophy to social science.[25] Now, it is the Americans who defend pessimistic realism, insist on the frailty of reason, and prescribe military solutions to every sort of problem. Gone are the heady days following the collapse of communism when Francis Fukuyama predicted that Europe and America were leading the way into a peaceful, posthistorical era of triumphant liberal capitalism.[26] American sees itself mired in history, trapped in an anarchic, Hobbesian world, while Europe, foolish Europe, thinks it can live, in Kagan's words, in "a self-contained world of laws and rules and transnational negotiation and cooperation . . . a post-historical paradise of peace and relative prosperity."[27]

American anti-Europeanism has several roots. There is fear about the global economy and America's place in it, for whatever Europe's economic problems, and they are many, the 1990s American boom, based on stock market speculation and the high-tech sector, is over and with it the hope or fear that that was the model that others must emulate.[28] The weak dollar and American dependence on massive foreign investment engender anxiety about the potential power of the EU and the Euro. Militarily, America is frustrated that it cannot persuade Europe to spend and deploy more, while leaving all decisions about goals and strategy in U.S. hands.[29] Finally, the United States is annoyed and perplexed that, despite its military might and a defense budget greater than all other countries combined, not everyone defers to American wishes.

American unilateralism has oscillated between internationalist gestures and interventionist actions, with or without a "coalition of the willing."[30] In either mode, Bush and his supporters have labeled any criticism as anti-Americanism—despite the vehement objections of the critics[31]—and responded with anti-Europeanism. This leaves no room for reasoned critique, nuanced debate, or legitimate disagreements. In the words of Zbigniew Brzezinski, America tells its European allies to "'line up' as if they were part of some 'Warsaw Pact.'"[32] This counterproductive approach has deepened divisions within the EU and NATO, threatened the Atlantic alliance, and corroded the special German-American relationship built over the cold war decades.

. . .

The growing German criticism of America is more than a contingent response to current U.S. policies. To understand it more fully, we need to turn from contemporary international relations to long-term domestic developments and trans-Atlantic exchanges, which reshaped both German society and discourses of anti-Americanism. From the 1920s on, Germany was transformed not as part of some ill-defined processes of modernization or westernization but rather in specifiable ways that built on German structures, institutions, values, and practices but borrowed from American models in many fields and were shaped by American active interventions. There were selective borrowings, negotiated appropriations, wanted and unwanted interventions. What did these produce in the areas central to discourses of Americanism and anti-Americanism—mass production, mass consumption, and mass culture?

Let us begin with economic Americanization. As German capitalism evolved from the rationalization of the 1920s through the Nazi war economy to postwar variants of Fordism and post-Fordism, America served as a model to be emulated or avoided, as an ensemble of technologies and managerial practices to be appropriated selectively. It suggested new ways to imagine consumption, rethink economic growth, and revamp the social relations of work and leisure. But, until the 1960s, economic Americanization was rhetoric more than reality, a distant object of desire or disdain, not a central element of everyday life.

Nonetheless, Germans anguished about mass production and mass consumption. During the 1920s, capital and the Right admired American efficiency, minimal state intervention, and weak unions, while defending German specialized production, "quality work," and an export strategy. Labor and the Left embraced the assembly line and accepted deskilling but demanded higher wages and more consumption in return. All classes and parties criticized American materialism, standardization, and homogeneity and were at best profoundly ambivalent about the liberated women and dollar-obsessed men that American economic prowess purportedly fostered. The Nazis moved hesitantly toward more Americanized forms of production and payment, even as they viewed America as decadent and weak, because it permitted racial mixing, but also dangerous because it was ostensibly dominated by Jews.[33] The Nazis, however, were much more open to mass consumption than were Weimar conservatives (or 1950s Christian Democrats).

In both West and East Germany, post-1945 economic recovery resulted from increased worker productivity and exports, not from investment in new technology.[34] In the mid-1950s, East and West Germany looked more like each other, and more like their interwar predecessors, than like America. The breakthrough to Americanized mass production with extensive mechanization, rationalization, and new management techniques, and to the mass consumption of fridges, vacuums, cars, washing machines, modern furniture, and TVs, came only in the late 1950s in the West and, on a more modest scale, in the 1970s in the East.[35] By the late 1960s, West Germany had become the premier European economic power, a position it has maintained despite deindustrialization, reunification, and globalization. It is both the most Americanized of European economies and the one that, alone and now as part of the EU, represents the major economic challenge to the American model.

Even as Americanized mass production and consumption triumphed in the West German economic miracle of the long 1950s, anxieties about mass consumption persisted. There were anguished efforts to educate and discipline the potentially unruly female consumer.[36] In the East, where a socialist mass consumption emerged later, the focus was on alternative, more egalitarian consumer values and practices, on consuming American-style goods but not in American ways.[37] The '68 generation was the first to embrace modern mass consumption unequivocally and it remained as infatuated with American mass culture as its '50s predecessor or its East German counterpart.

From the 1970s on, older anxieties about the corrosive effects of Americanized mass production and mass consumption dissipated. Consumption became pervasive, socially sanctioned, and personally acceptable. Moreover, the very success, not to say excess, of West German mass consumption became a premier weapon in the cold war. In the 1950s religion, family and private property were the hallmarks of West Germany's self-proclaimed superiority over the godless, communist East. (Allegiance to democracy was initially more formal than deeply felt.) By the 1960s, it was the mass production of consumer goods of every sort and quality and the conspicuous consumption of leisure and travel that proved the Federal Republic's material and moral worth. This too was a form of Americanization, for the United States had pioneered consumption-oriented cold war politics and propaganda in the 1950s—recall the Brussels World's Fair and the

Kitchen Debate.[38] Only in the former GDR are there still echoes of the earlier unease about the effects of consumption on identity and culture. *"Ostalgie,"* the nostalgia for consumer goods specific to the GDR, has swelled after the first years of frantic consumption of the once longed-for West German/Americanized goods.[39]

Economic Americanization was accompanied, indeed preceded, by the spread of Americanized mass culture. In the 1920s, it was Hollywood films, jazz musicians, and the Tiller Girls precision dance troupe. The Nazis reworked elements of American popular culture to create what Michael Geyer has called the nationalist variant of modern mass culture.[40] After World War II, American mass culture, spread by occupation forces and ambitious entrepreneurs, took on whole new dimensions. During these decades, German anti-Americanism attacked Hollywood films, jazz, and rock 'n' roll as seductive and dangerous. Like mass consumption, mass culture ostensibly catered to the lowest emotions and the least developed classes and races. Together, they reflected and promoted a feminization of the public sphere and an Americanization of gender relations; they encouraged a clever but shallow *Homo faber* as opposed to the European *Home sapiens*. Mass culture and mass consumption produced a society of confusingly similar surfaces and superficiality, of facile optimism and empty materialism.

These tropes, elaborated most insistently by the Right and by men but echoed by many others, were not definitively challenged until after World War II and then only slowly. The American occupation and the Marshall Plan, as well as the cultural programs of both the U.S. government and American foundations, brought Americans and Americanization to Germany in dramatically new forms and encouraged Germans to visit and study in the United States. Hollywood films and rock 'n' roll flooded German theaters and airwaves. American mass culture served multiple functions—as a weapon in the cold war for the West and as proof of socialist superiority for the East, as the terrain of generational struggle, and as a diversion from the bleak postwar present in both East and West.

As American "high" and "low" culture were consumed—avidly by some, ambivalently by others—perceptions of American culture grew more complex.[41] Liberals made their peace with youth culture, and even the Christian Right modulated its criticism of American movies and music. By 1968, the student generation happily consumed American mass culture, while directing its anti-Americanism in political directions. American mass culture became an integral part of everyday West German life. By the 1980s, for example, the entire nation watched *Dallas* religiously and without lamenting about threats to *Kultur*.[42] This embrace of American mass culture reflected both choice and necessity. The French could vehemently defend their civilization against McDonald's and Hollywood, but the task was much harder for Germans, given the complicity of educated elites and cultural institutions in Nazism.

Economic and cultural Americanization has thus eroded the ambivalence about and hostility to modernity and capitalism that pervaded earlier German anti-Americanism. There are, to be sure, criticisms of unregulated capitalism, minimalist social policies, and McDonald's, but only among the radical Greens have these entailed a total rejection of capitalism, industrialism, and modernity. Since the 1970s, political anti-Americanism, or *Amerikakritik*, to use a more apt German term, has come to the fore.

Although Americanization eroded older forms of anti-Americanism in Germany, it did not transform Germany into a mini-America. Germany became distinctly modern, but it differs from America in four key areas: religion, social policy, peace and ecology, and memories of war. These are crucial to explaining the emergence of a new *Amerikakritik*.

In constitutional theory, church and state are more separate in the United States than in Germany, where churches get federal funds and religion is taught in schools. The United States has no party comparable to the CDU/CSU, with its close ties to both the Protestant and the Catholic Churches. In the first postwar decades, Germany was as religious as America; both had large church memberships; religiosity and respectability were closely associated, and religious rhetoric was a key element in anti-Communism. (In West Germany, religion also featured prominently in the attack on an excessively materialistic, morally lax Americanism.)[43]

Since the 1970s, Germany has become more secularized, even if official Church membership has not declined significantly.[44] Religion does not permeate everyday life or pervade politicians' speeches; fundamentalism has not taken root. Whereas two-thirds of Americans go to church weekly, only 20 percent of West Germans and 14 percent of East Germans do.[45] "Whenever an American president links his Christianity with a wish to reorder spheres of interest in the most harmonious way, Europeans react with deep skepticism," wrote *Der Spiegel* in early 2003. Yet, *Der Spiegel* continued, one can understand America only if one takes religion seriously.[46] The article, accompanied by pictures of Bush speaking in front of a towering painting of Jesus and cabinet members praying together, revealed how difficult such understanding is and how starkly Europe's secular visions differs from a religiously transformed America.

Social policy as much as secularization divides Germany and America. With the abandonment of Keynesianism and the neoliberal attack on the Social Democratic model, little attention has been paid to social policy and labor law, the least Americanized aspects of Germany.[47] They are seen by Americans as anachronistic if not objectionable. Germany has, to be sure, reduced many of its most generous social policy provisions in the name of competitiveness, but it has not embraced the fighting creed of neoliberalism championed by the United States and Great Britain. Codetermination persists, and social policies remain much more extensive than American ones ever were.[48] Germany offers a much more empowering and protective framework for workers, for the elderly, and for those of all ages in need of health care. Claus Leggewie argues that the Rhenish model of capitalism aims at social integration and the minimization of poverty, while the Anglo-Saxon model fears unemployment but tolerates insecurity and high levels of inequality.[49] The East German welfare system put even greater value on equality and basic security. These welfare states created not only a different material context in which Americanized mass production and mass culture have been consumed but also a different vision of the good life and the just society. Both shape current German reactions to American policies and values.

Although both Germany and the United States have relatively non-ideological, catchall parties, in Germany new social movements, which link peace, anti-nuclear, and environmental issues, are much more important. Germany has Europe's largest and most successful Green party, which is sustained by extensive social activism and is represented in many local and state governments and currently in the federal government, as well. As a result of the Greening of Germany, regulations about air, water, factory emissions, and recycling are much more stringent than in America, and the commitment to transnational environmental cooperation is much greater. While the United States rejected the Kyoto Accord with little thought and little popular protest, Germans see Kyoto as a key environmental pact and the U.S. rejection of it as an indication of America's determination to pursue national economic interests and neoliberal principles whatever the environmental costs or opposition abroad.

The Greens' initial success was rooted in Germany's vulnerable geopolitical position in the cold war and in America's nuclear weapons and oil policies and the contradictory SPD responses to them. It was sustained in part by the appeals of their nonnational or postnational program and identity.[50] Finally, the linking of ecology and peace reflected and responded to a fear of war that grew from and is still nourished by memories of World War II and the Holocaust.

In profound ways, Robert Kagan is correct that "America is from Mars and Europe is from Venus."[51] For America, World War II was the good war, a just war, the war it hopes to fight again instead of another Vietnam.[52] And it was a war fought elsewhere, not at home. Europeans, above all Germans, learned different political lessons from the first half of the twentieth century. For Germany, World War II was a nightmare of destruction and guilt by which it is still haunted.

Since 1945, Germans have been trying to "come to terms with the past," to employ the ambiguous terms so frequently used, but the past continues to inhabit and shape the present. In the early cold war, the West acknowledged that "unspeakable crimes have been committed," while failing to name the perpetrators, and paid restitution to Jews and Israel. In the East, responsibility was put on capitalism and the successor West German state in which it survived. But these early strategies did not put memory to rest or assuage guilt. The Eichman trial of the 1960s; the American television film *Holocaust* in the 1970s, and the German series *Heimat* in the 1980s; and the Historians' Debate of the late 1980s forced the Germans publicly and privately to revisit war and genocide. Nor did the end of the cold war and reunification bring the desired reprieve. There was Daniel Goldhagen's *Hitler's Willing Executioners,* Victor Klemperer's diaries, the controversial photo exhibition *War of Annihilation: Crimes of the Wehrmacht, 1941–1944,* and, most recently, the spate of books on the bombing of German cities in World War II.[53] War is associated not with heroism but with guilt for genocide and with the suffering of German civilians and POWs. Long after the material rubble was cleared away, both those who experienced the war and subsequent generations live with the cultural and psychological rubble caused by a war of unprecedented destructiveness to civilians and soldiers. The romance of war is hard to sustain in the face of that.

The ways in which Germany has diverged from the U.S. model of modernity are mutually reinforcing and sustain a set of commitments to peace, ecology, and social welfare that have changed the terms in which Germans criticize America. There was not one turning point but rather a series of shifts that gradually eroded the appeals of cultural anti-Americanism while enhancing concerns with American foreign policy and neoliberal economics. For the '68 generation in Germany, like its counterpart in Western Europe, a "passion for American culture" went hand in hand with a criticism of American interventionism, above all in Vietnam, but also in Iran and Latin America. But the cold war on the one hand and a shared commitment to Keynesianism, regulatory social policies, and industrialism on the other limited conflict. Anti-Americanism of a different sort emerged in the 1980s. There was a growing critique of the norms, forms, values, and costs of the model of industrial capitalism, rationality, and growth that the United States had pioneered and the Federal Republic adopted.[54] Closely related in terms of program and personnel was the widespread opposition to nuclear weapons and to U.S. energy policies that came to a head with bitter disputes over the stationing of Pershing II and Cruise missiles in Europe.[55] There were also disputes about seabed mining, the marketing of baby formula in the third world, and abortion. By the mid-1980s, in Sanford Ungar's diagnosis, America had become estranged from an increasingly complex world, was unwilling to try to understand or negotiate with even its economically powerful European allies, and insisted that others accept its policies and priorities, its definition of a world simplistically divided into good guys and bad ones.[56] From the perspective of 2004, both the unilateral behavior of the United States and the political critique of Europeans sound strikingly familiar. But the cold war context contained rhetoric and reactions on both sides, disciplining German and European dissent but not bitterness, and limiting U.S. willingness to launch a full-scale attack on countries and international institutions that failed to do its bidding.

In the post–cold war period, foreign policy has continued to dominate German views of America. "In no other European country did the Gulf War engender such fear, concern—one might say hysteria—on such a massive level in virtually every social groups as it did in the newly united Germany."[57] The disintegration of Yugoslavia provided occasions for cooperation as well as disagreement, but with the Iraq war

Germany and the United States, the governments and the citizens, are once again at loggerheads.

In the 1950s, the hegemonic right-wing anti-Americanism supported U.S. foreign policy and the dominant U.S. military presence in West Germany but was deeply anxious about American culture and ambivalent about American-style consumer capitalism. Now a more left-wing *Amerikakritik* that focuses on politics while embracing American mass culture and advocating a more socially equitable and environmentally conscious form of capitalism is ascendant. This resembles neither the West German anti-Americanism of the 1950s and 1960s nor the East German variant, with its sweeping attack on American militarism, imperialism, capitalism, and culture but uncritical acceptance of industrialism and productivism and insensitivity to environmentalism.

Much of what is currently labeled anti-Americanism claims to be and is a legitimate and important critique of American unilateralism, preemption, and imperialism. But it is a critique that silences and marginalizes some issues even as it articulates others. "Anti-Americanism" focuses obsessively and exclusively on Germany's relationship to America and on Germany's opposition to an imperial order, imposed by a single metropole. Simultaneously, anti-Americanism represses Germany's colonial past, replete with atrocities, and masks the unequal, often neocolonial relationships of individual European states, Germany included, to the global south.

Anti-Americanism emphasizes the unprecedented military spending and power of the United States, while conveniently ignoring the massive export of arms—from both "old" and "new" Europe—to the Middle East, Africa, Asia, and Latin America. Emphasis on American militarism papers over questions about what sort of military power the EU should develop. In criticizing American neoliberalism, Germans avoid exploring what sort of economic power the EU has become and whether it represents a neoliberal challenge to the German and European social democratic alternatives.

These intended and unintended consequences of anti-Americanism need further exploration, but they do not nullify the differences between Europe and the United States.[58] Germany and much of Europe have built a different model of modernity, have a different conception of social justice, are committed to international law and cooperation, and are moving toward a postnational identity. Anti-Americanism and

Americanism in their twentieth-century forms were based on the simultaneous hope and fear that in the end all the world would become America. That no longer seems either possible or desirable. Despite American military prowess and global aspirations, America has been decentered as an economic model, a cultural mecca, and a political beacon. Germans increasingly look to themselves and to the real and the imagined Europe when debating their distinctly modern future. Without that centrality of America, anti-Americanism looses its sweeping appeal, its ability to ventriloquize a multitude of social concerns and cultural anxieties. Anti-Americanism has become about military might, intervention, and Empire. So, too, has America.

NOTES

1. Henri Astier, "La Maladie française," *TLS,* January 10, 2003. For a review of the spate of recent French books on French anti-Americanism, see Tony Judt, "Anti-Americans Abroad," *New York Review of Books,* May 1, 2003, pp. 24–27.

2. Dan Diner, *Feindbild Amerika: über die Beständigkeit eines Ressentiments* (Munich: Propyläen, 2002), p. 8.

3. Stanley Hoffmann, "The High and the Mighty: Bush's National Security Strategy and the New American Hubris," *American Prospect* 14:1 (January 13, 2003): 28–31. Tony Judt, "Its Own Worst Enemy," *New York Review of Books,* August 15, 2002; Claus Leggewie, *Amerikas Welt: Die USA in unseren Köpfen* (Hamburg: Hoffmann und Campe, 2000). The Pew Global Attitudes Project's report *What the World Thinks in 2002* argues that, "in general, antipathy toward the U.S. is shaped more by what it *does* in the international arena than by what it *stands for* politically and economically" (italics in original). December 4, 2002, p. 69. Available at www.people-press.org.

4. Pew Global Attitudes Project, *What the World Thinks in 2002,* p. 2.

5. Pew Global Attitudes Project, *America's Image Further Erodes: Europeans Want Weaker Ties,* March 18, 2003. Available at www.people-press.org.

6. William Wallace, "Living with the Hegemon: European Dilemmas," in Eric Hershberg and Kevin W. Moore, eds., *Critical Views of September 11: Analyses from Around the World* (New York: New Press, 2002), p. 101.

7. Petra Goedde, *GIs and Germans: Culture, Gender, and Foreign Relations, 1945–1949* (New Haven, Conn.: Yale University Press, 2002), passim.

8. Andrei S. Markovits, "On Anti-Americanism in West Germany," *New German Critique* 34 (winter 1985); Andrei S. Markovits and Philip S. Gorski, *The German Left: Red, Green and Beyond* (New York: Oxford University Press, 1993), pp. 25–26.

9. Claus Leggewie, "A Laboratory of Postindustrial Society: Reassessing the 1960s in Germany," in Carole Fink, Philipp Gassert, and Detlef Junker, eds., *1968: The World Transformed* (Washington, D.C.: German Historical Institute and Cambridge University Press, 1999), pp. 285–289.

10. For a provocative discussion of activism and terrorism in West Germany, see Belinda Davis, "Activism from Starbuck to Starbucks, or Terror: What's in a Name?" *Radical History Review* 85 (winter 2003): 37–57.

11. Wallace, "Living with the Hegemon," p. 101.

12. Charles A. Kupchan, *The End of the American Era: U.S. Foreign Policy and the Geopolitics of the Twenty-First* Century (New York: Knopf, 2002), pp. 70, 156.

13. *The National Security Strategy of the United States of America,* September 2002. Available at www.whitehouse.gov/nsc, p. 5.

14. *The National Security Strategy*; Anatol Lieven, "The Push for War," *London Review of Books* 24:19 (October 3, 2002); Hoffmann, "The High and the Mighty."

15. Michael Ignatieff, "The Burden," *New York Times Magazine*, January 5, 2003. Available at www.newamericancentury.org. See also Jay Tolson, "The American Empire: Is the U.S. Trying to Shape the World? Should It?" *U.S. News and World Report,* January 13, 2003.

16. Kupchan, *The End of the American Era*, p. 157.

17. Lieven, "The Push for War."

18. Robert Kagan, "Power and Weakness," *Policy Review* 113 (June–July 2002). See also his book on the same theme, *Of Paradise and Power: America and Europe in the New World* Order (New York: Knopf, 2003). See also Karl Zinsmeister, "Old and in the Way," *American Enterprise* 13:8 (December 2002).

19. See Timothy Garton Ash, "Anti-Europeanism in America," *New York Review of Books,* February 13, 2003, for a review of the epithets and an assessment of the varied American forms of anti-Europeanism.

20. Cover headline, *New York Post,* January 24, 2003.

21. William Safire, "'Bad Herr Dye,'" *New York Times,* January 23, 2003.

22. "Wir kriegen sie nur über as Geld," *Der Spiegel,* March 22, 2003. Available at http://www.spiegel.de/wirtschaft/0,1518,241645,00.html.

23. *New York Times,* April 23, 2003. Powell interview on Charlie Rose Show, PBS, broadcast April 22, 2003.

24. Joseph Joffe, "The Greening of Germany," *New Republic,* February 14, 1983, p. 18.

25. Volker Berghahn, *America and the Intellectual Cold Wars in Europe* (Princeton: Princeton University Press, 2001).

26. Francis Fukuyama, *The End of History and the Last Man* (New York: Free Press, 1992).

27. Kagan, "Power and Weakness."

28. Leggewie emphasizes how attractive elements of the 1990s American economy were to Germans. *Amerikas Welt*, p. 87.

29. Kupchan, *The End of the American Era*, pp. 119–159.

30. Perry Anderson, "Force and Consent," *New Left Review* 17 (September–October 2002): 5–30.

31. "Amerikakritik ist ein Freundschaftsdienst." Interview with Günter Grass, *Der Spiegel*, October 10, 2001. Available at http://www.spiegel.de/Kultur/gesellschaft/0,1518,161446,00. See also Alfred Grosser, "Les hors-la-loi," *Le Monde*, April 26, 2003, p. 8.

32. Patrick Tyler, "Threats and Responses: The Outlook," *New York Times*, March 4, 2003.

33. Diner, *Feindbild Amerika*, pp. 105–106. Adelheid von Saldern, "Ueberfremdungsängste: Gegen die Amerikanisierung der deutschen Kultur in den zwanziger Jahren," in Alf Lüdtke, Inge Marssolek, and Adelheid von Saldern, eds., *Amerikanisierung: Traum oder Alpentraum in Deutschland des 20.Jahrhunderts* (Stuttgart: Steiner, 1996).

34. Several historians have noted that both East and West Germany in the late 1940s and 1950s recovered economically not through new technology but through more productive and extensive use of labor. Gerold Ambrosius, "Wirtschaftlicher Strukturwandel und Technikentwicklung"; Joachim Radkau, "'Wirtschaftswunder' ohne technologische Innovation? Technische Modernität in den 50er Jahre"; and Wolfgang Mühlfriedel, "Zur technischen Entwicklung in der Industrie der DDR in den 50er Jahren," all in Axel Schildt and Arnold Sywottek, eds., *Modernisierung im Wiederaufbau: die westdeutsche Gesellschaft der 50er Jahre* (Bonn: J. H. W. Dietz, 1993), pp. 107–169.

35. Exactly what was borrowed and what remained distinctively German is still being debated. See Christian Kleinschmidt, *Der productive Blick: Wahrnehmung amerikanischer und japanischer Management- und Produktionsmethoden durch deutsche Unternehmer, 1950–1985* (Berlin: Akademie Verlag, 2002); Volker Berghahn, *The Americanization of West German Industry, 1945–1973* (Cambridge: Cambridge University Press, 1986); S. Jonathan Wiesen, *West German Industry and the Challenge of the Nazi Past, 1945–1955* (Chapel Hill: University of North Carolina Press, 2001).

36. Erica Carter, *How German Is She? Postwar West German Reconstruction and the Consuming Woman* (Ann Arbor: University of Michigan Press, 1997); Jennifer A. Loehlin, *From Rugs to Riches: Housework, Consumption and Modernity in Germany* (Oxford: Berg, 1999).

37. Ina Merkel, *Utopie und Bedürfnis: Die Geschichte der Konsumkultur in der DDR* (Cologne: Böhlau Verlag, 1999).

38. Walter L. Hixson, *Parting the Curtain: Propaganda, Culture and the Cold War, 1945–1961* (New York: St. Martin's Griffin, 1997), pp. 90, 151–183. Robert H.

Haddow, *Pavilions of Plenty: Exhibiting American Culture Abroad in the 1950s* (Washington, D.C.: Smithsonian Institution Press, 1997), pp. 106–111, 201–229. Karel Ann Marling, *As Seen on TV: The Visual Culture of Everyday Life in the 1950s* (Cambridge, Mass.: Harvard University Press, 1994), pp. 242–283.

39. Martin Blum, "Remaking the East German Past: *Ostalgie*, Identity, and Material Culture," *Journal of Popular Culture* 34:3 (2001): 229–253.

40. Philipp Gassert, *Amerika im Dritten Reich: Ideologie, Propaganda und Volksmeinung, 1933–1945* (Stuttgart: Franz Steiner Verlag, 1997), pp. 164–182; Hans Dieter Schäfer, *Das gespaltene Bewusstsein: Ueber Kultur und Lebenswirklichkeit 1933–1945.* Konrad H. Jarausch and Michael Geyer, *Shattered Past: Reconstructing German Histories* (Princeton: Princeton University Press, 2003), pp. 289ff.

41. Maria Höhn, *GIs and Fräuleins: The German-American Encounter in 1950s West Germany* (Chapel Hill: University of North Carolina Press, 2002); Uta Poiger, *Jazz, Rock and Rebels: Cold War Politics and American Culture in a Divided Germany* (Berkeley: University of California Press, 2000); Berghahn, *America and the Intellectual Cold Wars in Europe.*

42. Höhn, *GIs and Fräuleins*; Kaspar Maase, *BRAVO Amerika: Erkundigungen zur Jugendkultur der Bundesrepublik in den funfziger Jahren* (Hamburg: Junius, 1992); Poiger, *Jazz, Rock and Rebels.*

43. Maria Mitchell, "Materialism and Secularism: CDU Politicians and National Socialism, 1945–1949," *Journal of Modern History* 67:2 (June 1995): 255–277; Höhn, *GIs and Fräuleins.*

44. "Umfrage: Nur noch jeder dritte ein Christ," *Der Spiegel*, December 24, 1979, pp. 70–78.

45. "Krieg aus Naechstenliebe," *Der Spiegel*, February 22, 2003, p. 95.

46. Ibid., p. 91.

47. Wade Jacoby, "'Ization' by Negation? Occupation Forces, Codetermination, and Works Councils." Available at http://www.ghi-dc.org/conpotweb/westernpapers/jacoby.pdf.

48. Patricia Davis and Simon Reich, "Globalization, Gender, and the German Welfare State: The Maldistributive Consequences of Retrenchment," in Carl Lankowski, ed., *Breakdown, Breakup, Breakthrough: Germany's Difficult Passage to Modernity* (New York: Berghahn Books, 1999), pp. 175–211.

49. Leggewie, "Laboratory of Postindustrial Society," pp. 91–92, 109.

50. Markovits and Gorski, *The German Left*, pp. 18–25.

51. Kagan, *Of Paradise and Power*, p. 3.

52. Marilyn Young, "Dreaming of World War II, Living with Vietnam." Available at http://www.nationinstitute.org/tomdispatch/index.mhtml?pid =354.

53. For complex politics of memory, see Robert Moeller, *War Stories: The Search for a Usable Past in the Federal Republic of* Germany (Berkeley: University

of California Press, 2001); Mary Nolan, "The Politics of Memory in the Berlin Republic," *Radical History Review* 81 (fall 2002): 113–132; Geoff Eley, ed., *The Goldhagen Effect, History, Memory and Nazism—Facing the German Past* (Ann Arbor: University of Michigan Press, 2001); Omer Bartov, Atina Grossmann and Mary Nolan, eds., *Crimes of War: Guilt and Denial in the Twentieth Century* (New York: New Press, 2002).

54. Markovits, "On Anti-Americanism"; Markovits and Gorski, *The German Left*.

55. For a survey of the growing importance of political anti-Americanism, see David Ellwood, "Comparative Anti-Americanism in Western Europe," in Heide Fehrenbach and Uta G. Poiger, eds., *Transactions, Transgressions, Transformations: American Culture in Western Europe and Japan* (New York: Berghahn, 2000), pp. 26–44.

56. Stanford J. Ungar, "The Roots of Estrangement," in Stanford J. Ungar, ed., *Estrangement: America and the World* (New York: Oxford University Press, 1985), pp. 14–18.

57. Markovits and Gorski, *The German Left*, p. 23.

58. Perry Anderson and Tariq Ali have both dismissed differences and international institutions. Anderson, "Internationalism: A Breviary," *New Left Review* 14 (March–April 2002): 5–25; Tariq Ali, "Recolonizing Iraq," *New Left Review* 21 (May–June 2003): 5–19.

8

The French Declaration of Independence

Kristin Ross

THE UNITED STATES has long been accustomed to representing the inequality between itself and other nations in terms of velocity. Other nations drag their feet, they delay, they haplessly trail behind the kind of unmarked modernity or spirit of inevitability that the United States embodies. To the extent that such a temporal rhetoric has become accepted—even naturalized—the fundamental political discursive struggle, from the American point of view, has already been won. Free-market positions and the most inegalitarian values become systematically identified with modernity and are then understood in a way that goes without saying as representing "the modern."

The struggle has been won, in part, by introducing the vocabulary of the marketplace itself into the field of foreign relations. This was particularly apparent during the weeks building up to the U.S. invasion of Iraq in the spring of 2003. Again and again, foreign criticism of the United States boomeranged to render critics "unmodern," "outmoded," nostalgically clinging to the contours of the backward bog or swamp they call home—or, in the preferred word of the Bush administration, irrelevant. And all the more so if the critique emanated from France, a country described four years ago in the *Wall Street Journal* as "not even a liberal democracy" but rather "the last Soviet republic."[1] Nations critical of the United States (like critical individuals or groups within consensus democracies like the United States) are represented as obsolete—in other words, as well past their "sell by" date, as dinosaurs.

Where, then, can opponents of social adaptation to the constraints of the market go for terminology to describe their position? Unmodern, traditionalists, resisters of progress, Luddites (as the U.S. trade representative Robert Zoellick called the French for resisting genetically modified agriculture), Poujadistes (as French conservatives call those

144

French critical of the United States), "fading into history," as George Bush called the United Nations—or, perhaps, simply, anti-American. Thus, the ideological accusation of "anti-American," when made by conservatives, whether American or French, transforms ideological critique and struggle into a futile opposition to the whole forward movement of history. The unmarked normativity of the American way manages to present itself and be accepted in terms of rational technique and consensus by setting itself up against that which it claims the power to designate as naïve, hysterical, outmoded, or irrelevant. Increasingly, any representation anywhere in the world in which struggle, and particularly class struggle, is present in any form whatsoever becomes anti-American. Any critique of market logic, whether French, Americans, or Venezuelans make it, becomes "obstructionist" or worse: an indication of magical thinking.

In France, French conservatives of my generation performed much of this ideological labor themselves. The most vocal and prominent of these—at least in the mainstream media where they are comfortably ensconced—are the reformed '68 *gauchistes*, the aging New Philosophers, and advocates of capitalism with a human face. They have now loyally served the New World Order for a quarter of a century. These are the French apologists for the United States, neoliberalism, and economic globalization, the loud defenders of human rights (mostly in Bosnia), unconditional supporters of the Israeli government, and incessant critics of the third-worldism of their own youth. The André Glucksmanns, Pascal Bruckners, and Bernard-Henri Lévys of France, who got their start by establishing themselves as the official memory custodians of May '68 and the social upheavals of the French 1960s, are not a uniquely French phenomenon—they have their counterparts in the United States in the form of media-seeking pundits like Paul Berman and Todd Gitlin. But I want to highlight this group of what Serge Halimi calls "philo-Américains," in part because they allow us to set up a periodization of the present that extends back to May '68 and to the third-worldist ideology that undergirded that event.[2]

The Murdoch press, in its attempt to denigrate the French for their criticism of the American invasion of Iraq, preferred a different historical frame, one in which World War II emerged as the key or defining lens through which to view contemporary developments. The Fox News television network and Murdoch tabloids in the United States and Britain made a concerted effort during the spring of 2003 to incite or encourage Anglo-American Francophobia, culminating in a *Daily News* cover photograph of acres of American GI graves in Normandy: iconic shorthand for French ingratitude and historical amnesia.[3] But framing contemporary events with the 1960s allows us to return to the last moment when American imperialism was widely perceptible, not only to the French but to people around the world. It was also the last moment that American imperialism was widely theorized, as well. The prevalence of international dislike for American hegemony and dominance during the 1960s and 1970s suggests that this moment provides a more compelling optic onto the present than does World War II; perhaps, in part, the optic being revived in some form today reopens the debate over what can be said or perceived about the 1960s.[4] Thirty years ago, half a million American troops were still engaged in bloody warfare in Vietnam. Much of the extensive theoretical writing about imperialism from that time, however, did not derive imperialism's existence from the fact of the war in Indochina. On the contrary, as the Indian economist Prabhat Patnaik reminds us, the existence of wars was explained in terms of imperialism.[5] Imperialism was understood to be not only present in overt instances of actual military conquest but also heavily reliant on the mechanisms of trade, finance, and investment. What U.S. aggression in Iraq in part serves to make newly perceptible is the fact that the system of economic relations covered under the rubric of imperialism has hardly changed at all in the past thirty years.

The French critique of American imperialism of the 1960s and 1970s was informed by a third-worldism that was highly specific.[6] Anti-colonialism that developed in France did so in a country that clung tenaciously to its colonies through its own seven-year war in Vietnam, followed by another eight years of intense war in Algeria, and in a country that then went on to become a far from disinterested observer of the U.S. war in Vietnam. Such an anti-colonialism developed perforce outside the French Communist party (which took a kind of wait-and-see position on Algerian independence), in far-left circles, where it combined with a virulent anti-capitalism. French third-worldism in this important sense differed markedly from the Anglo-American version. The latter was born and evolved under the auspices of philanthropy and Christian charity and within an ideology of modernization and developmentalism manifest in the massive aid campaigns launched by the United States at the end of World War II. The aid went to "underdeveloped"—the term was invented by those same aid campaigns—countries the United States feared were in danger of becoming communist after having achieved independence. Third-worldism in France, on the other hand, which arose in part as a critical response to the same American aid campaigns, was dominated by an analysis based on class relations. "Colonial subject" and worker were fused into a single agent of class struggle, and all of the universalizing power of the proletariat was projected onto the rebellion of the colonized.[7] Throughout the twenty-odd-year period of radical left political culture in France, from the mid-1950s through the mid-1970s, the discourses of anti-imperialism and those of anti-capitalism were thus inextricably merged.

French third-worldism had an exceptional impact, at a mass level, on the political life of the country. It was the leading catalyst of May '68—an event that was itself the largest mass movement in French history, the biggest strike in the history of the French labor movement, and the only "general" insurrection the overdeveloped world has known since World War II. The prehistory of 1968 in France lies in the radical anti-colonialism associated with French and Francophone thinkers like Jean-Paul Sartre, Jacques Vergès, Frantz Fanon, and Albert Memmi and with the Asian, African, and Latin American theorists translated into French in the inexpensively priced paperback series the Petite Collection Maspero—required reading for everyone on the left throughout the 1960s and 1970s. It lies in the attempt to link the stakes of Algerian independence to a leftist alternative in France. For the war in Algeria provided the background noise of the childhood of the militants of 1968; striking workers and their supporters in the streets had all seen, in the context of the final years of that war, to what use the Gaullist regime put its police. At the level of political practice, a new kind of mass organizing (against the Algerian War in the early 1960s and later against the Vietnam War, the last great third-worldist cause) took students outside the university to workers' housing and popular neighborhoods in the outskirts of the city; it brought previously segregated social groups into a new level of contact and sociability. Organizing that involved physical dislocation ended up becoming a dislocation in the very idea of politics, moving it out of its place, its proper place, which at that time for the Left meant the Communist party. Subsequent efforts by self-appointed memory functionaries of '68 did succeed in, in effect, "Americanizing" the memory of the event into a playful, countercultural, libertarian eruption of free expression. And it did so in part by forgetting or excising that prehistory. But the ideological targets of the movement—at the time, at least—were crystal clear. These were three: American imperialism, capitalism, and Gaullism.[8]

When, in the mid-1970s, some of yesterday's third-worldists re-emerged into the public eye, they did so as born-again "New Philosophers," on a new crusade under the banner of the United States and the defense of the capitalist West against barbarism. It took a major ten-year effort on the part of several repentant '68-ers, prominently placed in terms of media access (or, rather, in the process of gaining that place in return for the repentance for their errors), to disguise their own personal enthusiastic conversion to the values of the market as a cultural, spiritual, and, above all, ethical revolution on the part of the Left as a whole. For it was not enough for them to simply proclaim an impassioned denunciation of their former blindness. The case against third-worldism had to be made in tandem with an attempt to rehabilitate ethical values that supposedly transcended outdated ideological divisions at the international level—values that were nevertheless seen to emanate entirely from the West: namely "liberty" and "human rights."[9] Well before Samuel Huntington's "clash of civilizations," Glucksmann, Bruckner, Bernard-Henri Lévy, and other reformed '68-ers had reconfigured the world beyond Euro-America into a kind of invading force of absolute alterity against which it would now be the vocation of a small elite group, namely Western intellectuals, to remain ever vigilant.[10]

It was at this moment then, sometime in the late 1970s, that French media intellectuals—a new phenomenon in and of itself—came to embrace slogans identical to those of the capitalist United States and began to proclaim themselves and the Left (since they still claimed to speak for it) as happy within horizons limited to a dream of modernized capitalism. And it was here that they began to facilitate an eclipse of politics in favor of ethics that, if I may finally evoke something resembling national difference, is really far more in tune with the theological patriotism of contemporary American ways of being than it is with the French national symbolic. If we recall the manifesto a group of American intellectuals published after September 11 in support of George Bush's policies, this text proudly proclaimed that the United States is first and foremost a community united by common moral and religious values—a "city on a hill," an ethical community, not a political one.[11] And "ethos," as Jacques Rancière reminds us, actually meant "lifestyle" long before it meant a system of moral values. For Rancière, the assertion of an unmediated identity between the way a community lives—its lifestyle—

and a universal system of values is what allows crime perpetrated against Americans to be viewed as crime perpetrated against the Good by which the community is founded, or ultimately, against Good itself.[12] Such crime then elicits a reciprocal, Jehovah-like response: that of "infinite justice," as the U.S.-led war against terrorism was briefly called. The eclipse of politics and the rise of ethics have accompanied all of the forms by which the United States and the West have intervened abroad, all of the various "humane interventions" of the past twenty years. And to the extent that the French have fought side by side with the United States in all of its recent wars except Iraq—in the Persian Gulf in 1991, in Kosovo in 1999, and in Afghanistan in 2002—it seems clear that the dominant motivation of a good part of the French ruling elite is not at all the hostility to the United States that Fox News would have Americans believe but rather hatred for what incarnates France for non-French as well as for many of the French themselves: namely the Revolution, the Republic, and the values of liberty, fraternity, and, above all, equality inscribed above the doorways of mayoral buildings in countless small towns across France.

Hatred of the French Revolution in France, which dates back to Joseph de Maistre, was revived in the interwar years in the writings of fascist and fascist-leaning figures like Rebatet, Brassilach, and Drieu la Rochelle.[13] It blossomed again with enormous vigor in the conversion narratives of the reformed *gauchistes* of the 1970s, for whom the Soviet gulag—and eventually Pol Pot!—were the necessary destiny of the French Revolution and for whom Stalin was already alive in Robespierre. Working in tandem with the historian François Furet, the New Philosophers disseminated the new critical vocabulary centered on the term "totalitarianism." A ready-made doxa emerged in their texts, according to which the "excesses" of the French Revolution were named as the territory where totalitarian discourses and practices had taken root, in effect producing the equation that revolution = communism = totalitarianism.[14] Their work was enormously facilitated by the emergence for the first time in France, in the 1980s, of American-style "think tanks" like the Fondation Saint-Simon. Presided over by Furet, who once defined anti-Americanism as "the jealous fantasy of the poor vis-à-vis the rich,"[15] this foundation brought together for the first time in France a mix of government leaders, academics, industrialists, and media people around a nebulous "modernizing project," with modernity being understood to mean conformity to economic constraints. The goal was to bring the social sciences into direct service to the state, and the result was clearly a further consolidation of the intellectual's position as that of "expert" or consultant to the state, clear-eyed and cognizant of hard economic realities. Intellectuals engaged in pragmatic problem solving, liberated from abstraction, would encounter social problems unbiased by ideological considerations. They would exhibit the tranquility of a social class engaged in transforming society and the world in the image of its own interests. The American ideal of Weberian-Parsonian "value-free" social science found a home at the Fondation Saint-Simon. Any adversaries—critical intellectuals or those engaged in social movements—could be disqualified in advance as flaming ideologues, irresponsible, hellbent on swimming against the tide of history, or, in a word, "anti-American." And to be called anti-American in France in the 1980s was tantamount to being accused of fascist tendencies, Stalinist tendencies, or both at the same time—a kind of post-Arendtian red-brown fusion.

The new intellectual-expert was of course wildly suspicious of the people at large, whom he considered incapable of understanding not only the economy but, more important, the whole air of economic necessity given to neoliberal politics. And he was right to be suspicious. For it was those people at large—hundreds of thousands of them—who took to the streets in the winter of 1995 in support of massive public-sector strikes against proposed governmental cuts in the social security system, a movement that can now be seen as the first great mass anti-American demonstration of the 1990s. The uprising was provoked by the announcement of a government plan, designed by Prime Minister Alain Juppé, to introduce a kind of additional tax to pay off the social security debt. The plan also called for raising the number of years before state workers could have access to their pensions and for transferring control over health care spending from employer/employee organizations to the government—reforms designed to bring France in line with the international financial establishment. The mainstream media as a whole, as well as the usual array of media intellectuals—André Glucksmann, Bernard-Henri Lévy, Pascal Bruckner, the Fondation Saint-Simon people, Daniel Cohn-Bendit—all leapt to congratulate the government, in a text published in *Le Monde,* for a courageous and fundamental reform. Night after night, these and other experts could be seen on the evening news, patiently explaining the importance of the government reforms to the people, characterizing the strikers as archaic in their wishes and concerns, stubborn, clinging to the past, anachronistic, out of touch with global realities, dinosaurlike, and conservative. Aging workers were portrayed as backward-looking, exhibiting nothing more than their own pathetic retreat from the modern world, their fear of moving forward into the kind of liberal society that was expanding and flourishing, as anyone with eyes could see, everywhere in the world. The questions these workers ultimately raised—what kind of society do we want to live in? How can we take charge of our collective lives? How is intelligence shared out in the social body?—were decidedly unmodern.[16] The retrograde, egalitarian fantasies of workers and their supporters were just an unfortunate eruption of nostalgia in the ongoing narrative of the disappearance of class and political disagreement in a modern consensus democracy like France.

But no amount of explanation on the part of experts, technocrats, and ex-*gauchistes,* it seems, could convince the millions of striking workers and their supporters that the plan was anything but a greased slide into an Americanized system of social benefits—which is to say, a system of minimal health services and shaky pensions. For the people in the streets, the plan represented a frontal attack on the national health system and public services—sectors long privatized in the United States but not entirely subservient to market forces in France. For several weeks, more than two million workers brought France's cities to a virtual standstill, and hundreds and thousands of their supporters participated in the largest demonstrations seen in France since May 1968.

France, like Germany, had had no Ronald Reagan or Margaret Thatcher in the 1980s, no ultraconservative restructuring of its society. The Juppé plan, from the point of view of the organ of neoliberal consensus, the *Economist,* for example, was long overdue, representing reforms France had delayed in performing, especially a modernization of the public sector that would oblige France to espouse certain traits of the American model. To a certain extent, the Juppé plan and the strike it engendered made Juppé's position analogous to that of Thatcher or Reagan in their first years in office. In Britain, Thatcher had established her program of "reforms" by crushing the miners' strike in 1984–1985, while Reagan had inaugurated his conservative revolution by breaking the air-traffic controllers strike and firing sixteen thousand workers. Juppé and Chirac adopted a similar position of nonnegotiation in an attempt to smash the 1995 strike, but the response on the part of hundreds of thousands of French, oblivious to the inconveniences the breakdown of transportation services had caused, was to take to the streets in support of striking workers. "For the first time in a rich country," wrote an editorialist in *Le Monde,* "we are witnessing today a strike against globalization, a massive collective reaction against economic globalization and its consequences."[17] Viewed from across the Channel, the scene in France looked quite different to a representative of Anglo-Saxon modernity writing on the same day in the *Economist*: "Strikers in the millions, battles in the streets: the events of the last two weeks in France make the country resemble a banana republic in which a besieged government tries to impose the politics of austerity on a hostile population."[18] In addition to forcing Juppé out of office, the strike obliged the government to negotiate and to back down on some, but not all, of its programs.

In the context of a discussion of French anti-Americanism, the example of the 1995 strikes in France is important to remember for a number of reasons. First, it shows that well before the American invasion of Iraq, there were signs in France of a reaffirmation of certain French political specificities, specificities—like the fact that the French had a social revolution and the United States did not—that entail a distancing from or disidentification with the United States. Already in the 1990s, the tide was beginning to turn away from the neoliberal consensus of the previous decade. An impatience with the liberal order was tangible in France, and strong misgivings about social inequality in the United States were regularly expressed. Books critical of the naturalized laws of the economy and of what had been called in the 1980s (when the word "ideology" was itself too ideological to mention) "la pensée unique" topped the best-seller list—the immediate predecessors to the best-sellers of today on the theme of anti-Americanism.[19] In the countryside, the radical activities of the agricultural union, the Confédération Paysanne and its leader, José Bové, were and continue to be greeted with strong popular support, both in France and abroad. The Fondation Saint-Simon auto-dissolved in 1999 after the death of Furet, citing in one of its final publications the persistence of a profound "anti-liberal" strain in French political life.[20]

Second, the strike shows that there exists a real conflict between the United States and France (and Europe more generally), a conflict that cannot be attributed to national character or written off as any of the various forms of *ressentiment.* The disagreement is situated at the level of political culture: vast numbers of French resist the notion of a state, like the American state, that is designed to serve the economy and nothing else. The strong contribution of the workers' movement to the formation of modern French political culture means that French (and, more broadly, European) society may have what American society does not—namely the ideological means to allow it to resist the dictatorship of capital.[21] The long-standing American hostility to the French model—with its decent wages, working conditions and social benefits—was most recently apparent in the United States's undisguised championing of the accession of East European countries, with their low wages and repression of labor, to the European Union. Undermining the social standards of the big industrial countries, France and Germany, could only benefit the United States. The economist Samir Amin, whose political trajectory is that of an unreconstructed third-worldist in the French sense, takes the argument one step farther. The United States does not share fairly the profits it accrues from its role as the military defender of the neoliberal interests it shares with the European ruling elite. European (and Japanese) contributions of capital, he reminds us, cover the essential part of the American deficit. Were Europe to "delink," so to speak, and withdraw the contributions it makes to an asymmetric liberalism that benefits the United States, were it to use that capital instead to launch a European economic and social renewal, the artificial health of the U.S. economy would collapse. Europe cannot afford to believe that the United States will give up the practices that allow it to compensate for its own social and economic deficiencies. Europe will either be on the left, he concludes, or it will not be at all.[22]

Can France and Germany constitute a left alternative to the United States? Having observed the deficiencies of the American system, can the French succeed in not imitating it? This is not at all certain. In the last week of June 2003, French military police broke down the door of José Bové's house in the Larzac in a commandolike raid, seizing him with a violence lifted straight out of the pages of Les Misérables to begin his prison term for destroying a field of genetically modified rice. Bové's supporters were not alone in viewing the brutality of his apprehension as a blatant criminalization by the Raffarin/Sarkozy government of syndicalists, and political activists more generally. The volatile issue of pension reform is once again on the government agenda, with Chirac poised to attempt to push through the reforms he failed to do in 1995.

Recent political commentary in the United States and elsewhere tends to attribute French hostility to the United States to a visceral French aversion to the personal style and mannerisms of George Bush, if not to a French perception of an American government as taken over by a cabal of neoconservative hawks who engineered the invasion of Iraq. Other commentators emphasize various forms of intercapitalist rivalry. U.S. aggression in Iraq may have increased the visibility of American imperialism and provoked widespread popular outrage among the French, but the economic system of relations underlying that war has been subject to French critique since the early 1990s, just as it was in the l960s and 1970s. If we give that critique the name "anti-Americanism," then its revival in the past ten years or so in France is best understood—as is Francophobia (American or French), as well as French third-worldism—not in culturalist, psychological, or affective terms but in class terms. Anti-Americanism is, then, something akin to a project: the attempt to counteract the ideological slippage toward oligarchy and the rule of experts that dominated the l980s. When Pascal Bruckner was quoted in the *New York Times* in March 2003 as fearing that French popular opposition to the American war in Iraq constituted a return of "the old Frenchy passion for third-world ideologies,"[23] he was actually expressing fear of a gathering mass struggle against the *imperium* of the United States. And his fear may be justified.

NOTES

1. Guy Sorman, cited in the *Wall Street Journal,* March 27, 2000.

2. See Serge Halimi, "Un Mot de trop," and "Les 'Philo-américains' saisis par la rage," in *Le Monde Diplomatique* (May 2000).

3. Murdoch-orchestrated Francophobia had its humorous moments. When viewers of Fox News were shown a photograph of the French ambassador to the United Nations, Dominique de Villepin, and encouraged to send in lists of insults inspired by the photograph, one viewer included "well-groomed" on his list.

4. See Marilyn Young, "Dreaming of World War II, Living with Vietnam." Available   athttp://www.nationinstitute.org/tomdispatch/index.mhtml?pid =354.

5. See Prabhat Patnaik, *Whatever Happened to Imperialism and Other Essays* (New Delhi: Tulika Press, 1995), pp. 102–106.

6. See chapter 10 of Pierre Jalée's *L'Impérialisme en 1970* (Paris: Maspero,

1969), for an example of Vietnam-era French theorizing about American imperialism.

7. The ubiquity of this analysis can be measured by a phrase written in 1956 by Roland Barthes, who was not at all known primarily as a third-worldist: "Today it is the colonized peoples who assume to the full the ethical and political condition described by Marx as being that of the proletariat." *Mythologies* (New York: Hill and Wang, 1972), p. 148.

8. For a sense of the ideological dimension of the movement, read the texts and pamphlets assembled by Alain Schnapp and Pierre Vidal-Naquet, *Journal de la commune étudiante. Textes et documents. Novembre 1967–Juin 1968* (Paris: Seuil, 1969). On the memory of May '68 in France, see my *May '68 and Its Afterlives* (Chicago: University of Chicago Press, 2002).

9. For a more extended version of this argument, see chapter 3 of my *May '68 and Its Afterlives;* see also Jean-Pierre Garnier and Roland Lew, "From the Wretched of the Earth to the Defense of the West: An Essay on Left Disenchantment in France," *Socialist Register* (1984), pp. 299–323. The best-known anti-third-worldist book is Pascal Bruckner's *Le Sanglot de l'homme blanc* (Paris: Seuil, 1983), which appeared in English as *Tears of the White Man* (New York: Free Press, 1986).

10. And vigilant they have remained. From the early 1980s, when Lévy signed a petition published in *Le Monde* urging Ronald Reagan to increase support to the Contras in Nicaragua and Glucksmann supported the French invasion of Chad, to the present, the politics of these extremely vocal editorialists has remained consistent. During the U.S. invasion of Iraq, they were characteristically loud in proclaiming their fraternal alliance with the United States. Their stance was that of solitary, isolated, dissident men of justice, bone-weary from being forced to lead the battle for liberty and modernity against what Bruckner and Glucksmann, referring to widespread French opposition to the war, called "the quasi-Soviet ambiance that has welded together 90% of the population into the triumph of a monolithic way of thinking," and, in the same text, "the nationalism of imbeciles." From "La Faute," in *Le Monde,* April 15, 2003. While Lévy claimed afterward to have opposed the war, any opposition he expressed was drowned out by his adamant self-characterization as an "anti-anti-American."

11. The manifesto, which issued from the Institute for American Values, was published in a number of newspapers in Europe and Japan and appeared in *Le Monde* on February 15, 2002, under the title of "Lettre d'Amérique." Signed by sixty American intellectuals and college professors, including Michael Walzer, Francis Fukuyama, Daniel Patrick Moynihan, and Samuel Huntington, the text proposed a number of definitive ethical values characterizing the American Way of Life, a way of life targeted by the attack on the Trade Towers.

12. See Jacques Rancière, "Le 11 septembre et après: une rupture de l'ordre

symbolique?" in *Lignes* 8 (May 2002): 35–46. A short version of this piece has been translated on the Web by Norman Madarasz as "Prisoners of the Infinite" in *Counterpunch*, April 30, 2002. Available at http://www.counterpunch.org/rancière0430.html. See also his more recent critique of the Iraq invasion, "De la guerre comme forme suprême du consensus ploutocratique avancé," *Lignes* (October 2003): 32–39; English translation forthcoming in *Contemporary French and Francophile Studies/Sites* 8:3 (2004).

13. For a history of French hatred of the French Revolution and the Republic, see David Martin-Castelnau, *Les Francophobes* (Paris: Fayard, 2002).

14. For an example of this kind of writing in English, see Tony Judt, *Past Imperfect: French Intellectuals, 1944–1956* (Berkeley: University of California Press, 1992).

15. François Furet, cited in Halimi, "Les 'Philo-américains.'"

16. Far from being a sectional or corporatist revolt, the 1995 strikes, in the words of one union delegate, were "a conflict of existence" (cited in M. Kail, "Tous ensemble. Une grève se gère par les grévistes," *Les Temps Modernes* 587 (March–April 1996): 549; as one railway worker remarked one week into the strike, "We are no longer fighting for ourselves; we are on strike for all wage earners. To start with, I was on strike as a train driver, then as a railway worker, then as a public sector worker, and now it's as a wage earner that I'm on strike." A nurse, active in the strikes, recounts: "If I felt concerned again it's because this time it was about essential demands, political demands. . . . It was the rejection of a capitalist society, the rejection of money. People were mobilized more against that than against the Juppé plan" (cited in Jim Wolfreys, "Class Struggles in France," in *International Socialism* 84 (1999): 37.

17. Erik Izraelewicz, "La Première révolte contre la mondialisation," *Le Monde*, December 9, 1995.

18. *Economist*, December 9, 1995, cited in Serge Halimi, *Les Nouveaux Chiens de garde* (Paris: Editions Raison d'Agir, 1997), p. 71.

19. See, for example, Pierre Bourdieu's *La Misère du monde* (Paris: Seuil, 1993), and Viviane Forrester's *L'Horreur économique* (Paris: Fayard, 1996). Recent popular books dealing with American imperialism or anti-Americanism include Philippe Roger's *L'Ennemi américain: essai d'une généalogie de l'antiaméricanisme français* (Paris: Seuil, 2002); Noel Mamère's *Non merci, Oncle Sam* (Paris: Ramsay, 1999); Nicholas Guyatt's *Encore un siècle américain?* (Paris: Enjeux planètes, 2002); Emmanuel Todd's *Après l'empire: essai sur la décomposition du système américain* (Paris: Gallimard, 2002); and Jean-François Revel's *L'Obsession anti-américaine* (Paris: Plon, 2002).

20. See Philippe Raynaud, "Les Nouvelles Radicalités: de l'extrême gauche en philosophie," in *Le Débat* 105 (May–August 1999): 90–116.

21. See Samir Amin, "Confronting the Empire," *Monthly Review* 55:3 (July–August 2003): 15–22.

22. Immanuel Wallerstein makes a related argument. The U.S. attack on Iraq, in his view, was designed primarily to intimidate Europe: "This was an attack on Europe, and that is why Europe responded in the way that it did." Peter Gowan shares this perspective: "The American attack on Iraq had a number of objectives . . . but among the global targets, ending the growing cohesion and influence of Western Europe was central." See Immanuel Wallerstein, "U.S. Weakness and the Struggle for Hegemony," *Monthly Review* 55:3 (July–August 2003): 23–29; Peter Gowan, "U.S. Hegemony Today," in the same issue, pp. 30–50.

23. Pascal Bruckner, cited in Richard Bernstein, "Press and Public Abroad Seem to Grow Ever Angrier about the United States," *New York Times,* March 27, 2003.

9

The Dogs of War

Myths of British Anti-Americanism

Patrick Deer

THE RECENT RESURGENCE of widespread anti-American sentiment in Britain provoked by the aggressive neo-imperial foreign policy
of the George W. Bush administration, supported by Prime Minister
Tony Blair despite a groundswell of popular dismay, is nothing new.
Certainly, British protests against the unilateral Anglo-American war
on Iraq caught many in the United States by surprise, with opinion polls
showing a broad majority opposed in the days before the invasion,
numbers at times comparable to those across "old" Europe.[1] Despite the
seductive mythology of a "special relationship" between the United
States and the United Kingdom, the postwar era has seen frequent and
repeated outbursts of British anti-Americanism as the former superpower struggled to adjust to its subordinate position in the cold war Pax
Americana. But the present conjuncture, I argue, reveals some crucial
shifts. Current manifestations of British anti-Americanism must confront the active involvement of the Blair government in this aggressive
drive for U.S. global hegemony, which is justified by a state of permanent warfare against an ill-defined worldwide terrorist threat. Unlike
previous protests during the cold war, there are few immediate signs or
sites to suggest that the United States as an occupying power threatens
the territorial integrity of the British nation. The recent revival of the
"special relationship" is revealed as an affair of trans-Atlantic elites, an
alliance of arrogant, distant powers perceived to threaten the civil
rights, safety, and well-being of the broad majority of the population.

Second, the pervasively popular nature of this latest outburst of
British anti-Americanism reveals that, contrary to the rhetoric of politicians on both sides of the Atlantic, there is not a common majority cul-

ture based on shared trans-Atlantic values[2]—especially when these "values" include the open advocacy of what Condoleezza Rice, the president's national security adviser, has called an "imperial but not imperialist" role for the United States in international affairs.[3] To adapt George Bernard Shaw's observation, the United States and Britain are now more than ever two nations separated by the same language. What persists is the continued British engagement with American counterculture and oppositional traditions of popular protest that has been a constant feature of relations between the two countries since World War II. Paradoxically, even in Britain, where global U.S. culture marks almost every aspect of everyday life, America continues to provide resources for resisting globalization and the neo-imperial U.S. foreign policy.

Like the seductive mythology of the special relationship, the new emphasis on "anti-Americanism" in Britain threatens to mask the instability and volatility of the present situation, in which a gulf has opened up between the aggressive war agenda of the trans-Atlantic elites and the various alarmed and bitterly critical sectors of British public opinion that oppose this latest phase in the Bush administration's drive for U.S. global hegemony. The situation is indeed strange: the new Labor government is acting as a proxy force for the distant Republican administration, and Tony Blair is embodying the remoteness of power traditionally imputed to the "cowboys" in the White House. Prime Minister Blair seems to have taken on the qualities of Graham Greene's Quiet American, memorably recaptured in a recent film adaptation:[4] he is moralistic, apparently naive, motivated by uneasy desires, with a secret purpose that we cannot comprehend, and he displays a singular lack of irony. With George W. Bush's help, he seems to have reversed the polarity of the special relationship, in which the irony was supposed to run in the British direction. So much for Americans not having a sense of humor; Blair seems to be still waiting for the punch line, hopelessly earnest in the face of German and French verbal sparring about "old Europe" or even the wise-cracking, wily, and sarcastic circle around George W. Bush. The historical ironies proliferate. The French refuse to collaborate; the Germans restrain U.S. military aggression. And the more the British change, the more they stay the same.

What's wrong with the discourse of "anti-Americanism" in the British context is that it projects an image of uniformity upon some extremely unstable alliances. The discourse gives popular opposition to war in Britain the appearance of a nationalist exceptionalism, as if British critiques of U.S. foreign policy are essentially different in kind from those of French, German, or Spanish protesters in "old Europe" or of other members of the dissenting international community.[5] This supposed exceptionalism mirrors Tony Blair's singular conversion to the Bush doctrine at a time when it is opposed by the majority of the European Union, or the Bush administration's own one-sided vision of the United States's "imperial but not imperialist" geopolitical role. Like the mythic "special relationship," it also obscures the significance of Blair's pro-U.S. foreign policy in relation to the delicate game new Labor is playing with British suspicions about greater European integration.[6]

The most powerful unifying thread in current anti-American discourse in Britain is the justified, but exaggerated and often racist, fear that U.S. military aggression and occupation in Iraq will unleash Middle Eastern terrorist reprisals against British targets. Ironically, the enormous shock, sympathy, and compassion extended toward the United States and more especially to New York City in the wake of the September 11 attacks have soured into a profound anxiety that "we will be next." The repeated refrain runs: "It's all right for them to go after Iraq. But what about us? We're right here." By targeting the United States as a distant aggressor over which the British people have no control or influence, these fears of proximity conveniently forget the origins of the terrorism produced in response to Britain's own history of colonial rule in Northern Ireland, the Middle East, and South Asia.[7] They also tap into the long tradition of anxieties at Britain's temporal proximity and cultural closeness to the American future and a fear of colonization of British sovereign territory. These are fears that can also be mobilized in the name of counterterrorism against immigrant communities from South Asia and the Middle East. As many have observed, this anxiety has in large measure to do with Britain's—or, more accurately, England's—inability to fully assimilate its postimperial geopolitical position and cultural identity. From elsewhere in the disunited kingdom come more nuanced critiques of U.S. policies that resist the seductions of the "special relationship" or of imperial nostalgia for Britain's lost international moral authority.

TRANS-ATLANTIC PROJECTIONS

The limited number of previous studies of British anti-Americanism have been overshadowed by the elite logic of the special relationship. They have tended to offer typologies of the different political, cultural, or class bases for anti-American sentiment, as if the phenomenon were a nebulous minority pursuit rather than a constant feature of the post–World War II era.[8] By emphasizing discontinuity, these typologies tend to obscure the underlying thread to British anti-Americanism, namely the traditions of popular protest against the human costs of the close ties between trans-Atlantic elites. As Paul Gilroy's groundbreaking work on the "Black Atlantic" or Daniel T. Rodgers' study of the "Atlantic crossings" of cosmopolitan left progressives during the first half of the twentieth century remind us, the discourse of the "Atlantic" has been defined most successfully out of oppositional projects of resistance and critique.[9]

Attempts to project a positive spatial imaginary for official Anglo-American relations since 1945 have foundered in the nebulous imagery of Atlanticism. In his famous "iron curtain" speech at Fulton, Missouri, in 1946, Winston Churchill projected Britain as the "swing power" balancing "three circles of influence"—the American, European, and Commonwealth—but the image depended for its force on Britain's imperial power.[10] Half a century later, with the sun set on the British Empire, Tony Blair's current notion of Britain as a "bridge" between America and Europe is a far more unstable fantasy.[11] Even if savvy French and German travelers from bad "old Europe" wanted to go to the "new world" these days, why take the bridge and tunnel through London when you can fly direct? The British role as bridge between the United States and Europe seems to have the gone the same way as the U.S. special role as mediator between the British government and the parties to the peace process in Ireland. The collapse of British authority in Europe, like the Bush administration's disengagement from Ireland, only recently seemed unthinkable. Whatever Tony Blair's original agenda in relation to the EC or NATO, it is now apparent that the British "bridge" is being used as a wedge by the anti-European Bush administration to divide "old Europe" from "the new" in matters of common defense policy.

The continuing power of the mythology of "special relationship," despite constant conflicts between the partners since World War II, lies in the fact that it evolved as a structure that claimed to keep friends close and potential enemies closer, always tempering intimacy and closeness with bracing doses of anti-Americanism. The special relationship combined spatial metaphors, of Greece and Rome, Atlanticism, and so on, with a more compelling and predominantly masculinist rhetoric of kinship that shifted drastically depending on the personalities involved. But the consistent feature of this radically asymmetrical relationship on the British side was that the balance of power lay with the wrong partner. The callow American colossus needed British guidance; despite intense, often hostile U.S. economic and political pressure, beginning with the signing of the Atlantic Charter in August, 1941, the fantasy was that the British could manipulate and control the U.S. leadership to serve their own global interests.[12]

From the first, the British side of the Anglo-American elite took a famously suspicious and often hostile attitude toward their U.S. counterparts. During the formative years of the Second World War, even the most benign fantasies about the British capacity to manipulate and control the underschooled and overpowerful America had at their core a marked patrician condescension. Here is Harold Macmillan (who would serve as a Conservative prime minister from 1957 to 1963) holding forth to the young Richard Crossman (a future Labor minister of the 1960s) at Allied Force Headquarters in Algiers in 1943:

> We, my dear Crossman, are Greeks in this American empire. You will find Americans much as the Greeks found the Romans—great big, vulgar, bustling people, more vigorous than we are and also more idle, with more unspoiled virtues but also more corrupt. We must run AFHQ as the Greek slaves ran the operations of the Emperor Claudius.[13]

One of Macmillan's diary entries for 1944 reveals both private mandarin disdain and the seductive fantasy of control at stake in the Atlanticist hierarchy of Greeks and Romans:

> They either wish to revert to isolation combined with suspicion of British imperialism, or to intervene in a pathetic desire to solve in a few months by the most childish and amateurish methods problems which have baffled statesmen for many centuries. Somehow between

these two extremes we have got to guide them, both for their own advantage and ours for the future peace of the world.[14]

All the stereotypes are there, held in check by English self-restraint and guile. Little wonder there were American suspicions of a "well nigh inexhaustible store of superior cunning" among the British.[15]

During the cold war, despite constant conflict, the old magic seemed to work. The greatest success story was Margaret Thatcher's trans-Atlantic romance with Ronald Reagan, in which he played the adoring younger brother.[16] But as its historians have noted, the special relationship was plagued by constant conflict over foreign policy, defense spending, nuclear weapons strategy, European integration, and decolonization. Nevertheless, stereotypical disdain for the untutored, brash "American empire" was held in check by English self-restraint, statesmanship, and guile. Perhaps this is what Tony Blair meant when he bafflingly referred to British anti-Americanism as a "foolish indulgence": you feel it, but you don't give in to it.[17]

BULLDOGS, POODLES, AND BLOODHOUNDS

The radical asymmetry of the relationship, in which the subordinate British partner must struggle for control, is parodied in the recent tide of complaints about Tony Blair's position as "Bush's poodle." The "axis of poodle," as analysts might call this phenomenon if they lacked good taste or a sense of decorum, has a venerable history as a term of British political abuse. Lloyd George called the House of Lords "Balfour's poodle" as early as 1908; after the 1983 U.S. invasion of Grenada, the Labor MP Denis Healey referred to Mrs. Thatcher as "Reagan's poodle."[18] All this is most unfair to the dog, of course, as the head of the British Poodle Owners Association recently complained.[19] The poodle was a German hunting dog first introduced to France during the Napoleonic wars and embraced for its valor by the Emperor Napoleon himself. The point, of course, in the majority of recent criticism of the British premier, is less that Blair should be playing the Churchillian bulldog instead of the poodle than that the wrong beast is at the end of the leash. Britain, no longer shamed by its subordinate position in the U.S. global hegemony, should be leading the way. But, as the disdain for the

Franco-German "poodle" image suggests, for many Britons opposed to the war, the way does not necessarily lie in the direction of Europe.

Prime Minister Blair's dogmatic support of the Bush doctrine may have to do with the close trans-Atlantic ties between those other dogs of war, the military and intelligence communities. The recent discourse of British "anti-Americanism" highlights the very specific institutional and political alliances between the transnational elites that plan, finance, and arm "from above" aggressive acts of military intervention like the present war in Iraq. As one recent study has observed:

> During the Cold War, at least following the repeal of the McMahon Act in 1958, the U.K. enjoyed privileged access to nuclear information from the United States. This, along with the intermeshing of U.S. and British intelligence under the UKUSA agreement of 1947, formed the essence and beating heart of the Cold War relationship.[20]

The 1947 treaty, described as "quite likely the most secret agreement ever entered into by the English speaking world," intimately linked the intelligence-gathering agencies of the United States, Britain, Canada, Australia, and New Zealand.[21] Britain has its own signals intelligence (SIGINT) eavesdropping stations at home and abroad, run by its Government Communications Headquarters (GCHQ), based in Cheltenham, and provides installations for the U.S. National Security Agency (NSA) in Britain. There are also joint GCHQ and NSA sites at the Ascension Isles in the South Atlantic and on Diego Garcia in the Indian Ocean, islands that proved of strategic significance in both the 1982 Falklands war and the 2003 invasion of Iraq.

The major NSA station at RAF Menwith Hill, in Yorkshire, for example, which bristles with satellite tracking aerials and dishes, was "built into the heart of Britain's national communication system" by the British Post Office and has, since the mid-1970s, "sifted the communications of private citizens, corporations and government for information of political or economic value to the U.S."[22] After September 11, 2001, one British newspaper reported that "Britain is so linked into the U.S. intelligence system through the UKUSA accord . . . that intelligence support was automatically supplied."[23] British stations like Menwith Hill and Morwenstow, Cornwall, remain crucial hubs in the highly secret Echelon system, which gives the UKUSA partners unprecedented power to spy on worldwide nonmilitary communications. Indeed, Echelon was deemed threatening enough to business interests and individual privacy in Europe that the European Parliament made it the subject of two special investigative reports.[24] Beyond Echelon, there are the Orwellian projects of Total Information Awareness (TIA) and Carnivore. On April 2, 2003, the British government announced even closer intelligence ties with the newly created Department of Homeland Security in the name of the global war on terrorism.[25]

The nuclear and conventional armed forces of both countries are also closely allied. The 2003 war against Iraq came after a decade of close military cooperation and bombing by the RAF and USAF there to enforce UN no-fly zones, most notably in the massive December 1998 aerial campaign, Operation Desert Fox. Intelligence cooperation in the war on terrorism, as well as Britain's continued reliance on U.S. nuclear weapons technology for its Trident submarines, and Britain's commitment to the U.S. Nuclear Missile Shield, all suggest that the post–cold war strategic relationship remains a force to be reckoned with.[26]

To these close intelligence and military ties must be added the British presence in the global arms trade. The British defense ministry and arms manufacturers must compete against the market dominance of the U.S. permanent war economy: the U.S. currently commands 64 percent worldwide, while Britain has the next largest share, around 20 percent.[27] But they also share domestic markets and powerful vested interests in promoting arms transfers to developing countries, many of which, such as Iran, Iraq, Argentina, and Chile, have been states with dismal human rights records. As Neil Cooper and John Pilger have asserted, despite its rhetoric of "ethical foreign policy" and cleaning up the "pariah" arms trade in "uncivilized, un-Western" weapons like land mines, the Blair government has relaxed restrictions on sales to countries like Indonesia and Turkey.[28] By pressuring the market in low-tech "pariah" arms, the British have joined the United States in promoting a new generation of extremely expensive high-tech precision weaponry, whose prohibitive costs can be sustained only by a vigorous export market. Instead of land mines, trans-Atlantic arms manufacturers produce and promote cluster bombs. This new generation of weaponry also includes the manufacture and use of shells, bombs, and missiles tipped with depleted uranium, which leaves targets widely contaminated by carcinogenic dust that causes cancer and birth defects.[29] These are exactly the "humanitarian" weapons used to such devastating effect in Kosovo, Afghanistan, and Iraq.

FROM FORTRESS BRITAIN TO AIRSTRIP ONE

For half a century, it was the American airbases and bombers in Britain that haunted the imaginary of British popular anti-Americanism. During World War II, popular resentment of the American GIs and air force personnel stationed in Britain was expressed in the familiar terms of a disturbing proximity: they were, notoriously, "oversexed, overpaid, and over here."[30] Once Attlee's Labor government agreed to build air bases in eastern England for U.S. B-29 nuclear bombers in 1946, these outposts of the American frontier became a permanent feature. In his novel *1984,* George Orwell famously satirized Britain's position in the superpower bloc Oceania as "Airstrip One." Even that dogged imperialist and Atlanticist the part-American Winston Churchill complained bitterly to his doctor during his second spell in government in 1953 that Britain had been reduced to an "aircraft carrier" for Eisenhower's America.[31]

Around the bases in the late 1940s crystallized the familiar, unstable elements of British anti-Americanism: resentment for the punitive terms of the 1946 U.S. loan to Britain; at American demands for a 50 percent increase in the defense budget that hamstrung the Labor reconstruction program and for a more rapid dismantling of the British empire; for the pressure for greater British integration into a postwar European union; for the U.S. refusal to share nuclear weapons secrets that encouraged Britain's own costly pursuit of an independent nuclear deterrent; for America's material prosperity and unbridled consumerism at a time of enforced austerity; above all, for the enforced recognition that Britain was a subordinate player in the U.S.-Soviet cold war.[32] Perhaps understandably in a country with a distant maritime empire that had just lived through the threat of invasion and the Blitz on its civilian population, the greatest outbursts of popular anti-Americanism occurred when the special relationship brought home the vulnerability of "Fortress Britain." The fears were compounded of this contradictory blend of proximity and distance. Post–World War II, British anti-Americanism erupted most forcibly when the United States's remote actions threatened both Britain's sense of territorial integrity and its prestige as a sovereign power in the *pax Americana*.

The first major postwar outbreak of anti-Americanism on a large scale was during the "A-bomb" scare in 1950, when offhand remarks by President Truman on November 30 about the possible use of nuclear weapons in the Korean War sparked widespread alarm and protests. The then-Labor MP Roy Jenkins recalled an unprecedented "mood of near panic."[33] The situation was sufficiently alarming that Labor prime minister Clement Attlee himself was dispatched to Washington. Despite U.S. reassurances, opinion polls early in 1951 showed that 60 percent of the British public thought there was a real risk of general war, and though 58 percent expected the Soviet Union to be the guilty party rather than the United States, only 40 percent approved of American policy.[34] In a striking parallel with the bitterly divided diplomatic situation before the 2003 war against Iraq, only Britain and Turkey had committed troops in Korea, and the United States was trying to force a resolution through the UN condemning China as the aggressor and imposing sanctions. In his attempts to avoid a cabinet mutiny, Ernest Bevin argued for quiet persuasion rather than open dissent against "the well-intentioned but inexperienced colossus."[35] Fortunately for the special relationship, the Chinese rejected a ceasefire, allowing Britain to support UN condemnation in February 1951.

Anti-Americanism flared up during the 1956 Suez Crisis among those angry at the United States for blocking the Anglo-French imperialist adventure in Egypt. But though the events proved bitterly divisive in Britain, shattered the special relationship, and brought down the Conservative prime minister, Anthony Eden, the majority remained sympathetic toward the United States.[36] The nuclear fears of the late 1950s and the emergence of the Campaign for Nuclear Disarmament (CND) and the New Left reactivated widespread anti-American sentiment. Calls from the Left for unilateral disarmament, and for British leadership of a "third force" with the Commonwealth and nonaligned nations, were articulated in an unstable blend of imperial nostalgia and romantic invocations of "Deep England" and of the heroicized collective spirit of the Blitz and Dunkirk that persist to the present.[37] This contradictory mix of nationalism and internationalism could have unpredictable consequences. In 1961, for example, Hugh Gaitskell played left-wing anti-Americanism against anti-nuclear feeling, persuading the Labor party conference to drop unilateral disarmament from its manifesto by arguing that without its own nuclear weapons Britain would have to hide behind American might.[38]

During the Vietnam War, the bombing of Hanoi and Haiphong in 1966 swung public opinion sharply against the United States. Diplomatic relations reached an all-time low in the winter of the following year over Vietnam, as well as over policy in the Gulf states.[39] British protests against the war focused anger against the U.S. Embassy in Grosvenor Square in 1967–1968 but clearly distinguished between opposition to U.S. and U.K. government policy and solidarity with the "other America."

THE OTHER AMERICA

British hostility to U.S. cold war policy did not necessitate hostility to the American populace or its high and low culture. As early as 1947, reporting on the House Un-American Affairs Committee, the journal *Our Time* published a piece entitled "We Want to Be Un-American," which argued that the "Hollywood witch trial" was a diversion from "much more serious infringements of thought, constituting a cold war against intellectuals in America," and saw a similar possible threat in Britain. In an article in the same issue, "cold censorship . . . red-baiting and war-mongering stories" were blamed for the often inarticulate British suspicion of American political intentions: "Ignorance of what Americans are really like today, what decent Americans are doing, and how much, is inevitable because the Americans themselves are blocked off from nearly all means of expression."[40]

Though the New Left was intensely critical of the Americanization of British popular culture during the 1950s, with the founders of British cultural studies, Richard Hoggart and Raymond Williams, often sounding like the fiercely reactionary F. R. Leavis, the 1950s had seen a far more fluid and sympathetic appropriation of U.S. popular culture, in jazz, the blues, abstract expressionism, Pop Art, and the Beat writings. Lindsey Anderson's 1959 pro-CND documentary film, *March to Aldermarston,* for example, showed a postprotest scene of youngsters dancing to jazz, with the voice-over commenting, "It's no use being against death if you don't know how to enjoy life when you've got it."[41] The 1960s offered the examples of hippie counterculture and psychedelia, student revolt, the civil rights movement, and Black Power, to name but a few. Subversive appropriations of U.S. counterculture were strongly present in the British protests against Vietnam, culminating in the riotous protests in Grosvenor Square.[42]

Punk rock flirtations with anti-Americanism in the late 1970s by bands like the Clash, the Fall, and the Gang of Four were similarly double-edged, aimed as much at the dominant British culture as at the "Yankee soldier" of the Clash's "I'm So Bored with the U.S.A."[43] During the "new cold war" of the early 1980s, the U.S. airbases once more became the focus of widespread anti-American and anti-nuclear feeling, and strong alliances were formed with the European peace movement. Ronald Reagan's twilight romance with Margaret Thatcher gave the special relationship new life, and the U.S. deployment of cruise and Pershing missiles on British bases, as well as the talk of neutron weapons and a limited nuclear war strategy for northern Europe, reinvigorated the CND.[44] The women's peace camp outside USAF Greenham Common was to protest and survive until the last cruise missiles were withdrawn. Duncan Campbell's 1985 exposé, *The Unsinkable Aircraft Carrier*, once again portrayed Britain as occupied territory, a frontline American base. The 1986 bombing of Libya by American F-111's from British bases with Thatcher's consent confirmed the sense of popular outrage. A MORI poll on April 17, 1986, showed 70 percent of Britons hostile to U.S. policy.[45] Yet CND remained more popular than the opposition Labor party's unilateral nuclear disarmament platform, and the Conservatives won the 1983 and 1987 elections over a weak and divided opposition.

But the Falklands-Malvinas adventure of 1982 had shown there was life in the old dogs yet, allowing Mrs. Thatcher to declare memorably at Cheltenham racecourse that Britain was great once more, and that "nothing had changed."[46]

FROM ETHICAL FOREIGN POLICY
TO HUMANITARIAN WARFARE

The 1991 Gulf War saw widespread anti-war protests in Britain, but the brevity of the conflict as well as the UN-sponsored multinational coalition limited the outrage. For many commentators, however, the special relationship had seen its last hurrah.[47] Complaints about the U.S. refusal to send ground troops to stop the genocide in Bosnia were complicated by the European Union's own conspicuous failure to deal adequately with the murderous violence on its own borders. Tony Blair's willingness to act as the point man for the Clinton administration's "humanitarian intervention" using U.S. and NATO air power in

Kosovo drew public hostility, but the official appropriation of the rhetoric and institutions of international human rights complicated the position of those opposed to the bombing.[48] Prime Minister Blair had learned his lesson. When the new Labor premier flew to support his friend Bill Clinton during the dark days of the Lewinsky scandal and to discuss the runup to the bombing campaign against Milosevic's Serbia, Blair asked President Clinton nervously what would happen if the bombing didn't work—to which Clinton reportedly replied in a faraway voice, "We keep on bombing. We can bomb forever."[49] Despite widespread international skepticism about the motives for the 2003 war against Iraq, given the absence of evidence of weapons of mass destruction to date and the flawed intelligence analyses used to justify the unilateral intervention, the Blair government continued to invoke the rhetoric of human rights as the last trump card to justify the massive use of precision bombing, ground war, and colonial policing techniques honed for thirty years in Northern Ireland. Armed with the Bush doctrine, the White House has less need to mask its plans for the Middle East in humanitarian rhetoric. It too can bomb forever.

The current anti-war movement draws in part on the sustained protests of the 1980s, one current CND group in Gloucestershire offering to send volunteer weapons inspectors into the remaining U.S. air bases and radar and surveillance sites in Britain.[50] But the disturbing difference about the present situation is that there are few visible signs of American occupation to protest and that humanitarian rhetoric is being used to justify military aggression. To contest the U.S. drive for global hegemony, in February 2003 more than a million British anti-war protestors had to take to the streets of their own capital. For all the moral indignation and imperial nostalgia in some strains of British anti-Americanism, there is the disturbing fact of continuing British complicity in a militarist drive for U.S. global hegemony. The lesson of the cold war era of British protest is that anti-war movements cannot just wait for the wars to break out; they also have to contest during peacetime the mythology of the technologies and strategies of permanent war. Instead of revealing the mendacious euphemisms of nuclear overkill, those opposed to permanent war now must expose the manipulative projections of postmodern "humanitarian" warfare. No doubt Tony Blair gambled his "moral" stance on the ability of the overwhelming U.S. military firepower to minimize American and British body counts, but, for all the rhetoric of precision bombing, high-tech warfare produced thousands of Iraqi casualties.[51] The occupation's military and civilian death toll continues to mount. The war on Iraq may appear bloodless, precise, and "morally justified" only because we were not permitted to see the full horror of the dogs of war in action.

NOTES

1. Though opposition to the war held steady around 52 percent before the invasion, public opinion swung behind the British troops after the intervention began on March 17, 2003; after the initial phase of military action failed to uncover Iraqi weapons of mass destruction (WMD), criticism of the war and occupation mounted once more. For the shifting public responses to the Bush-Blair war agenda, see Alan Travis and Ian Black, "Blair's Popularity Plummets," *Guardian*, February 18, 2003; John Curtice, "On the Brink of War: Public Opinion: Polls Tilt towards Blair, but This Is Still the Most Unpopular War for Decades," *Independent*, March 19, 2003; Travis, "Surge in War Support Confirms Dramatic Shift in Public Opinion," *Guardian*, April 15, 2003; Travis, "War in the Gulf: Support for War Surges," *Guardian*, March 25, 2003. According to one report, a MORI poll in early March 2003 tracked British opposition to war against Iraq in the absence of a "smoking gun" or a second UN resolution at 67 percent. Catharine Fay de Lestrac, "Blair between a Rock and a Hard Place on Iraq," Agence France Press, March 8, 2003. For British public opinion during the occupation and the controversy over the dubious intelligence reports regarding Iraqi WMD produced by the Blair cabinet to justify unilateral invasion, see Ben Whitford, "Labour Damaged in Polls by WMD Claims," *Guardian*, June 17, 2003.

2. On the question of shared values and strong divergences among the United States, Britain, and "old" and "new" Europe, see the *Economist*'s recent special report based on the findings of surveys by the Pew Research Center, the German Marshall Fund, and the Chicago Council on Foreign Relations, unsigned, "Special Report: American Values: Living with a Superpower: Some Values Are Held in Common by America and Its Allies. As Three Studies Show, Many Others Are Not," *Economist*, January 4, 2003.

3. Peter Beaumont, "Now for the Bush Doctrine," *Observer*, September 22, 2002; Peter Beaumont and Ed Helmore, "Will Bush Go to War against Saddam?" *Observer*, September 1, 2002. The formulation was first promoted in Bush foreign policy circles by Richard Haass, then director of policy planning for Colin Powell's State Department, in a November 11, 2000, paper entitled "Imperial America"; see John Bellamy Foster, "Imperial America and War," *Monthly Review* 55:1 (2003): 1–2. A veteran of the first Bush administration and originally in the moderate wing of the architects of the Bush doctrine, Haass was reported as

telling Nichólas Lemann "there is a big difference between imperial and impe-rial*ist*" in an interview for a *New Yorker* article; Nicholas Lemann, "The Next World Order: The Bush Administration May Have a Brand-New Doctrine of Power," *New Yorker*, April 1, 2002, p. 46. For an incisive critique of the intellec-tual genealogy of this "new kind" of U.S. empire, said by its ideologues to be "divorced from national interest, economic exploitation, racism, or colonialism, and that exists only to promote freedom and human rights" and to emulate a supposedly "enlightened" nineteenth-century British informal imperialism, see Foster, especially pp. 3–4. The phrase "imperial but not imperialist" has since become a commonplace in British news reporting about the Bush doctrine, but Condoleeza Rice's remarks have not been reported by any major U.S. news sources to date.

4. *The Quiet American*, dir. Philip Noyce (U.S.A./Germany/Australia: Mi-ramax Films, 2002), screenplay by Christopher Hampton based on the 1955 novel by Graham Greene. Michael Caine plays Fowler, the cynical *London Times* correspondent in Vietnam; his mistress, Phuong, is played by Do Thi Hai Yen, and his rival, the "quiet American," the CIA covert operative Alden Pyle, by Brendan Fraser.

5. For a discussion of British exceptionalism in relation to the United States and Europe, see Kenneth O. Morgan's conclusion to his lucid survey *The Peo-ple's Peace: British History 1945–1990* (New York: Oxford University Press, 1990), pp. 508–520, especially p. 519.

6. In a much-publicized speech to British ambassadors in January 2003 out-lining the "seven principles" of British foreign policy, Prime Minister Blair placed the close alliance with the United States as the top priority. Somewhat optimistically, given the vigorous French and German diplomatic opposition in the United Nations to U.S. and U.K. pressure for support for the war against Iraq, he declared as the second principle: "Britain must be at the centre of Eu-rope. . . . To separate ourselves from it would be madness. If we are in, we should be in wholeheartedly. That must include, provided the economic condi-tions are right, membership of the single currency. For fifty years we have hes-itated over Europe. It has never profited us. And there is no greater error in in-ternational politics than to believe strong in Europe means weaker with the U.S. The roles reinforce each other. . . . We can indeed help to be a bridge between the U.S. and Europe and such understanding is always needed. Europe should partner the U.S. not be its rival." Tony Blair, "The Prime Minister's Address to British Ambassadors in London," *Guardian*, January 7, 2003, p. 1. (See also note 17.) On British political ambivalence and outright resistance to U.S. pressure for greater European integration after 1945, see Kathleen Burk, "War and Anglo-American Financial Relations in the Twentieth Century," in F. M. Leventhal and Roland E. Quinault, eds., *Anglo-American Attitudes: From Revolution to Partner-ship* (Burlington, Vt.: Ashgate, 2000), pp. 253–254; C. J. Bartlett, "*The Special Re-*

lationship": A Political History of Anglo-American Relations since 1945 (New York: Longman, 1992); and John Dumbrell, *A Special Relationship: Anglo-American Relations in the Cold War and After* (New York: St. Martin's Press, 2001), pp. 173–195.

7. See Bernard Porter, *Britannia's Burden: The Political Evolution of Modern Britain, 1851–1990* (London: E. Arnold, 1994).

8. John Dumbrell, for example, gives a representative survey of the typologies of British anti-Americanism, which include the cultural (comic stereotyping, the supposed American inability to recognize irony, class-based critiques of Americanization of everyday life); leftist (critiques of U.S. militarism, nuclear exterminism, cultural imperialism, globalization); nationalist (High Tory resentment at the U.S. hand in the end of empire, or at U.S. pressure for European integration); and pro-European (the United States as more foreign culturally than continental Europe, the EU as the future for Britain rather than the United States); see Dumbrell, *A Special Relationship,* pp. 24–32. See also the *Economist's* lively characterizations of British anti-Americanism in unsigned, "Bombs Away: Britain's Anti-War Movement Is Booming but Divided," *Economist,* February 15, 2003. For an eclectic, politically conservative survey that includes some useful literary examples, see Paul Hollander, *Anti-Americanism: Critiques at Home and Abroad, 1965–1990* (New York: Oxford University Press, 1991), pp. 371–377.

9. See Paul Gilroy, *The Black Atlantic: Modernity and Double Consciousness* (London: Verso, 1993), and Daniel T. Rodgers, *Atlantic Crossings : Social Politics in a Progressive Age* (Cambridge, Mass.: Belknap Press, Harvard University Press, 1998).

10. Dumbrell, *A Special Relationship,* p. 7.

11. For a recent critical view, see David Clark, "Britain's Bridge across the Atlantic Is Fated to Collapse," *Guardian,* May 14, 2002.

12. See, for example, Katherine Burk's sobering account of U.S. *realpolitik* in its financial dealings with wartime British governments throughout the twentieth century. Burk, "War and Anglo-American Financial Relations," pp. 243–260.

13. Dumbrell, *A Special Relationship,* p. 14.

14. Ibid.

15. Bartlett, *"The Special Relationship,"* p. 12.

16. In her memoirs, Margaret Thatcher remains cordially analytical in her appraisal of her relationship with President Reagan, but the dedication to the color photograph of a seemingly diffident Reagan gazing up at the Iron Lady holding forth at a July 1988 dinner in his honor at 10 Downing Street suggests something of the ironic quality of the romance: "Dear Margaret—As you can see, I agree with every word you are saying. I always do. Warmest Friendship. Sincerely Ron." Margaret Thatcher, *Margaret Thatcher: The Downing Street Years, 1979–1990* (New York: HarperCollins, 1995), p. 435. For a more critical appraisal, see Porter, *Britannia's Burden,* pp. 376–377.

17. Tony Blair, "Prime Minister's Address to British Diplomats in London," reprinted in the *Guardian*, January 7, 2003. The prime minister declared as the first of seven principles of U.K. foreign policy: "We should remain the closest ally of the U.S., and as allies influence them to continue broadening their agenda. We are the ally of the U.S. not because they are powerful, but because we share their values. I am not surprised by anti-Americanism; but it is a foolish indulgence" (1). As the second principle, Blair declared: "Britain must be at the centre of Europe. . . . To separate ourselves from it would be madness. If we are in, we should be in wholeheartedly" (see also note 6).

18. Bartlett, *"The Special Relationship,"* p. 157.

19. Nick Cohen, "Without Prejudice: Is Blair Bush's Poodle? That's Unfair to Poodles," *Observer*, February 25, 2001. A survey of recent British news sources suggests that the image of Blair as Bush's poodle emerged in February 2001 following his visit to George W. Bush's ranch in Crawford, Texas, in a dissenting whispering campaign by Labor traditionalists, then spread in critical comments of new Labor "insiders" in the summer of 2001, and was given prominence in a *Newsnight* interview with the BBC political journalist Jeremy Paxman broadcast on May 15, 2002, in which the prime minister was made to deny that he was Bush's poodle. It was taken up in July 2002 by the tabloid *Daily Mirror* as the centerpiece of a campaign critical of New Labor foreign policy and subsequently became a slogan in national anti-war street protests. One of the more controversial creative products of the recent anti-Blair/anti-American poodle boom was George Michael's satirical music video to his song "Shoot the Dog," which featured the British prime minister as loyal cartoon lapdog to the gun-toting cowboy president. See George Michael, "Shoot the Dog," *Shoot the Dog E.P.* (Polydor, 2002).

20. Dumbrell, *A Special Relationship*, p. 124.

21. Jeffrey T. Richelson and Desmond Ball, *The Ties That Bind: Intelligence Cooperation between the Ukusa Countries—the United Kingdom, the United States of America, Canada, Australia and New Zealand* (Boston: Allen and Unwin, 1985), p. 142.

22. Ibid., p. 197. In addition to the secret ties in U.K./U.S. SIGINT, Richelson and Ball also discuss the cold war secret special relationship in air defense, aerial and satellite surveillance, ocean surveillance, the monitoring of radio broadcasts, covert action and assassination, human intelligence, the production of intelligence estimates, and the conduct of security investigations and training (pp. 135–238). They also emphasize, of course, that the cold war relationship was frequently vexed. See chapter 11, "Discord, Non-cooperation and Deceit with the UKUSA Community," pp. 239–268. For the post–cold war period, see Jeffrey Richelson, *The U.S. Intelligence Community*, 4th ed. (Boulder, Colo.: Westview Press, 1999), pp. 291–296. One recent report on the £800 billion new site for GCHQ suggests that 95 percent of the SIGINT handled there is American; see

Richard Norton-Taylor, "Big Brother: The Eavesdroppers: Lords of the Ring: Britain's New GCHQ Is a State of the Art Listening Post. But Who Is in Control, Asks Richard Norton-Taylor," *Guardian,* September 14, 2002, p. 10.

23. Michael Smith, "Britain Could Deploy Tomahawk Missiles," *Daily Telegraph,* September 13, 2001.

24. The European Parliament's findings were strongly critical of the ultra-secret Echelon system's breaches of privacy in the name of U.S./U.K. economic espionage, going so far as to recommend the use of encryption technology to protect email confidentiality, but the Temporary Committee was subsequently disbanded. See European Parliament and Temporary Committee on the ECHELON Interception System, *Report on the Existence of a Global System for the Interception of Private and Commercial Communications (Echelon Interception System) (2001/2098[Ini])* (Strasbourg: European Parliament, 2001). For an overview of the controversy, see also Duncan Campbell and Mark Honigsbaum, "Britain and U.S. Spy on World: Big Brother Satellites over Indian and Pacific Oceans Intercept Internet, Fax and Phone Messages," *Observer,* May 23, 1999; Jeffrey T. Richelson, "Desperately Seeking Signals," *Bulletin of the Atomic Scientists* 56:2 (2000); James Bamford, "Big Brother: The Eavesdroppers: What Big Ears You Have: Listening Stations Ring the World, Capturing Our Personal Conversations: Perched Like Chattering Magpies above the Earth, Satellites Channel Millions of Private Messages—Straight into Echelon's Global Eavesdropping Net," *Guardian,* September 14, 2002; and the American Civil Liberties Union's highly informative online Echelon article, "Echelon Watch: Answers to Frequently Asked Questions about Echelon," available at http://archive.aclu.org/echelonwatch/faq.html.

25. For recent congressional checks to the TIA initiative, see Adam Clymer, "Threats and Responses: Electronic Surveillance; Congress Agrees to Bar Pentagon from Terror Watch of Americans," *New York Times,* February 11, 2003. The ACLU website provides a useful overview of TIA and the Carnivore e-mail surveillance system at http://www.aclu.org/SafeandFree/SafeandFree.cfm?ID=12719&c=207. For the recent announcement of closer U.K./U.S. intelligence cooperation to combat terrorism, see Alan Travis and Home Affairs editor, "War in the Gulf: Britain and U.S. to Join Forces in Fight against Terrorist Threat," *Guardian,* April 2, 2003; and Audrey Hudson, "U.S., Britain to Train Jointly for Terror Attacks," *Washington Times,* April 2, 2003.

26. For a lucid overview of the British struggle for a nuclear deterrent "with a union jack on it," as Ernest Bevin put it, see Sean Greenwood, *Britain and the Cold War* (London: Macmillan, 2000).

27. On the permanent war economy, see Seymour Melman, *The Permanent War Economy: American Capitalism in Decline* (New York: Simon and Schuster, 1985), and Melman, *After Capitalism: From Managerialism to Workplace Democracy* (New York: Knopf, 2001). See also Mary Kaldor's survey of the recent debates;

Kaldor, "Do Modern Economies Require War or Preparations for Warfare?" in Robert A. Hinde, ed., *The Institution of War* (New York: St. Martin's Press, 1992).

For the British share in the global arms trade through 1999, see Mark Phythian, *The Politics of British Arms Sales since 1964* (New York: Manchester University Press, 2000), pp. 22–23, as well as the more conservative U.S. Department of State figures in *World Military Expenditures and Arms Transfers, 28th Edition* (WMEAT), "Arms Transfers: Arms Export Trends," February 6, 2003: 6. The report is available online at http://www.state.gov/t/vc/rls/rpt/wmeat/1999_2000/.

28. On the British role in the global arms trade, see Neil Cooper, *The Business of Death: Britain's Arms Trade at Home and Abroad* (London: I. B. Tauris, 1997); John Pilger, *The New Rulers of the World* (London: Verso, 2002); and Phythian, *The Politics of British Arms Sales*. See also Neil Cooper's powerful critique of the use of the discourse of "Western values" to promote high-tech "humanitarian" weaponry in Cooper, "The Pariah Agenda and New Labour's Ethical Arms Sales Policy," in Richard Little and Mark Wicham-Jones, eds., *New Labour's Foreign Policy: A New Moral Crusade?* (New York: Manchester University Press, 2000).

29. See Depleted Uranium Education Project, *Metal of Dishonor, Depleted Uranium: How the Pentagon Radiates Solders and Civilians with DU Weapons* (New York: International Action Center, 1997). According to the British-based Campaign against Depleted Uranium, these weapons have also been manufactured and tested in Britain, see http://www.cadu.org.uk.

30. For a lively discussion of the presence of American GIs on the wartime home front, see Angus Calder, *The People's War* (London: Pimlico, 1969), pp. 307–311.

31. Porter, *Britannia's Burden*, pp. 288–290.

32. Morgan, *The People's Peace*, pp. 52–60; Porter, *Britannia's Burden*, pp. 272–274.

33. Bartlett, "The Special Relationship," p. 49.

34. Ibid., pp. 50–51.

35. Ibid., p. 50.

36. See Morgan, *The People's Peace*, pp. 145–157.

37. Meredith Veldman, *Fantasy, the Bomb, and the Greening of Britain: Romantic Protest, 1945–1980* (Cambridge: Cambridge University Press, 1994), pp. 143–144.

38. See Veldman, *Fantasy, the Bomb, and the Greening of Britain*, pp. 186–187; Morgan, *The People's Peace*, pp. 180–184.

39. Bartlett, "The Special Relationship," pp. 113–115; Dumbrell, *A Special Relationship*, pp. 147–159.

40. Margaret Garlake, *New Art, New World: British Art in Postwar Society*

(New Haven, Conn.: Published for the Paul Mellon Centre for Studies in British Art by Yale University Press, 1998), p. 72.

41. Alan Sinfield, *Literature, Politics, and Culture in Postwar Britain* (Berkeley: University of California Press, 1989), p. 262. See also Sinfield's discussion of the contradictory attitudes to U.S. popular culture in "Left culturism" and the New Left (pp. 232–252; 258–266); and Alistair Davies and Alan Sinfield, *British Culture of the Postwar: An Introduction to Literature and Society, 1945–1999* (London: Routledge, 2000), pp. 103–109.

42. Robert Hewison, *Too Much: Art and Society in the Sixties, 1960–75* (New York: Oxford University Press, 1987), pp. 158–163.

43. The Clash, "I'm So Bored with the U.S.A.," *The Clash* (CBS Records, 1977). Of one of the Clash's last U.S. live performances in 1984, Greil Marcus noted, "In 1978 in Berkeley, 'I'm So Bored of the U.S.A.' was a gesture of contempt to a bourgeois audience; this night it was offered to the audience as their own, and they took it. Some of *our* culture to *another* culture," in Greil Marcus, *Ranters and Crowd Pleasers: Punk in Pop Music, 1977–92* (New York: Doubleday, 1993), pp. 304–305. Other notable punk reflections on British anti-Americanism might include the dour Mancunian irony of Mark E. Smith of the Fall, "C'n'c-S. Mithering," *Grotesque (after the Gramme)* (Rough Trade Records, 1980), and the notorious anarchistic provocations of Crass, which resulted in prosecution and censorship by the Thatcher government; see Crass, "Smash the Mac," *Best before . . . 1984* (Crass Records, 1984). On punk and anti-Americanism, see George McKay, "Anti-Americanism, Youth and Popular Music, and the Campaign for Nuclear Disarmament in Britain," in Sylvie Mathe, ed., *Anti-Americanism at Home and Abroad* (Provence: University of Provence Press, 2000). For other lively overviews of the transatlantic genealogy of punk, including its roots in the Black Atlantic, see also Greil Marcus, *Lipstick Traces: A Secret History of the Twentieth Century* (Cambridge, Mass.: Harvard University Press, 1989); Dick Hebdige, *Subculture: The Meaning of Style* (London: Routledge, 1988).

44. Bartlett, *"The Special Relationship,"* pp. 157–163; Dumbrell, *A Special Relationship*, pp. 128–132.

45. Bartlett, *"The Special Relationship,"* p. 158, Dumbrell, *A Special Relationship*, pp. 102–104.

46. Dumbrell, *A Special Relationship*, pp. 159–168, Burk, "War and Anglo-American Financial Relations," pp. 255–256.

47. Dumbrell, *A Special Relationship*, p. 158.

48. For discussions of the shift to postmodern "humanitarian warfare," see Christopher Coker, *Humane Warfare* (London: Routledge, 2001); James Der Derian, *Virtuous War: Mapping the Military-Industrial-Media-Entertainment Network* (Boulder, Colo.: Westview Press, 2001); Slavoj Zizek, *Nato Kao Lijeva Ruka Boga? Nato as the Left Hand of God?* Bastard International ed. (Ljubljana, Slovenia:

Arkzin, 1999); and Will Bartlett, "'Simply the Right Thing to Do': Labour Goes to War," in Richard Little and Mark Wicham-Jones, eds., *New Labour's Foreign Policy: A New Moral Crusade?* (New York: Manchester University Press, 2000).

49. Andrew Rawnsley, *Servants of the People: The Inside Story of New Labour* (London: Hamish Hamilton, 2000), p. 270. See also Richard Hodder-Williams, "Reforging the 'Special Relationship': Blair, Clinton and Foreign Policy," in Richard Little and Mark Wicham-Jones, eds., *New Labour's Foreign Policy: A New Moral Crusade?* (New York: Manchester University Press, 2000).

50. See David Wilson, "Meet the Gloucester Weapons Inspectors: The Protest at the Fairford Stealth Bomber Base," *CounterPunch*, January 30, 2003. See also Gideon Burrows, "Return to Action: After a Period of Relative Inactivity, Direct Action Is Once Again Beginning to Make Its Presence Felt," *Guardian*, April 30, 2003.

51. As of March 7, 2004, verified news reports of Iraqi civilian deaths caused by the invasion and occupation of Iraq ran between 8,437 and 10,282 killed; see http://www.iraqbodycount.net/bodycount.htm#total. For an overview of Iraqi civilian casualties, see http://www.iraqbodycount.net/. The website provides a highly informative overview of this and other monitoring projects, at http://www.iraqbodycount.net/editorial_aug0703.htm and http://www.iraqbodycount.net/editorial_june1203.htm. Because of Saddam Hussein's regime's secrecy and U.S. Central Command's refusal to disclose estimates of Iraqi military casualties, the number of Iraqi soldiers killed and wounded may never be known. Estimated numbers killed generally agree on "the low thousands," though between two thousand and three thousand Iraqi soldiers were reported killed in the final armored assault on Baghdad alone; see Andrew Sullivan, "America Sets the Agenda for Wars of the Future," *Sunday Times*, April 13, 2003; Amy Goldstein, Jonathan Weisman, and Margot Williams, "Casualties: Low Number, Many Causes; Nearly 40 Percent of U.S. Deaths Were Not at Enemy's Hand," *Washington Post*, April 13, 2003; Peter Ford, "Surveys Pointing to High Civilian Death Toll in Iraq," *Christian Science Monitor*, May 22, 2003. By March 7, 2004, there were confirmed reports of 551 U.S., 59 British, and 42 "other nationality" military casualties. Of the total 652 deaths, 195 (or 29.9 percent) resulted from accidents or friendly fire. See Reuters, "Table of Casualties in Iraq," July 2, 2003, http://www.alertnet.org/thenews/newsdesk/NL24165019.htm and "Iraq Coalition Casualty Count," at http://lunaville.org/warcasualties/Summary.aspx.

10

The Beekeeper,
the Icon Painter, Family, and Friends

"November 17" and the End of Greek History

Vangelis Calotychos

ON THE EVENING OF JUNE 29, 2002, an icon painter and a bee-keeper took a stroll on the quayside at Piraeus, the port of Athens. The bomb in the icon painter's hands exploded unexpectedly. He fell to the ground, critically wounded. The beekeeper fled into the night. Soon, it became clear that this was no ordinary bomb but a Pandora's box that would bring to trial Europe's most enduring terrorist organization, the Revolutionary Organization November 17 (17N).[1] Since its appearance in 1975, 17N had been linked to twenty-three killings, including those of four Americans, countless bombings, rocket attacks, and a series of robberies. Twenty-seven years later, no member of the organization had been apprehended.

A gun dropped at the site was traced to a police officer shot in a bank robbery carried out by the notorious 17N on Christmas Eve, 1984. Two days later, the published photograph of the icon painter led Greece's Anti-Terrorism Unit to two Athens apartments, which were raided and found to be stocked with rockets, guns, grenades, and revolutionary proclamations. In the meantime, police had announced that the icon painter's fingerprints matched ones found on a bag left at the scene of a 17N assassination of a ship owner in 1997. The authorities pressed the hospitalized icon painter for a confession and informed him of provisions provided for by the Anti-Terrorism Law of April 2001, which foresaw the exchange of leniency to remorseful terrorists for co-operation in identifying colleagues and rooting out of a terrorist group.

In the days that followed, news reports maintained that the bomb in the dark was not a shot in the dark for Greece's Anti-Terrorism Unit, which had reputedly been closing in on the group after twenty-seven years. The release of East Germany's Stasi files in 1993 had revealed information about another terrorist group, ELA (an older, more prolific but far less deadly group that had collaborated with Carlos the Jackal), and this information had effectively forced ELA to cease operations since 1995. Lower cadre members of 17N had also been under surveillance since 1993, and consultations with French police had provided authorities with a convincing profile of the man eventually identified by police as the group's leader. Events unfolded dramatically. Within days of the bombing, the police arrested the icon painter's youngest brother, who was herding goats at the time,[2] and an older brother, a maker of traditional Greek musical instruments (*bouzoukis*), who, for days, had been accompanying his parents on hospital visitations to the icon painter. Both provided confessions to the authorities. A fisherman was hauled in; a schoolteacher, two cousins, three friends from the same village near Albania—seventeen in all—and, finally, in a careful police operation, one Alexandros Yotopoulos was apprehended on a quiet island in the Dodecannese, where he owned a conspicuous pink summer house. The son of Mitsos Yotopoulos, or "Witte," who was second only to Trotsky in the worldwide Trotskyist movement in the 1930s, the younger Yotopoulos, now in his sixties, was soon proclaimed to be the leader of 17N. One month later, the Greek justice minister, once a Trotskyist himself, cautiously announced that nearly all the members of 17N had been apprehended. The icon painter, the goatherd, the *bouzouki* craftsman were hauled off to a high-security prison. In the year of Hollywood's "big, fat Greek family," it was looking as if Greek terrorism was also a family business.

But what of the beekeeper, Dimitris Koufodinas? He was family, too. Koufodinas was married to the icon painter's first wife (who, at this point, was herself a suspect and was later arrested). Police had launched an unprecedented hunt for the man who had pulled the trigger in most of the organization's operations since 1984. Working from the principle that the best way to hide is to be most exposed, Koufodinas spent the summer, naked, on a nudist beach near Athens until his surrender to authorities in September. But his disappearance all summer had spawned all manner of speculation. First, it was thought that he had "ratted out" all the other members of the group and had even planned to botch the bombing. Some argued he was in a witness protection program, never to be seen or heard from again, or, that he was about to be double-crossed by the authorities and killed. Journalists swarmed around U.S. ambassador Thomas Miller to ask whether he knew of Koufodinas's whereabouts and whether the Americans themselves had whisked him out of the country? This last question did not necessarily imply that the Americans had apprehended him. For some, the question implied that Koufodinas had "sold out" to the United States or had even been working for them all along. A segment of public opinion believed the Americans to be in a pact of sorts with the Greek government and that "the extended family" on trial was destined "to take the fall" for the real masterminds. One opinion poll, conducted less than a month after the bombing, showed that one in five of those polled considered the bombing and arrests a fiasco and that the suspects "were not the real 17N."[3] Furthermore, 26.6 percent of those polled believed that the government was concealing the real members of the organization. Certainly, there was a feeling that the Greek government would be pressured to hand over the key suspects to the United States to face the death penalty and, subsequently, be executed, an eventuality doubtless feared by the suspects themselves. This scenario was evoked to explain the remarkable appearance of detailed confessions reputedly given by most of the defendants to Greek district attorneys within days of their capture. For, to everyone's surprise, nearly all the defendants, with the notable exceptions of Yotopoulos and Koufodinas, had allegedly signed detailed testimonies of their actions in the organization. A group that presumably had enforced deadly discipline to keep secret such an organization for twenty-seven years was now unraveling in a matter of hours. In fact, members' testimonies were "leaked" to newspapers in what can only be described as a midsummer deluge. One day after the next, newspapers were plastered with long testimonies. And these remained unquestioned until Koufodinas turned himself in to police authorities in September. It was only then, once Koufodinas had accepted full political responsibility for the organization's actions, that a number of the defendants retracted their earlier testimonies and charged that these had been submitted under duress. Indeed, the icon painter maintained that his confession was taken while he was incapacitated, under the influence of mood-altering drugs, and not in the presence of a lawyer.

The whole scenario is stunning in its way—an organization that the United States had spent millions of dollars trying to apprehend; that had assassinated American diplomatic and military personnel, injured

American citizens, and damaged American property; and that had ruined the careers of a series of CIA officers was perceived by some as an
American-backed outfit.[4] How could this be so? American officials attributed such a view to a Greek penchant for conspiracy theory and to
a political immaturity that always strives to place responsibility elsewhere.[5] Some Greeks would accept this explanation. Others might
argue that conspiracy theories are the product of a social and political
milieu that has seen its fair share of conspiracies and cover-ups since
American involvement in Greece in 1947.[6] They are aspects of a cultural
idiom ordinary people employ to understand their realities, their relation to power, and to make sense of their place in history and in their
specific society. In this idiom, for many Greeks, the issue of terrorism is
less about the Greek state's laxity toward its perpetrators and more a
discourse wielded by the Americans against Greece, and Greek governments, in order to produce destabilization, apply pressure, and
press home a diplomatic, commercial, or (geo)political gain.

The issue of terrorism and 17N may not be the most obvious vehicle for discussing the strong sentiment against American economic, political, and, more recently, environmental policy in Greece. American attitudes are seen at the heart of Greek concerns about threatening neoliberal market forces and practices and about an erosion of worker
rights and an assault on the social welfare safety net. A perceived U.S.
tilt toward Turkey on a host of issues and the staunch belief in American acquiescence, though more commonly culpability, for inaction over
the country's military junta (1967–1974) and over the Cyprus problem
has fueled deep resentment over intervention in the Balkans and elsewhere. The U.S.-led bombing in Kosovo also raised an environmental
concern about the possibility of radiation from military ordinance
falling in the air and rivers and only served to galvanize further strong
Greek public opposition to American sponsorship of genetically modified foods in the EU. But the issue of 17N—topical as it is—provides an
interesting example of the ways in which the discourses and interests of
anti-Americanism in Greece are organized, deployed, and then reconfigured to live and fight another day. For the discourse of anti-Americanism informs, is informed by, and fits with the culturally specific
forms of a cognitive mapping. There is no space here to present ge-
nealogies of this cognitive mapping, only to stress that any in-depth
study of anti-Americanism in Greece must also take into account the
more general modes Greeks employ to relate to power, authority, and

justice *within* Greek society itself. The sketch given in this essay of Greek political history alongside the fortunes of its own "war on terror," which has raged (or not raged quite enough) since 1975, and the trajectory of the 17N group during this time will prove instructive as to the ways by which anti-Americanism exploits, and is exploited by, a variety of actors.

When 17N's first target, the CIA station chief in Athens, was gunned down outside his home on December 23, 1975, Greece had just emerged from a seven-year military dictatorship that was supported (and not just tolerated)—and, for many Greeks, sponsored—by the United States. The regime fell from power in 1974. But its days had been numbered long before this. On November 17, 1973, students at the National Polytechnic in Athens had risen in revolt against the junta but were put down brutally by the military. The junta survived that night of November 17, but events of that night, and its date, November 17, became symbolic of democratic resistance both to the junta and to foreign interests seen as propping it up. With their back against the wall, one year later, the junta colonels launched a desperate coup attempt in Cyprus to incorporate the troubled island, with its Greek and Turkish Cypriot populations, into Greece. It proved a debacle. Worse still, it triggered mainland Turkey's invasion and illegal occupation of the north of the island, which stands to this day. Despite countless UN resolutions affirming the need to return to the status quo ante, these events have not been reversed. While European anti-Americanism may very well reside traditionally with the Left,[7] the Cyprus issue has had the effect of broadening anti-American sentiment in Greece. Greeks from across the political spectrum, from both the right and the far left, consider the U.S. government at least complicit in the coup whether because they believe that Turkey would not have acted without U.S. consent or because the United States was unwilling to intervene and prevent the Turks from invading Cyprus. A recent book by Brendan O'Malley and Ian Craig, *The Cyprus Conspiracy: America, Espionage, and the Turkish Invasion* (1999), has only emboldened such opinion by revealing, in an interview with the then British prime minister Lord Callaghan, that Britain, one of the island republic's guarantor powers, was ready to intercept the Turkish invasion but was dissuaded from doing so by the U.S. secretary of state, Henry Kissinger. Ironically, the tragedy of Cyprus led to the junta's collapse, and democratic rule returned to Greece in summer 1974. But, for the majority of Greeks, the American stance on the junta and on Cyprus has rendered subsequent U.S. proclamations of support for the international order and human rights both hollow and hypocritical. American unwillingness to heed countless UN resolutions and put pressure on Israel to end its occupation of the West Bank and Gaza is often compared to its reluctance to openly challenge Turkey to remove its troops from northern Cyprus. It is easy to see how, in 1975, 17N's first action did not elicit a public outcry.

Resistance to the junta between 1967 and 1974 was organized both in Greece and among exiles abroad. Despite the official Greek Communist party's denunciation of a number of radical groups, these groups prepared for armed urban struggle in Greece and for the overthrow of the entire capitalist system. Their members were vigorously opposed to U.S. foreign policy; they perceived the Americans as having taken over from the British in supporting the Greek government against communist forces in the savage civil war that ravaged the country from 1944 to 1949. With the defeat of the communists—the first victory of the Truman Doctrine—Greece entered NATO; the United States invested heavily in Greece in the 1950s, and thousands of communists fled into exile behind the Iron Curtain. The United States also had a heavy hand in a series of governments that purged leftists, banned their parties, interned them in camps, and rigged elections. Throughout the 1950s and 1960s, the United States kept Greece on its side of the Iron Curtain but did so by resorting to collaboration with arms of the so-called parastate—the military, the security services, and the Palace—to repress aspiring democratic forces. When the opposing forces emerged and a center-left party came to power in 1964, the "parastate" used undemocratic means against it. The resulting polarization in political life eventually prompted the military's takeover in 1967.

During junta rule, the alleged future leader of 17N, the "professor" Alexandros Yotopoulos, was involved with just such groups in Paris, and he even spent a year (1968–1969) in Cuba studying urban guerrilla warfare tactics.[8] In retrospect, their action was limited. When the military junta collapsed in 1974, he returned to Athens and participated in discussions over future action at a series of now-mythical clandestine meetings with other members of the extraparliamentary Left. The majority resolved to back the new democratic system, however precarious and inadequate. The newly elected conservative government of Constantine Karamanlis was hardly to the liking of the Left, but, as the renowned composer Mikis Theodorakis famously put it, the choice was between "Karamanlis or the tanks." However, a few, like Yotopoulos, reputedly resolved to continue *armed* struggle and so—the police maintain—he and others founded 17N and carried out their first, previously cited high-profile assassination of the Athens CIA chief. In its early phase, up until 1980, 17N's so-called first generation settled scores with police officers from the junta who had received amnesty after 1974.

In 1981, the victory of Andreas Papandreou's Panhellenic Socialist Party, or PASOK, on a platform that promised to take Greece out of NATO and out of the European Economic Community, coincided with a lull in the group's activities. The group's assassination of American military personnel late in 1983 and early in 1984 marked 17N's "second generation." From 1981 to 1983, the first generation recruited a new team of operatives drawn from the so-called extraparliamentary Left, among whom the beekeeper was to become the leading figure. In the 1980s, the group targeted Greek businessmen and industrialists, many of whom were involved in the denationalization and privatization of state industries. Its long anti-American, anti-capitalist, and Marxist proclamations, allegedly written by Yotopoulos himself, offered rationales for their attacks. In a society where public opinion passionately believes that corruption at the highest levels of power, at the interface of political and economic power, always goes unpunished, a segment of the public saw in 17N a just executioner and was swayed by the mythology it cultivated for itself. The perils of the politics of polling aside, there are no polls to substantiate this or, indeed, other ways to quantify the support for the group's activities in the 1970s, 1980s, or even early 1990s, let alone comprehend what such "support" entailed, how deep-seated it might have been, or how contingent such stated support was on the rhetorical context or the interviewer's identity. It pays to be cautious in such assessments. Elsewhere, scholars studying Greek interpretations of the Kosovo War have noted that statements about anti-Western, Great Power machinations were conveyed with irony, humor, and, often, an admission of their hypothetical basis![9] However, it is my impression that there was great tolerance for 17N in the 1970s, more qualified acceptance in the 1980s, and a mounting feeling that the group had fallen out of step with the times in the 1990s. To my mind, journalistic commentary since the capture of suspects in 2002 has downplayed the support once enjoyed by the group, and this, if nothing else, shows how current perspectives and politics color the past and make characterizations (like my own) problematic. It is worth noting that, in the 1989 Greek national elections, the group had the gall or the confidence to claim that the blank and despoiled electoral ballots were votes *for* their activities. By this gesture, the group showcased both its ultimate ambitions and, perhaps, its recognition that they were unachievable. For, true to principles propounded by revolutionary anarchists such as Errico Malatesta and others, the group selected its strikes symbolically and strategically with a view to convincing the working class that terrorist action could unmask the capitalist state's inability to respond to acts directed at its demise. But the group failed dismally to attract *this* form of grassroots "support."[10] Social revolution was never on the cards. However, a segment of Greek society did feel that 17N was striking a blow *for* it. The only valid antidote to such support in Greek society, writes the respected constitutional legal scholar Nikos Alivizatos with impeccable clear-sightedness, is, simply, "the proper establishment of a state of laws and due process."[11]

In the 1980s, 17N targeted American military personnel at a time when the Reagan administration was enraged by the Papandreou government's anti-American rhetoric, its demand for the ejection of the American "bases of death" from Greek soil, and its support for the PLO and Libya. At one level, Papandreou's anti-American rhetoric served to consolidate his political party and to bring together forces from the center Left and the Left, made up in part by citizens who had been excluded from the political process since the civil war. Greek-American relations were marked by suspicion, and this was very evident around the issue of terrorism. The Reagan administration exerted pressure on the Greek government to enact special anti-terrorism laws, but Papandreou resisted such pressure for fear that citizens' rights would be eroded and by arguing that criminal laws in place were strong enough. The U.S. administration punished Papandreou by criticizing security measures at Greek airports. Then, in June 1985, it reacted to a highjacking initiated in Athens by issuing a travel directive to its citizens to avoid Greece, thus wrecking the tourist sector in the mid-1980s. American officials went so far as to maintain that Papandreou's government was complicit with the 17N terrorists and that some PASOK deputies, once affiliated with anti-junta organizations in the early 1970s (especially one group known as PAK), were now behind 17N. The leader of the conservative Greek government that succeeded PASOK in power from 1990 to 1993, a longtime foe of Papandreou whose son-in-law had been assassinated by 17N in 1989, reiterated this view. However, his government did not fare any better in tracking down 17N or preventing its attacks. Regardless, talk of matching specific 17N operations in the 1980s to the pressing interests and concerns for Papandreou's party at the moment such acts were carried out, and uncovering their logic, continues to this day in a highly engrossing form of political punditry.

Terrorism became a plaything of party politics as cooperation among the FBI, the CIA, and the Greek police reached a low, from which it never recovered. Just three years ago, ex-CIA chief James Wolsey stridently proclaimed that members of the Greek Parliament were involved in 17N. In response, a Greek parliamentary committee and an Athens prosecutor's office invited Wolsey to show the appropriate cooperative spirit in the war on terror by sharing his information. But Wolsey declined and then proceeded to glibly assert that he was fearful of coming to Greece lest he be assassinated. But Wolsey was not alone in taking this stance. In January 2002, Ed Bradley, of the CBS program *60 Minutes,* interviewing in the moralizing and paternalistic tone the show reserves for foreign officials from certain parts of the world, asked the Speaker of the Greek Parliament, one of the most principled members of Greek political life, if he was a member of 17N. The Speaker refused to answer the question. The Greek press and official sources brushed aside the insult and commented only on its status as a harbinger of renewed pressure from the American establishment regarding Greece's record on terror before the Olympic Games, to be held in Athens in 2004. In general, many Greeks felt that their country did not deserve to be labeled a terror haven; after all, they argued, their country was often cited as the safest EU member state, according to EU crime statistics. Other European allies, like the United Kingdom or Spain, were judged far more leniently. Despite the more widespread violence perpetrated by Loyalists and the IRA in the United Kingdom and by ETA's secessionists in Spain, neither Britain nor Spain was ever cast as a "terrorist haven." There was widespread recognition in Greece that the police force was ineffectual. But, some argued that evidence from other terrorist cases, like the IRA, demonstrated that it was exceedingly difficult to root out organizations that worked in small, tightly knit cells. Generally speaking, since the 1980s, there was increasing public suspicion that the continuing presence of the 17N organization was the result of a cover-up of some sort and that someone was hiding behind the organization. Indeed, right up to 2002, one poll showed that three of five Greeks believed that certain forces were "hiding behind" 17N: only one in five believed that 17N was an autonomous organization. More specifically, one in two surveyed considered that the Greek government was involved in the group, while nearly 15 percent believed it to be infiltrated by the CIA or other secret services. Only 3.4 percent felt that 17N amounted to a group of "leftist extremists."[12] There lingered the suspicion that if the perpetrators were homegrown, then even the less-than-distinguished Greek police force should have been able to find the culprits among the so-called known-unknowns of extraparliamentary or anarchist circles. The failure to do so fueled suspicion that domestic intelligence services had infiltrated or controlled the group, or, in a variant version, that elements within these domestic services were working on behalf of foreign security services. In this guise, they were using the cover of 17N to destabilize the country and so to allow the Americans in particular to apply assorted pressures at will on the Greek government. After Cyprus, even rightists believed the Americans capable of such "hidden hand" tactics and manipulation. For much of the past thirty years, Greeks have deemed immoral American support of Turkey on a host of regional issues, and it was generally understood that this policy depended on a carefully calibrated "hot and cold" policy toward Greece and Turkey. Periodically, other issues like the outcry against the U.S.-led intervention in the Yugoslav wars and an anti-Serbian (and, for some, an anti-Orthodox) bias only exacerbated this sentiment and stoked the fires of speculation about ulterior U.S. geopolitical designs for the region. Progressively, in the 1990s, the Greek government strove patiently to steer Greek-Turkish bilateral issues and the Cyprus solution *through* the EU and the UN and away from the United States as far as was feasible. Greece had come out resolutely against the Iraq war and sided with French and German positions before the American action began. It was no coincidence, either, that, in early 2003, it was during Greece's turn to assume the presidency of the EU that EU ministers held an emergency meeting to affirm a common EU policy on Iraq in the hope of heading off an internal split within the organization. Greeks were wary of an increasingly recognizable American axis of Britain, Turkey, and the new Eastern European states within the Union.

The 17N organization's third phase, in the 1990s, was characterized by rocket attacks on commercial interests, as well as attempts on businessmen and politicians. But it was marked also by a nationalist bent (in keeping with the times in Greece and the Balkans) and by greater criminality (in the strict sense).[13] Turkish diplomats were gunned down in the early 1990s; in the late 1990s, during the Kosovo crisis, the group planned, but did not carry out, a rocket attack on NATO forces passing through northern Greece. And, all the while, the organization carried out bank robberies and daring raids of army barracks and police stations for money, arms, and weapons. What turned out to be the group's last act, the assassination of British Brigadier Saunders, in 1999, came with the unsubstantiated justification that Saunders was pivotal in the military planning of the NATO bombing of Serbia, which was opposed by the overwhelming majority of Greeks. But times were changing. Saunders's murder now seemed an anachronism as the group met with opposition from the vast majority of the Greek public. A nationwide poll conducted nine months before the bombing as part of a regular survey of the Greek public, in September 2001, showed that 83.4 percent of the population held a negative opinion of 17N (10.2 percent of the remainder "did not have an opinion").[14] (Even fervent anti-American conspiracy theorists were puzzled as to why Americans would cross their traditional allies, the British.) The victim's grieving but dignified widow cut a stoic figure. And her image was exploited by the Greek media to concentrate the public's negative opinion and to build support for hunting down 17N. British police assistance was welcomed (conspicuously) and was persistently compared favorably against the haughtiness that accompanied the erstwhile American cooperation. Where the Americans were described as imperious and culturally insensitive, the British were ever cooperative and methodical. Mindful of the pressure on it to "shape up" before the 2004 Athens Olympics, the Greek government saw the assassination as an opportunity to work on public opinion by showing that terrorism was not in keeping with the government's broader policies of modernization. The Socialist government under Costas Simitis, which had improved Greece's image abroad after Andreas Papandreou's death in 1996, particularly by way of its policies in Europe and the Balkans—it had also met the criteria to enter the European Monetary Zone—now needed to rid itself of terrorism's stigma. Prime Minister Simitis, who himself had once placed bombs in trash cans during the junta years, proclaimed that terrorism was passé.

Conspiracy theories that placed responsibility elsewhere, he argued, had become an exhausted paradigm or a false belief in metanarratives, incompatible with the workmanlike approach of a technocratic administration keen to disseminate the self-reliance that comes with modernization. The discourse of anti-Americanism was incompatible with a society striding confidently out of the ranks of the world's disaffected, the underdogs, and trying to prove to itself that it had entered the sunlight of democracy, capitalism, and modernity. To cast November 17 as the last vestige of an old order would cleanse Greek society of the last effects of a tale of ideological rancor and strife. But this also had to be done with care so as not to tarnish the parliamentary Left with terrorism's brush, especially since two of the defendants, prominent opponents of the junta and longtime trade unionists, stand trial on the flimsiest of evidence. Their presence adds an indirect, and perhaps unwanted, criticism lodged against the wagers of a militant class struggle, a wholly un-American objective and the anathema of neoliberalism. As I write, the trial has not begun, but it seems clear that this aspect of the trial will be brought into focus as the governing party itself strains to shed the populism and socialism of its founder, Andreas Papandreou, without losing its grassroots constituency. It is very likely that both men will not be convicted or, at least, that they will serve little time. In general terms, the trial will demonstrate that Greece has turned a corner; it will mark a step beyond the civil war, the parastate, the junta, and the period of post-junta democratic consolidation. It will mark the end of Greek history (or a period of it).

As a result, when the bomb went off in the icon painter's hands, it was in the government's interest to go along with—if not propagate—the big, fat Greek family scenario. It served its agenda to underwrite the tale of the beekeeper, the icon painter, their friends and family. For this homegrown brand of terrorism had a face that was positively homey: the public was soon on a first-name basis with the suspects. It learned of their ordinary professional lives and their passions (e.g., soccer); it dissected their religious beliefs (the icon painter's father was a priest and his uncle a onetime priest-turned-pagan who hoped to rescue hellenism from the clutches of Orthodoxy). All in all, this was a motley crew incompatible with the sophistication of many of today's transnational terrorists. The group's suspects "did not look the part," as the *New York Times* also asserted. But, in effect, this familiar set of neighborhood figures fit their roles perfectly well.

For its part, the Greek public remains suspicious and dissatisfied with the tale. It reaches for subtexts. The defendants' purported testimonies describe in detail how each crime was carried out and by whom. But there is little in them about the choice of targets or the way in which decisions were taken. Nor is there any indication about from where some of the group's information on victims (if accurate) might have been derived. Indeed, some of the defendants said they killed people without knowing whom they were killing. The "professor" and, perhaps, the beekeeper knew. But they are not talking—Yotopoulos, the professor, maintains he has nothing to do with the organization and that, even if he did, he would not be its leader, since such hierarchical taxonomies are traditionally inimical to the organization of such leftist groups. And Koufondinas, the beekeeper, upon his surrender, took full political responsibility for the group's actions but would say nothing about any details relating to the attacks. Another cover-up? Modern Greek history is full of them, but now that history is supposedly over and such categories are not meant to apply, we are all urged to move on. Regardless, anti-Americanism in Greece has only been reinvigorated by the swagger of the Bush administration's policy in Iraq: the role of intelligence services in "manufacturing" or "sexing" up a threat, the disregard of the United Nations—that is, the American, and not the Iraqi, disregard; these have all touched raw nerves.[15] Few minds have been changed in Greece; indeed, the only high-profile change of heart of late in Greece was that of Brady Kiesling, a senior State Department official, who declared himself opposed to Bush administration policy and whose resignation received a great deal of publicity. Kiesling just happened to be holding the post of political counselor in the American Embassy in Athens at the time.[16]

On the eve of the trial, there is a prevailing sense that members of the group's first generation are not standing trial; that those "behind" this group will never stand trial; that some of the defendants are innocent and will probably be found so, though only on appeal, when the case is no longer on people's minds—and this, only after the 2004 Olympics. Whether there is any evidence for or truth in the allegations about the role of the United States in identifying the suspects or in acting behind the scenes to oblige the Greek government to accept an American "list" of prime suspects, the charge will doubtless be exploited by forces in Greek political life and used by them against one another. But there is also the suspicion that branches of the American government will eventually revive the issue for their own ends. It is likely that new laws currently being agreed upon by the European Union and the United States for cooperation on matters of terrorism, which include provisions that make it easier for citizens from EU states to be handed over for trial, or retrial, in the United States, may facilitate a new phase of American pressure on the Greek government *after* the Greek justice system has run its course with regard to these suspects— that is, *after* the 2004 Olympics. After all, the Games must go on.

NOTES

1. The information cited in this chapter is derived from newspaper articles and the published testimonies of the arrested suspects. As is explained in the article, some of the defendants have since retracted these testimonies. A number of books on events since the bombing in June 2002 by investigative reporters and commentators are also largely based on similar evidence. The most well-known and discussed books are the following: Alexis Papahelas and Tassos Telloglou, *17: The November 17 File* (in Greek) (Athens: Estia, 2002); Vassilis G. Lambropoulos, *Corner of Patmos and Damareos Street: 17N, ELA, 1st May, Revolutionary Cells: Answers to the Secrets of Domestic Terrorism* (in Greek) (Athens: Synchroni Orizontes, 2003.) Both books make detailed use of police sources. The former's authors have been criticized for this, most notably from the "Ios" columns of the Athenian daily newspaper *Eleftherotypia*. Relevant columns and an exchange (in Greek) can be accessed from the website www.iospress.gr (see especially January 26, 2003; February 9, 2003). A commentary and an interpretation of the group are to be found in the work of one other prominent journalist: Yannis Pretenteris, *The Confrontation: Life and Death of "November 17"* (Athens: Estia, 2002). One of the few books written before the bombing, and now available in English, is George Kassimeris, *Europe's Last Red Terrorists: The Revolutionary Organization 17 November* (New York: New York University Press, 2001).

2. Papahelas and Telloglou, *17: The November 17 File*, p. 250.

3. The poll was taken by Metron Analysis for the July 27, 2002, edition of the newspaper *Imerisia*.

4. For a listing in English of the group's attacks, see Kassimeris, *Europe's Last Red Terrorists*, pp. 211–218.

5. For a discussion of the habit of neoconservative American policy commentators of attributing economic and political development to cultural values and psychological attitudes, see David Sutton, "Poked by the 'Foreign Finger' in Greece: Conspiracy Theory or the Hermeneutics of Suspicion?" in Keith S.

Brown and Yannis Hamilakis, *The Usable Past: Greek Metahistories* (Lanham, Md.: Lexington, 2003), pp. 191–210.

6. Briefly, I cite the assassination of the CBS correspondent George Polk during the Greek civil war in May 1948 and the very likely framing of Gregory Staktopoulos to implicate the Left in staged proceedings that involved Greek, American, and British government officials and journalists. See Edmund Keeley, *The Salonika Bay Murder: Cold War Politics and the Polk Affair* (Princeton: Princeton University Press, 1989); also the murder of peace activist Grigoris Lambrakis by the rightist parastate. The latter was memorialized in Vassilis Vassilikos's novel *Z* and in a film by that name directed by Costa Gavras.

7. See Timothy Garton Ash, "Anti-Europeanism in America," *New York Review of Books*, February 13, 2003.

8. Papahelas and Telloglou, *17: The November 17 File*, pp. 27–30; Lambropoulos, *Corner of Patmos and Damareos Street*, pp. 34–42.

9. K. S. Brown and D. Theodossopoulos, "The Performance of Anxiety: How Greeks Make Sense of Kosovo's Contradictions," *Anthropology Today* 16:1 (2000): 3.

10. For an analysis of the group's ideology and strategy, see Kassimeris, *Europe's Last Red Terrorists*, chapter 5, pp. 106–151.

11. Nikos Alivizatos, "The Hidden Charm of Violence" (in Greek), *Ta Nea* newspaper, August 24, 2002, p. N12.

12. There is little documentation on public opinion until very recently. The issue of terrorism had long been taboo, and so few, if any, surveys appeared in the last twenty years. The survey cited here was performed by ALCO for *Press* magazine (April 19, 2002), which is published along with the *Eleftherotypia* newspaper. Of those polled, 60.5 percent believed that there were people hiding behind 17N; 22.3 percent believed that it was an autonomous organization; 47.8 percent believed that one or more political parties or organizations were behind the group; 12.5 percent believed these to be the Socialist party and the current government, PASOK, while 9.1 percent believed it to be the CIA, 4.5 percent thought it to be the Greek secret services, 3.4 percent believed it to be leftist extremists, 2.9 percent the far Right, and 2.1 percent PAK (an anti-junta revolutionary group from the 1970s).

13. The issue as to whether the 17N suspects are guilty of "political" or "criminal" violations is a critical one. The constitution of the court assigned to hear the case—it is not to be a trial by jury—assumes that the suspects are "criminal," and not "political," prisoners.

14. I am grateful to Christos Vernardakis and the VPRC public opinion survey firm for providing me with the results of their poll. The results are about to be published in a VPRC publication, not available at this time of writing, as

Vassilis Meïdanis, "A Note on Greek Society's Positions on the 'November 17 Organization.'"

15. See, for example, Anthee Carassava, "Anti-Americanism Is Reinvigorated by War," *New York Times,* April 7, 2003.

16. I am referring to Kiesling's much-quoted resignation letter in March 2003. His reasons for resigning are captured in Brady Kiesling, "Athens in Wartime," *New York Review of Books,* May 15, 2003, pp. 16–17.

PART IV

EAST ASIA

11

An "Etiquette of Anti-Americanism"

Being Japanese in the American Imperium

Harry Harootunian

> Our goal is not to create a dependency in Iraq. To the extent that you are too heavy a footprint, you don't help them, you hurt them because foreign forces in a country are an anomaly.
>
> —Secretary of Defense Donald Rumsfeld,
> *New York Times,* September 14, 2003

THE RULES OF THE GAME

Not withstanding recent claims that anti-Americanism is simply a short-lived, spectral apparition, a homemade commodity easily exportable abroad, or even a prod to arousing nostalgia for the consequences of other, now past imperial orders, the phenomenon has always played an active role in the modern history of Japan. The echoes of that history are still audible in recent events. The event of September 11 immediately reverberated throughout the Japanese press and intellectual world to stoke dim memories of a history reaching back to the midnineteenth century, when Commodore Matthew Perry arrived unannounced and uninvited in Japan with his warships and presented a request—demand is probably more accurate—to the shogun's government that it open its ports to American ships. This episode, marking the "opening" of a Japan that had pursued a policy of seclusion from the rest of the world for 250 years, led to an exchange of documents, which were read differently in Japanese and in English, causing misunderstanding about the agreement to open up Japan and exchange ambassadors. As a result, Japanese were even more surprised when the first American ambassador, Townsend Harris (memorably played with stone-faced discipline by John Wayne in an unforgettable movie called *The Barbarian and the Geisha*), showed up a few years later to negotiate a commercial treaty. In a certain sense, this inaugural act of misrecognition and misunderstanding has formed and deformed the relations between the two countries ever since.

In the wake of September 11, the assault on Afghanistan, and the subsequent invasion of Iraq (Japan supplied only cash to the United States in the previous and now lamented Gulf war), what instantly "flooded the brain" of one Japanese writer, Kan Sanjun, "was the famous film made during World War II by Frank Capra called '*Why We Fight*.'" Kan's recalling of the film was prompted by the publication of a manifesto signed by "representative" American intellectuals such as Michael Walser and Jean Elshtain titled "What We're Fighting For."[1] The statement gave an account of the reasons for the Afghan expedition and thus shared a kinship with Capra's famous documentary. Kan clearly recognized that the motivation behind the making of the film had been to bolster the morale of fighting troops on the Pacific Islands. This film and other documentaries about the war were not only vulgar expressions of propaganda but were also single-minded expressions of the desire to emphasize the "exceptional universalism" of the American state according to a political theology. "As for universalism," Kan remarked, "America is the world and the world, like America, points to the realization of 'universal human values.'"[2] Kan's article, like so many in the past two years, easily saw through the claims used to underwrite yet another "just war" fought by the United States in a document that stirred memories of "Americanism" and its baneful history, with which Japanese have lived continuously since the opening of the country by Perry.

Japanese writers have been quick to notice that in the triumphal "Americanization of the world," the model that best exemplifies the course that must be followed is the U.S. military occupation of Japan after World War II. And this despite the fact that other examples, like the Rhee regime in South Korea and the "return" of the Shah in Iran, are also available. Although the Japanese experience has often been described as a success, for many Japanese the occupation represented an unwanted and unwarranted transformation of society and polity, the beginning of an oxymoronic democratic imperialism that led ultimately to the Iraqi war and that military occupation. But the success of the

Japanese model is the result not only of an enforced regime change but also of the fact that the United States effectively gave the Japanese back their prewar political structure. The United States decided to retain the Emperor and assured him of indefinite military protection and accessibility to the bountiful American market. If the logic of the analogy holds, the attempt to apply the Japanese model to Iraq would therefore entail the reinstating of Saddam Hussein who, like the absolute imperial figure symbolized by Hirohito, would serve as the lynchpin of a received and authoritative political order renamed as democratic and reinforced by a commitment to indefinite military occupation. Despite Donald Rumsfeld's warning against the anomaly of American forces on foreign soil and the "hurt" they can cause, the logic of an analogy that appeals to historic models such as Japan demands that we recognize that it is in fact even more anomalous to maintain empires without permanent military occupation. At the same time that the incident of terror enlisted to justify the military assault on Iraq recalls the image of Pearl Harbor in the United States, it is necessary to understand how Pearl Harbor has become an historical trope with different associations for Americans and Japanese. For Americans the trope authorizes analogies that permit easy identification with terrorism, while in Japan Pearl Harbor has come to symbolize the struggle with white imperialism. In Japan, a new and more virulently right-wing anti-Americanism has thus appeared, which, driven to rectify the understanding of the wartime past and to revise school history text books, promises to provide what historian Amino Toshihiko and others call real teeth to postwar historiography.

If left/liberal writers see traces of the American policy enacted in Japan in the new historical conjuncture inaugurated by war in the Middle East, the right has used the figure of an "American empire" as a painful reminder of Japan's own experience with it—an experience that many Japanese are still living through, as though in a precinct of permanent parenthesis. For many on the right, the U.S. military occupation and its policies directed at reforming Japan constituted the first step in the subsequent "Americanization of war." Writers like the conservative cartoonist Kobayashi Yoshinori and cultural critics like Kato Norihiro have all pointed to the ways Japan was deformed and disfigured by its forcible transformation into a client status, inaugurating what has come be known as "the long postwar" Japanese have been living since 1945. It is important to remember that Japan and South Korea have known foreign military occupation continually for more than fifty years now, as if it were a natural armature of the everyday life of these countries. Although conservative opinion has usually eschewed being labeled anti-American, it has in recent years formulated what it calls an "etiquette" (saho) of anti-Americanism that seeks to account for Japan's long subordination to the United States by insisting on establishing a relationship based upon difference and the recognition of equality. In fact, the etiquette, shared as well by the liberal Left, actually refers to the importance of being Japanese as a declaration of difference and distance from the Americanization of postwar Japan and the subaltern status Japanese believe they have been made to occupy. It is in part the rules, or good form guiding this etiquette, that reveal a common ground attractive to both the left/liberals and the right wing. As Kobayashi explained in a recent discussion with Nishibe Susumu, a conservative critic who formerly taught at Tokyo University and a self-confessed admirer of Ortega y Gasset, since the "terror," it has become urgently important for conservatives to think about a program that might communicate doubts concerning the present-day conduct of the United States.[3] In this regard, he has advised conservatives that they might do well to emulate the Left, which has historically monopolized anti-American criticism in Japan in their consistent opposition to war. At the heart of this conservative critique is the rejection of American meddling and intervention in the internal affairs of other, sovereign states. This policy, vigorously pushed by Bush in his "axis of evil" speech, has been dubbed the "terrorization of war," and it is not always clear in conservative discourse which state is considered more terroristic, the United States or its enemies in the Middle East and North Korea. In Nishibi's words:

> When you confront a world geography with the United States at its center, the Japanese archipelago, in all of its frightful smallness, has no existence other than being at the edge of this world. It is that kind of consciousness that is in Americans' heads. . . . But the source of this image is the feeling of a fumbling country, hideously puny, that is Japan. I've heard that Bush has said Prime Minister Koizumi Junichiro looks like a sergeant. In other words, I think a phrase like "axis of evil" incites violent associations that make one think of the three axis powers [of World War II].[4]

Nishibe was convinced that Bush and the American leadership were lit-tle more than "mad" and proposed that "mad times" invariably throw up "mad leaders." Later in the discussion, Kobayashi opined that "Bush might possibly be the Hitler of today" and that Japan might at some fu-ture date have to refer to the United States as an "axis of evil."[5] To this end, Nishibe, who had no doubts that America was a "barbarian civi-lization" that "worshipped the trinity of Americanism, globalization and vulgarism," was convinced that the principal task of the day was to explain why "more than one hundred million people who live on this archipelago" are blinded to the American problem, or, more precisely, to America itself. The solution must take the form of a manifesto de-claring a new form of "Japanism" that will show Japanese how to break the spell and find the correct "manner" or "etiquette" to overcome their "inferiority" to the United States.[6] But the appeal to an "etiquette," a mannered and polite decorum, already compromises the sincerity and the logic of the argument, since it fails entirely to match the actual lan-guage used to describe how Japanese feel about the United States.

What seemed to bother Kobayashi most was the reluctance of con-servatives in Japan to speak out publicly on these issues and to express opinions they have held for a long time. To offset this timidity, he rec-ommended that Japanese once more meditate on the words of Nishibe Susumu, who advised that "there is a proper manner of being anti-American." Kobayashi was convinced that while the older forms of anti-communism, once linked to pro-Americanism during the long duration of the cold war, no longer possess any real political utility, to be pro-American in Japan now that its anti-communist antipode has disap-peared, has also lost its meaning and has been reduced to simply a feel-ing of intimacy with the country that had defeated Japan.[7] Yet, the recur-ring memories of a devastating war with the United States have always been available, even in the economically palmy days when they seemed to recede. It is important to recall that Japan was not defeated by China and Russia but by the United States. Hence, the "most important man-ner we must employ for protection is nothing more than showing respect toward the ancestors of corpses fallen in battle that have accumulated for hundreds of generations for the purpose of protecting us today."[8]

No voice has been more vociferous in pushing Japan's claims for re-spect from and equality with the United States than the current, popu-lar governor of Tokyo, Ishihara Shintaro. Nor has anyone been more consistently outspoken in his denunciations of the American Imperium. A former novelist and author, a few years ago, of a best-selling book titled *The Japan That Can Say No!* Ishihara, a longtime conservative politician and former member of the Diet, is known for his tough stand on the urgent necessity of abolishing Article 9 of the constitution and fully rearming Japan. In his thinking, the Japan that can say no is a country that need no longer bend to the whims of the United States and is perfectly capable of setting its own economic, political, and military policies in the post–cold war era.

Ishihara's book called for Japan to win acknowledgement from the United States as an equal partner. According to some observers, Ishihara is actually devoted to "Americanism," rather than anti-Americanism, even though he has been consistently critical of the Japan-U.S. relationship since the end of the war. One commentator has compared Ishihara to a child who is always eagerly trying to win recognition of its claim to equal authority from its father.[9]

"No" was the opening shot in a campaign that has recently turned toward a more militant agenda. In a recent speech, Ishihara referred to "third nations" that pose a threat to the global order as represented by megalopolises like Tokyo, New York, and London. The figure of "third nations," quickly conjuring up the image of the former third world in a postcolonial context, reflects for him an international division between the rich and the poor. Ishihara has imagined an almost Schmittian scenario of constant struggle between the rich and the poor, who are now found both within and without the great urban complexes of the developed world. Historically, Korea and China before the war represented this threat, which today has begun to repeat itself with even greater force. Armed with this figure, Ishihara has managed to link the civil "disorder," now caused daily by migrant laborers in Tokyo (in his opinion), with the threat posed by underdeveloped countries like North Korea, Iran, and the former Iraq, not to mention China, to the stability of the global economic order. The purpose of this fractured vision of a futurescape in which the great centers of world economic power must defend themselves against the ever-present assault of the wretched of the earth, who are seen as both economically and racially inferior, is, in fact, shaped by his desire to secure from the United States recognition of the importance both of Tokyo and of Japan's role in Asia in the coming battle to preserve the current world order.[10] It is for this reason that Ishihara has insisted on a remilitarization of Japan capable both of providing for the protection of Tokyo—his state within a state—and of mounting interventions throughout the Asian continent whenever and wherever such threats appear. Such a strategy barely conceals the repetition of Japan's prewar imperial adventures that envisaged regional integration under the rubric of the East Asia Co-Prosperity Sphere and that led to a disastrous and destructive war in Asia. The only difference today is that Japan, in Ishihara's imagining, constitutes the eastern flank of a hierarchical world economic order constituted of G-7 nations with Tokyo as the condensed miniature of the larger hierarchy that now divides the globe between the rich and the poor. (This view is simply an attenuation of an earlier conceit whereby Japan identified itself with the industrial West as it distanced itself from the third world, even functioning as an honorary Aryan nation for South Africa.)

It is unlikely that Ishihara, whose chances of eventually becoming prime minister in the near future are good, will secure from the United States an arrangement that envisions an hierarchical world order with Tokyo as one of its principal apexes. While it is entirely probable that the United States will one day support the elimination of Article 9, if for no other reason than to lessen its own burden of military expenditures in Japan and to encourage the subsequent expansion of Japanese military capacity beyond its present extent, it is inconceivable that this will lead to a partnership of parity in which Japan will have a free hand in military adventures in East Asia. The problem with Ishihara's putative postcolonial vision for maintaining order in megalopolitan Tokyo and East Asia against "third nations" is that the figure of third nations now refers to China and North Korea, which, no longer colonized, are acutely sensitive to any sign of the resurfacing of Japanese militarism.[11] As a fantasy designed to dramatize the necessity of inducing the United States to recognize Japan's claim to equality, Ishihara's discourse has much in common with the grumbling of the comedian Rodney Dangerfield, always complaining that he gets no respect, and amounts to little more than the thinly veiled obfuscation of a sovereign nation trying to have it both ways.

According to some observers, Ishihara's version of pro-Americanism founders precisely because it is virtually impossible to construct a strategy based on equal partnership between the two nations, despite the long experience of friendship. What stands in the way to accomplishing this goal is the nature of the friendship itself: Japan's long postwar experience of groaning for its own voice and silhouette in the shadow of the United States. Hence, the yearning for an impossible parity simply expresses a deeply imbedded anti-Americanism (and nationalism) that is shared by a good majority of articulate political opinion. Friendship for Japanese has cemented the conviction that the United States has always looked down upon Japan, treating the country (even before the war) as simply an appendage to American power in the Asian Pacific. In an empire, there can be equality only between subordinates. With the disappearance of any critical perspective on politics in contemporary Japan, except for interesting post–New Left groups now gathering on the horizon of an everyday life lived by the poor and migrant laborers—Ishihara's internal enemies terrorizing the streets of Tokyo—all that remains is a reflexive anti-Americanism whose choice of forms of expression is all that divides one group from another. As Nishibe suggested, the rules of etiquette that govern anti-Americanism must always begin with recognizing Japan's difference from the United States. But that recognition invariably slides into outbursts of cultural solipsism.

THE ISLAND OF DR. MOREAU

Before the war, the philosopher Watsuji Tetsuro, no friend of what in those days was called "Americanism," wrote an enduringly perceptive account of American national character.[12] The long essay, published in 1940, represented an informed and often prescient application of social theory, popular in the immediate prewar period, that promised to delineate national character. In this respect, Watsuji's study resembled Ruth Benedict's later book *The Chrysanthemum and the Sword,* written for the Office of War Information toward the end of the war to supply Americans with specific knowledge of the enemy's behavior before they began the arduous task of military occupation and postwar recovery. Benedict's hugely successful book reduced Japanese behavior to the second term of a simplistic and ahistorical binary pattern composed of guilt and shame cultures (occupied by West and East, respectively). Japanese, it seems, had always been socialized into behavior driven by the fear of public shame, that is, the fear of acting against the group or collective interest, as opposed to a culture of guilt, which emphasized personal interests based on individual conscience and a transcendental point of reference. Watsuji's searing account of American behavior, on the other hand, was informed by a shrewd understanding of the history and ethic of capitalism and the frontier experience. The inaugural moment of American national character was formed by a confluence of a savage Hobbesian war of all against all and a Baconian emphasis on scientific rationality and the primacy of materiality to produce a society driven by a desire for acquisition—possessive individualism—that led to the genocide of the native population and an ethics of competition devoid of morality.

What had marked Watsuji was an interwar encounter with American material culture in the 1920s and 1930s ("Americanism") that had already transformed life in Japan into a replica of a society of consumption. The sternest critics of this "Americanism" called attention to how commodities, consumption, new forms of popular pleasures—Hollywood films repetitively portraying material consumption, dance halls, bars, and cafés—promised individual liberation but resulted only in diluting the received spiritual culture, as well as loosening moral standards of conduct. With the ending of the war and the implementation of the postwar period, Japan was thus subjected to a second wave of "Americanism," albeit involuntary this time, which was increasingly reflected in the interminable status of the "postwar" itself: a chronological parenthesis that has lasted down to the end of the twentieth century. The photographer Tomotsu Shomei described this "Americanization," as he called it, as dominating the scene in the early 1960s, concluding that it "had originated from the American military bases" and thus from the time of the occupation. "I have the impression," he wrote as late as 1981, "that America gradually seeped out of the meshes of wire fences that surrounded the bases and before long penetrated the whole of Japan."[13] Although the actual military occupation lasted until 1952, with the completion of the peace treaty, continued American presence was guaranteed by the signing of the Japan-U.S. Mutual Security Pact in which the United States pledged to provide Japan with military protection. In no time at all, additional economic and political arrangements transmuted former foe into friend but not partner, an autonomous nation into a dependent client of a new, postwar imperium.

The American military occupation of Japan was directed by General Douglas MacArthur, Supreme Commander of the Allied Powers from 1945 to 1952, who, shamelessly playing the role of an imperial Roman proconsul lacking only a toga, effectively ruled the country as a distant colony of a vast empire. The way in which the U.S. occupation differed from other, historic examples of imperial colonization origi-nated in the decision to remake the Japanese and their society. The mil-itary occupation signaled the end of a long and murderous war in the Pacific and on the Asian mainland, stretching back to 1931, one that, at an ideological level, Japan had fought to rid the country of an "Ameri-canism" already implicated in the reshaping of culture and society. It also signified the defeat of a fascist regime aligned with Mussolini's Italy and Hitler's Germany in what might be called the paradigmatic axis of evil. Despite the Japanese claim to liberate Asians from white man's domination, Japan's armies throughout East and Southeast Asia behaved as brutally as those of the Western nations they were now seek-ing to replace. War's end brought momentary relief to the Asia of the defunct Co-Prosperity Sphere and immediate decolonization in Korea, Formosa, and parts of Southeast Asia, usually by enlisting defeated Japanese troops until the allied powers could return and redeem their former colonies. While a war-weary population in Japan failed to greet the coming of American troops, or even to dance jubilantly in the streets (here they probably shared a sentiment with the Iraqis), it offered no re-sistance. Destruction and devastation marked the country everywhere, while the civilian population, exhausted from dodging incessant air raids, working around the clock in war factories on too little sleep and food, and incurring incalculable personal losses, were instructed by the emperor to lay down their arms and cooperate with the invading army. Rather than merely fulfill its military obligation to protect the defeated country from itself, the American military occupation sought to remake Japan into a functioning democracy, once authorities recognized in 1947 that Japan would have to occupy the role as leading ally in East Asia be-cause of the imminent collapse of the nationalist regime in China. At this juncture, planners and implementers would discover their model of transformation in the figure of what can only be described as an ide-alized vision of American society, even though they believed they were importing the real thing.

Under the sanction of this new charge, the occupation envisaged Japan as a vast social and political laboratory, devoted to "experiments" that would alter the deepest behavioral and institutional patterns. These experiments often resembled those performed by the cruel, mad, but "masterful physiologist" Dr. Moreau in his island laboratory, but on a scale never imagined in H. G. Wells's novel. It was believed that, through a series of political, economic, educational, and social reforms,

Japanese could be changed from a conformist, shame-ridden population susceptible to authoritarian rule into a democratic citizenry capable of making responsible and informed decisions in their own interest. Yet the "experiments" uncannily recalled Moreau's failure to mold lower animal life into complete humans, "five men," as they called themselves, proudly holding up five fingers rather than hoof or claw.[14] But because it was an unprecedented social experiment (with some unintended biological dimensions) under controlled conditions established by the military occupiers, Japanese were made into unwilling objects, to be sculpted like clay to become, one day, it was hoped, full-fledged democratic subjects. Yet, the experiment prefigured its result of reducing Japanese to second-class clients, perpetually waiting for the recognition of an equality that never comes—clients who, in the eyes of many critics, were literally "deformed," "bent," "disfigured," and made alien to themselves. In a certain sense, Japanese never outlived the experience of having been involuntary objects of "experimentation."

Capping these reforms was the issuing of a new constitution, written principally by Americans, that represented a refinement and even an improvement of the federal constitution and offered citizens the guarantee of fundamental rights when before they had possessed only duties, and the famous Article 9 that foreswore war. But at the same time the reformers were busily transforming the Japanese, the occupation decided to retain the Emperor, rather than try him as a war criminal and hold him and the institution over which he presided responsible for the war, effectively setting the stage for the undoing of democratization.

Since the military occupation, the trajectory of anti-Americanism has proceeded in two, not always mutually exclusive, directions. From the 1950s on, there has been a broad-based leftist opposition, characterized by organized collective action, climaxing in the mass demonstrations against the ratification of the Security Pact; peace movements opposed to American intervention in Vietnam; periodic protests in the 1960s and 1970s targeting the berthing of nuclear-powered submarines; event-driven outbursts over the sinking of a Japanese vessel off the Hawaiian coast by a hotdogging American submarine; and barely visible marches against the war in Iraq. On a parallel temporal track, the Right, increasingly aligned with the dominant Liberal Democratic party, has articulated an anti-Americanism aimed at calling into question the diminution of national sovereignty, fueled by denunciations of the claim of unconditional surrender and the American-inspired constitution, the ever-present threat to cultural difference posed by the Americanization of society, and the quartering of troops on Japanese soil. In the boom years of the 1960s and 1970s, this form of anti-Americanism was often employed to underscore the legitimacy of Japan's claims in the trade wars with the United States. By the 1980s, once the economic balloon began to deflate, anti-Americanism regenerated a new nationalism fueled by a more virulent form of negativism, denouncing the occupation and its postwar legacy. Protests against American military bases in Okinawa increased, and continuing assaults on the civilian population since 1995 have actually failed to either energize the Left or animate the Right.

Regardless of the form of expression, the common ground shared by Left and Right has been a sense of abject subordination and dependency mirroring the hierarchical relationship between Japan and the United States. Behind this anti-Americanism that cries out for difference but respect can be heard the muffled but barely perceptible murmurs of Moreau's "experimental" humans, asking, "Are we not men?" Since the 1950s, Japanese have increasingly described this unequal relationship as a form of feminization and infantilization that has ultimately undermined any claim to forming a stable self-identity—what it means to be Japanese. The outpouring of the discourse on Japanese culture (*Nihon bunkaron*) in countless books and articles since the occupation's end attests to how deeply imbedded is the conviction that the repetitive projection of difference still offers a guarantee of equality or compensation for its absence. But what anti-Americanism manages to recall in Japan is the earlier encounter with modernity and the addiction to Western imports and the lure of imitation. By the end of the 1930s, just before the war, this surfeit of borrowing provoked attempts to "overcome modernity" in order to find a modernization path less dependent on Euro-American models and made in Japan. In many ways, the United States has filled the space vacated by modernity to become yet another Japanese addiction. This time, however, the addiction was not self-induced but an unwelcome affliction inflicted by an army of occupation and successive U.S. regimes. And it was sustained by the eagerness of Japanese political classes to accept a subordinate role in return for military protection (against whom has never been made clear) and the seductions of the American market. A devil's pact, if ever there was one.

"GO BACK HOME, YANKEE"

The most important and politically consequential outburst of anti-Americanism in Japan came early in the postwar period and, failing to achieve its goal, went on to enjoy an afterlife as the central, historical experience of collective action. It might also be remembered as the Left's finest hour and the beginning of the end of what, for political intellectuals like Takeuchi Yoshimi, had promised to be the first stage in the coming Japanese Revolution. In 1960, thousands of people gathered in Tokyo to demonstrate against the resigning of the Japan-U.S. Mutual Security Pact, which had been agreed upon at the time of the peace treaty and had committed Japan to what the conservative prime minister Hatoyama Ichiro lastingly described as a state of "subordinate independence" under American military power.[15] By 1960, the presence of permanent American bases in Japan had already produced a large inventory of popular resentment over their environmental effects—noise, destruction of land, pollution—and the steady increase of violent incidents like rape by military personnel whose conduct fell under the "extraterritorialized" jurisdiction of U.S. military law. By the time of the mass protests, there were already forty-six thousand troops stationed on the main islands and an additional thirty-seven thousand billeted in Okinawa. The quartering of troops, provided for by the terms of the treaty, was further exacerbated by the formation of a peace movement devoted to nuclear disarmament. A few years earlier, a Japanese fishing trawler, called the "Lucky Dragon," was contaminated by radioactive fallout from a test blast on the island of Bikini. While this event encouraged the organizing of a great deal of anti-nuclear activity, it also managed to lay the groundwork for the staging of subsequent protests in the 1960s and 1970s against the visits of nuclear-powered submarines to Japanese ports. The dispute in 1960 was ignited when both Japan and the United States elected to extend the duration of the original pact by ratifying its renewal. The structure of the pact remained unchanged: the United States agreed to offer military protection to Japan, as well as to the Asian perimeter around China, while Japan consented to help pay for bases and the stationing of troops. But Japan was effectively liberated from financing and implementing its own military defense, even though it later developed a national self-defense force and accumulated a rather large defense budget. A vast coalition of the political Left (socialists and communists), students, members of labor unions, and women's groups announced their objections to what all believed was the most recent sign of Japan's subordinate status. Driven by the fear that Japan would be drawn into a wider international conflict, owing to the terms of the treaty, demonstrators staged numerous protests in Tokyo in April and continuing well into June, forcing the government to ram the vote through the Diet, preventing President Dwight Eisenhower from visiting Japan (and forcing his press secretary at the last moment to seek escape from angry demonstrators by boarding a waiting helicopter), and resulting in the death of a young woman, attributed to police brutality.

A decade later, pacifism resurfaced to contest the American intervention in Vietnam. Once more, Japanese were propelled not only by the fear of being dragged into the struggles but also by a forceful conviction that American military intervention in what appeared to be a civil war constituted a singular act of imperial aggression. To this end, a loose federation of peace groups came together in a new organization called *Beheiren*—Vietnam Peace—which orchestrated large-scale antiwar demonstrations and actively assisted military deserters in finding safe havens in countries like Sweden. In 1970, the peace movement was instrumental in organizing the largest single protest demonstration in Japan in response to the automatic renewal of the Security Pact, recruiting over 750,000 people who denounced Japan's "dependence."[16] After this moment passed, the enthusiasm for mass protests against the United States seemed to slowly dissipate, partly as a result of Japan's staggering economic success, paralleled by the rapid demise of the Left during the 1970s and 1980s. These years marked Japan's global, economic hegemony, increasing trade disputes with the faltering industries of the United States, and a momentary but delusional desire in the capitalist world to emulate the Japanese model and its successful managerial techniques. Events would eventually conspire to remind Japan of its dependent status and subordination to the United States. In 1971 President Richard M. Nixon made known his plan to visit China and normalize relations. He also moved to take the United States off the gold standard to allow the value of the dollar to float against other currencies, especially the yen, which had remained at a fixed rate since the occupation.[17] What these actions signified for the Japanese was simply a reminder of their subordination—an existence led in the "shadow of America," as the critic Kato Norihiro would later describe it. A year later (1973), the administration of the island of Okinawa reverted to

Japan, even though American bases and troops stayed on, ultimately undermining the desire of both the Japanese state and Okinawa to secure the recognition of equality.

The issue of Okinawa, especially since 1995, represents the last major expression of organized protest against the United States. Unlike earlier organized outbursts, the Okinawan protest movement stems principally from the island itself, and its leaders are drawn from among the resident population whose everyday lives overlap spatially and temporally with the United States military bases. The dispute has been provoked by noise, pollution, and violence, echoing earlier grievances on the main islands, and also contestation over the military occupation of large chunks of scarce island real estate. Most estimates put the actual amount of expropriated land at roughly at 20 percent of the island's total. Moreover, this problem has been exacerbated by a growing number of highly publicized incidents since 1995 involving rape and even murder by soldiers. Here, the protests and the publicity have succeeded in persuading the military authority to transfer the jurisdiction over criminal behavior to the Okinawans.

Although the reversion of Okinawa resulted in policies that turned the island into a theme park and a war memorial for tourism, the continuous conflict over land and over the violent presence of the military occupiers in the everyday life of Okinawa is complicated by the collision of Okinawan aspirations and Tokyo-made policies, which are not always in accord. It should be remembered that, despite the fact that the campaign for reversion was based on the putative presumption of the Japanese identity of Okinawans, suggesting that the islanders were finally returning "home," Okinawa has since that moment consistently insisted on its own ethnic, linguistic, and cultural identity. In this triangulated relationship that links Okinawa, Japan, and the United States, the Japanese state must be seen as responsible for having put Okinawa under military occupation, despite the reversion. As a result, Tokyo can offer no credible support for complaints over land expropriation, because of its own commitments to and dependence on American military protection growing out of the Security Pact. Unavoidably, Okinawa is caught in a bind between a wish for sovereignty and the return of its land and Japan's ironclad subordination to the United States and the American determination to retain the island as the keystone of its Pacific defense strategy.[18] Since the time of the reversion, discord and struggle have escalated precisely because Okinawans recognize that the expenses for the bases have been entirely assumed by the Japanese government, even though they acknowledge the principal American role in the depletion of the soil.[19] At the same time, this resentment is reinforced by the constant resurfacing of memories of the savage nature of the war that ravaged Okinawa but spared the home islands, memories that animate the resident population mercurially like a vast "underground magma that explodes and gushes forth with anger."[20] The history of American expropriation of land in Okinawa has no real solution (other than the decision to simply pull out), since it is now fused with America's global and imperial status. What the Okinawa-Japanese case shows is the force of an imperial design that prefigured its later maturation into a full-fledged empire.

The second and more enduring form of anti-Americanism transmuted an earlier critique of modernity that had aimed to overcome its reliance on foreign emulation and imitation. It is important to add that the earlier call to overcome the modern was used as an ideological enhancement of the decision to go to war. In the postwar period, the United States was substituted for the figure of Western modernity in this critical form and became the object to be overcome. Like its predecessor, this criticism invariably veered toward asserting the claims of an irreducible cultural identity that assured Japanese of their difference from Americans. This was undoubtedly the purpose of Kojima Nobuo's best-selling novel of 1965, called *Family Embrace* (*Hoyo kazoku*), which caught the attention of a number of conservative literary and cultural critics in the 1970s and 1980s. The novel, imbedded in the context of the first flush of postwar affluence produced by income doubling and the high economic growth policies of the LDP, was principally concerned with thematizing the effect of the American presence in contemporary Japanese society. The relationship between America and affluence was not an accidental coupling and was subsequently dramatized by Mishima Yukio, who excoriated his countrymen and women for having succumbed to the blandishments of consumption—Americanization—just before his spectacular suicide in 1970. In Kojima's novel, the principal sign of the new affluence is the figure of the housemaid, who embodies progressive, or modern, thinking and who induces the housewife to embrace the new, liberal, American style of life that ends in her decision to enter into an adulterous affair with a young American soldier.[21] (By the same measure, the reader is told that, since the maid's arrival, the house has never been so clean.) Some writers have argued that a narrative centered on an affair between a middle-class housewife and an American soldier repeats at the microcosmic level the larger relationship between a masculine United States and a feminine Japan, already symbolized by the historic photograph of General MacArthur and Emperor Hirohito taken in 1945.[22] The photo shows a small, almost shrinking, seated Hirohito, dressed formally in cutaway jacket and pinstriped trousers, next to an open-shirted big Mac, who is standing, dwarfing the emperor, to compose a picture of a bourgeois wedding. This feminization was later reinforced by the marriage of Crown Prince Akihito (currently the Heisei emperor) to the commoner Shoda Michiko in 1959. Great effort was made to close off discussions that described Japan as a feminized society, as a household, represented and symbolized by Michiko. But Kojima's novel brought it out into the open. The head of the household, the cuckolded husband, Shunsuke, is shocked upon learning of the affair from the housekeeper, Michiyo. During the final meeting of the three to discuss the affair, the husband listens to the explanations offered by the wife, Tokiko, and the soldier, George, and calls attention to the differing interpretations of the event each conveys. Tokiko offers a simple accounting of the episode, usually indicated by the phrase "anyhow, I. . . ." Acknowledging that he feels some responsibility in the matter, Shunsuke addresses the soldier: "I'd like to hear why you don't feel any responsibility." "Responsibility?" the soldier replies. "To whom do I feel responsible? I feel responsibility toward my parents and the state." Shunsuke interprets this as the voice of the American army. The army always responds to any question in the following way: "I feel no responsibility. I have no responsibility other than to my parents and the United States": George will not assume the responsibility for having committed an immoral act. The wife reacts scornfully to this explanation, while the husband, after declaring that he despises Americans, puts an end to the episode by unexpectedly blurting out the phrase *"go baku homu yanki"*—go back home, yankee.

By the 1980s and 1990s, the verdict on America's Japan and the damage exacted by continuous Americanization initiated by the occupation had become a colonizing of the mind that critics like Kato Norihiro have recently called "twisted" (*nejire*): an experience that has led to "50 years of disavowal and denial."[23] In the current postbubble environment, what both Kato and the historical revisionists seem to have accomplished has been to make the postwar, as such, an almost timeless temporality and an offense to proper historical chronology. Produced by the American determination both to alienate Japanese from themselves and to present their national history as unrecognizable, the postwar becomes a prolonged parenthesis between a remembered past that never existed and a future that promises the Japanese reunion with what had been forcibly taken away from them. In this vision, only the imagined past is filled with futurity, while the present is fated to never see beyond its own horizon.

For Kato, war, defeat, and especially the American occupation made it impossible to recover those conditions of the past that had structured the identity of the collectivity. The U.S. military occupation swept away the claim to a different identity by implementing a harsh and unjustified policy of literary censorship.[24] Kato reasons that the act of denying access to the history that had once constituted the group's identity—being Japanese and the irreducible difference it marked—meant accepting its subsequent determination in the postwar era. Here is the real meaning of "war's defeat" (*haisen*), its capacity to make available a space for a structure of denial and self-deception, even self-loathing, that results in the formation of a new identity, severed from the historical past and indeed time itself but rooted in an endless present that Japanese are obliged to live as "difficult lives" (*nejire*), which could only produce only a "twisted" and "perverse" narrative.[25] It is not surprising to see how postwar Japan represents a "heterogenous temporality" that Japanese have been forced to shoulder because of defeat and a settlement that imposed the inescapable judgment that the country had fought an "unjust" and "unprincipled war" (only the United States, it seems, is in a position to fight "just" ones). Hence, Kato observes, Japanese have been obliged to live in this indeterminate, timeless zone called the postwar because they have not yet "apologized" to those countries on which they have been accused of inflicting untold destruction and death. Kato focuses on the memory of Japan's war dead, rather than on the actual offense of having waged total war against Asia. Instead of acknowledging the brutality committed by Japanese armies of occupation, he broods about how Japan was coerced into accepting a new constitution under the menace of the American army and how Japan has been destined to live difficult lives "stained" (*kegare*) by perversity and pollution. This reminder of pollution, enlisted from the arsenal of native religious practices, which have always demanded some form of purification in order to make the world right again, involves the collective action of the community as the means of restoring to it its lost solidarity and forfeited identity. The removal of "error" and "mistake" would, Kato believes, open the way to retrieving a subjectivity answerable to Japan's history and reinstalling a nationality founded on a "unified personality." But the price that must be paid for this commemorative catharsis required mourning for Asia's twenty million dead only after expressing profound regret for the three million heroic dead of Japan. In other words, the act of mourning meant conversing first with the heroic spirits of Japan as a necessary condition for communicating with the dead of Asia. Even in commemoration, it seems, Kato has managed to recuperate the structure of colonialism among the dead, attending first to the ghosts of empire and then to its unfortunate victims. Kato's discourse is driven by the longer view of Japan's history, a history of successive waves of cultural invasion that have dispossessed Japanese of words to express their innermost sentiments and forced them to find other outlets. Not only has the occupation censorship policy fulfilled this historical role, but also America has, according to Kato, prevented Japanese from mourning their own war dead.

Kato's anti-Americanism has usually been differentiated from the campaign of historical revisionists and proponents of a new, self-confident arrogance (*gomanizumu*), which invites Japanese to take pride in the war. But what they all share is the conviction that postwar Japan has been the site of a painful record of self-denial and self-deception motored by a "historical conception of self-oppression" caused by a mistake that must now be rectified. All also agree that the United States has been responsible for denying Japan access to its past and for effacing its national identity in the shadows of its imperium. Revisionists such as the tireless proponent Fujioka (as well as an army of supporters who are found in every prefecture of Japan today) have resorted to slash-and-burn tactics to diminish Japan's wartime responsibility for events like the Nanjing massacre and the forcible recruitment of Korean women for prostitution in the effort to airbrush history and to create a "correct narrative" for textbook consumption. It is hard to exaggerate the economic dimensions of this movement to revise textbooks and the almost overnight proliferation of organizations and the avalanche of barely readable publications that purportedly demonstrate the enormity of the textbook problem, linked to both Liberal Democratic party politics and conservative and even right-wing publishing houses. Behind this strategy is the figure of *gomanism,* so persistently portrayed by the cartoonist and conservative polemicist Kobayashi Yoshinori, and his program to induce Japanese to express arrogance, haughtiness, and self-satisfaction for their wartime achievements. His most celebrated work, a fat comic book approaching the size of a telephone directory, titled *On War* (*Sensoron*), which was published in 1998 and which sold more that half a million copies, has simply inverted the familiar violence associated with pornographic *manga* (comic books) into an affirmation of national *amour propre*. While Kobayashi is on record for having criticized pornographic comics, the violence portrayed in his own illustrations makes such claims sound hollow. The comic book *On War* adds up to a sustained screed against the disavowals that have resulted in Japan's descent into self-deception, often recalling Mishima Yukio's claims that peace has only softened Japanese by substituting American-style "individualism" (the private sphere) for self-sacrificing duty to the public, that is, the nation. In one panel, Kobayashi's hysterical protagonist, resembling himself, shouts out that the individual in Japan is only a consumer and nothing else, since there are no people left who are willing to die for the "ancestral country."[26] "Human rights, equality, and feminism have all entered the country from the American presence in the postwar"[27] as products of democratic thought. The young of today do not even know that Japan and the United States fought a war and should be now taught to applaud the scale of struggle waged by a "small, island country in Asia." They should also be made to understand that the war was fought to rid Asia of the white man's domination.[28] In many ways, Kobayashi's comic book resembles an illustrated *Cliff Notes* to the revised textbooks Fujioka and others were producing.

At the center of the problem of textbook revision is what Fujioka called the "liberalistic historical view." Masquerading behind an appeal to liberalism, this conception of history has declared war on historical narratives believed to have been shaped by both the Tokyo War Crimes Tribunal and the Soviet Comintern. Fujioka's denunciation of the tribunal was by no means an exceptional undertaking by conservatives, since the Left had already been on record as dismissing its judgments. But the key to this critique shared by Right and Left alike was the simple assumption that both the Americans and the Soviets had promoted a foreign interest in Japan. The narrative developed by the Tokyo trials encouraged a plan for "brainwashing the Japanese by the United States Army of Occupation that held the [prewar] state responsible for the war," while the Comintern view was designed to discredit Japan's successful modernization under the leadership of the Emperor.[29] Both of these narratives, not really very far apart from each other, converged to overdetermine the production of postwar historiography that has "darkened Japan's history," inviting "self-oppression" and the "poisoning of historical education . . . in the writing of textbooks."[30] The cartoonist Kobayashi attributes this toxicity to the "left-wing atmosphere" that prevailed in the postwar and especially to teachers, dominated by left-leaning unions, who thoughtlessly embraced values of human rights introduced by the United States that became the ground for condemning the war and Japan's history. In this respect, he appeared eager to portray the War Crimes Tribunal as a party devoted to "lynching justice that disregarded international law."[31] The task of a genuine historical education intends to return Japanese, especially contemporary youth, to a national experience that was deliberately buried by the postwar oppression and thus to exorcise the self-loathing that has made Japan ashamed of its military achievements. Fujioka described this old "new" history as "energetic" and enumerated its basic principles for an upbeat version: (1) a healthy nationalism, (2) realism, (3) an end to ideology, (4) a critique of bureaucracy, especially those agencies that had presided over textbook selection. The only interesting thing about Fujioka's liberalistic history is its insistence on linking the United States to the Soviet Union, which even before the war, he was convinced, had been bonded in a common campaign to block the movements of the Japanese state since the decade of the 1920s. That this view of history became mainstream meant that people embraced conceptions of history that literally negated Japan's modern history before 1945. But, on closer inspection, Fujioka's "liberalistic history" appears to be nothing more than a rewriting of Hayashi Fusao's earlier incendiary book that "affirmed" Japan's war as the culmination of a century-long struggle to free East Asia from white imperialism.

As a practical measure for the production and adoption of proper textbooks, Fujioka proposed, in his most celebrated work, *The History Textbooks Don't Teach* (1996), a set of themes as a guide for "grasping the constitution."[32] The most important point was the need to revisit the ruin wreaked upon Japan by the military occupation and by the continuing America presence, which dominates Japan's contemporary history. "In over fifty years, what has protected the peace of Japan has not been Article 9 but the Security Pact." Moreover, the "military occupation forced on Japan violent resolutions resulting in the revision of education and the [overthrow] of the Meiji Rescript on Education." (This

Rescript of 1889 outlined in starchy Confucian language the moral duties each subject was obliged to perform as the task of national education.) The defects and the damaging influence that have accompanied the forcible imposition of educational "reforms" have been immense. By "throwing dust in the eyes in this way, Japanese no longer possess spiritual self-reliance and independence."[33]

CONCLUSION: HATING AMERICA AND LOVING IT

In a recent *New York Times* article reporting the findings of a Pew Foundation survey on global anti-Americanism (it is always problematic to quantify such a slippery category), Japan was not even mentioned, even though the country had been polled.[34] The Pew Research Center issued a similar report for the year 2002, when 72 percent of the respondents in Japan expressed a favorable view of the United States. The importance of both the *Times*'s decision to omit Japan from the article and the earlier findings attest to the widespread belief that Japanese appear more friendly toward the United States than others and that anti-Americanism in Japan poses no serious problem. It also reflects the widespread conviction in the United States that Japanese cannot really be anti-American because of their dependence on American economic and military support—so much so that they are really like Americans. All of this only shows the indifference of Americans toward Japanese, who have been seen, since the end of the war, as a dependent client that the United States has protected and sustained economically. But this also depends upon how anti-American attitudes are read. Japanese have been addicted to the United States, and their expressions of anti-Americanism must always be understood through the refractions of this particular optic. Like any addiction, whether voluntarily or involuntarily acquired, it is difficult, if not impossible, to shake off, which means that the addict loves and hates it at the same time. In a sense this is what Japanese anti-Americanism consists of: the recognition of Japan's dependence on the United States and the desire to win equality, respect, and recognition of partnership, an impossible double-bind that has no real resolution other than a continued desire to have it both ways. This is the reason that Japan has lived such a long postwar, which will end only when the nation is able to resolve its ambivalence about the United States. Despite the construction of a discourse promoting an irresolvable paradox, it is really the status of Okinawa that exposes the contradiction of Japanese anti-Americanism and unveils the hypocrisy of wanting it both ways. Japan was momentarily deluded into believing that Okinawa's reversion would finally lead to the restoration of sovereignty and the recognition of Japan's full partnership with the United States. Instead, reversion reflected only the agreement to retain the military occupation designed to accomplish the transfer of financial responsibility for American bases to the Japanese government. While Japan could have made an issue of this, especially in the wake of a propaganda campaign that had actually represented Okinawa and its culture as Japanese, and thus dramatize the opening gambit of a larger strategy demanding the restitution of full sovereignty, it failed to do so. In the end, the pull of the Security Pact, the habit of having American troops on Japanese soil, and the benefits Japan had come to expect and depend upon won out. The country chose to remain safely wedded to the United States in a marriage that allows endless opportunity for fantasizing about what it means to be Japanese without the necessity of actually acting on those fantasies.

NOTES

1. The Japanese translation was published in *Gendai shiso,* vol. 30, no. 8 (2002).

2. Kan Sanjun, "Amerika o shiru koto no imi," *Gendai shiso,* vol. 30, no. 12 (2002): 70–71.

3. See Kobyashi Yoshinoru and Nishibe Susumu, *Hanbei to iu saho* (Tokyo: Shogakkan, 2002).

4. Ibid., pp. 44–45.

5. Ibid., p. 47.

6. Ibid., p. 308.

7. Ibid., p. 310.

8. Ibid., pp. 310–311.

9. Kan Sanjun, "Datsu reisen to Higasha Ajia," *Gendai shiso,* vol. 28, no. 7 (2000): 62.

10. Ibid., pp. 61, 64.

11. Ibid., p. 65.

12. For an account in English of this important document, see Harry Harootunian, *Overcome by Modernity* (Princeton: Princeton University Press, 2000), pp. 277–281.

13. Cited in Sandra S. Phillips and Alexandra Monroe, and Daido

Moriyama, *Daido Moriyama: Stray Dogs* (San Francisco: San Francisco Museum of Art, 1999), p. 16.

14. See H. G. Wells, *The Island of Dr. Moreau* (New York: Signet, 1988).

15. Cited in Andrew Gordon, *A Modern History of Japan* (New York: Oxford University Press, 2003), p. 77.

16. Ibid., pp. 282–283.

17. Ibid., p. 291.

18. See Kokubu Kotaro, "Gendai sekaishi no naka Okinawa," *Gendai shiso,* vol. 28, no. 7 (2000): 86–88.

19. Ibid., p. 93.

20. Ibid., p. 94.

21. My account of Kojima's novel follows Kato Norihiro, *Amerika no kage* (Tokyo: Kawade shoboshinsha, 1985), pp. 56–69.

22. See Osawa Masachi, *Sengo no shiso kukan* (Tokyo: Chikuma shinso, 1998, pp. 74–75. The argument is derived from Eto Jun, *Seijuku to soshitsu* of 1967.

23. Kato, author of an earlier book, *America's Shadow* (1985), argued that American assistance to Japan had essentially made the Japanese state into one of its props. Japan suffered from a political structure that could not do without the United States, and the long postwar was made to stand in. Actually, Kato's argument glossed the earlier argument made by Eto Jun, which proposed that that the American army exceeded the claims of the Potsdam Declaration of 1945, which ended the war, especially its putative authorization of unconditional surrender and the military occupation of Japan, which subsequently implemented policies that led to a veritable regime change. See Harry Harootunian, "Japan's Long Postwar: The Trick of Memory, The Ruse of History in Postwar Japan," in Tomiko Yoda and Harry Harootunian, eds., *Millennial Japan,* a special issue of *South Atlantic Quarterly* 99:4 (fall 2000): 715–739.

24. Kato Norihiro, *Haisengoron* (Tokyo: Tokyo, 1997), pp. 156–158.

15. Ibid., p. 17; Osawa, *Sengo no shiso kukan,* pp. 38–39.

26. Kobayashi Yoshinori, *Sensoron* (Tokyo: Gentosha, 1980), pp. 18–19.

27. Ibid., p. 23.

28. Ibid., p. 31.

29. Tawara Yoshifumi, *Kyokasho kogeki no shinsho* (Tokyo: Gakushu no yusha, 1997), p. 58.

30. Ibid., pp. 58–60.

31. Kobayashi, *Sensoron,* p. 44.

32. Fujioka Nobukatsu and Jiyushugi Shikan Kenkyukai, eds. *Kyokasho ga oshienai rekishi,* 4 vols. (Tokyo: Nyusu sabisu, 1996–1998).

33. Tawara, *Kyokasho Kogeki no shinsho,* p. 17.

34. The *New York Times* report on the Pew survey appeared on September 11, 2003. The survey itself is available at http://people-press.org/reports/display.php3?ReportID=185.

12

Desires for North Korea

Hyun Ok Park

FOR ALL THEIR DIFFERENCES, the expressions of anti-Americanism that erupted late in 2002 and 2003 in South Korea and in North Korea, respectively, convey the capitalist desires of Koreans and other Asians in the post–cold war era. They are distinctly post–cold war events, not just because Koreans pursue their national sovereignty independently of the United States so as to amend previously unequal relations, but, more important, because the displays of anti-Americanism are symptoms of an inflected aspiration for a new Northeast Asian community, which the two Koreas and their neighboring countries have begun to envision for their collective future.

The appeal for a new Northeast Asian community has recently emerged as a spatial and temporal fix to the capitalist crisis in Asia, especially in South Korea and in Japan. Whereas South Korea had emulated America and Japan during the cold war, it is now collaborating with Japan to configure a northeast Asian economic bloc comparable to the European Union. The economic bedrock of the cold war establishment was the bilateral relationship between each Asian country and the United States that inhibited Asians from developing multilateral relations with other parts of the world, let alone among Asians themselves.[1] National identity was either conflated with or diametrically opposed to American imperialism. Examples include the participation of Japan and South Korea in the Korean and the Vietnam wars, respectively, the well-known anti-American movement in South Korea during the 1980s, and the persistent discourse of "the postwar" that still holds the American occupation accountable for social and cultural unevenness in Japan. If neither the Koreans nor the Japanese were capable of imagining an Asian community during the cold war, the emerging fetish of the Asian community under the economic crisis distinguishes the post–cold war era. The American trade embargo has disrupted the economic growth of Japan since the late 1970s and South Korea since the late 1980s. With the trauma of the IMF crisis and the subsequent consolidation of neoliberal reforms, Asians now see a northeast Asian community as an alternative to previous dependence on American capital and markets.

South Korean participants and spectators of the current anti-American protests have expressed anxiety about America. This emotional complexity, in my view, reflects social discontent in futile search of a resolution. In November 2002, about a million candlelight protesters in South Korea flooded a central district of Seoul, and the protest still continues on a smaller scale.[2] At first, they demanded that South Korea and the United States reform their Status of Forces Agreement (SOFA), which has granted a routine amnesty since the mid-1960s to thousands of American civilians and military personnel guilty of crimes, including two soldiers responsible for the death of two schoolgirls in June 2002. The scale and the tone of this anti-Americanism have surprised Koreans as much as the outside world. For the skeptics of the proliferating NGO movement, the protest is a sign that political unity is still possible in an age of fragmented movements. For some others who conflate globalization with transnationalism, the recent anti-American sentiment is the return of the nationalist chauvinism of the past. Afraid of undermining an already contested relationship between South Korea and the United States or of discouraging foreign investors, some politicians and intellectuals construe the protest as merely a reaction to the past, as a move to offset the past hierarchical relationship between the two countries.[3]

E-POLITICS

The most prominent sign of anxiety is, however, the call for spontaneity among individual participants. Self-expression and unconventional forms of public protest must supersede conventional practices of social movements. This orientation is a trademark of virtual citizens, or "netizens," whose identity emerged with the November 2002 candlelight vigil that their Internet communications created.[4] They called upon one another to express themselves freely and uniquely, instead of chanting familiar slogans such as "anti-America" and "SOFA reform." Since June 2002, a long-standing unification movement organization (*Pomminryon*), in collaboration with several dozen social movement organizations and NGOs, endeavored in vain to organize protests against the schoolgirls' deaths. However, it was not until November that the protest began a phenomenal surge due to mobilization via the Internet. To express their opposition to the American war against Iraq, netizens have extended the candlelight vigils to the global anti-war and peace movement, distancing themselves from established movements that still focus on the relationship between South Korea and the United States. Fearing desertion by this emergent netizen crowd, the media, politicians, and well-known movement organizations have sought to follow the voice of netizens. Accordingly, the candlelight vigils are given the status of a new politics where participants lead the movement. This status reverses the usual institutional formula for social movements and signals that the protests are also an attempt to reclaim popular space from organized politics.

The insistence on spontaneity signifies a desire for new democratic expression that conventional social movements have failed to fulfill. Although spontaneous politics must be linked to a worldwide youth culture, the participation of diverse age groups and the pervasive fascination with spontaneity permit us to embed the spectacle within a social crisis that poses problems for representation. The simultaneous progression since the 1990s of long-awaited democratization and sweeping market liberalization has prevented various movement organizations from comprehending the reality of the current situation. Flourishing NGOs tend to espouse liberalism instead of censuring it: for instance, the economic concerns of leading NGOs include the monopoly of conglomerates, the rights of small stockholders of conglomerates, and corruption; only recently have they begun to discuss the problem of the growing number of part-time workers. Labor unions have been abandoning the role they played in the 1980s and have become more like interest groups for employees of conglomerates than a vanguard for the majority of workers who are not unionized. Human rights organizations continue to represent the victims of the previous authoritarian regime, such as tortured and long-term prisoners and families of the disappeared. In this context, the candlelight protests are opening a space for various groups and generations that have ambivalent and contradictory feelings about neoliberal democracy.

The search for a new democratic expression entails a capitalist dream that includes North Korea. The tension with the United States over nuclear weapons successfully pressured North Korea to stop procrastinating and to start implementing its plan for market reform as a gesture to offset the American portrayal of North Korean military ambition and to sustain ongoing negotiations with South Korea, Russia, China, and Japan for economic cooperation. This new development has rekindled South Korean public support for the Sunshine Policy of engagement with North Korea that South Korea has implemented since 1998.[5] The new policy of engagement centers on economic cooperation between the two Koreas and is called "national cooperation" (*minjok kongcho*).[6] This is the post–cold war replacement for the earlier South Korea–U.S. cooperation (*hanmi kongcho*) and for North Korea's negotiation first with the United States and later with South Korea (*sonmihunam*). National cooperation further consolidates capitalist hegemony over both the form and the process of the Korean unification, which has been increasingly economic in nature since the 1990s. This is evident in the transformation of national cooperation from trade and subcontracting agreements mediated by Korean diasporas to the direct investment of South Korean capital in the market reform in North Korea. According to the South Korean business community, North Korean laborers are cheaper yet better skilled than their Han Chinese or Korean Chinese counterparts, who are relied on by South Korean firms. North Korea emerges not just as a market for South Korean surplus production but also as a promising new site for investment in industrial production.[7]

A NEW REGIONAL BLOC

The enthusiasm of South Koreans for North Korea's immanent future is marked by a distinctive historical time consciousness. Although economic liberalization failed to deliver on its long-promised redistribution of wealth, the trauma of the 1997 IMF crisis nevertheless invoked the specter of developmentalism. Deregulated foreign capital performed the dirty work for South Korean capital in mobilizing diverse sectors of society to rally again for national unity in support of capitalist expansion. In the current historical juncture, where the nation's cultural appeal is significantly reduced, the memory of the IMF transports the radiant dream of the past into the future.[8] Will the opening of the North Korean market alleviate the social crisis, taming the neoliberal capitalist drive begun in the 1990s that expanded the part-time labor force to more than half the total labor force, eliminated job security, and reduced the size of the middle class? When neoliberal reforms have emptied out the meaning of democracy in the economic space, will the capitalist dream for North Korea help to reconcile democratization and economic growth? While South Koreans are condemning American imperialism, they are oblivious to their own fascination with North Korea, which may not be as imperialistic as America but is just as inequitable. The construction of an American Other—whether in the form of enchantment (NGOs' internationalism or the insistence on keeping the American forces in South Korea) or of denunciation (anti-Americanism)—deters Koreans from confronting their own social reality in the present.

North Korea constitutes the last link in the completion of the Northeast Asia economic bloc. Whereas China and Russia have steadily expanded their economic relations with South Korea throughout the post–cold war era, they have begun to renormalize relations with North Korea only since the late 1990s, pledging aid to North Korea and further cooperation. Japan and North Korea have also attained a milestone in their process of normalization by reaching an agreement on compensation instead of reparation for the colonial occupation of Korea by Japan. (Official normalization has been stalled because of Japan's fury over the abduction of Japanese nationals by North Korean security agents.) A shared vision of a Northeast Asian bloc enabled each neighboring country to formulate a trilateral relation with the two Koreas. This vision foresees the trans-Siberian freight route linking the natural resources and manpower of Russia and North Korea with the capital, technology, and surplus production of South Korea, Japan, and even China. The Asian community is projected not only to consolidate itself among northeast Asia players but also to expand its power into Europe and Southeast Asia.

The actualization of the Asian community is forestalled by other territorial disputes, competition for hegemony, and disagreement on the American war against Iraq. Yet the capitalist crisis in Asian countries invigorates the aspiration for unity. These are favorable circumstances for South Korea, Japan, Russia, and China to oppose the American aggression against North Korea, which they regard as threatening the sovereignty of North Korea or the military power of China—often said to be the true target of the American offensive in North Korea—and as threatening their common interests just when they are beginning to coalesce.

Some of the interests of the United States and North Korea appear to be already fulfilled as a result of their nuclear standoff, possibly obviating the need to undertake a widely unpopular war between them. Heightened military tension accompanied by a surge of anti-Americanism in the Korean peninsula might help America kill two birds with one stone. First, it would give the Bush administration a rationale to execute the plan to withdraw its troops from South Korea without giving up this strategic post in Asia. Second, it might enable the United States to replace its groundforce-based security program with a missile defense program. While helping North Korea negotiate for more American economic aid, the nuclear tension inadvertently enables North Korea to temper the speed of national cooperation under the control of South Korean capital. It also offers North Korea an opportunity to boost its declining legitimacy with the people of both South and North Korea in the wake of North Korea's rampant famines. The peace treaty with the United States demanded by North Korea is superior to the South Korean proposal for making the Korean peninsula nuclear-free. Whereas the South Korean proposal requires the two Koreas to eliminate nuclear weapons but fails to prohibit the United States from bringing nuclear weapons to the peninsula in an emergency, the North Korean proposal categorically prohibits the use of nuclear weapons by all sides—including the United States. The peace treaty is capable of lending North Korea political currency in the process of putative national cooperation and the construction of the Northeast Asian community.

A NEW MILITARY ORDER

Riding a wave of popular enchantment with a promising future, economists and policy makers have struck up conversations about a single currency and new maritime transit centers for the Asian economy.[9] As with the embryonic discussions, the flow of discourse is shaped by far-fetched projections about the potential mutual benefits among the Asian countries, rather than the realities of power and lived history. Skeptics and critics seemed to be muted by the turbulent economic recovery embodied in irregular stock market performance. When the anti-American protests are tangled up with the aspiration for a regional bloc, they gloss over the multifaceted reality of the Asian region under post–cold war reconstruction.

Undercutting the seemingly unified rally for viable regional unity is the old and new notion of national sovereignty. As the experiences of the European Union illustrate, the formation of a regional bloc can progress alongside the reinvention of the nation-state system. Despite a growing cosmopolitanism, the more powerful nation-states are still the major decision makers in the EU, whether they involve the institutionalization of the supranational governance, the freedom of labor migration across the borders within the EU, or the denizenship and other political and social rights of migrants and noncitizen residents. Two significant expressions of national sovereignty in Asia merit further elaboration: the new military buildup of key Asian players and the lived history of a newly emerging Korean nation.

Nothing attests better to the dissolution of the cold war order than the diplomatic normalization of relations on the part of China and Russia with South Korea; however, these countries' strained relations with North Korea also express a muddled post–cold war order. While China disagrees with the American plan for a regime change in North Korea, it has sought to discipline North Korea, often using food aid and oil supply as carrots and sticks. Market reforms in North Korea are essential to the formation of the northeast regional bloc, but North Korea's first groundbreaking move for such transition was hampered by Chinese opposition to the North's economic plan in a city adjacent to a Chinese economic industrial complex. While Russia has pursued military and economic relations with the South, whether it will achieve comparable cooperation with the North remains to be seen because of the two countries' strained relationship during the 1990s and their recently renormalized relations.[10]

The most ominous sign of the complex challenges facing a viable regional unity is the emboldened attempts of the United States to re-integrate Japan and South Korea in its new strategic plan for Asia. As the United States is reorganizing the Middle East under the pretext of an antiterrorist regime change in Iraq, a similar process based on the nuclear threat of North Korea is under way in Asia. Jae-Jung Suh observes that the American policy toward North Korea is marked by a combination of contradictory elements—engagement with and containment of North Korea.[11] The 1994 Agreed Framework between America and North Korea outlines their cooperation and compromise toward full normalization of relations. In exchange for Pyongyang's return to the Nuclear Nonproliferation Treaty and its dismantling of nuclear reactors, Washington promised to provide economic assistance and to move toward diplomatic normalization. Simultaneously progressing with this engagement policy toward North Korea is the American rearmament of Asia that has repositioned military equipment and armies in preparation for immediate and flexible deployment of forces.

Japan has entered a new military alliance with America in the wake of the September 11 attacks on the World Trade Center. Japan's support for the American offensive in Afghanistan and the preemptive strikes against Iraq provided Japan with an opportunity to shed the postwar restrictions on armaments and to press its new dream of militarization in the name of self-defense. During the last phase of negotiations for diplomatic normalization with North Korea, North Korea's recognition of its responsibility for the kidnapping of Japanese civilians not only halted the turbulent negotiations but also intensified public support for changing the constitution that would lead to the legalization of self-armament. The security alliance between Japan and America has been continuously expanded through a series of declarations, including the U.S.-Japan Joint Declaration on Security of 1996, the new Guidelines for the U.S.-Japan Defense Cooperation in 1997, and a law governing "situations in areas surrounding Japan" in 1999. These security measures have fundamentally changed the self-defense forces of Japan. They removed constraints on America-Japan security cooperation and enabled American military forces to use Japanese bases for operations outside Japan, including on the Korean peninsula.[12] The continued outcry among Japanese over the kidnapping of Japanese by North Korea and an overstated vulnerability to missile attack are fanning support for Japanese military expansion and displacing the concerns over the economic recession.[13]

South Korea has fortified its defense force since the 1990s. The synergy of the U.S. pressure to procure high-tech equipment and South Korea's enduring fixation on self-defense has led South Korea to augment its defense budget and to become the second largest importer, behind China, of conventional weapons. In 1995 alone, Korea imported from the United States a range of armaments including machine guns, personnel carriers, tanks, and submarines, which cost $957.4 million, or about 56 percent of the total amount spent on arms procurements. The South Korean government successfully negotiated with the United States to develop a missile with a longer range and to expand its budget for research and development of weapons. Since 1996, military cooperation has been developing between South Korea and Russia. South Korea still maintains a sense that its alliance with America is a cornerstone of national defense and security, but South Korea's continued purchase of weapons from the United States is not to be equated with American control of the South Korean military. It is not clear whether South Korea will remain a faithful ally of the United States or will take sides with North Korea. As the threat of North Korea is a deeply embedded psychic structure in this divided country, South Korea is still habitually bolstering its defense capacity, even when the disparity between the two Koreas seems to grow with North Korea's significantly decreased investments in armaments during recent years.[14] With the renewal of the received past, South Korea has yet to forge new military and political relations with America and North Korea.

A NEW KOREAN NATION

South Korea's economic restructuring since the late 1980s has transformed the contour of its nation through its newly developing economic and cultural relations with North Korea and Korean diasporic communities. Rising labor costs, the unavailability of cheap labor, increasingly expensive land costs, and other increases in production costs have undermined economic growth in South Korea. In the aftermath of the financial crisis in the late 1990s, the state and the business sectors have further scrambled in their search for new ways to maintain the viability of South Korea's economy. The economic crisis has produced a new discourse and policy on transnational Korea. The Korean diaspora has been continuously recognized as an "enormous asset" capable of advancing the status of Korea in the international community, a prospect comparable to what the Chinese diaspora brought to coastal regions of China.

At the beginning, the language of inclusiveness of Korean transnational ethnicity was striking. Yet, beneath the inclusive language was a new construction of difference. In its drive to find Koreanness, the South Korean state presented its own practices and interpretations of Korean culture and language as the truthful rendition of national spirit (*minjok ol, minjok chonggi*). It asserted that overseas Koreans, especially those who lived under socialist regimes, had strayed too far from their Korean roots. According to the South Korean constitution, South Korea was the only legitimate national entity in the Korean peninsula. Those who held North Korean citizenship, including sixty thousand out of two million Korean Chinese, were subsumed into South Korean citizenship. As South Korea began to formulate the new terms of its relationship with overseas Koreans, such contrived provisions were not applied uniformly to all overseas Koreans. Of all the diasporic groups, only the Korean Americans emerged as privileged partners of South Korea, and they were invited to converse with South Korean elites about such issues as dual citizenship, property rights, voting rights, military service, and requirements to pay taxes. Some Korean Americans won races in the 1994 South Korean legislative elections. Leading South Korean politicians and presidential candidates in 1994 and 1997 pledged to promote dual citizenship for Korean Americans while proposing restrictions on similar privileges for other diasporic groups, such as the Korean Chinese.

If Korean Americans fit the image of flexible diasporic members in the current literature of the diaspora, other Korean diasporic groups in Japan, Russia, and Sakhalin remained forgotten, despite their expressed desire to visit South Korea—if not return permanently. Koreans in China deviate from both recent and older descriptions of the diaspora. While playing significant roles in mediating economic interactions between South Korea and North Korea and working in South Korean factories, like other foreign migrant workers, most Korean Chinese have taken the back door when visiting South Korea. Korean Chinese could legally visit South Korea only for family visitation, industrial training programs, and marriage with South Koreans. Among these channels, the industrial training program is the only legal avenue for Korean Chinese who wish to work and earn money in South Korea, and only a very few were accepted into the program. Most other Korean Chinese have been visiting though the back door, illegally overstaying family visitations or paying brokers $8,000 to $10,000, the equivalent to two or four years of earnings for an individual worker in mainland China.

Korean Chinese have distinguished themselves from other foreign workers. Not long after it became apparent to Korean Chinese that their ethnicity would not bring them any rights in South Korea, they began to represent themselves as "returnees" to their parents' homelands. For some Korean Chinese, the memory of the colonial experience also became the source of a historical power to circumvent discrimination and a lack of rights in South Korea. Korean Chinese have considered their humiliation in South Korea and the experience of being defrauded by brokers as betrayal in their ancestral homeland and a crime against the nation.

As the economic cooperation between the South and the North moves forward as planned, it is probably a matter of time before North Koreans migrate to the South and replace Korean Chinese and other migrant workers as cheap laborers. It is expected that this will further heighten the tension between Korean Chinese and North Korea that has existed for years. Sharing kinship ties and borders for decades until the early 1990s, Korean Chinese and North Koreans had extended economic support to each other during times of hardship and natural disasters. With the worsening of the economic crisis in North Korea since the mid-1990s, about 200,000 to 300,000 North Koreans have been illegally migrating to the Korean Chinese community adjacent to the border between China and North Korea.[15] North Korean migrants have developed interactions with Korean Chinese in China like those that Korean Chinese migrants maintain with South Koreans in South Korea: working as illegal migrants for their ethnic kin. While the Chinese authorities barred North Koreans from work and residence, Korean Chinese have been hiring North Koreans as farm laborers and to work in fisheries and in the wood-cutting industry. Without legal status, North Koreans often find themselves working for Korean Chinese for low or irregular wages, leading to violent wage disputes. This relationship may deteriorate further with the anticipated flow of North Korean labor to South Korea. It remains to be seen how the South Koreans will treat incoming North Korean migrant laborers. The discourses of national cooperation obscure the issue of the unequal relationship among various groups of Koreans that is at the heart of the Korean globalization and its new ethnic network.

CONCLUSION

Anti-Americanism and efforts to consciously distance oneself from it, as well as the insistence on spontaneity, suggest a crisis of representation. They highlight an undeniable desire for a new national popular space that has not yet been fully defined. The North Korean state is an accomplice in the construction of neoliberal structures that are producing these energies in South Korea and that are propelling Asians to envisage their unity. If South Korean anti-Americanism is to yield concrete results capable of organizing a regional economic bloc, the protesters and spectators must turn their attention to the multifaceted regional and global order, in which the economic yearning for a regional unity has become entangled with the old and new military configuration in Asia. If anti-Americanism is to be effective in actualizing a new national relationship with North Korea, it must also interrogate the meaning of a newly constructed national cooperation.

NOTES

1. A short version of the paper was published in *Radical Philosophy* 2003 (May–June): 2–5. On the economic relations during the cold war period, see Woo-Cumings, "Market Dependency in U.S.–East Asian Relations," in Arif Dirlik, ed., *What Is in a Rim? Critical Perspectives on the Pacific Region Idea* (Boulder, Colo.: Westview Press, 1993), pp. 135–160.

2. For detailed footage of the candlelight protests, see the official website of this movement (www.antimigun.org). See also Kim Ji-eun, "Chaju p'yonghwa yomwon chopuleun kyesok denda" [Candlelights for independence and peace will continue], www.ohmynews.com, January 26, 2003; Kim Ji-eun, "Ajikeun chopul kkulddaeka anijanayo" [It is not yet a time to put out candlelights], www.ohmynews.com, January 18, 2003.

3. For various discussions of anti-Americanism in South Korea, see Kwon Pak Hyo-won and Nam So-yean, "Chopulsiwinun panmi anin noyesari kopu" [The candlelight protests are not anti-Americanism but the rejection of slavery], www.ohmynews.com, January 12, 2003; Seung-Hwan Kim, "Anti-Americanism in Korea," *Washington Quarterly* 26:1 (2002–2003): 109–122; Kang Songkwan, "Yangsimi itnunhan han najun koe sisonul dulgot" [I will lay my attention to a low place, as long as I have a conscience], www.ohmnews.com, January 8, 2003; Hong Song-sik, "Pulpyongdunghan 'sopa' hyondaepan nobi munso, oeseka mandun sesangeun kajago howi" [The unequal SOFA, a modern slavery, the world made by the foreign power is fake and fiction], www.ohmynews.com, January 8, 2003; Kim Ji-eun and Kwon Park Hyo-won, "Han'guke panmi kamjong yombong dolko idda. Namhannae dojong kanch'op 5manmyong hwaldong" [A contagious disease of anti-Americanism in South Korea, the 50,000 North Korean spies are currently working in South Korea], www.ohmynews.com, January 19, 2003; Howard French, "Shifting Loyalties: Seoul Looks to New Alliances," *New York Times*, January 26, 2003.

4. For an example, *NGO Times,* December 31, 2002.

5. For a comprehensive discussion of the Sunshine Policy, see Chung-in Moon, "The Sunshine Policy and the Korean Summit: Assessments and Prospects," in Tsuneo Akaha, ed., *The Future of North Korea* (New York: Routledge, 2002), pp. 26–46.

6. For a recent discussion n the South Korea-North Korea cooperatives, see Bae Chong-Ryel, "Development of Inter-Korean Economic Relations," *Korea Focus* 11:1 (2003): 110–135.

7. On the prospect of the North Korean economic reform, see Doowon Lee, "The Economic Outlook for Reconciliation and Reunification," in Kongdan Oh and Ralph Hassig, eds., *Korea Briefing 2000–2001: First Steps toward Reconciliation and Reunification* (Armonk, N.Y.: M. E. Sharpe, 2002), pp. 43–77. On the recent agreement between South Korea and North Korea, see "Hyondae, Daepuksaop 'pokwal dokjomkwon' numkil" [Hyundai, the North Korea Project 'A Comprehensive Monopoly Right'], www.hani.co.kr, February 9, 2003.

8. On the South Korean economic reforms before and after the IMF crisis, see Eliot Kang, "Segyehwa Reform of the South Korean Developmental State," in Samuel Kim, ed., *Korea's Globalization* (Cambridge: Cambridge University Press, 2000), pp. 76–101.

9. As an example of such discussions, see Kim Cae-One, "Moving Ahead with Economic Integration of Northeast Asia," *Korea Focus* 11:2 (March–April 2003): 96–119.

10. On the relationships of Russia and China with South Korea and North Korea, see Victor Cha, "The Security Domain of South Korea's Globalization," in Samuel Kim, ed., *Korea's Globalization* (Cambridge: Cambridge University Press, 2000), pp. 217–241; Samuel Kim, "China, Japan, and Russia in Inter-Korean Relations," in Kongdan Oh and Ralph Hassig, eds., *Korea Briefing 2000–2001: First Steps toward Reconciliation and Reunification* (Armonk, N.Y.: M. E. Sharpe, 2002), pp. 109–148; and Robert Scalapino, "Korea: The Options and Perimeters," in Tsuneo Akaha, ed., *The Future of North Korea* (New York: Routledge, 2002), pp. 9–25.

11. Jae-Jung Suh, "The Two-Wars Doctrine and the Regional Arms Race: Contradictions in U.S. Post–Cold War Security Policy in Northeast Asia." *Critical Asian Studies* 35:1 (2003): 3–32.

12. Tetsuo Maeda, "Japan's War Readiness: Desecration of the Constitution in the Wake of 9-11," *Gunshuku* 226 (December 2002): 6–11, trans. Victor Koschmann and cited from *Japan Focus* (www.japanfocus.org); Sangjung Kang, "The First Agonizing Step towards Stabilizing Northeast Asia," *Ronza,* November 2002, cited from *Japan Focus.*

13. Ko Mishima, "The Ghost of Ultra-Nationalism Haunts Japan," *SAIS Review* 19:2 (1999): 251–255.

14. Yang Byung Kie, "Changes in North Korea's Military Policy and East Asian Security," in *Korea Focus* 11:1 (2003): 51–71.

15. Kelly Koh and Glenn Baek, "North Korean Defectors: A Window into a Reunified Korea," in Kongdan Oh and Ralph Hassig, eds., *Korea Briefing 2000–2001: First Steps toward Reconciliation and Reunification* (Armonk, N.Y.: M. E. Sharpe, 2002), pp. 205–226.

13

China's Repressed Returns

Rebecca E. Karl

AT THE BEGINNING OF JUNE 2003, a peculiar situation developed in Beijing. Saddam Hussein's ambassadorial envoy to the People's Republic of China, Muwafak al-Ani, refused to relinquish his post. He barricaded himself inside the Iraqi embassy in Beijing and proclaimed that the "Iraqi authorities" who had recalled him to Baghdad were merely puppets of the United States occupation and thus had no authority over him at all. Meanwhile, the United States called upon Beijing to designate al-Ani persona non grata and urged Chinese authorities to expel him from the country, by force if necessary. China, which had opposed the U.S. invasion of Iraq in the United Nations Security Council, resisted U.S. requests for al-Ani's expulsion by claiming that the fallout from the war was an "internal problem" and that China does not interfere in such matters. The Chinese added that they were reluctant to alienate their "Muslim friends around the world" and thus would take no overt action. They did, however, cut off contact with the Iraqi embassy. On July 31, al-Ani left the embassy, apparently voluntarily. As al-Ani's successor, al-Khudairi, noted, he departed exactly fifty-five days after the incident's inception. Curiously, al-Khudairi added that this fifty-five-day stretch "brings us to the memory of *55 Days at Peking*," referring to the 1963 film starring Charlton Heston and Ava Gardner and set during China's Boxer Rebellion of 1900, with Heston portraying a muscular U.S. marine who leads recently installed Philippine-based American troops into Peking [now, Beijing] to rescue diplomats and their families under siege in the foreign legation.[1]

The rescue of the diplomatic quarters in Beijing in 1900 was hardly the exclusively heroic American affair that the film depicts; however, perhaps it was one of the first times what we might now call a "coalition of the willing" was assembled to invade a nominally sovereign country so as to impose, among other things, free trade and political-economic subservience to new global norms (at that time, the coalition, known as the "allied powers," consisted of eight powerful imperialist nations eager to redistribute among themselves what was left of China's profitable economic sectors). The outcome of this rescue is well known: a large-scale and indiscriminate massacre by rampaging allied forces of any Chinese suspected of being or sympathizing with the Boxers; urban destruction and looting by the foreign troops; spiraling social, economic, and political instability in the capital and beyond; and a weakened, discredited dynastic court forced first to flee the capital and then to sue for peace at the price of financial ruin and the ceding of more sovereignty. By the time the Boxer Protocol was negotiated in 1901, the provisions of the treaty were so punitive that, within a decade, they helped lead to the collapse of the Qing dynasty and to nearly half a century of political turmoil that came to a close only with the success of the Maoist revolution in 1949.

In June 2003, a very different "coalition of the willing" dominated by the United States and composed not of the major powers of our day but rather of minor states and mercenary corporations held Iraqis under siege, while China was exhorted in effect to lay siege to the Iraqi embassy in Beijing. In this light, it might be unclear what al-Khudairi meant by referring to *55 Days at Peking,* other than as a banal indication of the similar length of time and location of the incident. By the same token, his calls for the rescue of the Iraqi embassy somehow do recall the pleas of those other foreign diplomats over a century ago; in his *55 Days* reference, he thus inadvertently pointed to something interesting.

For, despite the dominant depiction in U.S. media and in academic and policy circles of China and Chinese as xenophobically ethnocentric for the length of their history—a depiction that was whipped into modern hysteria by the Boxers' purposeful attacks on missionaries, foreign-owned property, and any Chinese viewed as foreigner-friendly—and despite the insertion of more recent so-called Chinese anti-Americanism into this supposedly continuous tradition of xenophobia, any specific Chinese "anti-Americanism" has a complex history that was born of and in the violence of the turn of the twentieth century. As connected to events perpetrated by the United States and the European imperialist powers upon China as it is tied to changing interpretations within China of modern Chinese history itself, "anti-Americanism" in China—both its practice and its depiction, its specificity as well as its linkages to larger anti-imperialist political currents—must grapple with this violent past, rather than depend upon a timeless notion of Chinese xenophobic ethnocentricity. I thus take al-Khudairi's remark as an inadvertent referencing of this historical problematic.

At that level of generality, this essay is a meditation on "anti-Americanism" in China, with reference to the century-long history of its various moments, and with a particular focus on the repressed returns in the past decade or so of this past in new guises. The essay is by no means a comprehensive account of the issue but rather an attempt to think about how we might constitute "anti-Americanism in China" as an object of inquiry at all. Indeed, as a general proposition, "anti-Americanism" is often dated from the postwar period (1945) and what is taken as the formal onset of the cold war, although this periodization, for China as for many other places, is shortsighted and incomplete. Representing this parochial version, the right-wing critic Jay Bryant recently stated that "Modern anti-Americanism is a legacy of the Cold War, when skillful communist propaganda energized and directed a hard core of activists who continue to foster the metastasization of distrust and hatred of U.S. motives and policies."[2] As I argue, for all their manifest fascination with and attraction to the United States, Chinese have not had to rely upon propaganda to come to critical conclusions about the United States or about imperialism in general. As frequent targets of direct or indirect American and imperialist violence over the past century, they have rarely fallen under the illusion of America's original state of grace, or its unfailingly "good intentions."[3]

Although the Chinese are said to have harbored a "special relationship" with the United States from the late nineteenth century on, the rhetoric and ideology of this relationship was subjected to severe critique throughout that time. By the same token, in the past decade in China, perspectives on historical and therefore on current Chinese experiences of the United States—or, more broadly, of "Americanism" construed as modernization—have become an arena of heavily contested re-interpretation among intellectuals; these contestations have been animated by and situated within the context of broader rethinkings of modern Chinese history and the future of China in the world. Understanding some of the complexities of these rethinkings requires first locating them within shifting modes of historical periodization; I thus first turn to some general problems associated with the problem of periodizing.

The German philosopher Karl Löwith begins his life history, written in 1940 at Harvard University and titled *My Life in Germany before and after 1933,* with this observation on the relationship among historiography, temporality, and individual consciousness:

> The division of European history into "before" and "after" Christ still dominates the calendar . . . , but no longer the mind. The dictatorships emerging from the World War [i.e., World War I] laid claim to dating the whole of history in a new way, just as the French Revolution had done. And indeed, it cannot be denied that everything is different from the way it was before.[4]

As Löwith subsequently acknowledges, this pervasive sense of a total historical break both accedes to and concedes too much. It accedes too much to an equivalence between individual experience and the abstract temporality of history; it also concedes too much to the abstraction of temporality as a real reflection of the historical. Nevertheless, Löwith implies, it is in explicitly posing the historical problematic of the tension between this simultaneous accession and concession—of the incommensurable gap between abstract temporality, the historical, and individual experience—that perhaps can be found what he elsewhere calls "meaning in history."[5]

As a German intellectual in exile, Löwith had as one of his main goals not only to understand what he saw as the singular rise of German fascism and the descent into world war but to explore, as a matter of historical and deeply personal urgency, the theoretical constitution of a relationship between "historical events" and individual experience in the wake of fascism. Löwith's *Meaning in History,* written in 1949, was thus conceived in the explicit belief that "we find ourselves more or less at the end of the modern rope. It has worn too thin to give hopeful support."[6] Indeed, as he well knew, fascism—the very theological-secular "hope" of history that forms the unspoken critical object of the book's backward historiographical tour from Burkhardt and Marx to the Bible—remained a latent possibility in the postwar world. As he despairingly wrote at that time, "we have learned to wait without hope, for hope would be hope for the wrong thing."[7] The pervasive sense of historical rupture of which Löwith wrote in his wartime autobiography, then, is qualified both by his return to Germany from exile and by his evaluation of the potential break represented by the "postwar" in Ger-

many and of the new theological tendencies being shaped at the inception of the cold war in the secular historiographical revisionisms of the
time.[8]

Löwith's ambivalence about the postwar as a category of history—
or, more broadly, about periodization and individual experience as a
matter of theological/secular concern—has recently arisen in the Japanese and Chinese contexts, albeit in different form and from a different
historical perspective. Indeed, with the end of the cold war—a period
often understood to be roughly synonymous with the postwar—a debate began about periodizing the "postwar" in Japan, the United States,
and China (among many other places). In Japan, the debate soon de-
volved into a right-wing attack on the limitations of the postwar Japanese constitution, imposed upon Japan by the American occupation after
World War II. Only with the lifting of the constitutional restrictions on
remilitarization, it was said, could the postwar in Japan and the cold
war in Asia be considered completed.[9] This right-wing version relied
for its persuasiveness upon a representation of Japan as the national victim of the United States. The end of the postwar in Japan thus came to
signify the completion of the unfolding of a theological abstract temporality leading to the triumphal return to an essential "Japanese-ness." In
the United States, by contrast, the debate on the postwar with reference
to Japan took shape as a liberal reaffirmation of the positive role played
by the United States in consolidating so-called Japanese democracy in
the aftermath of the war. In this liberal rendition, the postwar was understood as the fruition of a timeless American present—those eternally
"good intentions"—that precluded any analysis of politics or history.

Both Japanese right-wing and liberal American versions embraced
a vision that appealed to an essential, frozen, national past existing in
the present outside of history. In the Japanese case, this vision was
founded upon an eternal Japan returning to its suppressed self; in the
American case, it is founded upon an eternal America that continues to
express its good self.[10] In the current moment, when pre- and post–September 11 seems to have restructured historical horizons around the
world (to differing degrees and in various registers), the Japanese right-
wing "anti-American" position and the congratulatory liberal American position seem to have converged: the postwar in Japan is now over,
it is said, because the American occupation of Japan after the war is now
not only touted as an appropriate goal (if not also a model) for postwar Iraqi reconstruction—capitalist democracy and political-economic

subservience to the United States eternalized as destiny—but also because Japan is well on its way to overtly re-entering the global military arena by contributing troops to the Iraqi theater of war and to remilitarization in general.[11] In short, it appears as if the tension between the two positions, at least at national policy levels, has been resolved.[12]

For different albeit not altogether unrelated reasons, in the 1990s in China, a debate about how to properly characterize the post-Mao era emerged in relation to the end of the cold war, or at least, to the fall of the Soviet Union. Soon after the suppression of the 1989 social movement (commonly called the "Tian'anmen Incident/Massacre"), the question was raised in intellectual circles: when did the post-Mao period end? *Did* it end? There was widespread disagreement. While the successes of Deng Xiaoping in the 1980s in reorienting the economy, politics, culture, and perceptions away from three decades of Maoism led some commentators—often now called neoliberals—either implicitly or explicitly to christen the Mao period as tantamount to a nightmarish "pre-Deng" era (thus in effect repudiating the whole socialist moment), the persistence of the Chinese Communist party (CCP) and its selective suppressions of dissent led other commentators—now called liberals—to imply that the post-Mao was a sham (that is, that Deng Xiaoping, in strengthening the rule of the CCP, was continuing the political stranglehold of the Maoist era).

For the neoliberals, the Deng era of economic reform came to be construed as China's true postwar period, in the sense that China in the 1980s had finally—normatively and belatedly—joined the global capitalist mainstream after three decades of socialist aberration. Meanwhile, for the liberals, the despised political strength and endurance of the CCP constrains the more triumphal pronouncements that Maoism and the traumas of modern Chinese history have been overcome. Among liberal democracy activists in China and in exile—the favorite sources on China of most American mainstream media—only with the toppling of the CCP can the post-Mao/post–cold war really begin. For both liberals and neoliberals, postwar and post–cold war are sometimes synonymous and sometimes not. Often conflated with post-Mao, in China, postwar usually connotes a normative U.S.-led capitalist and geopolitical standard of modernization against which modern Chinese history can be measured and understood. In this version, the three decades of socialist economic development and politics in China (1949–1979) are relegated to a nonhistory of lunacy—somehow outside time altogether.

And yet, with China continually imbricated in U.S.-led revanchist cold war–type politics (e.g., with reference to North Korea or as a primary target of American military contingency planning prior to September 2001) the cold war cannot be said to be over in China. Here, China is mired in a double timelessness: stuck in enmity toward the Mao period and yet with the Mao period appearing as an eternally repressed return.

The strategic and historical differences between the debates in China and Japan over the postwar/post–cold war are clear: in the Japanese case, the debate is a symptom and reflection of Japan's post-1945 and ongoing strong national *presence* in the world of capitalist modernization, whereas, in the Chinese case, the debate is essentially posed as a lament about China's prolonged national *absence* from that same world. Yet, I suggest that one way of understanding the significance of debating the postwar at the moment of the supposed end to the cold war is precisely in problematizing, as Karl Löwith attempted for his era, the ways in which an incommensurable relationship between individual experience and abstract historical temporality are mobilized for historical interpretation. Indeed, while this problem is often elided in contemporary Japanese, Chinese, or American evaluations of postwar fealty to a timeless American-defined norm of capitalism and political obeisance, it is precisely the supposed deviation from this norm that leads to the American accusations of "anti-Americanism" leveled at China and Japan. Thus, at a political-philosophical level, it is precisely by posing the historical problem of incommensurability that there exists the basis for recognizing the particularities of a critique of "Americanism" in much of the world today, even while the U.S. invocation of "anti-Americanism" against all who oppose U.S. government policies erases this problem by drawing upon a profoundly anti-historical and anti-political notion of an original state of American grace.

Long before the cold war began and in the midst of the woefully misnamed Spanish-American War at the turn of the twentieth century, Chinese intellectuals, attempting to cope with the precariousness of the Chinese political, social, economic, and cultural situation, were just beginning to see the world as a structured whole.[13] For many of them, the march of the United States across the Pacific—via Cuba, Puerto Rico, Hawaii, and Guam to the Philippines—was a sure sign of a vast shift in global temporal, spatial, and historical dynamics. As in Latin America, albeit rather less totalistically in China, it is in this shift—particularly reflected for the Chinese in the betrayal by the United States of the Philippine revolution against Spain—that one can pinpoint the beginnings in China of an articulated skepticism about the United States in particular, a skepticism that happened to arise in tandem with a recognition of the dynamics of imperialism in general. That is, this skepticism was based upon an incipient grasp of an abstract synchronic temporality operating at a global scale that linked all objects of U.S. desire to a specific experience of this particular unsettled moment in China. Yet, unlike in Latin American countries, where 1898 could mark, in Greg Grandin's words, the beginning of a distinctive "arc" of popular and normative opposition to the United States,[14] in the early twentieth century in China, this was an incipient possibility at best.

For, China had not yet consolidated a nation-state polity or a stable conceptualization of China's place in the modern world. Chinese intellectuals were thus unable to lay claim to a strong articulation of a "pre-" and "post-" historical consciousness that could mark a definitive rupture with the past: too many dispiriting events, both domestically and internationally, vied for attention in those years of extreme dissolution, even as too many historical markers of internal and global disruption proliferated for such apparent ruptural breaks to gain the status of historical periodization and consciousness-altering historicity.[15] Certainly, in various realms and at various times, major movements and events became historically and individually iconic, the best-known among them being the Boxer Rebellion, the fall of the Qing dynasty, and the cultural and national anti-imperialist May Fourth Movement (1919). In fact, however, it was only by Mao Zedong's time, in the 1950s, and then by Deng Xiaoping's, in the 1980s, that a strong "pre-" and "post-" consciousness had become absolutely integral to the figuration of an individual (and national) experience of historicity and historical temporality.

In the Mao era (1949–1976), official history was marked as pre- and postliberation [*jiefang qian/jiefang hou*], and opposition to the United States consolidated around U.S. economic, military, and political support for Chiang Kai-shek's Nationalist party (Guomindang); this opposition came to be articulated in terms of anti-American imperialism—part of anti-imperialism, *tout court*—often followed by the phrase "and its running dogs" (indicating Taiwan, Japan, and South Korea).[16] During this revolutionary period—actually starting during the Chinese civil war in the late 1940s and reaching two distinct apogees during the

Korean and Vietnam wars—the United States, along with all reactionary and counterrevolutionary forces, was designated a paper tiger: that is, to be taken seriously but not unduly feared.[17] (By contrast, as evidenced by the general tenor of the early 1950s and the devastation of the field of China scholars achieved by the McCarthyite "who-lost-China" witch hunts, China's rhetoric was taken seriously *and* unduly feared in the United States.)

In the Deng Xiaoping era (1979 onward), much of this changed. History in China came to be strongly marked by the language of pre- and postreform—or, Mao and post-Mao. Indeed, the previously ubiquitous term "liberation" (*jiefang*) came into increasingly cynical or merely official rhetorical use. Usually indicating the normalization of society in the wake of the Cultural Revolution (1966–1976), post-Mao also came to connote China's opening to the world and, most centrally, the normalization of diplomatic, economic, and other relations with the United States. By the mid-1990s, in this idiom of normalization and normativity, there was a complete repudiation of Maoism and its claims to the "liberation" of China, which, along with the collapse of the Soviet Union, led in many quarters to a wholesale rejection of socialism as a systemic alternative to capitalism. At this point, what Serge Halimi has called "Americanophiles" in post-1968 France made an appearance in China, under many of the same guises that they used in France: anti-revolutionary and with primary concern for personal ethical and economic matters, rather than political ones.[18]

With these developments, the debates over when the post-Mao/postwar began and ended simultaneously took the form of debates over what was deemed a necessary depoliticization of China's past and future course; in this process (which was really a repoliticization, albeit in a different guise), the problem of the *divergence* between individual experience and an abstract notion of the historical (whether utopian, revolutionary, or otherwise construed) became a central and polarizing issue. That is, where, previously, the individual was understood to converge and coincide exactly with the national and the abstract historical—for example, general liberation was synonymous with individual liberation—now the relationship was discredited, if not altogether denied. With the assertion of the absolute divergence between individual and abstract historicities—*not*, as with Löwith, the posing of this issue as an historical problematic with political consequences (e.g., the return or not of fascism)—debates over China's past, present, and future came to be framed in almost mutually exclusive terms: either in the abstract terms of "modernity" (revolutionary, socialist, capitalist, global, whatever) *or* in terms of the individual experience of repression (during the Mao period) and subsequent redemption (in the Deng period). This was no mere retreat from Marxist class analysis, although it was that; rather, this shift represented a return to a suppressed and repressed liberal perspective on the problem of the historical.

The mutual exclusivity of the abstract and experiential perspectives is most readily apparent in the explosion of Cultural Revolution memoirs from the late 1980s and 1990s that focus on the repression during that era of intellectuals, many of whom have now become successful public figures either in China or abroad. For them, individual experience—emblematically configured as the experience of intellectuals that stands in for national experience—is everything, and the problem of incommensurability is neither posed nor acknowledged. It is also apparent in the ongoing spate of publications of such right-wing, explicitly state-centered nationalistic books as *China Can Say No* (*Zhongguo keyi shuo bu*) or the more recent *Unlimited War.*[19] In those books, national experience—reductively understood as the strengthening of the state in the current geopolitical and economic climate—is all that counts. However different these two genres are, they nevertheless both privilege the category of experience in an ostensibly apolitical, ahistorical, and a priori fashion.

Meanwhile, those who engaged the debates in the 1990s by arguing most consistently in the critical terms of modernity, a theoretical appeal to abstract temporality, emerged as a small group of intellectuals, many of whom came to be lumped together under the label "the New Left." Most had individually experienced the Cultural Revolution and Maoism, but most also were convinced that experience had to be problematized more broadly. The New Left label was affixed by self-identified liberals and neoliberals to their intellectual opponents and was intended both to stigmatize these intellectuals with the discredited taint of leftism leftover from the Mao era—known as a period of ultra-leftism—and, at the same time, to differentiate the "new" leftists from the remnant elder generation of "old" leftists, who are now, in any case, most often called "conservatives" (that is, anti-reformist, old-style Maoists, whose specter continues to haunt the Chinese body politic).

It is here that a new "anti-Americanism"—asserted by one faction of Chinese intellectuals against another—inserts itself in the interstices of the mutually antagonistic positions on the historical primacy of experience or abstract historicity that itself is part of the debate over China's past and future *and* over fealty to presumed global norms (defined by the United States). These intra-Chinese anti-Americanism charges proceed much in the spirit of Paul Hollander's definition of anti-Americanism for the United States. Hollander names American anti-Americanism as an infantile disorder emanating from the irresponsible 1960s that led to the widespread estrangement of American intellectuals. In this vein, Chinese liberals and neoliberals accused China's "new leftists" of "anti-Americanism" for the latter's urgent critiques of China's 1990s version of primitive capital accumulation and disastrous social stratification. That is, because of an explicitly *politicized* critique of capitalism and modernity, and because they refused to admit to the "fact" of the primacy of experience in historical interpretation, "new leftists" came to be labeled "anti-Americans." Thus, again much like Hollander's jeremiad against critical intellectuals in the United States (Hollander's book was positively reviewed in the *People's Daily* in 1996), China's "new leftists" are accused by liberals and neoliberals alike of anti-Americanism through a conflation of three things: first, their critical attitude toward capitalism generally; second, their purported attachment to 1960s radicalism, evidenced by the foreign critical theorists they read and introduced to China (such as Fredric Jameson and Michel Foucault); and, third, their critical and politicized stance vis-à-vis the systematization of economic inequality and exploding social inequity in China during the 1980s and 1990s.

As such, in Chinese intellectual circles most recently, anti-Americanism refers to the right-wing nationalist form (often, in any case, dismissed by professional intellectuals as craven distortion for the ignorant masses); yet, it also most insistently came to connote any critical attitude toward the modernizationism of the Dengist reforms, understood as the crucial aspect of the post-Mao period. This charge of anti-Americanism was further buttressed by the observation that many "new leftists" had thriving crossover careers in the United States and/or Europe. This fact dovetailed with Hollander's charge that intellectual estrangement was a hallmark of post-1960s American "anti-Americans," as this supposed estrangement was claimed to be the precise sine qua non for Chinese intellectual success in the United States. That is, those Chinese who did not conform to the purported "anti-American" bias of U.S. academia could not possibly have supporters

among anti-American American intellectuals who supposedly dominate the academy.[20] Hollander's view, more general media and government pronouncements in the United States, and liberal and neoliberal
Chinese sentiment alike, then, all conspire to construe any overtly critical and politicized attitude toward the past, the present, or the future
as "anti-American."

In the several weeks preceding the Iraq War, this accusation of
"anti-Americanism" against critical Chinese intellectuals erupted anew
and reached some sort of absurd apotheosis, with the signing by many
"new leftists" and other concerned Chinese of an anti-war petition intended to contribute to the global anti-war movement. (Barred from
public demonstrations of anti-war sentiment, despite their support for
China's Security Council opposition to U.S. policy, Chinese critical of
the impending war decided that a petition was the best way to signal
support for the February 15 "World against the War" global movement.) Neoliberals in China mostly toed a prowar line, presumably in
hopes of reaping the economic benefits of cooperation with the United
States, even if that put them in opposition to the Chinese government's
official position. Someone of the neoliberal camp apparently forged a
number of signatures on the anti-war petition and then, with these signatures as evidence, proceeded to lambast, over the Internet, Chinese
"leftist" intellectuals for their knee-jerk anti-American slavishness and
for their supposed exaggeration of Chinese resistance to the proposed
American war. This cynical move was followed by Internet battles that
were astonishing in their vituperation, not least for their insistent conflation of a critique of would-be American hegemony and U.S. duplicity with a blanket "anti-Americanism."[21]

Naturally, this type of complicated intra-Chinese episode is not on
display in the U.S. media. Indeed, such an analysis would indicate a
complexity to the unitarily understood "Chinese mind"—ethnocentri-
cally and xenophobically bound even while government manipulated—that might confuse American newspaper readers about the true
character of Chinese communism and its apparently docile, sheeplike
people. Rather, the U.S. media are generally happier to wallow in the
caricature of Chinese "anti-American nationalism," reported as gov-
ernment-induced and essentially contradictory (they eat McDonald's/drink Coke/wear blue jeans but don't like us, the mantra goes.)
The U.S. media version of Chinese "anti-American nationalism" was

particularly on display in two now remote but recent episodes of social disturbance in China: the outraged reactions to the bombing of the Chinese embassy in Kosovo and the impassioned response of many Chinese to the death of their fighter-jet pilot in his confrontation with the American spy plane near Hainan Island. There were large urban protests in the wake of both incidents.

In the embassy bombing case, Chinese "Americanophile" liberals and neoliberals, accustomed to blindly glorifying American superiority as an appropriate model of economic and military, if not political, development, were caught a little offguard: they simply could not believe that the bombing was a mistake. In the spy plane case, most Chinese insisted that Americans were willfully intervening in China-Taiwan relations, construed by Chinese as a domestic issue and by Americans, despite all rhetoric to the contrary, as an international one. Thus, these two popular assertions of Chinese outrage against the United States were only ambivalently embraced in ethos even while also embarrassedly disavowed by Chinese liberals and neoliberals: embraced because there had been a clear violation of international norms, disavowed because of the uncontrolled explosion of the purportedly basest instincts of an ignorant Chinese populace, which raised the specter of "mob rule" that has haunted the dreams of this decidedly unpopulist group. Whatever the complexity of Chinese motivations for the demonstrations against the United States, these explosions of anger were instantly seized upon by the U.S. media as reminders of the essentially anti-American antagonism of that unitarily understood, infinitely manipulable "Chinese Communist" mind.

While we might be skeptical about Löwith's insistence that "meaning in history" may somehow be found, his caution about the insistent contradiction between the abstraction of historical temporality and an experiential notion of historicity continues to require a complex negotiation. This is particularly true in these perilous times when "post–September 11" is used in the United States, and post-Mao/pre-Deng is being used in China, to suppress all previous histories in the name of a theologically antagonistic simplicity that is often based upon the primacy of experience as an interpretive trope. In China, this theology is most often construed by neoliberals as an insistence on "joining tracks with the world" (*he shijie jiegui*) at whatever price to the Chinese or any other people. In explicit attacks on any who might critique this view, the ostensible secularism of experience is reconnected to an abstract temporality to coercively reinforce a normative U.S.-defined theology of capitalist modernizationist good.

Friedrich Nietzsche warned in *Human, All Too Human*, that "many a person fails as an original thinker simply because his memory is too good."[22] This essay could be construed as an argument against memory; however, the point is that it may be too long to wait for critical memories to fade for us to insist on historical complexity and a certain amount of clarity. For, anti-Americanism as defined and reified both inside and outside China cannot be allowed to appear as a form of an eternal depoliticized present whose repression from a politicized past is always ready for return. For, the erasure of politics thereby achieved merely contributes to what Rey Chow has perceptively called and explored, in a different context, the "fascist longings in our midst."[23]

NOTES

I would like to thank Kristin Ross and Andrew Ross for organizing the conference for which a version of this chapter was first prepared and Harry Harootunian for asking me to participate in that conference. As usual, I am also very grateful to Marilyn Young for her careful reading, critique, and editing. The essay was initially written in February 2003, on the eve of the U.S. invasion of Iraq. Much of a dispiriting nature has happened since then, and my revisions, undertaken in late August and early September 2003, attempt to account at least partially for more recent events.

1. This account comes from a report titled "Standoff between Iraq's ex-envoy to Beijing and staff ends peacefully," dated 4 August 2003, from www.channelnewsasia.com (a Singapore-based site). Accessed on August 29, 2003.

2. This remark is in Bryant's review of Max Boot's book, *Savage Wars of Peace*. See http://www.townhall.com/columnists/GuestColumns/Bryant20030829.shtml. Site accessed on August 29, 2003.

3. "Good intentions" was most recently argued by Michael Ignatieff, "Why Are We in Iraq? (and Liberia? and Afghanistan?)," *New York Times Magazine*, September 7, 2003.

4. Karl Löwith, *My Life in Germany before and after 1933*, trans. Elizabeth King (Urbana and Chicago: University of Illinois Press, 1994), p. xix.

5. Karl Löwith, *Meaning in History* (Chicago: University of Chicago Press, 1949).

6. Ibid., p. 3.

7. Ibid.

8. For a discussion of these incipient tendencies, albeit in different terms, see Wolfgang Schivelbusch, *In a Cold Crater: Cultural and Intellectual Life in Berlin, 1945–1948* (Berkeley: University of California Press, 1998).

9. With the recent decision to send Japanese troops to Iraq (July 2003), this final barrier has presumably been breached.

10. While it is true that this dynamic—American "good intentions"/Japanese resurrection of self—in a general sense is not limited to U.S./Japan relations, nevertheless, this has specific resonances in Asia, where the choice between the United States and Japan as models for development and politics has been repeatedly posed. The resolution, therefore, that erases the Japanese historical role in Asia is particularly telling within the context of broader historical erasures on a global scale.

11. Although, in actuality, Japan was never really absent from the global military arena.

12. For some indicative essays on the debates, see Andrew Gordon, ed., *Post-War Japan as History* (Berkeley: University of California Press, 1994). Clearly, the rise of the North Korean nuclear issue, the growing strength of China, and "terrorism" in the Philippines and Indonesia has given even more life to arguments about Japan's total remilitarization.

13. For an in-depth argument on this period, see Rebecca E. Karl, *Staging the World: Chinese Nationalism at the Turn of the Twentieth Century* (Durham: Duke University Press, 2002). The account that follows is derived from this book.

14. See Greg Grandin, "The Narcissism of Violent Differences," in this volume.

15. We could mention the Chinese defeat in the first Sino-Japanese War (1894–1895); the 1898 reform movement; the Boxer Rebellion; the abolition of the civil service exams; the formation of the Revolutionary Alliance; the monarchical constitutional movement; the rights-recovery movement; the fall of the Qing dynasty; and so on.

16. In recent translations of Mao Zedong's speeches, talks, and so on, the phrase "running dogs" has most often been changed to "lackeys," presumably because the latter is deemed less offensive than the canine reference. For example, see the translations included in the compendium Mao Zedong *On Diplomacy* (Beijing: Foreign Languages Press, 1998).

17. In a talk with Harry Pollitt, chairman of the British Communist party, in April 1955, Mao Zedong stated that the United States is an "iron tiger" at first, but its inner core, or essence, is a "paper tiger." That is, "it has the form of an iron tiger but the substance of a paper tiger." See Mao Zedong, "The United States, Though Frightful, Is Not So Frightful," *On Diplomacy* (Beijing: Foreign Languages Press, 1998): 158–159.

18. See Kristin Ross, "The French Declaration of Independence," in this volume.

19. *China Can Say No* was published in the mid-1990s and posed itself as an awakening from an "American dream" (*Meiguo meng*). It was essentially a declaration that China could and would chart its own path in the world, no matter what the United States's response to that path would be; at the same time, it was a rejection of the spirit of the 1989 student movement, which was more cosmopolitan than, if not as worldly as, the book. *Unlimited War* (*Wuxiande zhanzheng*), also published in the late 1990s, was a call to strengthen the Chinese military in not only basic technological but also tactical/strategic terms. It became a China-bashing cause célèbre for the American right.

20. This supposedly obligatory "anti-Americanism" is of course implicitly or explicitly contrasted to that of the post-1989 exiled "democracy activists," many of whom became leading "Americanophiles" and contributors to "China-bashing" in the United States in the 1990s, through their affiliations with political science departments (with or without specific links to the U.S. government), think tanks, and policy circles. Never for a moment seriously critical of the United States, these Chinese intellectuals, as victimized "native informants," have been crucial in strengthening "anti-China" perceptions in the United States.

21. It was possible to read a summary of the "debates" and news reports about them in the online version of *Nanfang zhoubao* [Southern Weekend Weekly]; the website that provided this summary, however, seems to have been dismantled and/or disabled. At the very least, at my last attempt to access (June 2003), I was unable to find it again. Certainly, it would be possible to consult a print archive on the February–March brouhaha over this issue.

22. Friedrich Nietzche, *Human, All Too Human: A Book for Free Spirits*, trans. R. J. Hollingdale (Cambridge: Cambridge University Press, 1986).

23. Rey Chow, *Ethics after Idealism: Theory-Culture-Ethnicity-Readings* (Bloomington: Indiana University Press, 1998).

14

"We Threaten the World"

U.S. Foreign Policy through an Asian Lens

Moss Roberts

AMID THE DIN OF SELF-CONGRATULATION over the dissolution of the Soviet Union, the occasional voices of quieter caution went unheard. In an article called "Why We Will Soon Miss the Cold War," the University of Chicago professor of political science John J. Mearsheimer wrote, "We may, however, wake up one day lamenting the loss of the order that the Cold War gave to the anarchy of international relations."[1] Mearsheimer's focus was limited to the structuring effect of the Soviet *threat* on the West (he generally ignores the third world). Others who have studied the cold war saw "mutual deterrence," an American threat equivalent to or even greater than the Soviet threat, resulting in a military balance of power that set certain limits on global conflict. A smaller subset of scholars, mostly studying the third or colonial world, rejected the rigid dualism of cold war ideology; they saw a different game: aggressive U.S.-European neocolonialism, for which the cold war was but a rhetorical device to transform third world or colonial issues into communist ones. "In 1958, W. E. B. Du Bois proclaimed the dubious distinction conferred by our military and industrial ascendancy, 'No nation threatens us. We threaten the world.'"[2] Reversing the formula, Du Bois transformed the communist question into a colonial one. Now, more than a decade later, marginalized prophecies such as Mearsheimer's acquire new salience, for the self-acclaimed American victory in the cold war has brought no peace but a widening gyre of threats and wars.

From the Du Bois point of view, the perspective of the conscious colonial subject, the sequel to cold war neocolonialism is globalization, a euphemism for narrow corporate interests promoted under regimes of unequal and coercive trade enforced by the IMF, the World Bank, the

Department of Commerce, and the Pentagon. A sampler of actually existing trade relations reveals the situation: the Department of Commerce imposes tariffs on South Korean semiconductors that threaten to cause bankruptcies and liquidations of South Korean firms, "a process that many foreign analysts think would be healthy for the semi-conductor industry and the Korean economy but that Korean officials fear would precipitate more business failures."[3] An op-ed piece reveals the devastating effect of U.S. protection of domestic cotton production on African cotton farmers.[4] Protection for American honey has already ruined the Argentine industry (which had developed production under an AID grant). Chile and Poland are induced to squander billions on unneeded American military equipment. Meanwhile, inhumane overcharging for medications, ruinous nontariff barriers to first-world markets, and massive subsidies to first-world agriculture inflict grave economic damage on vulnerable populations.[5]

Then there are the Chinese Communists and their precariously thriving new order of state-guided capitalism, under a party government still strong enough to compel fair trade and to control China's currency. Through more than a century of oppression and revolution, the Chinese have been commuting to hell and back. In the process, they have managed *through building state power* to overcome much of their colonial past, no thanks to the Americans, who during the cold war conducted embargoes and sabotage against them. Able to draw lines, touchy when pushed, determined to control their own economy and their own politics, the Chinese leaders have to be handled with care. They have their memories. At the same time, in the post–cold war world, Chinese leaders must negotiate a tricky path. While some American officials and business leaders are satisfied with the evolution of China into trading partner, investment environment, and possibly even regional security asset (parallel to the role Japan played for Britain and the United States during the first three decades of the twentieth century), others seek a replacement for the Soviet "enemy." This faction of militarist politicos and their pundits, sometimes called the "blue team," try to cast China in the vacant role of official enemy and seek to mobilize for war. The Chinese, however, seem unwilling to oblige, arguing against any move to revive cold war conflict.

This war faction's policy push reached a high point when a U.S. spy plane was unlawfully sent to probe Chinese airspace in April 2001; the policy continued to gather force until September 11, 2001. After the destruction of the World Trade Center by Saudi elements that U.S. officials had recklessly recruited as allies against Russia, U.S. policy makers reluctantly moved their anti-China project to a back burner and lowered the light. The "dove" faction (or "red team"—Zbigniew Brzezinski, Henry Kissinger, and others) was vindicated by the contingencies of history, but this faction also gains negotiating traction from the belligerence of the "hawks" and so gives only limited public opposition to them. The Chinese, for their part, try to dodge confrontations engineered by the United States and have moved tactically and tactfully after September 11 to seize the opportunity for a peaceful interval in U.S.-China relations. At the same time, the Chinese, like the Americans, exploit the so-called war on terrorism to pursue their state interests and control popular aspirations.

The sphere of Chinese ambition is regional, however, not global. The Chinese oppose U.S. unilateralism and advocate regional organization and a multipolar global order. They emphasize the authority of the United Nations and strive for good relations with all China's neighbors, hoping to thwart U.S. efforts to re-encircle China militarily. Inside the United States, subsidized rumors of Chinese aggressiveness circulate, but they are not widely believed even inside our borders. The Chinese remain in defensive mode.

Taiwan is at the heart of Chinese anxiety. A *Wall Street Journal* article describes Pentagon officials and their corporate cronies "pushing" the Taiwanese to buy a new Patriot missile system, though the Taiwanese are balking at the expense (and perhaps the politics, too; the article did not say).[6] Here is one last field of U.S.-Russian rivalry, the China arms race, with Moscow selling to the Chinese and Washington to the Taiwanese.[7] In our discourse about China, it is an article of faith that China threatens Taiwan and not the other way around. Few Asians would agree. Moreover, among Taiwan's political and business leaders, there is a growing preference for peaceful integration with China and increasing resentment at the threat of being dragged into a war arranged by the United States. The once robust Taiwan war constituency has shrunk since Lee Teng-hui, a favorite of the U.S. war faction, lost the Taiwan presidential election of 2000, and mutual economic interests that bind China and Taiwan surged in profitability. What if blood proves thicker than water? Now the U.S. war faction, to the dismay of the South Koreans, has shifted strategy and brought back North Korea as the leading pretext for raising tensions and purchases of U.S.

weapons in the area. Whether China can defuse the Korean crisis too remains to be seen. The fact that China hosts large first-world holdings in and of itself serves as a partial deterrent against the U.S. penchant for using force. One suspects that Mao initially opened the door to Western investment with this measure of military insurance in the back of his mind.

Apart from arming Taiwan, to a significant degree the Yugoslav and Iraq wars and the new military bases in Central Asia are also intended to threaten the Chinese. While the Chinese prefer to ignore these probes and thrusts, one occasionally finds a sharp response. One English-language Chinese journal published a lengthy critical analysis placing hegemony before terrorism as a cause of violence around the world. This article is more representative of opinion inside China than English-language sources might suggest. The author, Wang Yusheng, writes, "The [U.S.] preemptive theory reminded people of the Brezhnev Doctrine in the Soviet period, and the new interventionism of the Clinton administration, which initiated the theory of limited sovereignty. But the preemptive theory goes further, directly challenging the basic principles of the U.N. charter and international law."[8] With the Brezhnev Doctrine, the Soviet Union arrogated to itself the right to intervene anywhere in its sphere of influence to defend the Soviet system. In addition, the *Beijing Review* article uses terms like "hegemony," "spheres of influence," and "imperialism" to point up the nineteenth-century backwardness of the new world order. The article concludes that the modern world is too diverse to be controlled in this way: "The United States is finding that it is not so easy to control the world all by itself. Not all small countries will listen to it, neither will the major powers . . . and the U.N. will not allow itself to be transformed into the United States."

In speaking here for national sovereignty and for collective security, a global as much as a national interest, the Chinese are taking an international leadership posture that confounds and infuriates those U.S. policy officials and their spokesmen who assume that they, and they alone, can speak for more than their own nationalism. On the American side, this reaction bespeaks a kind of classic paranoia, mirroring the amateur diagnosis of Chinese leaders that American journalists and scholars often indulge in. In addition to testing the waters as world leaders, the Chinese are also reflecting the lived historical experience of most Asians during the past half-century. For them, the throwaway phrases of U.S. foreign policy mantras—"freedom," "democracy," "human rights," "security," "stability," "rule of law"—are promises not meant at best and spurious justifications of war and subversion at worst. A number of U.S. policy makers and their spokesmen who advocate "democracy" for China mean by that little more than the formation of a rival party through which they can orchestrate a system of bribery and political pressure, as has been done in Japan, Italy, and other countries. (Policy makers have shown no interest in democratizing governments already conditioned to follow Washington's orders; sincere advocates of political ideals are ignored unless momentarily useful.)

As for Du Bois, so for most Asians the cold war names an American policy and not an objective general conflict, a policy bereft of substantive ideals and devoted to the continuation of the colonial project of recent centuries. Hard, harsh facts support this view. The ashes of Hiroshima and Nagasaki had not cooled when Truman and his secretary of state, James Byrnes, restarted World War II in Asia by intervening in China's civil war, by supporting French aggression in Indochina with arms and money, and by re-imposing the Japanese colonial structure in South Korea. Like anti-terrorism today, in postwar Asia anti-communism justified all evils of recolonization. This uncold war meant live battle and high civilian death tolls. In China, Korea, Indonesia, Vietnam, Laos, and Cambodia, millions of noncombatants were slaughtered in American or American-instigated wars against peoples barely emerging from the stranglehold of European-Japanese colonialism. In the 1930s, American corporations supplied the Japanese war machine in Asia; in the 1950s and 1960s, Japanese corporations supplied the U.S. war machine in Asia. The merchant and the samurai had exchanged their classic roles; the victims stayed the same.

One wonders how far the so-called Japanese miracle would have gone without the billions in war contracts showered on Japanese companies during the Korean War. And during the Vietnam War, South Korean businessmen and officials joined the Japanese in reaping major benefits from war contracts; they also could do what the Japanese could not: supply the Americans with 300,000 mercenaries. (A few years ago, the South Koreans sent a delegation to Hanoi to apologize for their wartime crimes, but the Vietnamese authorities displayed little interest in such formalities, saying in effect that those who feel the need to apologize were welcome to do so. Free of guilt, the Vietnamese are more interested in rebuilding their country than in raking up the past.)

It goes without saying that these events on the far side of the world, compared to postwar European events, have figured only faintly in American public memory. In the interest of preserving a relatively uncomplicated (and narcissistic) story line for the second half of the twentieth century, the prevailing pattern in American intellectual and cultural life was to downplay the actual existing history of the diverse nations of Asia and wherever possible to omit or gloss over the American role. There are some in the Asian field who cooperate with this agenda, and there are others who do not, who try to place modern Asian history in a genuinely objective and comprehensive discourse. However, major public venues of discourse are not often open to the latter. In an effort to restore some of the markers of this neglected record, the remainder of this essay reviews some of the major moments of Asian history over the past fifty years and reflects on the pattern that they form.

BEFORE AND AFTER WORLD WAR II IN ASIA

For more than a decade before their "infamous" Pearl Harbor raid, which ignited the war with the United States in the Pacific, the Japanese had been at war with China. That "unknown" and "forgotten" war is called the China War (1931–1941). In September 1931, the Japanese Imperial Army attacked Manchuria and the following year set up its puppet state, Manchukuo. Britain, Japan's ally since 1902, was then the leading colonial power in East Asia; American capital had a junior but growing role. Neither Britain nor the United States meaningfully opposed the Japanese war in China, for they expected the Japanese to protect their principal investments and keep the Chinese people under control. By 1940, however, the Anglo-U.S. détente with Japan was breaking down over the issue of dominance in China, the grand prize, and the U.S. rulers were angling to replace both Britain and Japan as the chief power in Asia. In the course of World War II, Japan's bid for dominance in Asia failed, and British power faded. The tsunami of the Chinese revolution was low on the horizon. Accordingly, in the postwar, the Americans assumed they would rule the roost in China and in Asia.

By 1944, however, China's three decades of civil war had deeply divided the nation, and the Americans had to take sides. Thoughtful American China specialists like John Service (a political officer serving there under General Stilwell), cautioned against allying with Chiang

Kai-shek's anti-communist Nationalist party and advocated cooperation with the Communists as the best way to fight Japan in China and
build a postwar peace. Roosevelt rejected this advice and recalled Stilwell. Both men, Stilwell and Service, were ordered to keep quiet. In the
summer of 1945, as the war was reaching its end, the new president,
Harry Truman, was determined to ensure U.S. dominance in China. He
thought military support of Chiang's party was the way to do it. The
United States also tried (and failed) to indict John Service, the first of the
government's many transparently political gestures in judicial disguise.

In China, the promoter of U.S. interests (and his own) was Chiang
(Jiang) Kai-shek. Truman continued to give material support to Chiang
and refused to negotiate with the Communists on a mutual basis. This
was a foolish and shortsighted choice on Truman's part, one of his
many ill-advised decisions. Another Asian specialist, Owen Lattimore,
who had worked as an adviser to Chiang but retained his perspective
and judgment, tried to convince Truman to pursue a more sensible policy. Truman gave Lattimore a three-minute audience before showing
him the door. U.S. military and financial support for Chiang prolonged
the civil war in China for years, causing great suffering and loss of life
and property and leaving a legacy of ill will. At the time, General Alfred
Wedemeyer, who late in 1944 had succeeded the recalled Stilwell as
commander of American forces in China, warned the U.S. government
about the perils of this policy. "[Wedemeyer] reiterated to Chief of Staff
General Eisenhower that the U.S. had to decide whether it was going to
follow its stated course of avoiding involvement in China's 'fratricidal
warfare,' or reverse course and ignore public opinion and the principle
of self-determination by providing sufficient air, naval, and ground
forces to unify China and Manchuria under Jiang."[9]

Ignoring Wedemeyer's practical caution, Truman chose to back
Chiang and prolong the civil war in China another four years, from
1945 to 1949. But the tsunami of revolution swept all before it. Chiang
fled in disgrace to Taiwan. Truman's duplicities had fooled some Americans but few Chinese. In Chiang he had backed the wrong horse, and
he and his advisers could hardly contain their fury. The failed bid to
take over Japanese and British positions in China for U.S. corporate interests "lost" not only China but, more important, an opportunity to exercise leadership in shaping a general peace in East Asia, a role in which
he could have won the respect and gratitude of millions of Americans
and Asians and made the Korean War unnecessary.

The U.S. wars in Asia are best (if rarely) understood as an effort to reverse the unpleasant surprise outcome of World War II in the Pacific, namely the loss of a major part of the spoils. The march of folly toward reversing history's unsympathetic verdict led to Korea and Vietnam as surrogate wars against China. Understandably nationalistic, American scholarship generally assumes that there was no way to avoid the conflict with China, but one wonders. In the spring of 1949, months before the new Chinese government was established, the new leadership suggested a willingness to negotiate a new relationship with the American leaders. As the Communist party leader Mao Zedong wrote, "[The Chinese government] proclaims to the governments of all other countries that this Government is the sole legal government representing all the people of the People's Republic of China. This Government is prepared to establish diplomatic relations with any foreign government which is willing to observe the principles of equality, mutual benefit and mutual respect of territorial integrity and sovereignty."[10] Since this meant in practice abandoning their special relationship with Chiang Kai-shek, the Americans declined to explore the possibilities of a new deal with China.[11] There was great fluidity in the China scene and plenty of room for innovative policy making in the crucial months between the establishment of the new Chinese government (October 1949) and the start of the Korean War (June 1950). A positive response to Mao's offer was not out of the question. But U.S. Secretary of State Dean Acheson, the formulator of foreign policy at the time, showed no interest in negotiating. Refusal to recognize the new government (a virtual declaration of war) was his and Truman's banal choice.

Much as George W. Bush today portrays himself as a friend of the Iraqi people, Acheson portrayed himself as a friend of the Chinese people. Mao Zedong made the following assessment of U.S. Secretary of State Dean Acheson's theory that U.S. government policy paralleled the interests of the Chinese people: "To bore into China by all possible means and turn China into an American colony—this is the basic policy of the United States. Helping Chiang Kai-shek with six billion American dollars in the last few years to butcher several million Chinese people—this is the so-called no conflict but parallelism between American interests and the interests of the people of China."[12] Backed by a mass movement with seasoned anti-colonial politics, China's leaders for the next few generations would define independently their nation's own path. They might have preferred a peaceful and productive relationship with the United States, but they set strict limits to the terms they would accept for it.

VIETNAM AFTER HIROSHIMA

In the fall of 1945, in tandem with their support for Chiang, U.S. decision makers gave aid and comfort to the French military in retaking their Indo-China colonies. (France had been a collaborator in the Third Reich, and its colonials were mostly Fascist.) That was the beginning of the postwar French War in Vietnam, which lasted until the spring of 1954 and was continuously underwritten by the U.S. government. There is little public awareness in the United States of how early this support to the French cause came, because it "looks better" to mask colonialism as anti-communism, that is, to frame that support as a response to the Chinese revolution and the Korean War. Direct testimony about this early aid was filmed for a British documentary of the late 1990s, called "Uncle Sam/Uncle Ho." Officers of the Office of Strategic Services (OSS) who had worked with Ho Chi Minh during the war, speaking on camera and with the clarity and bitterness of enlightened hindsight, expressed their anger at Truman's betrayal of Ho to the French. Some said that the United States should have supported Vietnamese independence as the right thing to do, others that the government should have recognized the rescue services that the Vietnamese Communists had performed for U.S. airmen in the war against Japan. To my knowledge, this British film has not been shown in the United States.[13] After the Chinese revolution and during the Korean War, U.S. aid to the French war effort in Vietnam increased markedly and continued after the Korean truce of 1953 (the same year that the CIA overthrew the democratic Mossadegh government of Iran, initiating a new chain of bad karma that led to Saddam Hussein and the current Iraq wars).

THE KOREAN WAR AND CIVILIAN CASUALTIES

In American public memory, the Korean War remains in shadow; the Vietnam War holds the spotlight. The Korean War is often called the "forgotten" or the "unknown" war. The Vietnam War stands out dramatically in both our politics and our culture. Elites like to portray it as a frightful mistake or aberration, but at the middle and lower levels of society it continues to weigh on the American conscience, a moral anxiety that policy makers have called a sickness, the Vietnam syndrome.

The relation of the two wars is rarely examined. Was the Korean War a postlude to World War II, or was it a prelude to the Vietnam War? Was it a war against Communist tyranny, a civil war, or a war of colonial domination? Was it caused pure and simple by Communist aggression or by the synergy of U.S. and North Korean policies? What did American policy contribute to the outbreak of war? And how was the war fought? What care did the vastly superior American forces take to protect innocent noncombatants? Such questions are not easily raised in public venues.[14] But for this last and all-important question, the record is not obscure or ambiguous. It shows wanton disregard for human life on the part of the American decision makers, especially in the second half of the war, when negotiation possibilities were most promising. U.S. aerial bombing was modeled after the fire bombings of Japanese cities and towns in the last year of World War II and culminated in the bombings of the Suiho hydroelectric plant and finally the dykes that sustained Korean agriculture. This demonstration of raw power was directed as much at the Chinese as at the Koreans.[15] American policy thus prolonged the Korean civil war, just as it had prolonged the Chinese civil war and the Vietnamese independence struggle—with harrowing humanitarian consequences.

U.S. Air Force general Curtis LeMay describes the bombing: "We burned down just about every city in North and South Korea both . . . we killed off over a million civilian Koreans and drove several million more from their homes."[16] As Callum MacDonald notes, the U.S. Air Force was using napalm made in Japan, and many a Japanese merchant turned a tidy profit supplying the Americans with everything from napalm to prostitutes. The policies of Truman and Eisenhower served no conceivable American national interest; rather, they worked against the national interest by making any negotiated peace with the new Chinese government impossible. Moreover, because of the war, internal Chinese policy developed in a harsher direction, socially and ideologically. Perhaps this was an unstated goal of the war makers.

The Korean War left unfinished business on all sides. The resistance of the Korean and Chinese people forced a humiliating stalemate on the American war rulers and whetted their appetite for a comeback. However, with catastrophic losses for the Koreans and major American casualties, browbeaten American citizens had begun asking awkward questions of their own. To check domestic concern over the war before it evolved into serious criticism of their Asian policies, the war leaders sought and found a scapegoat—American servicemen. Tying their accusations to the coattails of the McCarthy hysteria, they calumniated as "brainwashed" American POWs who had not in their judgment sufficiently resisted their Korean captors or who had actually had the unthinkable thought that there was a measure of right on the Korean side. Denouncing the servicemen for "character weakness" and failure to resist "enemy indoctrination," grandstanding authorities and experts issued their bold condemnations from positions of comfort and safety.[17]

VIETNAM AND THE PHILIPPINE WAR

The Vietnam War may be viewed as an Indochinese war, since it also involved Laos and Cambodia. All three countries were subjected to severe bombing, and accurate civilian death tolls have never been compiled. There can be no serious discussion of the colonial question unless the death toll is put front and center as a point of reference, both factually and morally. For Vietnam, we hear the number four million bandied about, sometimes two million, but that's for Vietnam alone. And within what time frame? If we split the difference, we have half a holocaust, three millions. Measured by a true time line, the death toll exacted by French colonial forces in the decade 1945–1954 has to be added in, as well as the casualties suffered under the Diem and subsequent U.S. puppet regimes.

In 1995, former Secretary of Defense Robert MacNamara, referring to the Vietnam War, told Americans: "We were wrong, terribly wrong. We owe it to future generations to explain why."[18] His conscience-stricken statement may be applied to the entire course of our conduct in Asia, going as far back as the Philippine War at the beginning of the twentieth century. Today, few remember the prophetic warnings that were issued in opposition to that colonial war. William James, Benjamin Harris, Charles Eliot Norton, and Mark Twain, to name some of the eminent men who opposed the war, prophesied that if the United States went the way of the European imperialists, its own republican institutions would be undermined. For managing an empire entails domestic repression. The more our rulers seek to dominate others, the more they must subjugate the citizenry to pursue their militarist project. This negative view of empire reverses the conventional wisdom of imperialism, namely that wars in the colonial world will objectively transfer the benign and advanced values of the invader country to the benighted or backward invaded country. This might be called the *New York Times* theory of modern colonialism as a secular mission.[19]

One of the leading opponents of the Philippine War, and the theory of spreading democracy through war, was Carl Schurz. Schurz came to America as a refugee from Germany after his participation in the 1848 uprisings there. A park in New York City is named for him. In his American career, he served as a senator, as a diplomat, and as an adviser to government. He opposed the Philippine conquest on the grounds that it would radically alter domestic political institutions. He formulated a law, Schurz's Law, that held that the "United States did not have to acquire new territories in order to achieve its international goals. . . . The most important provision of the Law, however, was the warning that the exercise of tyranny abroad would create tyranny at home."[20] In the event, the Philippines were laid waste and, after brutal slaughters of their people, annexed. A century later, their efforts to break free of American oppression have failed. The initial conquests of the Philippine people and of the Korean people were directly linked, since Japan agreed not to challenge U.S. control of the Philippines in exchange for U.S. acceptance of its domination of Korea. This ugly deal was performed secretly in the summer of 1905 and is known as the Taft-Katsuhara agreement. It paved the way for Japanese annexation of Korea in 1910. In March 1919, inspired by Wilsonian rhetoric about self-determination, a million Koreans marched for national independence. Wilson declared that colonies of victors were exempt from his ideals and turned a blind eye as Japanese police brutalized the protesters.[21] Contemporary Korean memory of that heroic moment remains distinct.

In U.S. public memory, the Philippine war has been even more intently forgotten than the Korean War.[22] Recently, however, problems with the colonizing of Iraq have jogged some memory of that century-old war. A thoughtful article, titled "Déjà Vu," quotes Emilio Aguinaldo, who led the Philippine independence struggle against

Spain.[23] Aguinaldo condemned the United States for its "violent and aggressive seizure [of his land] by a nation which has arrogated to itself the title 'champion of oppressed nations.'" The article also cites the war advocate Senator Albert Beveridge, of Indiana, who said, "Just beyond the Philippines are China's illimitable markets. We will not abandon our opportunity in the Orient. We will not renounce our part in the mission of our race, trustee under God, of the civilization of the world." Then no less than now, those "splendid little wars" in Asia—the Philippines, Japan, Korea, Vietnam, Laos, Cambodia, Indonesia—all lead back to China.

As the tide in the Vietnam War turned against them, the U.S. rulers decided to abandon the policy of proxy war against China and to reverse course. They turned to a policy of normalized commercial, diplomatic, and even military relations with China, a step that could have been taken at any time after the formation of the new Chinese government. The new Sino-American relationship has not brought paradise on earth, but it was a rational choice, one of the few that U.S. rulers have made in the third world. It was a vindication of the wisdom of George Kennan's political philosophy—know the limits of your power and respect them—and a rebuke to the insatiable ambition of Dean Acheson, whose "tomorrow the world" philosophy has been dominant and guides the Bush administration today.

The born-again U.S. policy toward China provoked, in a Vietnam War–weary world, no significant protest even in America; only the Russians were annoyed. The Vietnamese resistance, the Chinese revolution, and Russian aid all played a part in imposing this sensible decision on the Nixon regime, and the world breathed a sigh of relief as the Americans came to their senses, at least on the China question. Far preferable to perpetual war, the new order has benefited many throughout East and Southeast Asia. It is painful to reflect, all the same, on the refusal of the Truman administration to work with the new Chinese government when it had the chance to do so.

CAMBODIA

Finally, one must speak of Cambodia. Residual moral sensitivity among "ordinary" Americans to the Cambodian branch of the Vietnam War may explain why U.S. officials have been eager to set up tribunals to try

Khmer Rouge officials for war crimes. As a leading Cambodia special-ist, Professor Ben Kiernan, observes ironically: "Cambodia was now a lightning rod for afflictions of 'modern conscience.' . . . [William] Shaw-cross wrote that U.S. involvement in supplying the Khmer Rough from 1979 . . . 'will have long and disturbing repercussions on international consciousness.' The repercussions on Cambodia itself are of course quite another matter."[24]

Why the trials? The same officials insist (carrots in hand) that these trials be confined to the period 1975–1979, the period of Khmer Rouge rule under Pol Pot. The Cambodia War has a much longer time line than that. Why would American officials demand so narrow a window? Why should a (partial) accounting of the Vietnam War be displaced onto show trials in Cambodia?

U.S. pressure for putting its own assets on trial—Pol Pot, Saddam Hussein, Slobodan Milosevic, Noriega, to name the more notorious satraps—is an interesting new development in a propaganda effort at distance and denial and contrasts invisibly with the insistence on ex-emption for U.S. war criminals, whose trials would easily occupy the time of the World Court for a long time. As U.S. policies sink further and further into brutal lawlessness, the need for the appearances of vindi-cation increases. Another possible motive for the trials is simply to usurp the moral authority that Vietnam gained when its forces rescued Cambodia from Pol Pot and the Khmer Rouge. Historically, it was the Vietnamese counterinvasion of 1979 that drove Pol Pot from power and enabled Cambodia to achieve its return to normality. The awkward truth is that Washington and Beijing did all they could to thwart this hu-manitarian intervention: both came to Pol Pot's aid and sustained his cause for more than a decade.[25] Thus, the policy of prolonging a civil war was pursued for a fourth time in Asia—China, Korea, Vietnam, Cambodia—over the post–World War II decades.

While the United States put up the money and worked the diplo-matic levers to prevent a peace in Cambodia, the Chinese share of the division of the labor required them to supply arms and lend ideological cover. This enabled U.S. government propaganda to condemn Pol Pot as a "Maoist," even as the U.S. government was energetically promot-ing him. For close to another decade, America and China continued to support and arm Pol Pot and to protect his UN seat. Now the Ameri-cans are anxious to keep their own role out of the picture, so Cambodia war trials managers will be urged to steer clear of the post-1979 period.

Establishment journalists who refer to the war will be urged to observe the same taboo.

It will be equally necessary for any trial proceedings to pass over the pre-1975 period, during which tremendous U.S. bombing between 1969 and 1973 destroyed Cambodia's economy and culture, creating the conditions for Pol Pot's rise in the first place. The misrepresentation of the Cambodia War through war trials may also be intended to help retrieve, if only symbolically, the moral high ground that the U.S. state briefly enjoyed after World War II. Much as Soviet culture was anchored in the events of 1917, in our current cultural discourse, most of our colonial ventures are anchored by analogy to 1944 and 1945 as we revisit in Hollywood films and TV specials the battles, victories, and war-crimes trials of World War II. The Cambodia trials do not address the grief of the grieving. They are designed to produce scapegoats who will bear the crimes of the Khmer Rouge regime and protect the reputations of their backers.

With the conclusion of the Cambodian civil war in the early 1990s, the Indo-China wars have ended. The main story now is the Sino-American détente and the economic growth of China (now the main player in Cambodia). Neither government can admit it, but the Chinese and American people owe the Vietnamese (and the American peace movement) a debt of gratitude for containing U.S. ambitions in East Asia. The benefits to America from "losing" the Vietnam War were detailed in a serial retrospective in the *Wall Street Journal* in 1985, ten years after the war ended. Containment of U.S. power made peace possible then, but the advocates of war remain powerful and now dictate policy in the Middle East; their lust for war in East Asia has not abated, either.[26] To get a sense of the dimensions of China's economic growth (China is often called the world's factory floor), look through the *New York Times* and the *Wall Street Journal* for late August 2003.[27]

It has been said, sometimes affectionately, sometimes critically, that Americans want to be loved. Of course, most people wish for what they do not have, and the recent chorus condemning American leadership must be unpleasant to the ears of any concerned citizen. But, at the elite level, I suggest, Americans crave gratitude, not love. This craving often takes the form of a need to play (or perform) the role of rescuer. Stories of rescuing the innocent or helpless are a staple of our popular culture. These tales may (or may not) contain real heroes, but they also function as gratifying social dreams that disguise the grief and sorrow our rulers' policies have visited on people around the world, the innocent and helpless above all.

Those Chinese, unrescued and unrescuable, unlike the slightly too grateful Japanese, have "made it on their own," "pulled themselves up," American-style, rough and rugged, and thus can confront U.S. rulers and officials as equals on their very own terms, assert international leadership, and so on. At this moment, they may be rescuing the world (i.e., capitalist) economy themselves. (China holds close to $300 billion worth of U.S. government bonds.) This China seems to cause many elite Americans severe cognitive dissonance. For example, our financial pages routinely berate Chinese enterprise managers and state officials for defects in statistics, accounting weaknesses, and even corruption, as if the Enron and Worldcom scandals were irrelevant, as if their readers were unaware of the U.S. corporate crime wave identified by Ralph Nader. There are China scholars who have persuaded themselves that Americans understand China better than the Chinese and know what's better for China than the Chinese. Maybe so. But there is a corollary: the Chinese may understand America better than Americans do. Do we study and heed Chinese views of America as carefully as the Chinese study and heed American views of China?

In an attempt to put China problems back on the objective level, I find myself face-to-face with an old theory—that the fundamental inadequacies of capitalism compel its dependency on the state. Capitalism as a system is beneficial to so few and injurious to so many that it cannot maintain itself without reliance on state power for regulation. Capital utilizes state power in many ways—for infrastructure, from the federal highway system to bank deposit insurance, from the federal courts to the prison systems—and for domestic social equilibrium, from public education to social security and Medicare to trade protectionism. What stands out in the federal budget, however, is the allocation for war. The regimes of coercive international trade are so ruinous to weaker nations that, without nearly half a trillion dollars appropriated annually to maintain military dominance, actually existing trade relations could not long survive. The role of the U.S. military in international trade is to preclude a process of mutual level-field negotiation leading to voluntary agreements among nations. With the gun barrel in clear view at the table, we are still in a world of gunboat diplomacy, the midnineteenth-century high tide of Western war and plunder in Asia when piracy and Christianity joined hands to fight the Opium Wars in China, winning the right to push opium in the great China market. If few Americans think of the problem quite this way, many Chinese, and many Asians and Middle Easterners, do.

Paradoxically, it is an article of extremist U.S. ideology that the state is evil, something to dismantle (in its socially positive, not its militarist, functions). In third-world countries, the World Bank, the IMF, and the Pentagon demand a vulnerable nation, the Mobutu state as opposed to the Maoist state, a state too weak, too divorced from and detested by its own people to resist foreign demands, strong enough only to suppress democracy and the rise of a domestic middle class. This may help explain why today the world's most powerful state, which the world's most powerful economy requires absolutely, promotes an anti-state ideology abroad (and at home) while supporting compliant dictators all round the globe. It's only to humor American liberals that U.S. war leaders even bother to mouth the rhetoric of democracy, rule of law, and human rights. One lethal consequence of state-breaking in the third world has been the rise of extremist militant fundamentalism, which took over many of the positive social services that the United States forced third-world governments to abandon. These cruel state-breaking measures are an IMF specialty. The IMF targets any program conducive to the health and welfare of third-world populations, from milk subsidies to public education, from pollution limitation and energy conservation to affordable housing. The motive is as political as it is economic: not only to squeeze every possible penny out of the poor for corporate profit but also to extinguish any respect the people might have for their governors. Thus disempowered, third-world rulers bend to Washington's demands. In the past few years, populist governments in Venezuela, Brazil, and Argentina have begun to mount serious resistance. Counterpressure from Washington has been intense.

For the Chinese, and perhaps for the three other nations of Confucian Asia (Japan, Korea, and Vietnam), it is precisely the strong state as moral actor, a virtual parent to the people, that is the centerpiece of their concepts of civilization. This may help explain why the Chinese continue to use "modernization" rhetoric for their own national project, while American ideologues have replaced it with "globalization," a term that emphasizes privatization over state power and foreign corporate interests over national development. Is it the moral element in

Chinese state theory—now fully abandoned by U.S. policy makers—that explains repressed American envy of things Chinese?

NOTES

1. *Atlantic Monthly*, August, 1990.

2. John Edgar Wideman, Introduction to *The Souls of Black Folk* (New York: Vintage, 1990), p. xi.

3. "Seoul Warns Europe Not to Raise Tariffs on Hynix Chips," *New York Times*, July 5, 2003, p. C3.

4. *New York Times*, July 11, 2003.

5. For a systematic survey of the issues see Joseph Stiglitz, *Globalization and Its Discontents* (New York: Norton, 2003), and Lori Wallach, *The WTO: Five Reasons to Resist Corporate Globalization* (New York: Seven Stories, 2000).

6. "U.S. Urges Taiwan to Buy Missiles, Despite Risk of Irking Beijing," *Wall Street Journal*, May 9, 2003.

7. See the *Christian Science Monitor*, "Budding Allies: Russia and China; A New Agreement Expands Cooperation on Energy, Arms, Regional Security, and Space," June 4, 2003.

8. "Why Does the World Remain Unstable: Hegemony and Terrorism Constitute the Major Factors Affecting World Peace," *Beijing Review*, January 16, 2003.

9. Arnold Offner, *Another Such Victory: President Truman and the Cold War 1945–1953* (Palo Alto: Stanford University Press, 2002), p. 319; original documents in *Foreign Relations of the United States 1945*, vol. 7, *The Far East, China*, pp. 658, 659, 683.

10. From the "Proclamation of the Central People's Government of the People's Republic of China," delivered by Mao Zedong at the inaugurating ceremony of the People's Republic of China, published in *Mao Zedong On Diplomacy* (Beijing: Foreign Languages Press, 1998), p. 89.

11. For details and further reading see Moss Roberts, "Bad Karma in Asia," in Masao Miyoshi and Harry Harootunian, *Learning Places* (Durham: Duke University Press, 2002), especially pp. 330–335 and footnotes 27–42.

12. "In Refutation of Dean Acheson's Shameless Fabrications," article dated January 19, 1950, and published in *Mao Zedong on Diplomacy*, p. 98.

13. The OSS, or Office of Strategic Services, evolved into the CIA in the postwar period. In addition to this film, important studies of Vietnam in the late 1940s include Marilyn Young's *The Vietnam Wars* and Mark Philip Bradley's *Imagining Vietnam and America: The Making of Post-Colonial Vietnam, 1919–1950*.

14. Relief from the self-serving nationalist narrative of the war may be

found in Martin Hart-Landsberg's *Korea: Division, Reunification, and U.S. Foreign Policy* (New York: Monthly Review Press, 1998).

15. Bruce Cumings' two-volume history, *The Origins of the Korean War* (Princeton: Princeton University Press, 1981 and 1990), is unsurpassed. A shorter introduction to the main events and issues may be found in Callum A. MacDonald's *Korea: The War before Vietnam* (New York: Free Press, 1987).

16. MacDonald, *Korea*, p. 235; see chapter 12, "The War in the Air."

17. For names, see MacDonald, *Korea*, pp. 253–254.

18. Robert McNamara, *In Retrospect: The Tragedy and Lessons of Vietnam* (New York: Vintage, 1996), preface, p. xvi.

19. One contemporary critic of empire is the conservative political scientist Chalmers Johnson, whose influential book, *Blowback: The Costs and Consequences of Empire* (New York: Henry Holt, 2001), is a telling survey of the problem. Today it seems it is conservatives more than the liberals who understand how empire subverts democracy, perhaps because so many liberals suffer from adulation of the state. One liberal laureate of the empire is Michael Ignatieff, touted in the *New York Times Magazine* (September 7, 2003) as its "in-house historian and political philosopher." In an article for the January 5, 2003, issue of the magazine, called "The American Empire: The Burden," he writes, "[America] has become adept at using what is called soft power—influence, example, and persuasion—in preference to hard power. . . . The case for empire is that it has become, in a place like Iraq, the last hope for democracy and stability alike." His September 7 article, more soberly headlined "A Mess of Intervention," revisits his prewar optimism but remains of the York Harding–Alden Pyle brand of political philosophy. For a useful antidote see Gore Vidal's *Dreaming War: Blood for Oil and the Bush-Cheney Junta* (New York: Nation Books, 2002).

20. Robert L. Beisner, *Twelve against Empire: The Anti-Imperialists 1898–1900* (Chicago: University of Chicago Press, 1968), pp. 30, 32. Chapter 2 is devoted to Carl Schurz.

21. See Hart-Landsberg, *Korea*, pp. 30–31.

22. One important exception is Angel Velasco Shaw and Luis H. Francia's new book, *Vestiges of War: The Philippine-American War and the Aftermath of an Imperial Dream, 1899–1999* (New York: New York University Press, 2002); this book details the extent of the slaughter.

23. Cynthia Crossen, "Déjà Vu," *Wall Street Journal*, July 2, 2003.

24. Ben Kiernan, ed., Introduction to *Genocide and Democracy in Cambodia: The Khmer Rouge, the United Nations, and the International Community* (New Haven: Yale Council on Southeast Asia Studies, 1993), p. 12. Kiernan is criticizing a comment in William Shawcross's 1984 book *The Quality of Mercy: Cambodia, Holocaust, and Modern Conscience* (New York: Simon and Schuster, 1984). Shawcross is the author of an earlier and important work on Cambodia called *Sideshow* (New York: Simon and Schuster, 1979).

25. See Ben Kiernan's important chapter "The Inclusion of the Khmer Rouge in the Cambodian Peace Process," in Kiernan, *Genocide and Democracy in Cambodia.*

26. The warped quality of the public China discourse in the United States seems to have disturbed the former national security adviser Zbigniew Brzezinski. In his essay "Living with China," published in the *National Interest* (spring 2000), he writes, "Allegedly informed writings regarding China often tend to be quite muddled, occasionally even verging toward the hysterical extremes." This astute observation calls for further analysis; more than intellectual error is involved.

27. One striking piece is "China's Trade Lifts Neighbors," in the *Wall Street Journal,* August 18, 2003. This article describes a China that is a major international buyer, as well as a seller.

PART V

THE UNITED STATES

15

Hating Amerika

Anti-Americanism and the American Left

Linda Gordon

AFTER THE SEPTEMBER 11 ATTACK, conservative and liberal pundits informed us that the terrorists did what they did because they hated American values. Many on the Left replied that the terrorists were driven more by hatred for what the U.S. government *did*, for its policies, than for its values. It is certainly true that emphasizing "values" was a way to deflect attention away from U.S. policies. Moreover, the values talk involved caricaturing and constricting our understanding of the values of, say, al Qaida operatives or Palestinian suicide bombers. The talk of American values also set up a specious comparison between what "terrorists" do and what the United States says it believes. Inside this country, the anti-American-values epithet is manipulated as a club to stigmatize and suppress opposition.

And yet . . . can we really disregard "values" entirely in trying to understand our world? True, we would apprehend them more accurately if we induced them from the practices of a society rather than from its church pieties. American values are no more unanimous than any other nation's. Our hypocrisies are more blatant and more extreme, perhaps, as a result of the economic and military power of the American polity. Our homegrown Christian fundamentalists may well be genuine in proclaiming their hatred for the sexualized advertising, violence, and profanity of our commercial culture. But they defend the economic structures that give rise to these values and resist policies that could regulate them. Of course, foreign fundamentalists who proclaim the same revulsion toward these evils also love Nikes, Coke, hip-hop, and the Terminator. (When I first wrote this, I had no idea that he would become a governator, as well.)

What's more, the American Left also has a tradition of condemning American values, which is what I want to discuss here. This tradition is a less well understood aspect of anti-Americanism, but it has been extremely consequential in the history of that Left.

In the late 1960s and early 1970s, some black and white New Leftists, led by young macho guys, took to spelling America with a "K." That "K" gave off intense heat, recalling the bonfires of lynching, the white hoods of the Klan, the swastika, and the skinheads. It was a powerful condensation symbol, because it communicated so much with so little: anger at the exploitation, injustice, and suffering supervised and produced by the rulers of America, an anger stimulated above all by the brutal repression of the civil rights movement and the Vietnamese national liberation movement. The "K" was a more totalizing claim than burning a draft card or holding upraised fists when the national anthem was played at the Mexico City Olympics. People understood these as protests against the Vietnam War and against racism, while the "K" condemned the whole of America.

One objection to the "K" was that it exaggerated: America as a whole was not a Klan or Nazi power. In some contexts that "K" argued that the United States could not be reformed peacefully, that disruption, even violence would be necessary. Some of the "K" users convinced themselves that revolution could find mass support in the United States, a conviction that indicated a tremendous misconception about what American values were. The Black Panthers and the Weathermen developed this understanding of America as Amerika to promulgate a "by any means necessary" ethic that justified an extremely counterproductive violence. Older people in particular criticized that kind of exaggeration, because they had learned to lower their expectations, and feminists criticized it because they saw how much it derived from macho posturing. Still, in the midst of the Vietnam War, as we watched the "defoliation" of vast areas and children burning up with napalm, the "K" rang powerfully. As New Leftists came to understand what it meant to be residents of a superpower, they found it hard to avoid a condemnation of the whole because it is an integrated, if internally contradictory, nation. That is, those who rule the United States do so through hegemony as well as domination, through patterns of culture, the pleasures of consumption, and ideologies of freedom in which we cannot help but participate. Now that we are residents of *the* superpower, we are all the more its participants. And this very enforced participation puts us often in a rage, feeding a desire to condemn, reject, even secede from American "values," to become anti-Americans.

I want to suggest two things here about homegrown anti-Americanism: first, that it grew from centuries-old historical roots, so that understanding it takes us back into some well-known discussions of the nature of political opposition in the U.S. Left; second, that the Left itself was partly responsible for its weakness, for its degree of alienation from the polity and society in which we live. I want to suggest that the American Left contributed to the construction of the alleged binary between loyal Americans and anti-Americans. We did so not deliberately, and sometimes despite struggle against this dualism, but it remains true that the American Left rarely managed to make itself understood as "native." Instead, it often split between a "native" American radicalism in tension with a more cosmopolitan, urban, foreign-influenced Left that rejected America.

Of course, the notion of the "native" is already loaded with ideology, but this ideology is precisely what I'm talking about. Because the United States was a settler nation, its nationality was defined somewhat differently from that of nations that grew from long-resident populations. By the nineteenth century, "native" typically meant immigrants of northern European stock. But the exclusionary structure of this racism has been shaped also by an ideological distinction between those who belong and those who do not. As far back as Presidents Jefferson and Jackson, both "native," "white" Americans, we can see a germ of tension developing between a European-influenced liberalism and a populism that was able to get itself defined as "native." Throughout the nineteenth and twentieth centuries, this tension expanded and intensified.

So Americanism became an ideology, not a fact of citizenship or residence. That ideological construction reached its peak in the concept "un-American," which became so hegemonic during the cold war. What's unusual about that concept is that it was about ideology, about political opinion, and in that meaning it was not only new but structured in a way that, remarkably, was confined to the United States. Think about what "un-French" or "un-Russian" might have meant in that time—these terms would have implied an ethnic or racial difference or inferiority, perhaps referring to a Jew or a gypsy or a German-speaking Alsatian or a Ukrainian. There was a cold war everywhere in the world, but only in the United States did patriotism and national identity become so ideological. Although most of the Western democracies have fewer legal protections for civil liberties than we do, and although most glorify individualism less than our culture does, nevertheless the United States has been consistently more extreme than virtually any other Western democracy in its thoroughgoing suppression of the Left. Indeed, the Left became so un-American in this cold war discourse that it was criminal, treasonous. Of course, the international structure of the cold war and the Comintern allegiance of the American Communist Party allowed American Leftism to be branded as Soviet, but this was not and is not unique to that period of our history. A blond, WASP student told me that in the recent antiwar demonstration, a cop shouted at him, "Go back to Iraq."

But this ideological Americanism was conditioned in part by the nature of the U.S. Left itself. As illustration, focusing on the modern— that is, socialist and Marxist—Left, let me cite some admittedly schematic and therefore oversimplified and exaggerated oppositions. When Marxism came to the United States, in the late 1860s, with it came the factional and dogmatic tendencies of most systematic thought. The First International tried to suppress so-called utopian socialism (indeed, it contributed to making "utopian" a pejorative) with its prefigurative, communitarian projects. These earlier movements had emphasized issues such as sex equality, reproduction control, and health foods and simplicity in daily life, issues that the Marxists rejected as marginal, distracting from the scientific path of history, and even "bourgeois." The First International purged the "Yankees" for their strategic errors in working with the Woman Suffrage Associations and with African American civil rights movements; in response, American radicals whose theory and practice came from antebellum protest movements organized the rival New Democracy. Ever afterward, the Left in the United States wavered between or divided between scientific socialism, with its attempt at analytic rigor, and native-born democratic ideals. The IWW tried to hold together two constituencies at opposite ends of the "Americanism" measuring stick: East Coast immigrant-dominated cells in the textile and garment industries, often influenced by European socialist parties and unions, and western miners, lumbermen, and hobos, the "natives." The Socialist Party similarly tried to contain internal tensions between its eastern, big-city, largely immigrant membership and its midwestern, often small-town or even rural "native" or German (earlier immigrant) members, and these tensions contributed to the rupture that created the Communist party. The twentieth-century Communist Party-USA, in turn, oscillated between, on the one hand, its idolization of the Soviet Union and commitment to Leninist discipline and, on the other hand, its United Front, later Popular Front, turn to nonideological progressive coalitions. The civil rights movement divided between a grassroots organizing strategy directed toward the southern poor, couched in terms of American democratic ideals, and a northern-dominated urban nationalism that saw African Americans as part of the third world. The white New Left divided along the same lines: inspired at first by civil rights, a Whitmanesque search for authenticity against the commercialism and passivity of the corporate era, and commitment to prefigurative strategies and tactics, the movement fragmented under pressure from factions primarily influenced by "foreign" ideas, that is, Leninism, Maoism, Guevarism.

I am trying to define this dualism between the allegedly native and the allegedly foreign in a neutral fashion. I do this neither as a literary move nor in an attempt at social-scientific "objectivity" but because both represent vital aspects of oppositional politics in the United States. Both parts of the Left contributed energies and analyses to movements for social change, but also outrageous bias and dogmatism. "Native" American radicalism was often nativist, opposing "alien" ideologies and nurturing racist stereotypes of blacks, Jews, Mexicans, and the Irish. In the western labor movement, "American" often meant "white," thus discursively exiling both native-born and immigrant workers if they were Mexican-American or Asian-American. At the other end of this polarization, but nevertheless often coincident with such racisms, Marxist groups adopted strategies based on imported doctrine and, in the case of the Communist party, foreign priorities rather than analysis of local contexts. They maintained authoritarian organizational structures and intolerance for the justice demands of groups, such as women, people of color, and small businesspeople, that did not fit the honored scientific theories.

The Left was rarely able to transcend these divisions. Certainly, there were many historical obstacles to their doing so; my comments are aimed not at allocating blame but at identifying structures. In the second half of the twentieth century, these structures became larger and more imbedded. The New Left, unable to free itself from the dominant construction of "Americanism" in ideological terms, typically accepted, even celebrated its outsider status. To some degree, this was a performative, propagandistic choice. We see it vividly in the women's liberation movement as feminists appropriated terms of abuse applied to women—such as "bitch," "shrew," "trollop"—and made them collectively prideful, celebrated. Or, in black nationalism, which celebrated epithets like "bad." But the Left as a whole did not have the same ideological room to maneuver.

Left anti-Americanism tended to strengthen sectarianism. And there was a great deal of room for sectarianism, as the Left was divided not just among different tactical or even strategic approaches but among different goals. Some sought the overthrow of capitalism through Leninist strategy; others sought a liberal polity and regulated economy along the lines of social democracy; others prioritized civil rights and "identity politics." All these and other ideological positions were intensified in their purism and uncompromisingness by their members' sense of alienation from "America"; the further from the mainstream, the further from power, the greater the factionalizing impetus.

So, claiming the mantle of Americanism, appealing to a mainstream, seemed to some Leftists a capitulation, an immoral compromise, because of what it left unsaid, uncondemned. It sometimes seemed that every New Left leaflet, every demonstration, no matter what the cause, had to denounce every U.S. government and corporate sin, as if not to mention each one was to condone it. This fear of pollution by silence encouraged dullingly repetitive jargon and humorless, apocalyptic bombast. Building alliances by scaling back the Left's platform to a lowest-common-denominator agenda evoked fear of pollution through cowardice.

History could be called upon to support both those who feared compromise and those who feared alienation from the mainstream. Many liberals, progressives, and socialists have hoped and believed that the United States could be made more democratic in a coalition-building, step-by-step reform process: for example, first pass Social Security, then gradually expand it to meet the need; first get Medicaid and Medicare, then move on to health insurance for all. But, in actuality, that strategy often backfired, because the piecemeal approach divided the constituency of the coalition and weakened the demand for change. Not only did you never get beyond the first step, but, as we see so clearly now, a backlash eroded or even repealed these first small achievements. On the other hand, the discourses of systemic theory, arguing for total, transformative change because of the unity of various forms of oppression and aggression in our society and state, sometimes became a rhetorical absolutism, without warmth or outreach, speaking only to others as alienated as themselves.

Historically, as the United States rose to world power, criticisms of its violence and domination naturally grew. The rhetoric of anti-imperialism in the 1890s was less impassioned and less popular than that in the 1970s. The New Left examined the connections between the unspeakable atrocities of napalm and the domestic operations of the U.S. economy. A remarkable New Left feminist, Florika, made posters of juxtapositions that seem postmodern or mysterious today but that in 1969 spoke instantly and insistently: a young Vietnamese boy with one arm burned off next to a Dole advertisement reading, "Not all bananas are created equal"; a beautiful Vietnamese woman trying to protect her two children from napalm by clutching them in the middle of a river, next to an equally beautiful model promoting Chanel perfume. The message of these representations was a holistic anti-Americanism, condemning the culture, the standard of living, and the desire kindled by the selling of commodities. It is an anti-Americanism guilt-ridden, moralistic, and, yes, often self-hating. It says: consumerism kills third-world children. Eating bananas and coveting sexual attractiveness kill third-world children.

At an intellectual level, the debate about this guilt, these purisms, is sometimes organized as the American "exceptionalism" question. From the Puritan colonists to Wilsonian rhetoric about the League of Nations to Dubya's rhetoric about good guys and bad guys, standing alone on principle, and God's support for our foreign policy, there abides the idea that the United States is not just another state among the world's nations but a unique polity and society, uniquely standing for freedom. For nearly as long, some intellectuals have challenged this solipsistic, narcissistic ideology, but not without acknowledging and admiring the remarkable wild ride to wealth and power taken by this settler colony in two centuries. In other words, the set of categories that makes left politics unpatriotic *is* uniquely or at least predominantly American. With the collapse of Soviet power, America's unparalleled dominion produced epic anti-Americanism throughout the world, including here "at home."

These political emotions are, of course, never fixed. In this moment, after the U.S. government attacked an infinitely weaker Arab state and left its people without a government, without basic services, victimized by crime and fragmentation, it is difficult not to accept, even honor domestic anti-Americanism; difficult not to be drawn toward replacing the my-country-right-or-wrong rhetoric with my-country-always-wrong rhetoric. But that posture becomes muddled and counterproductive when we remember that most Americans did not want this war and yet continue to experience opposition to it as unpatriotic. We are faced with the continuing association of Americanism with loyalty to government and of army with conformity, of dissent with anti-Americanism. That set of associations is so deep and pervasive that it would be difficult to exaggerate the size of the resultant challenge to the Left.

16

The Domestic Front

Andrew Ross

THERE ARE FEW NATIONS WHERE DISSENTERS escape being judged unpatriotic, disloyal, or subversive. In the United States, however, they are required to face an additional charge. Those who dissent too vigorously may be judged in contempt of the *idea* of America and their views expelled from the orbit of public discussion about the affairs of civic nationalism. This does not make them persona non grata, however. On the contrary, the domestic anti-American is an integral component of the American Way, just as necessary to the national creed as the blasphemer or heretic is to the theological scourge.

On the one hand, this paradox seems unavoidable in a nation that so strenuously reaches after an ideal of perfectability, that imagines itself so zealously as the exemplary state of modern times, and whose evangelical self-affirmation is as righteous to believers as it is repugnant to most others. Piety of this order requires a steady supply of illiberal recreants to renew itself, and the conditions of eligibility are so flexible that suspects can always be found to fit the bill. In wartime, or in periods of state hysteria about national security, even the mildest expressions of nonconformity can qualify. In the repressive climate that followed September 11, when the Bush administration limited so many constitutional freedoms through legislation like the U.S.A. Patriot Act (the expansion of wiretapping and secret search powers, the deregulating of intelligence-gathering procedures, and the erosion of attorney-client privilege, media freedom, and immigrants' rights), the uses of the label "anti-American" mushroomed. Indeed, the term may well be headed for the same fate as "liberal," a word that the New Right has successfully converted into a pejorative so loosely wielded that it can now be used widely to demonize formerly centrist ideas. In this respect, then, anti-Americanism in the domestic sphere continues to be as serviceable to governing elites as anti-Americanism overseas has been to Washington's efforts to bolster puppet rulers in client states or to trigger instability in nonaligned and unfriendly ones.

On the other hand, anti-Americanism is not simply a bogeyman conjured up by state managers. For the Left, it is a very real point of entry into a debate about the shape and nature of dissent in the United States. Are there forms of politics that are perceived to be in the American grain and that are therefore consistent with radical republican values and home-grown protest traditions? If so, should they be promoted at the expense of politics that are perceived to take their primary inspiration from elsewhere and therefore do not have the same claim of right to domestic attention? This is a long-running debate, and, historically, it ebbs and flows in tandem with Washington's periodic swings between isolationism and engagement in international affairs. To many contemporary eyes, it may appear parochial at a time when the forces of economic globalization are directly challenged by an international protest movement with alternative ideas about global development. Yet, some understanding of this domestic debate may help us to see how the ballooning anti-Americanism of world opinion could be channeled in a useful direction.

One of the primary engines of overseas anti-American sentiment is the conviction that globalization, both economic and cultural, is being molded on a one-size-fits-all template, stamped with Washington's version of a materialist, market civilization fully serviced by a passive democracy. The culprit in question, then, is the faux universalism of a model that, on closer examination, appears to have been shaped exclusively by the peculiarities of U.S. history. For better or worse, the customary source for Washington's self-image of high moral purpose is the U.S. Constitution, which offered a safe haven for the radical ideas set in motion by the Enlightenment. The machinery of idealism was laid in place, and, with a little tinkering here and there, it has been steadily producing output ever since, much of it now exported alongside political and economic cargo that would have been anathema to the framers. However awkward the fit between eighteenth-century constitutional ideals and the muddled reality of modern American ideology, the effort to synchronize them is not only obligatory for left-liberals, it is also a source of gratification, since it is a surefire way of connecting with popular sentiment. Even so, most of the social progress recorded in the United States (whether or not it is recognized belatedly by the courts) has been a result of direct action, pursued outside established institutions of governance and often in violation of existing law.

Just as the political constraints of operating within the courts' interpretation of this eighteenth-century straitjacket have long been regretted, so, too, the inconsistency of Washington's attitude toward the revolutions and constitutions of other peoples has compromised nearly every shred of dignity that progressives are duly owed for their domestic achievements. This inconstancy started early, in the region that would become known as America's back yard. A mere three years after the adoption of the U.S. Constitution, Toussaint L'Ouverture gave expression to those same Rights of Man by successfully leading the largest slave revolt in history in what was then St. Domingue. The detailed career of the Haitian revolution (inspired, in part, by the independence struggle of the American colonists, in which some Haitian slave volunteers had actively participated at the siege of Savannah) demonstrates the difficulty, then and now, of separating class and race from a universal notion of natural rights.[1] But the U.S. response to the founding of the world's first black republic, and to the hemisphere's second declaration of independence, was just as telling. As president, George Washington put portions of the state's treasury and armory at the disposal of Napoleon's effort to quell the slave insurgencies and, after the success of the revolt, suggested that African American slave rebels be deported to Haiti.

There followed a brief interregnum, when John Adams' administration, eager to continue the sugar trade, recognized L'Ouverture's rule. But Thomas Jefferson's presidential term, beginning in 1801, saw the onset of a trade embargo and a policy of isolation and economic attrition toward the island republic that lasted until the United States officially recognized Haiti's independence in 1863, long after the liberated states of Colombia, Bolivia, and Venezuela, all motivated by Haiti's earlier example, had gained similar recognition. This punitive policy was, of course, driven by the fear of slave revolt spreading northward, but it was prophetic of how the United States would come to respond to other peoples' revolutions, even those inspired by its own. The most tragic example of the latter was embodied in Ho Chi Minh, a devout U.S. ally in the war against Japan, who modeled the Vietnamese declaration of independence in 1945 after the U.S. Constitution's description of "inalienable rights," only to learn how little such gestures meant in the world of Washington *realpolitik*.

FROM UN-AMERICAN TO ANTI-AMERICAN

By the time of the Vietnam War, it had became impossible to ignore the connections between the treatment Washington doled out to the modern equivalents of Haiti and the blocked promise of constitutional freedoms to citizens of color at home. The linkage of decolonization movements around the world to liberation struggles in the United States brought about a sea change in dissent that reshaped the domestic character of anti-Americanism. Increasingly, anti-Americanism would be identified by an empathy with what C. Wright Mills, in *Listen Yankee* (a book that heavily influenced the sea change) called "the hungry-nation bloc." How did this new perception of anti-Americanism displace and succeed the earlier designation of un-American activity?

The emergence of the "un-American" cannot be identified exclusively with McCarthyism, and it would be just as wrong to couple its demise with the discrediting of the junior senator from Wisconsin after the army hearings of 1954. The instincts and practices of anti-communism long preceded the congressional investigations launched by his infamous 1950 Wheeling speech. Three decades of post-Bolshevik lobbying, arming, and funding (for the Kuomintang, for example, in the first cold war crusade overseas), joined with the isolationist cause of "One-Hundred Percent Americanism" that carried the nativist Right through the wars, had more than prepared the breeding ground for McCarthyism. Nor did McCarthy make too many friends outside his sphere of influence. Cold war liberal intellectuals, elevated to unprecedented national importance in the pages of *Time* and *Life* for their resolution to "choose America," had every reason to be embarrassed by his Yahoo provincialism. So did the CIA, which, at the time, was funding anti-Communist efforts by covertly supporting the kind of left-wing, homosexual, European intellectuals who were abhorred by McCarthy and his acolytes. As Frances Saunders muses, in her book on the CIA's Congresses for Cultural Freedom, one of the reasons for the covert nature of the CIA's campaign to win over notable minds abroad may have been precisely that the CIA wanted to evade the scrutiny of the House Committee on Un-American Activities.[2] Forging consent for Atlanticism was a ceaseless contest for influence over foreign populations, and anything that would count as a propaganda asset was considered fair game.

By contrast, McCarthy's "great conspiracy" had the scale and the atmosphere of a circus sideshow. After all, the United States had one of the smallest Communist party memberships in the world. That it hosted one of the fiercest witch hunts was hastily explained away by cold war liberals as an aberration caused by chronic flaws in the national character—moral puritanism, anti-intellectualism, the paranoid style, status anxiety, irrational populism, and so on.[3] Revisionist commentators later disputed this view, establishing that McCarthy's support came from traditional Republican party quarters and arguing that the collusion of the FBI and other government agencies set the template for political repression in ways that were constitutive of federal power for decades to come.[4] Nonetheless, the PR opportunity offered by the spectacle of the HUAC hearings proved to be irresistible to political grandstanders throughout the land. Reds were soon found under every bed.

The degree to which the un-American label was broadly bestowed on fellow travelers, premature anti-fascists, neutralists, agnostics, peaceniks, New Dealers, and auto dealers with suspicious pasts was genuinely tragicomic in its dimensions. But, while the hysteria of the anti-Communist purgers was an overreaction, their rhetorical conviction that the neighbor across the way could turn out to be a Red was not all misplaced. The ordinariness of Ethel Rosenberg was palpable proof of how close to home—how close to the idea of America—communism had come. Before the war, communism was dogmatically expounded by the CPUSA as "twentieth-century Americanism," entirely in the lineage of "Washington, Jefferson, Paine, Jackson, and Lincoln under the changed conditions of today." Indeed, the Popular Front aimed at taking up residence in Middle America's living rooms and achieved some success in doing so. It was only recently that Americans had been able to express their patriotism through support for wartime ally Uncle Joe in Moscow, and so a special kind of applied psychology was required to turn the tide of national sentiment against the Reds. Like the clones in *Invasion of the Body Snatchers*, Communists had to be regarded as virtually indistinguishable from the average white suburbanite for cold war policy makers to fully exploit the heightened public paranoia of the era. On the other hand, many Communists had indeed occupied ordinary as well as key institutional positions in education, entertainment, and the labor movement, and they had learned to assimilate their politics accordingly. Consequently, the purges were all the more devastating to a Left that had become entrenched as never before.

If the Un-American could easily pass as an all-American, it was because the political character of the period had such a bipolar personality, in the clinical sense. Viewed from a certain angle, the cold war was waged by two utopian by-products of the bourgeois European imagination—the United States and the Soviet Union—each contending to be the champion of industrial modernity by outproducing the other, in everything from missiles to grain yields. Moscow had shown itself to be a player in the race for production and, if anything, a superior in the adoption of American industrial techniques like Taylorism. Production for use or production for profit? The means were congruent, even if the goals were not. It was the sheer symmetry, then, of the cold war in the North that gave birth to Un-Americans and made them so interchangeable with the other Euro-Americans filling the seats at the PTA meeting or coaching the Little League team.

No such symmetry would apply in nonwhite America, where citizenship was an incomplete experience, or in other parts of the world where the cold war took tens of millions of lives in the civil wars it scripted and generated. Decolonization and national liberation movements brought to the fore new political subjects for whom the Western and Soviet paths of forced industrialization were not a given and for whom postcolonial integrity required the embrace of more indigenous ideas about development. Decolonizing the mind in non-Eurocentric ways knocked sideways the sibling rivalry of the cultural cold war. Mao improvised a peasant-based model of continuous revolution that diverged from the Euro-Marxist Soviet paradigm of urban proletarianism, and when the Sino-Soviet split intensified, it bisected the international Left. The nonaligned movement promised "independent judgment" and unity to states combating imperialism and its effects, and the Cuban revolution flourished in Washington's back yard. These overseas developments had a profound impact on political consciousness at home, where the push for racial justice was rapidly unraveling the slaphappy pluralism of the cold war consensus. Fortified by new dreams of liberation, the freedom rides and marches in the South pioneered a participatory politics that inspired the many different movements of the New Left.

By the time the Pentagon was fully mired in Indochina, several new profiles of the anti-Americanist were in full bloom, for which the designation of "un-American" activity had ceased to be relevant. One of these profiles was filled out by minority nationalists who applied the theory of "internal colonialism" to black, brown, and red America.[5] They took their cue from the influential analyses of colonial underdevelopment in the third world, and their account of U.S. domestic imperialism was a wholesale rejection of the creed of "birthright liberalism" so vaunted by the cold war intelligentsia. The counterculture's rejection of technocracy was another strain of protest that broke with the official belief system. Among other things, it challenged a long-prized faith in the meritocratic rule of expertise that had distinguished the United States from nations with inherited feudal traits. This challenge also took some of its impetus from overseas—from ideas about local self-determination in poor countries cognizant of the ecological costs that came with the Western and Soviet client package of inappropriate technology combined with inappropriate development expertise. More conspicuous yet was the home-grown activist who visibly identified with third worldism, whether out of liberal guilt or compassionate solidarity. The idols of this tendency were Fanon, Mao, Ho, and Che, men whose romantic renderings of insurgent peasantry were a wildly popular successor to the Old Left's iconography of proletarian revolution. Their focus on the countryside, whether on rural communes or on the guerrilla encirclement of cities, was also a stark contrast to the predominantly urban imagery of industrial, technocratic modernity. Military resistance to imperialism, whether in Algeria, Cuba, Vietnam, or South Africa, was accepted as a just war of liberation, and it upped the ante of militancy at home. Armed self-defense and vanguardist confrontationism gained legitimacy among a number of movements (AIM, the Black Panthers, the Young Lords, and the Weatherman factions), whether in thrall to the romance of the street-fighting man or through indulgence of the right to bear arms in the face of state racism and government tyranny.[6]

By the end of the 1960s, it was easy to find voices on the Left willing to acknowledge that a line had been crossed, even if they were not necessarily willing to call it anti-Americanism. The 1970 manifesto of the New American Movement, one of the organizations that grew out of the implosion of Students for a Democratic Society (SDS), noted that "the focus on solidarity with the third world grew out of a correct reaction to United States national chauvinism—but it has gone so far in the opposite direction that it has lost all possibility of communicating with the American people, and has lost touch with reality." Because it substituted identification with the oppression of others for personal participation in daily struggles, third worldism was declared to be a betrayal of the radical democracy ethos that had emerged from Freedom Rides and anti-poverty organizing. The appetite for violence was considered an affront to the tactics nurtured in the peace and civil rights movements, and the revival of sectarianism was reviled as an outbreak of an Old Left disease. Revulsion with the hardcore belligerence of the male vanguards helped to fuel the breakaway groups that formed second-wave feminism.

These reactions could be regarded as incipient Left critiques of anti-American conduct, and, like many other Left self-criticisms of that period, they morphed over the next twenty-five years into neoconservative rhetorical weapons used to disparage all forms of dissent (consider the career of the term "political correctness," as it transitioned from its origin as an ironic caveat among movement insiders to its status today as a crude reactionary cudgel). Today, the sweeping charge of anti-Americanism still draws some of its moral heat from a perception, among some liberals and leftists, that political dissent at the end of the 1960s was somehow excessive and that "it lost touch with American reality" through its infatuation with armed liberation movements elsewhere. The events of September 11 set the stage for a full-dress revival of this scenario, with loudly scripted roles that allowed progressive patriots to wave their red, white, and blue credentials. Introducing a recent anthology on "American Rebels," Jack Newfield, for example, made the case for "authentic patriotism" by praising the "tradition of populist patriotism that I have felt a kinship with since the early 1960s." In pursuit still of "an alternative America which I could pledge allegiance to, " he declared proudly, "I never became anti-American." While Newfield's professed antagonists were "burglars of the flag," like Kissinger, Rockefeller, Helms, Hoover, Scalia, and Falwell, his claim to moral high ground was a more or less direct rebuke to Leftists who stray from the flag.[7]

Some (most prominently Christopher Hitchens) took the opportunity to publicly break with the Left over the legitimacy of "just wars" for the United States abroad—first in Afghanistan and then in Iraq.[8] Other left liberals of long standing revived the "out of touch with the American people" line to tar anti-war dissenters with the brush of anti-Americanism.[9] Given that the concept of the *bellum justum* was what allegedly pushed politicos of the 1960s onto the roads of anti-American excess in the first place, there was no small irony in the spectacle of belligerati with a New Left lineage promoting it as a humane policy for Washington to adopt in the name of self-defense. One by no means inconsiderable factor was the media recognition accorded those willing to agonize publicly over their "second thoughts." Liberal intellectuals converting to the war party in op-ed pages or in magazines of opinion are especially prized, if only because they provide the spectacle of an ostensibly free mind, capable of rational, and not ideological, deliberation. Another factor was the legacy of a decade of liberal debate about the justice of humanitarian interventions in Bosnia, Somalia, Kosovo, and Rwanda. This wrangling had prepared the way for rethinking war as an ethical instrument, even when administered by former imperial powers.

In principle, the case for such human rights interventions rests on the framework of a rule-based order, where decisions about the criteria for action are made through international diplomacy. The Bush administration's unilateral policies of intervention showed scant regard for such diplomacy. The New National Security Strategy (unveiled in September 2002) that reserved the right of the United States to preemptively attack other states was a clean break with the internationalism that the Washington Consensus helped to underwrite during the 1990s. It soon emerged that the plan to use an Iraqi war as a trial balloon for the new unilateralism had been proposed several years before September 11 by members of the Project for a New American Century, the neoconservative policy cabal that supplied the Bush administration with most of its ideologues. The new defense policy establishment publicly named other "rogue states" as potential targets for "regime change." Such developments brought forth a spate of commentary about a U.S. hegemony that was openly described as "imperial" in nature (see the discussion in the Introduction to this book). While hawks frankly advocated this imperial stance, many centrists and liberals saw it as an unavoidable, if awkward, consequence of U.S. military dominance in a unipolar world. Echoing the Victorian adage that the British empire was "acquired in a fit of absent-mindedness," Michael Ignatieff suggested that "if Americans have an empire, they have acquired it in a state of deep denial."[10] With the sudden ubiquity of fast talk about American empire, the traditional left-wing critiques of U.S. imperialism appeared strangely anachronistic. Even so, this did not prevent the branding of their advocates as fifth columnists for the tsunami of anti-American sentiment coursing around the globe before and after the war on Iraq. Nor did it lighten the charge of being out of touch with the American people, least of all in a jingoist climate when even the Dixie Chicks could be regarded as anti-American.

Today, when progressives berate each other for being anti-American, the charge often rests on a very particular interpretation of political history. At root, it is a story about an alleged leftist infatuation with racial justice, at home and abroad, which originated in the 1960s and has debilitated and fragmented the progressive cause ever since. Because of this obsession, it is asserted that the Left has unduly neglected the white working-class people who were once at the core of the New Deal coalition and have turned to the right as a result. Michael Kazin, writing in the wake of September 11, presents a typical version of this charge:

> Having abandoned patriotism, the left lost the ability to pose convincing alternatives for the nation as a whole. It could take credit for spearheading a multicultural, gender-aware revision of the humanities curriculum, but the right set the political agenda, and it did so in part because its partisans spoke forcefully in the name of American principles that knit together disparate groups—anti-union businesspeople, white evangelicals, Jewish neoconservatives—for mutual ends. . . . Most ordinary citizens understandably distrust a left that condemns military intervention abroad or a crackdown at home but expresses only a pro forma concern for the actual and potential victims of terrorism. Without empathy for one's neighbors, politics becomes a cold, censorious enterprise indeed.[11]

Not much distinguishes Kazin's sentiments here from the centrist advocates of the Democratic National Committee, for whom his invocation of "ordinary citizens" would be a codeword for the white, middle-class voter, fearful of a homeland in which other peoples' interests have any empowered place and of a larger world overseas in which Americans and their good intentions are misunderstood at best and irrationally resented at worst. For Kazin, the betrayal of this populist core had its origins in cold war liberalism but took on a mass dimension with the separatist legacy of the New Left and the rise of identity politics.[12] It is a point of view, loosely shared by a coterie of influential white male historians and journalists, that makes of Newfield's "authentic patriotism" a qualification for anyone who is serious about "persuading the nation."[13]

This school of thought has been widely rebutted for the assertions of its proponents that the politics of race, gender, and sexuality are acute distractions, marginalized as the domain of "special interests" by a likeminded white majority and proven ineffectual against the economic juggernaut of the New Right. On the contrary, as Lisa Duggan has shown, the sweeping progress of the neoliberal privatization revolution has depended on repeated appeals to identity and cultural politics (over welfare entitlements, law enforcement, tax reform, affirmative action, and federal funding, to name only a few) to pursue its goals of wealth privatization and redistribution.[14] Nor have such appeals been marginal to the networks of far-right patriot and militia groups whose racialist disenchantment with policies of the U.S. government (or ZOG, the "Zionist Occupation Government") would fill out a more consistent profile of anti-Americanism than virtually any left-wing tendency.[15] To overlook the domestic uses and power of these conservative appeals to racial and gender supremacy is to miss entirely the drift of modern American political culture.

In addition, Kazin and others' account of left-wing betrayal ignores how important it was, historically, for race militants to pull civil rights out of "piece of the pie" electoralism and to make common cause with the socially denied in other countries. Nor does this theory do justice to the monumental role that identity has played ever since in fundamentally altering the social personality of our times. So, too, its recommendation for the cause of liberal patriotism ignores our responsibility, as citizens and/or taxpayers, for the abhorrent consequences of several decades of U.S. counterinsurgent foreign policy (in this regard, it is justifiable to argue that none of us are what are often referred to as "innocent civilians"), and it glibly assumes that "ordinary citizens" do not care about worldwide resentment of the cavalier exercise of U.S. power.

The task of "persuading the nation" is no longer what it was in the heyday of the New Deal coalition favored by these authors, nor is it merely a matter of domestic concern. The peculiarities of the American electoral system require much of the world to be held hostage to the anticipated views of voters in the Iowa caucuses and the New Hampshire primary. The international community recognizes that certain aspects of U.S. foreign policy (perhaps even the war on Iraq, whose rational basis in policy seemed otherwise indefensible) are undertaken primarily to secure support of some provincial electoral constituency at home. In an age that has begun to take internationalism, if not world government, seriously, this parochial concern about the local spin on American ideals is almost ludicrous. Yet, when these ideals are zealously projected abroad as models for other nations to follow, they can hardly be ignored.[16] That does not justify their importance, but it does help to explain how a good deal of the retaliatory sentiment comes to be classified as anti-Americanism.

I have tried to show that the domestic profile of anti-Americanism, like its overseas counterparts, serves several functions. One of these is to regulate the limits of dissent and ensure that political debate is contained within the borders of civic nationalism, unswayed by the example of regional neighbors or by overseas influence. The Left has its own version of excommunication, where moralists seek to patrol the perimeters of opinion that they judge to be digestible to the public. But there are other, less censorious, functions of anti-Americanism. What if we were to use anti-Americanist discourse to remind us that idealism does not need to have a national personality? In the age of globalization, this should go without saying, but it is still all too often dismissed as a cosmopolitan fantasy, irrelevant to the mentality of Middle America. Even so, what effect, if any, has the recent, dramatic expansion of anti-Americanism had on the advocates of global justice?

IS ANTI-AMERICANISM THE ANTI-IMPERIALISM OF FOOLS?

A century ago, the German socialist August Bebel responded to populist denunciations of "anti-Semitic capitalism" by describing them as the "socialism of fools." Making scapegoats of Jewish bankers, he argued, distracted people from the real workings of capitalism. In reference to the Iranian revolution, Tariq Ali rephrased Bebel's comment by describing Islamic fundamentalism as the "anti-imperialism of fools." In the wake of September 11, others have wondered whether worldwide anti-Americanism is also "the anti-imperialism of fools." For example, old-style Trotskyist internationalists view such general condemnations of America as unfair to the mass of working people in the United States who have little influence over the imperial policy making of the Bush administration. Anti-Americanism, from this angle, is a distraction from the task of building an international working-class movement.[17] Yet the skepticism suggested by the phrase also resonates with the views of those in the movement for global justice (or the anti-capitalist, or alternative globalization movement, as it is sometimes termed) for whom the most recent outbreak of nation-bashing has been a distraction from the task of combating the dominance of transnational corporations.

The noisy disagreement over Iraq among the major powers resuscitated the grisly power game of rewarding and punishing nation-states and sparked the resurgence of the crude diplomacy of national stereotyping. An upswing of nationalist messianism at home was matched by the intensification of America-hating around the globe. All of these developments undermined the moral clarity of the international protest movement against free-trade institutions that have given large corporations unprecedented power to bypass or rescind any national regulations that hindered their rate of profit or market access. From the perspective of corporate managers reeling from a decade of sweatshop exposés and brand-busting, the restoration of nation-bashing came as a great relief. Public attention was turned away from the coalescing plutocracy that benefits from the World Trade Organization (WTO) to the feuding aristocracy that prevails over the UN. In recent years, the elites that determine the rules of world trade have been able to meet only behind barbed wire, and their ability to elevate the right to free trade over all other human, civil, and environmental rights has been hampered by massively successful protest campaigns. At the World Social Forum meetings in Porto Alegre, the movement to build on alternative ideas of global development had begun. Labeling countries as good or bad was considered anachronistic next to the hard task of imagining how to build globalization from below.

This world-view suffered when the Bush administration's response to September 11 reformatted the geopolitical map, substituting an old cartography of friendly and unfriendly states for the network of trade flows that makes up the geography of neoliberalism. The alternative globalization movement was nearly erased from U.S. public consciousness, even though its activities endured at ministerial meetings at Doha and Cancun, and the World Social Forum reconvened in Mumbai in January 2004. But the punitive wars that followed September 11 also delivered a reality check to activists whose sights had been fixed solely on institutions like the WTO, the IMF, and the World Bank or on big-brand global firms like Monsanto, Philip Morris, Pfizer, Disney, Time Warner, GE, Shell, Chevron, Wal Mart, Microsoft, ExxonMobil, Starbucks, and McDonald's. In particular, the assertion of U.S. militarism came as a reminder that corporate power depends on the threat of force to open up and to preserve markets. Neoliberal institutions appear to bypass nation-states, but they actually rely on states' monopoly of violence to guarantee the most favorable investment terms for clients. This rule applies not only in poor countries seeking to lure foreign capital with cheap labor pool, lax regulations, and authoritarian governance but also in rich ones where the profits are repatriated. While the IMF and the World Bank have exercised "soft" fiscal control over much of the world's population through structural adjustment policies and instruments of debt, the threat of harder discipline is only as far as the nearest U.S. military base—of which there are an estimated fifty-six spread around the globe, with more under construction, and 156 countries where U.S. troops are actively stationed.

Yet, for alternative globalization activists looking to learn new lessons, the fog of war only obscured the picture. What, after all, was the real motivation for the war on Iraq? There seemed to be one too many competing explanations for this exercise in Anglo-American adventurism. Conspiracy theorists had a field day, and the anti-war movement hosted a hundred tendencies. By comparison, the anti-WTO protests had been a model of lucidity, even though they involved a makeshift coalition of affinity groups with differing causes and targets. Part of the problem, it seemed, was the apparent incoherence of U.S. policy making. These days, it is much easier to diagnose (and to protest) corporate than "national" interests. Even more confusing, the hard line promoted by Bush policy hawks not only suggested a shift away from Atlanticism, rule-based multilateralism, and global diplomacy; it also seemed to indicate that the Washington Consensus was over. This was an accord, nurtured under Bush père and Clinton, under which U.S. Treasury elites managed world economic policy on behalf of the capital pools of the G-8 industrial powers, the world's major banks, foreign investors, and the leading transnational corporations. From the moment it took office, the Bush administration shunned most international agreements and opted for negotiating its own bilateral and regional trade pacts (most recently in Chile and Argentina). Financial elites in the NATO orbit took this badly. Accustomed to a dividend from U.S. dominion, they interpreted the allocation of contracts for the rebuilding of Iraq to U.S. companies as more than simply a matter of claiming the spoils of war. It also sent a highly visible message that the international sharing of the capitalist profit pie under the rubric of multilateralism could no longer be taken for granted. In contrast to the Bush Doctrine, which appeared to reward only a select pool of politically connected U.S. companies, the multilateral system had been much more favorable to the interests of *capital in general.* In the long term, the WTO's version of rule-based order provides much more stability and security for investments, especially since its rules are written to benefit the strongest players.

Nor do U.S. multinationals really want to do business with the backing of a bayonet, or a cruise missile, though they won't cry all the way to the bank if they have to do so. So why would Washington choose to throw its weight around in so cocksure a manner? Why would it assert its place at the top of the global food chain with such apparent contempt for global public opinion? Overseas opposition to U.S. policies has been a constant for several decades. Indeed, it could be said that anti-Americanism has long been a serviceable *source* of U.S. power. The record of its manipulation by Washington, which ebbs and flows according to domestic need, demonstrates how power constitutes and maintains its grip by nurturing and shaping its own opposition, its own enemies, in its own counterimage. Yet, the worldwide hostility generated by the Bush administration has been excessive, even by the standards of earlier high-water marks during the Vietnam War and in the Reagan era of Star Wars brinksmanship. The degree and intensity of anti-Americanism unleashed by Bush and his hawks far outstripped any capacity to use it expediently to affirm the righteousness of the American Way.

Perhaps, as David Harvey has argued, all the flexing of military might is a way to compensate for the erosion of real U.S. economic power.[18] Perhaps it is simply an exercise of raw state power on the part of testosterone-poisoned hawks, who finally found themselves in the drivers' seat of their dreams. Or perhaps it really does signal a shift to an entirely predatory appropriation of overseas resources and markets that no longer needs any legal cover. Either way, it has not been done with any degree of coherence or competence, not even from the perspective of those who talk wistfully of a new imperium. No one, it seems, really believes that the United States, and least of all the Dubya gang, has the will or the patience to apply itself to nation building in the colonial style (as witnessed, most recently, in the debacles of reconstruction in Afghanistan and Iraq).

Besides, even U.S. cultural imperialism—a long established staple—isn't quite what it used to be. U.S. media companies, for example, far prefer the strategy of localization to the old practice of dumping U.S. programming in foreign markets. The number of hours of American programming has dropped markedly in all European countries, while content at U.S. multinationals like CNN and MTV has been considerably de-Americanized; in 1996, 70 percent of CNN International was U.S. content, whereas now the figure is 8 percent. MTV broadcasts "funky but respectful" calls to prayer five times a day in Indonesia. Whether or not American content is a liability, these days—and in many parts of the world it clearly is—it is no longer as profitable as it once was. The appeal of American-identified cultural goods has been declining steadily for some time, and the gauge of their value no longer seems responsive to a reassertion of U.S. might as it has been in previous decades. U.S. citizens can travel abroad only warily, and the Stars and Stripes are as much a hindrance overseas as they are a virtue at home. The effort to implement the Bush Doctrine has only hastened the decline of brand USA. Investors are rapidly losing interest in backing a product that has retained its swagger but lost its romance. Yet, with multilateralism in retreat for the time being, the short-term profile of global capitalism still hangs in the balance.

What, then is to be done? For progressive globalists at home, the goal remains, as always, to think and act beyond the nation-state. Previous attempts to do so, based on proletarian solidarity or on student power, have not survived well, but the conditions for forging a new international seem more propitious today than they have been in several decades. Because of the lopsided impact of American politics on the world at large, the domestic row over how best to "persuade the nation"—a longstanding fixture on the American Left—cannot be regarded as a provincial matter. But, more than ever, the yardstick of homegrown protest must lie in its international linkage. Because of the impact of economic globalization, this rule applies to the domestic labor and social justice movements as much as it applies to the legacy of Seattle and Genoa. While the U.S. Left has often reflected the nation's strong leaning toward isolationism, exceptionalism, and protectionism, it has also seen admirable service on the frontline of internationalism: the Anti-Imperialist League of the late 1890s (which boasted a membership of half a million), the Popular Front of the 1930s, the civil rights, women's, and gay liberation movements, and the antiwar mobilization of the 1960s. These days, there is less and less choice in the matter. Ducking the challenge of internationalism is a recipe for irrelevance; facing down the charge of anti-Americanism is a small price to pay for taking it on.

NOTES

1. In *The Black Jacobins* (New York: Random House, 1963), C. L. R. James suggests that the sustaining source of the Haitian revolt lay more in the autonomous traditions of resistance forged by slaves—a black proletariat forged in the sugar factories—than in the ideas propagated by the French Revolution. James's treatment of Toussaint L'Ouverture's compromises with the white colonial remnant demonstrates the quandaries of reconciling the bourgeois legacies of French civilization with the reconstructionist needs of the new nation and its mass of former slaves. See Cedric Robinson's treatment of James's analysis in *Black Marxism: The Making of the Black Radical Tradition* (Chapel Hill: University of North Carolina Press, 1983), pp. 274–278.

2. Frances Stonor Saunders, *The Cultural Cold War: The CIA and the World of Arts and Letters* (New York: New Press, 1999). Even for those inclined to take Saunders's suggestion about the CIA with a pinch of salt, the general impact of her book has been far-reaching in its implication of a much wider cast of characters in the drama of dirty tricks and demonology. As a result, it is difficult for us now not to reread with suspicion almost everything that was said in the favorite organs of the liberal intelligentsia of the day.

3. I am paraphrasing views advanced by contributors to Daniel Bell, ed., *The New American Right* (New York: Criterion, 1955), who included Richard Hofstadter, Seymour Martin Lipset, Peter Viereck, Talcott Parsons, David Riesman, Daniel Bell, and Nathan Glazer.

4. Earl Latham, *The Communist Controversy in Washington* (Cambridge, Mass.: Harvard University Press, 1966); Athan Theoharis, *Seeds of Repression: Harry S. Truman and the Origin of McCarthyism* (Chicago: Quadrangle, 1971); Michael Rogin, *The Intellectuals and Joe McCarthy: The Radical Specter* (Cambridge, Mass.: MIT Press, 1967).

5. Robert Thomas's essay "Colonialism: Internal and Classic," published in the 1966–1967 issue of *New University Thought,* is considered to have had a seminal influence on the Native movement. The emergence of Black Power and black nationalism was modeled, in large part, on the anti-colonial and pan-Africanist movement; see Harold Cruse, *Rebellion or Revolution?* (New York: William Morrow, 1968); Kenneth Clark, *Dark Ghetto: Dilemmas of Social Power*

(New York: Harper and Row, 1965); and Stokely Carmichael and Charles Hamilton, *Black Power: The Politics of Liberation in America* (New York: Random House, 1967). Robert Blauner's *Racial Oppression in America* (New York: Harper and Row, 1972) was probably the most influential analysis of internal colonialism of the period. Rodolfo Acuña's *Occupied America: The Chicano's Struggle toward Liberation* (San Francisco: Canfield Press, 1972), is a classic Chicano critique of the occupied Southwest. Also see Manning Marable, *How Capitalism Underdeveloped Black America: Problems in Race, Political Economy and Society* (Boston: South End Press, 1983); Mario Barrera, *Race and Class in the Southwest: A Theory of Racial Inequality* (Notre Dame, Ind.: Notre Dame University Press, 1979); and Ward Churchill, *Since Predator Came: Notes from the Struggle for American Indian Liberation* (Littleton, Colo.: Aigis Publications, 1995).

6. Timothy B. Tyson, *Radio Free Dixie: Robert F. Williams and the Roots of Black Power* (Chapel Hill: University of North Carolina Press, 1999), investigates the traditions of armed self-reliance among black Americans.

7. Jack Newfield, introduction to dossier on "American Rebels," *Nation* (July 21–28, 2003), p. 13.

8. Hitchens's "break with the Left" was a long, drawn-out public affair, though it was conducted mostly in the pages of the *Nation,* where he resigned as a columnist in the fall of 2002. See Christopher Hitchens, "Taking Sides," *Nation* (September 26, 2002).

9. Todd Gitlin was only the most visible left-identified public commentator to take issue consistently with the anti-Americanism of "left-wing fundamentalism: a negative faith in America the ugly." For examples of his op-ed essays in this vein, see "Blaming America First," *Mother Jones* (January–February 2002); and "Liberalism's Patriotic Vision," *New York Times,* September 5, 2002, p. A23; "Liberal Activists Finding Themselves Caught between a Flag and a Hard Place," *San Jose Mercury News,* October 28, 2001; "The Ordinariness of American Feelings," *Open Democracy,* October 10, 2001, http://www.opendemocracy .net/debates/article-2-47-105.jsp.

10. Michael Ignatieff, "Empire: The Burden," *New York Times Magazine,* January 5, 2003.

11. Michael Kazin, "A Patriotic Left," *Dissent* (fall 2002). In a more even-handed contribution to the debate about jingoism, Howard Zinn argues that the distinction between "dying for your country and dying for your government is crucial in understanding what I believe to be the definition of patriotism in a democracy. According to the Declaration of Independence—the fundamental document of democracy—governments are artificial creations, established by the people, deriving their just powers from the consent of the governed and charged by the people to ensure the equal right of all to 'life, liberty, and the pursuit of happiness.' . . . When a government recklessly expends the lives of its young for crass motives of profit and power (always claiming that its motives

are pure and moral) ('Operation Just Cause' was the invasion of Panama and 'Operation Iraqi Freedom' in the present instance) it is violating its promise to the country. It is the country that is primary—the people, the ideals of the sanctity of human life and the promotion of liberty. War is almost always a breaking of those promises (although one might find rare instances of true self defense)." Available at *TomPaine.com* (Monday, May 5, 2003).

12. Kazin makes his case for the betrayal of left populism in *The Populist Persuasion: An American History* (New York: Basic Books, 1995).

13. Michael Tomasky, *Left for Dead: The Life, Death, and Possible Resurrection of Progressive Politics in America* (New York: Free Press, 1996); Richard Rorty, *Achieving Our Country: Leftist Thought in Twentieth-Century America* (Cambridge, Mass.: Harvard University Press, 1998); Michael Lind, *The Next American Nation: The New Nationalism and the Fourth American Revolution* (New York: Free Press, 1995); Steve Fraser and Gary Gerstle, eds., *The Rise and Fall of the New Deal Order, 1930–1980* (Princeton: Princeton University Press, 1990); Todd Gitlin, *The Twilight of Common Dreams: Why America Is Wracked by Culture Wars* (New York: Metropolitan Books, 1995); and various columns in the *Nation* by Eric Alterman.

14. Lisa Duggan, *The Twilight of Equality: Neoliberalism, Cultural Politics, and the Attack on Democracy* (Boston: Beacon Press, 2003). Also see Robin Kelley, *Yo Mama's Dysfunktional! Fighting the Culture Wars in Urban America* (Boston: Beacon Press, 1997); and Nikhil Singh, "Culture/Wars: Recoding Empire in an Age of Democracy," *American Quarterly* 50:3 (September 1988).

15. With a full-blown lineage in Ku Klux Klan and Nazi racialism, these right-wing movement of dissent are explicitly pro-American—their members consider themselves to be true upholders of the U.S. Constitution, defending national sovereignty against the New World Order of the UN. For recent literature on the topic, see Chip Berlet and Matthew N. Lyons, *Right-Wing Populism in America: Too Close for Comfort* (New York: Guilford Press, 2000); Daniel Levitas, *The Terrorist Next Door: The Militia Movement and the Radical Right* (New York: Thomas Dunne Books/St. Martin's Press, 2002); Linda Kintz, *Between Jesus and the Market: The Emotions That Matter in Right-Wing America* (Durham: Duke University Press, 1997); Lane Crothers, *Rage on the Right: The American Militia Movement from Ruby Ridge to Homeland Security* (Lanham, Md.: Rowman and Littlefield, 2003); Ann Burlein, *Lift High the Cross: Where White Supremacy and the Christian Right Converge* (Durham: Duke University Press, 2002); Sara Diamond, *Roads to Dominion: Right-Wing Movements and Political Power in the United States* (New York: Guilford Press, 1995); Diamond, *Spiritual Warfare: The Politics of the Christian Right* (Boston: South End Press, 1989); James Aho, *The Politics of Righteousness: Idaho Christian Patriotism* (Seattle: University of Washington Press, 1990); James Ridgeway, *Blood in the Face: The Ku Klux Klan, Aryan Nations, Nazi Skinheads, and the Rise of a New White Culture* (New York: Thunder's

Mouth Press, 1990); Catherine McNicol Stock, *Rural Radicals: Righteous Rage in the American Grain* (Ithaca: Cornell University Press, 1996).

16. As Eric Hobsbawm has put it, "The US, like revolutionary France and revolutionary Russia, is a great power based on a universalist revolution—and therefore based on the belief that the rest of the world should follow its example, or even that it should help liberate the rest of the world. Few things are more dangerous than empires pursuing their own interest in the belief that they are doing humanity a favour." Hobsbawm, "America's Imperial Delusion," *Guardian*, June 14, 2003.

17. David North and David Walsh, "Anti-Americanism: The 'Anti-Imperialism' of Fools." World Socialist website, September 22, 2001. Available at http://www.wsws.org/articles/2001/sep2001/rads-s22.shtml.

18. David Harvey, *The New Imperialism* (New York: Oxford University Press, 2003).

17

Vigilante Americanism

John Kuo Wei Tchen

TO FULLY UNDERSTAND ANTI-AMERICANISM, we have to step back and question what it means to be an "American." For President George W. Bush, it is a fanciful morality story of all-good versus all-evil. In a White House speech on September 23, 2002, he restated his definition of Americanism. "In America, everybody matters, everybody counts, every human life is a life of dignity. And that's not the way our enemy thinks. Our enemy hates innocent life; they're willing to kill in the name of a great religion. And as long as we love freedom and love liberty and value every human life, they're going to try to hurt us. And so our most important job is to defend the freedom, defend the homeland."[1] The true roots of the U.S. national empire could not be more different.

In 1845, John O'Sullivan, a New Yorker and the editor of the *United States Magazine and Democratic Review,* suggested that the prior colonial claims of European conquest did not matter; "Providence" was above all international treaties. Americans would make their own law.

> Away, away with all these cobweb tissues of rights of discovery, exploration, settlement, contiguity, etc. The American claim is by the right of our manifest destiny to overspread and to possess the whole of the continent which Providence has given us for the development of the great experiment of liberty and federative self-government entrusted to us. It is a right such as that of the tree to the space of air and earth suitable for the full expansion of its principle and destiny of growth.[2]

With Bibles and guns, crusading Euro-American Christian missionaries and soldiers, immigrants and entrepreneurs had indeed claimed the lands of the Native Americans, the French, the Spanish, and whoever was in the way of their "manifest destiny."

Violence was a necessary accompaniment. In a private 1893 correspondence, Frederic Remington, a New Yorker and a Yale-educated artist who helped create the mythic image of the American cowboy, frankly expressed his Anglo-Saxon Protestant nationalist view. "Jews, Injuns, Chinamen, Italians, Huns—the rubbish of the earth I hate—I've got some Winchesters and when the massacring begins, I can get my share of 'em, and what's more, I will. Our race is full of sentiment."[3] The clearance of these inferior peoples, along with those who advocated mixing together, enabled private land development and the flourishing of a white nationalism. Remington expressed a race warrior's enactment of manifest destiny. In President Bush's America, the definition of "our race" has expanded. It now includes Jews, Italians, and eastern Europeans as white and worthy. Rhetorically, it would also include "Injuns" and "Chinamen" and other others. Yet, the expansionist ambitions of O'Sullivan's American empire have remained fundamental to U.S. policy. Once it was bound by Canada to the north and Mexico to the south, Washington's dominion moved ever westward into the Pacific and into Asia. The post–September 11 Bush doctrine of U.S. right, might, and corporate freedom extends this expansionism onto a global scale. In the words he has repeated time and again: "I had made it clear to the world that either you're with us or you're with the enemy, and that doctrine still stands."[4] What does this history of empire-building mean for Americans today? And who truly counts as an American?

INQUIRING MINDS NEED TO KNOW: WHO IS AN "AMERICAN"?

Of course we are referring to those of the United States. And, technically, we are referring to U.S. Americans with full civil rights, as conferred by U.S. citizenship. Or are we using a definition determined by what Justice Sutherland (1925), in an infamous decision on citizenship, referred to as legitimate "common usage"? Or both? Clearly we are not speaking of the thousands of Arab and Islamic, or Arab-looking, or turban-wearing peoples rounded up, insulted, or beaten up after the bombing of the World Trade Center. "They" were not considered true Americans—whether they technically were U.S. citizens, held green cards, or had temporary visas. What of the figure-skating Californian Michelle Kwan? Remember the silly 1998 MSNBC headline when Tara Lipinski won the gold medal at the Nagano Winter Olympics: "American Beats Out Kwan"? The network apologized, but its slip-up was hardly innocent.[5]

Sometimes the mainstream speaks of Japanese-Americans as Americans, and sometimes not. We cannot forget that, after the bombing of Pearl Harbor in 1942, 120,000 Japanese-Americans, most of whom were born in the United States and thus American citizens, were sent to U.S. concentration camps. Many of these incarcerated Nisei men nonetheless volunteered to fight in the U.S. armed forces against fascism and became among the most highly decorated soldiers of the war. It took until 1992, after years of protests, for a U.S. president (Ronald Reagan, in this case) to officially apologize and to offer compensation to living internees in 1992. Not surprisingly, Japanese-Americans have been at the forefront of protests against the detainment of Arab and Muslim Americans during the Gulf and Iraqi wars.

What about Bhagat Singh Thind, a U.S. immigrant born in Punjab India who, when denied U.S. naturalization, appealed the ruling on the basis that he was technically of "Caucasian" ancestry? In his 1925 case, Supreme Court Justice Sutherland delivered the opinion that, in "common usage," Caucasian means "white persons," not persons from the Caucasus Mountains, in spite of "the speculations of the ethnologist." Since Thind was not "commonly recognized as white," he was considered ineligible to become a naturalized citizen of the United States.[6]

Or Wong Chin Foo, the New York journalist who, in 1887, stood toe-to-toe with the leader of the U.S. anti-Chinese movement, the Irish émigré Denis Kearny, at Cooper Union's Great Hall, and called him an un-American racist. Wong also coined the term "Chinese-American," at a time when Chinese-Americans could not hold citizenship simply because Chinese migrants were legally banned from naturalized citizenship.[7]

And, last, we surely do not have in mind the notable exiled former president of Peru, Alberto Fujimori. After all, he is a Latin American Americano, not an American American. Yet U.S. terminological usage trumps all definitions. Dare we ever imagine an Asian American as U.S. president?

REHABILITATED DEAD (ANTI-)AMERICANS

Last night, Mel Brooks's *Robin Hood: Men in Tights* (1993) ran on television. Brooks, the Eastern European Jewish-U.S. American comic genius, cast Dave Chappelle (formerly of Time Warner/Viacom's Comedy Central) as one of Robin Hood's loyal sidekicks. As the Asianized Ahchoo, Chappelle was the Moor-Sherwood Forestian martial arts expert. In the scene where the white Robin Hood is failing to rally his brothers to action, this dashing yet bland white man just can't rouse a crowd. His merry men are all snoring. Ahchoo comes to the rescue. Poised as the finger-pointing black militant, he saves Robin's *tuchis* by delivering a rousing "We did not land on Sherwood Forest! Sherwood Forest landed on us!" This Asian-black is acceptable to the white men in tights because he can rouse their otherwise unexpressed feelings.

Comedy flourishes at the boundaries of what society holds transgressive—one step removed. Brooks, the *Yiddishkeit* prankster defying still sensitive social taboos, is parodying Denzel Washington's Malcolm X speech about Plymouth Rock in Spike Lee's film *Malcolm X* (1992). Malcolm X—now there's a true blue anti-American American!!! He has become canonized as part of a *Time-Life* version of the '60s. An icon of the civil rights/Black Power movement, a movement mainstream whites perceive as a just cause marred by too-militant and too-uppity blacks. For Malcolm X, blacks were not part of the American dream. "No, I'm not an American. I'm one of the twenty-two million black people who are victims of Americanism. . . . I don't see any American dream; I see an American nightmare." To be an American for Malcolm X meant having full human rights, not the appearance of inclusion. "Well, I am not one who believes in deluding myself. I'm not going to sit at your table and watch you eat, with nothing on my plate, and call myself a diner. . . . Being born here in America doesn't make you an American. Why, if birth made you American, you wouldn't need any legislation; you wouldn't need any amendments to the Constitution; you wouldn't be faced with civil-rights filibustering in Washington, D.C., right now."[8] His ability to speak forcefully and plainly to everyday people (a power all too evident in reading his speeches today) made his free speech effective and all too dangerous to the powers that be. Malcolm's power extended internationally because he was thinking, earlier than Dr. King, beyond the boundaries of the United States. In 1963, at the early buildup of the U.S. war in Southeast Asia, Malcolm X did not want simply to preach nonviolence in the face of violent repression. He argued presciently: "If violence is wrong in America, violence is wrong abroad. If it is wrong to be violent defending black women and black children and black babies and black men, then it is wrong for America to draft us, and make us violent abroad in defense of her."[9] In condemning racial injustice and violence at home, he was laying the basis for a critique of militarism overseas. State-sanctioned violence perpetrated abroad continues to return home in the form of terrorism, echoing the trauma of violence with more unresolved violence. Some of this terror has been committed by homegrown former U.S. military soldiers gone berserk, plaguing our everyday life with domestic violence, sniper attacks, mass bombings, anthrax killings, and who-knows-what next. In 1963, these were brazen, analytic connections to draw. They broke through the surface peace of American political culture and helped build a bridge between the civil rights movement and the early antiwar movement.

Malcolm X, the untypical American, attracted unexpected admirers. In 1964, four Japanese journalists, each of them *hibakusha,* or survivors of the atomic bomb, came to New York City as delegates of the Hiroshima Nagasaki World Peace Mission. They requested a meeting with Malcolm X. The gathering was arranged in the modest Harlem apartment of Yuri and Bill Kochiyama. Under great duress because he had lately been ousted from the Nation of Islam, he spoke of the struggle of the people of Vietnam as the struggle of the third world for self-determination and human rights. This global vision is what attracted Bill and Yuri Kochiyama. She had been incarcerated in an Arkansas concentration camp, and he had been in the highly decorated all-Japanese American 442 Regiment. When Malcolm X was assassinated in the Audubon Ballroom on February 21, 1965, it was Yuri who held his bloodied torso on her lap.[10]

It was this same capacity to touch the hearts and minds of non-African Americans that made Dr. Martin Luther King Jr. ever more dangerous after the passage of the Civil Rights Acts of 1964–1965. In King's "Beyond Vietnam" speech at Riverside Church, on April 4, 1967, his prior critiques of poverty were augmented by a global critique of U.S. wars abroad. "The war in Vietnam is but a symptom of a far deeper malady within the American spirit. . . . We will be marching . . . without end unless there is a significant and profound change in American life and policy." King gave his most concise analysis of the link between domestic problems and global issues:

> I am convinced that if we are to get on the right side of the world revolution, we as a nation must undergo a radical revolution of values. We must rapidly begin the shift from a thing-oriented society to a person-oriented society. When machines and computers, profit motives, and property rights are considered more important than people, the giant triplets of racism, extreme materialism, and militarism are incapable of being conquered.[11]

Media analysts like Jeff Cohen and Norman Solomon have pointed out the conglomerate media's retrospective silence on this phase of King's political vision.[12] Moreover, while his holiday is now celebrated and he has become an icon of American history, the mainstream media loudly denounced King at the time. For example, *Time* magazine called his Riverside speech "demagogic slander that sounded like a script for Radio Hanoi." The *Washington Post* opined that "King has diminished his usefulness to his cause, his country, his people."[13]

In public political life, such challenges to the U.S. state are not taken lightly. We still do not know the full stories of the assassinations of Malcolm X or Dr. King. If they had lived, it is more than likely they would have suffered the same fate as the leadership of the Black Panther party—targeted and eliminated by J. Edgar Hoover's clandestine counterintelligence programs (COINTELPRO).[14] Regardless, Malcolm X's and King's more penetrating critiques of U.S. Americanism and the coalitional linkages they called for have been largely marginalized. In their common remembrance today, the complexity of their internationalist analyses has been reduced to caricatures: the dangerously militant Black Muslim anti-American American and the righteous, peaceful 100 percent American. Civil rights equality and justice have become naturalized as part of the national mythos. A sanitized King, with holiday and all, is now used, like Ahchoo, to save America's *tuchis*. Yet we are still far from conquering King's "giant triplets" and from making the promise of justice and equality a reality. In their place, new kinds of anti-Americans have been conjured up. Spies are once more said to be among us, and they are not the good spies, the Pierce Brosnan-James Bond types. They are stereotyped as foreigners, living in deep cover among immigrant and student communities within the United States.

As a result, whole communities are branded as suspect, and their rights go wanting.

A TWO-FRONT WAR?

These days, militarists and policy makers debate whether the U.S. armed forces are capable of waging a two-front war. Is the U.S. war machine technically capable? How solid will public support turn out to be (as measured by conglomerate-run opinion polls)? With the imagined victory over Iraq, shouldn't Iran be next? What of North Korea? What of the anti-guerrilla skirmishes in the Philippines and Indonesia? The study of Asian and Asian American histories can help us understand how U.S. wars in Asia (and now the Middle East) have always been two-front wars: the war at home and the war against [fill in the blank]. While the propagandists mobilize the public, internal enemies are typically identified, and anti-Asian or anti-Asian-American fears of fifth columnists are stirred up, followed by the inevitable violation of human rights in the name of wartime security. Ever since the U.S. Civil War, the phantom of domestic anti-Americanism has been manipulated to rally what Richard Slotkin called our "gunfighter nation."[15] Any citizens' dissent is quickly demonized and rendered unpatriotic. This vigilante justice is the failsafe system when legal means are perceived to have been exhausted. Self-defined "patriots" enact the duties of white, macho citizenship to exact true justice, and Justice Lynch presides. It is the direct action of fools and hatemongers, but also of the genteel power brokers, frustrated by standard legal channels.

In this current era, described by President George Bush Sr. as the "new world order," U.S. foreign policy continues to target regions of Asia. Before September 11, the target was most visibly China. Post–September 11, it has become Central Asia, Indonesia, the Philippines, and North Korea. And, with the Patriot Act and the Department of Homeland Security, once again foreign policy priorities were used to recast Americanism and loyalty within the United States. In the aftermath of the invasion of Iraq, U.S. troops and inspectors have found no verifiable evidence of "weapons of mass destruction"—the pretext for the U.S. military invasion of Iraq. Nor has Osama bin Laden been found. Yet, with the September 11 attacks, it is clear that America's new gunfighters, Paul Wolfowitz, Donald Rumsfeld, and John Ashcroft, have reformulated U.S. foreign policy and domestic politics to discipline and punish all who obstruct what can be loosely called "the American way."[16] The occupation of Afghanistan, the increased control of Arab and Central Asian oil and gas, and the incarceration of foreign nationals in the United States have become the flip side of the American Dream—an ever more fantastic, media-driven image of prosperity, opportunity, and security. The unrelenting U.S. push for unimpeded access to natural resources and rewards for its multinational corporations, such as Dick Cheney's Halliburton, only underscore the relevance of Martin Luther King's critique. The "giant triplets of racism, extreme materialism, and militarism" continue to drive U.S. interests and U.S. identity. In comparison with the newly centralized authority of the Department of Homeland Security, many fear that J. Edgar Hoover's secret "disruptions" will come to seem like child's play.

A CASE STUDY

The pre–September 11 case of the Los Alamos scientist Dr. Wen Ho Lee, wrongly accused of espionage in 1999, demonstrates well the underlying racial logic of U.S. political culture. The perpetual problematic of Americans treating Asians and Asian Americans as foreign and potential enemies is not a product of individual prejudice. It is a systemic feature of U.S. nationalism, hence at any given moment an expression of how Americans think of themselves and define others. The inclusion of U.S. citizens of Asian descent in the American Dream, therefore, is kept in systemic limbo—from group to group kept off balance (depending on which Asian nation is an enemy and which is an ally) by nationality and by dominant and shifting perceptions of racial incompatibility. In the course of a century and a half of American wars in the Pacific and Asia, this extralegal Americanism, tied to Justice Sutherland's judgment of "common usage," is what has defined vigilante Americanism.

Wen Ho Lee was put in solitary confinement and denied bail on charges of espionage. Like many of the brightest Asian students, he had sought out his American dream when he left anti-communist Taiwan in 1964 for graduate studies in mathematics and hydrodynamics at Texas A&M. He and his wife, Sylvia, had two American-born children, and he became a naturalized U.S. citizen in 1974. Working in the Los Alamos National Labs since 1978, he was falsely accused of "stealing the crown jewels" of U.S. nuclear arms for the People's Republic of China. Conveniently released at the same time, the Cox Commission Report claimed that China was stealing U.S. nuclear secrets and constituted a growing threat to U.S. national security. Lee was represented overwhelmingly by the media and the government as a foreign (Chinese) spy, likely to escape the country and therefore treated with undue severity.[17]

His case, when coupled with the reaction to a U.S. spy plane shot down over China, offered evidence that China was being set up by Washington hawks as the new alpha enemy of the United States.[18] The case clearly illustrates how powerful interests exploited racism against East Asian Americans and fabricated a case to support their claims about a Chinese nuclear threat. This threat, in turn, could be parlayed into justification for a large increase in the Pentagon budget, after the proclaimed "peace dividends" of the Clinton era had considerably reduced the armed forces.

Wen Ho Lee's egregious victimization was but the latest example of structural anti-anti-Americanism in U.S. history. While his American dream can be seen as the fruit of the 1965 reversal of the eighty-three-year-old Chinese Exclusion Act, the unfounded charges made against him fully foreshadow the Bush administration's militarists-in-power rhetoric of patriotism, national security, and competitive threats overseas (China bashing is a perennial favorite). If the past is any indication, the manipulation of public fear in a culture accustomed to anti-Asian racism and the resumed militarization of the United States combine to forecast great dangers ahead. Lee's case offers three relevant insights about the fundamental nature of vigilante Americanism in U.S. political culture.

When the situation calls for it, racially inscribed historical patterns trump any legal rights.

Lee got trapped in anti-Chinese/anti-Asian vigilante justice when a Justice Department leak to the New York Times created a media storm. The resulting feeding frenzy revealed his Chinese name and showcased his "Oriental" image. These two details, tied to specific accusations about his being an "enemy spy," were sufficient to trigger white racial fears in the U.S. public culture that violated all legal due process. These fears were subsequently manipulated to serve the ends of militarists and warmongers. Judge Parker's apology and the New York Times's unprecedented near-apology for their roles in fanning the flames highlighted the extralegal, yet highly consequential, power of this vigilante culture. For the victim, the accusations came as a personal attack, since Lee himself was largely unaware of the U.S. historical context that supported his targeting. He had been among the first generation of "Chinese" (in his case, Taiwanese) able to enter the United States with the repeal of the Chinese Exclusion Act and become a naturalized U.S. citizen. As an individual, he realized his American dream—a desirable and prestigious professional position that enabled him to have a family and pursue his passion for mathematics. But, as he also came to learn, Chinese, Taiwanese, Asians, and Asian-appearing peoples have never been fully accepted as full cultural citizens of the United States.

When deemed necessary, the gunslinger American (read: white, hetero-normative male power) trumps the rights of all "others" in the name of national security: White (Anglo-Saxon) national manhood is the bedrock of U.S. political culture. Indeed it was once the basis of U.S. citizenship. Property ownership, the original legal requirement for citizenship, also included the Protestant-defined "civilizational" quality of self-possession or self-ownership. Citizens had to be their own men, individuals not beholden to the Pope, tribal chief, nor proto-Fu Manchuesqe "heathen" despot. Chinese were excluded in 1882 because Chinese workers were viewed as semi-slaves—"coolies" who could not act as individuals, voting on their private, individual self-interests. They were believed to be attitudinally incapable of being Americans. As male non-Protestant European immigrants gained citizenship rights (followed by African Americans and women), the power of white vigilante civilizational moral righteousness became an extralegal quality of national cultural citizenship. Irish and Jews could become citizens and even vote, but the true spirit and power of Americanism belonged to those who harkened back to the founding origins of the nation and those who were their fellow travelers.

In times of grassroots moral crisis and/or international embarrassment, the realm of "we the people" has been expanded, but legal victories of inclusion have been only the beginning. It is in times of war that martial inclusion is most frankly enacted. Those men, and only recently women, who have proven their true loyalty to Americanism (i.e., risked their lives in battle) are then accepted as entitled to inclusion and certain benefits and rights. It was not until 1954, for example, that Chinese immigrants (many of whom fought against Japan in the U.S. armed forces) could be naturalized U.S. citizens, at a time when Chiang Kai-shek's Taiwan was represented as the "good Chinese" antidote to evil Communist China. The McCarran-Walters Act that approved naturalization was passed amid the witch hunts of the McCarthy era. Naturalization was premised on the willingness of would-be citizens to be proper, anti-Communist, self-sacrificing, true-blue Americans.[19]

The struggle for full inclusion into the deeper layers of U.S. political culture, beyond formal citizenship and formal inclusion, is an ongoing and unfinished project. We know from the various civil rights movements within the United States that legal inclusion is only the beginning of the fight for full inclusion in the core political culture. The legal inclusion of Jews into the United States and their inclusion into higher realms of the political culture have not yet resulted in a culture that would elect a Jewish U.S. president. African Americans as citizens are legally included but are en masse effectively excluded from "a level playing field," outside the realms of sports and entertainment culture. As the targeting of Lee demonstrated, the repeal of Chinese/Asian immigration exclusion has not redressed the ongoing marginalization of Asians from American culture and their racialized perception as "foreigners."

EMPIRE'S LIMITS

Two centuries of U.S. empire-building westward into the Pacific has met its match. Contemporary China will not be easily incorporated. It is simply too big and too nationalist. What Giovanni Arrighi has called the long twentieth century of U.S. political and economic supremacy is coming to an end. What will be its future?

In the fifteenth century, the European aristocratic dream of unfettered access to the perceived riches of "the Orient" drove the discovery of the New World. When the United States declared independence, the Euro-American quest for "free trade" and rapid access to the China market built the trade houses of New York City and the northeastern United States and helped accelerate the conquest of native American and Mexican territories to the West.[20] At the Pacific shore, the United States reached out to incorporate Hawaii, Guam, and the Philippines, and exacted military dominance throughout the Pacific Rim to extend the U.S. empire and, after 1949, to combat the threat of

Soviet and Chinese communism.[21] Yet, just as U.S. dominance seemed assured with the collapse of the Soviet Union and China's turn toward capitalism, Arrighi's book announced a fundamental conundrum for Americans. The United States enjoys a near-monopoly on weapons of mass destruction, yet it is chronically debt-ridden. World liquidity has shifted westward into Asia, even though the capitalists of Japan, China, and other Asian "tigers" do not have the military might to become the new global powers. As national and international capitalists intimately intertwine with U.S. capitalists, will this inaugurate a new U.S.-Asia/Pacific century? Or will it mark the onset of ever more dangerous rivalries?[22]

The culture of vigilante Americanism is deeply embedded in the sinews of U.S. white nationalism. Its current invocation imperils Americans of Chinese descent in the United States and threatens the possibility of triggering a twenty-first-century cold war with China. Is this what the American people want? Will this situation give rise to an even more reactionary anti-Asian U.S. nationalism vying to win over this next "evil empire"?

In the shadows of the liberalist rhetoric of inclusion, the specter of anti-Americanism always looms as a cultural resource, especially during periods of xenophobia and war. So I conclude with a quote from Langston Hughes's blues poem "Let America Be America Again." It embodies what I believe to be the best position for anti-vigilante Americans to take. Hughes writes with a cold-eyed realism and yet refuses to disengage. The poem ends with a fighter's spirit.

> O, yes, I say it plain,
> America never was America to me,
> And yet I swear this oath—
> America will be![23]

NOTES

This essay is dedicated to the memory of Jafar Siddiq Hamza, who fought for justice in Aceh, Indonesia, and New York City.

1. President George W. Bush, White House Speech, September 23, 2002.

2. Julius W. Pratt, "The Origin of Manifest Destiny," *American Historical Review* 32 (July 1927): 796.

3. Excerpt from private letter from Frederic Remington to Poultney Bigelow, a fellow Yale alumnus. Poultney Bigelow, "Frederic Remington: With Extracts from Unpublished Letters," *New York State Historical Association Proceedings* 10 (January 1929): 46. Also see Allen P. Splete and Marilyn D. Splete, eds., *Frederic Remington: Selected Letters* (New York: Abbeville Press, 1989), p. 171. The concept of vigilante Americanism is inspired by Richard Slotkin's important work. His trilogy, first published on the heels of the Vietnam War, clearly has ongoing relevance, especially to the Bush presidencies. For Remington's vigilantism, see Slotkin, *Gunfighter Nation: The Myth of the Frontier in Twentieth-Century America* (New York: HarperPerennial, 1992), p. 97.

4. Bush, September 23, 2002.

5. Rene M. Astudillo, "Michelle Kwan Headline Controversy Continues to Haunt Us," available at http://www.aaja.org/html/new_html/media_watch_020225.html.

6. *United States v. Bhagat Singh Thind*, 261 U.S. 204 (1923).

7. John Kuo Wei Tchen, *New York before Chinatown: Orientalism and the Shaping of American Culture, 1776–1882* (Baltimore: Johns Hopkins University Press, 1999), p. 281.

8. George Breitman, ed., *Malcolm X Speaks* (New York: Grove Weidenfeld, 1965), pp. 23–44.

9. Malcolm X, "Message to the Grassroots," November 10, 1963, Detroit, Michigan. Available at http://www.americanrhetoric.com/speeches/malcolmxgrassroots.htm.

10. *Yuri Kochiyama: The Fishmonger's Daughter,* interviewed by Arthur Tobier (New York: St. Marks Oral History Project, 1978).

11. Martin Luther King Jr., "Beyond Vietnam," in Clayborne Carson and Kris Shepard, eds., *A Call to Conscience: The Landmark Speeches of Dr. Martin Luther King, Jr.* (New York: IPM/Warner Books, 2001). The Martin Luther King Papers Project, Stanford University, website is at http://www.stanford.edu/group/King/publications/speeches/contents.htm.

12. Jeff Cohen and Norman Solomon, "The Martin Luther King You Don't See on TV," *Media Beat,* January 4, 1995, available at FAIR's website, http://www.fair.org/media-beat/950104.html.

13. Ibid.

14. Paul Wolf website at COINTELPRO, available at http://www.icdc.com/~paulwolf/cointelpro/cointel.htm. Also see "COINTELPRO: The Untold American Story," compilation by Paul Wolf with contributions from Robert Boyle et al. Presented to UN High Commissioner for Human Rights Mary Robinson at the World Conference against Racism in Durban, South Africa, by members of the Congressional Black Caucus who attended the conference, September 1, 2001. Available at http://www.derechos.net/paulwolf/cointelpropapers/coinwcar3.htm.

15. Slotkin discusses the frontier myth as a theory of development and the gunfighter as the theory's enabler. Slotkin, *Gunfighter Nation,* pp. 16–21.

16. On these hawks' longstanding relationships, see Elisabeth Bumuller and Eric Schmitt, "On the Job and at Home, Influential Hawks' 30-Year Friendship Evolves," *New York Times,* September 11, 2002.

17. House Report 105-851, *Report of the Select Committee on U.S. National Security and Military/Commercial Concerns with the People's Republic of China,* submitted by Mr. Cox of California, Chairman, available at http://www.access.gpo.gov/congress/house/hr105851/; Wen Ho Lee with Helen Zia, *My Country Versus Me* (New York: Hyperion, 2001), pp. 96–105; and Robert Scheer, "No Defense: How the *New York Times* Convicted Wen Ho Lee," *Nation,* October 23, 2000.

18. On April 1, 2001, a U.S. spy plane with a crew of twenty-four was shot down over Chinese airspace and a Chinese pilot was killed. This constituted George W. Bush's first major diplomatic crisis. Some Americans were calling for a boycott of Chinese-American restaurants and all Chinese-made goods, including those sold at Wal Mart.

19. For an example of the impact of such policies on an ordinary Chinese-American laundry workers, see Tung Pok Chin with Winifred C. Chin, *Paper Son: One Man's Story* (Philadelphia: Temple University Press, 2000), pp. 49–56.

20. Tchen, *New York before Chinatown,* pp. 3–62; Dana D. Nelson, *National Manhood: Capitalist Citizenship and the Imagined Fraternity of White Men* (Durham: Duke University Press, 1998); Slotkin, *Gunfighter Nation,* pp. 29–62; and Benjamin B. Ringer, *"We the People" and Others: Duality and America's Treatment of Racial Minorities* (New York: Tavistock, 1983).

21. See Michael H. Hunt, *The Making of a Special Relationship: The United States and China to 1914* (New York: Columbia University Press, 1983); Gil Loescher and John A. Scanlon, *Calculated Kindness: Refugees and America's Half-Open Door, 1945–Present* (New York: Free Press, 1986); and Angel Velasco Shaw and Luis Francia, eds., *Vestiges of War: The Philippine-American War and the Aftermath of an Imperial Dream, 1899–1999* (New York: New York University Press, 2002). The historical linkages between the U.S. frontier and possessions in the Pacific were first made by William A. Williams in *The Roots of the Modern American Empire* (New York: Random House, 1969).

22. Giovanni Arrighi, *The Long Twentieth Century* (London: Verso, 1994), pp. 352–354; and Arrighi, "Globalization and Historical Macrosociology," in Janet Abu-Lughod, ed., *Sociology for the Twenty-First Century: Continuities and Cutting Edges* (Chicago: Chicago University Press, 2000), pp. 117–133.

23. Langston Hughes, The Academy of American Poets, "Let America be America Again," available at http://www.poets.org/poems/poems.cfm?prmID=1473. From *The Collected Poems of Langston Hughes,* Arnold Rampersad, ed. (New York: Knopf, 1994).

Bibliographical Notes

Journalistic contributions to the debate surrounding the vision of a new U.S. imperium include Max Boot, "The Case for American Empire," *Weekly Standard* (October 15, 2001); Anthee Carassava, "Anti-Americanism Is Reinvigorated by War," *New York Times* (April 7, 2003); Robert Cooper, "The Postmodern State," *Observer* (April 7, 2002); Emily Eakins, "It Takes an Empire, Say Several U.S. Thinkers," *New York Times* (April 1, 2002); Jonathan Freedland, "Emperor George," *Guardian* (April 2, 2003); Michael Ignatieff, "Empire: The Burden," *New York Times Magazine* (January 5, 2003) and "America's Empire Is an Empire Lite," *New York Times* (January 10, 2003); John Ikenberry, "Getting Hegemony Right," *National Interest* (spring 2001); Robert Kagan, "The Benevolent Empire," *Foreign Policy* (summer 1998) and "Power and Weakness: Why Europe and the U.S. See the World Differently," *Policy Review* 113 (June–July 2002); Robert Kaplan, "Supremacy by Stealth: Ten Rules for Managing the World," *Atlantic Monthly* (July–August 2003); Paul Kennedy, "The Greatest Superpower Ever," *New Perspectives Quarterly* (winter 2002) and "The Perils of Empire," *Washington Post* (April 20, 2003); Nicolas Lemann, "The Next World Order," *New Yorker* (April 2001); Anatol Lieven, "The Dilemma of Sustaining an American Empire," *Financial Times* (January 2, 2003) and "The Push for War," *London Review of Books* (October 3, 2002); Michael Lind, "Is America the New Roman Empire?" *Globalist* (June 19, 2002); Sebastian Mallaby, "The Reluctant Imperialist: Terrorism, Failed States, and the Case for American Empire," *Foreign Affairs* (March–April 2002); Roger Morris, "From Republic to Empire," *Globe and Mail* (April 14, 2003); Ignacio Ramonet, "Transition to an Empire," *Le Monde Diplomatique* (May 1, 2003); Thomas Ricks, "Empire or Not? A Quiet Debate over U.S. Role," *Washington Post* (August 21, 2001); Edward Rothstein, "Cherished Ideas Refracted through History's Lens," *New York Times* (September 7, 2002); Andrew Sullivan, "America Sets the Agenda for Wars of the Future," *Sunday Times* (April 13 2003); Jay Tolson, "The American Empire: Is the U.S. Trying to Shape the World? Should It?" *U.S. News and World Report* (January 13, 2003); Daniel Vernet, "Postmodern Imperialism," *Le Monde* (April 24, 2003); and Martin Wolf, "The World's Lonely Imperial Power," *Financial Times* (November 26, 2002).

Books covering the liberal to centrist spectrum of the debate include Andrew Bacevich, *American Empire: The Realities and Consequences of U.S. Diplomacy*

(Cambridge, Mass.: Harvard University Press, 2003) and Bacevich, ed., *The Imperial Tense: Prospects and Problems of American Empire* (New York: Ivan Dee, 2003); Christopher Coker, *Empires in Conflict: The Growing Rift between Europe and the United States* (London: RUSI, 2003); and Joseph Nye, *The Paradox of American Power: Why the World's Only Superpower Can't Go It Alone* (London: Oxford, 2002).

Responses from the Left to the "new U.S. imperium" drawing on a neo-Marxist tradition include Samir Amin, "Imperialism and Globalization," *Monthly Review* (June 2001) and the *Monthly Review* issue on "Imperialism Now" (July–August 2003); Peter Gowan, *The Global Gamble: Washington's Bid for World Dominance* (London: Verso, 1999); David Harvey, *The New Imperialism* (New York: Oxford University Press, 2003); Harry Magdoff, *Imperialism without Colonies* (New York: Monthly Review Press, 2003); Michael Mann, *Incoherent Empire* (London: Verso, 2003); Leo Panitch, "The New Imperial State" *New Left Review* 11:1 (March–April 2000); and James Petras and Henry Veltmeyer, *Globalization Unmasked: Imperialism in the 21st Century* (London: Zed Books, 2001). The extensive debate about Michael Hardt and Toni Negri's *Empire* (Cambridge, Mass.: Harvard University Press, 2000), which envisages global power as de-centered and therefore detached from Washington's pivot, has helped to define differing leftist perspectives on the topic. Perhaps the most systematic counterbalance to Hardt and Negri's perspective can be found in Giovanni Arrighi, *The Long Twentieth Century: Money, Power, and the Origin of Our Times* (New York: Verso, 1994).

A leftist perspective somewhat less beholden to political economic analysis includes Tariq Ali, "A Short-Course History of U.S. Imperialism," in *The Clash of Fundamentalisms, Crusades, Jihads, and Modernity* (London: Verso, 2002); Eric Hobsbawm, "America's Imperial Delusion," *Guardian* (June 15, 2003); Chalmers Johnson, *Blowback: The Costs and Consequences of American Empire* (New York: Metropolitan Books, 2000) and *The Sorrows of Empire: How the American People Lost* (New York: Metropolitan Books, 2004); Norman Mailer, "Gaining an Empire, Losing Democracy?" *International Herald Tribune* (February 25, 2003); Arundhati Roy, *War Talk* (Boston: South End Press, 2003); and Gore Vidal, *Perpetual War for Perpetual Peace: How We Got to Be So Hated* (New York: Nation Books, 2003).

American Studies scholarship has a long history of analyzing expressions of U.S. imperialism. A very short list would include Eric Cheyfitz, *The Poetics of Imperialism: Translation and Colonization from the Tempest to Tarzan* (Philadelphia: University of Pennsylvania Press, 1977); Noam Chomsky, *Year 501: The Conquest Continues* (Boston: South End Press, 1993); Ward Churchill, *Fantasies of the Master Race: Literature, Cinema and the Colonization of American Indians* (Monroe, Maine: Common Courage Press, 1992); Robert Dean, *Imperial Brotherhood: Gender and the Making of Cold War Foreign Policy* (Amherst: University of Massachusetts Press, 2001); Ariel Dorfman and Armand Mattelart, *How to Read Donald Duck: Imperialist Ideology in the Disney Comic*, 2nd ed. (New York: Intl General, 1983); Richard Drinnon, *Facing West: The Metaphysics of Indian-Hating and Empire-Building* (New York: Schocken, 1990); Daniel J. Faber, *Environment under Fire: Imperialism and the Ecological Crisis in Central America* (New York: Monthly Review Press, 1993); Philip Foner, *The Spanish-Cuban-American War and the Birth of American Imperialism, 1895–1902* (New York: Monthly Review Press, 1972); James Gardner, *Legal Imperialism: American Lawyers and Foreign Aid in Latin America* (Madison: University of Wisconsin Press, 1999); Lloyd Gardner, *Imperial America: American Foreign Policy since 1898* (New York: Harcourt Brace, 1976); Lloyd Gardner, Walter LeFeber, and Thomas McCormick, *Creation of the American Empire: U.S. Diplomatic History* (Chicago: Rand McNally, 1973); Amy Kaplan, *The Anarchy of Empire in the Making of U.S. Culture* (Cambridge, Mass.: Harvard University Press, 2002); Amy Kaplan and Donald Pease, eds., *Cultures of U.S. Imperialism* (Durham, N.C.: Duke University Press, 1993); Walter LeFeber, *The New Empire* (Ithaca, N.Y.: Cornell University Press, 1963); Harry Magdoff, *The Age of Imperialism: The Economics of U.S. Foreign Policy* (New York: Monthly Review Press, 1969); Manning Marable, *How Capitalism Underdeveloped Black America: Problems in Race, Political Economy and Society* (Boston: South End Press, 1983); José Martí, *Inside the Monster: Writings on the United States and American Imperialism* (New York: Monthly Review Press, 1975); Walter Russell Mead, *Mortal Splendor: The American Empire in Transition* (Boston: Houghton Mifflin, 1987); C. Wright Mills, *Listen Yankee! The Revolution in Cuba* (New York: McGraw Hill, 1960); Emily Rosenberg, *Spreading the American Dream: Economic and Cultural Expansion, 1890–1945* (New York: Hill and Wang, 1982); John Carlos Rowe, *Literary Culture and U.S. Imperialism: From the Revolution to World War II* (New York: Oxford University Press, 2000); Angel Velasco Shaw and Luis Francia, *Vestiges of War: The Philippine-American War and the Aftermath of an Imperial Dream 1899–1999* (New York: New York University Press, 2002); Neil Smith, *American Empire: Roosevelt's Geographer and the Prelude to Globalization* (Berkeley: University of California Press, 2003); William Spanos, *America's Shadow: An Anatomy of Empire* (Minneapolis: University of Minnesota Press, 1999); David Stannard, *American Holocaust: The Conquest of the New World* (New York: Oxford University Press, 1992); Penny Von Eschen *Race Against Empire: Black Americans and Anticolonialism, 1937–1957* (Ithaca, N.Y.: Cornell University Press, 1997); Laura Wexler, *Tender Violence: Domestic Visions in an Age of U.S. Imperialism* (Chapel Hill: University of North Carolina Press, 2000); William Appleman Williams, *The Tragedy of American Diplomacy* (New York: Viking, 1955) and *Empire as a Way of Life* (New York: Oxford University Press, 1980); and Donald Worster, *Rivers of Empire: Water, Aridity, and the Growth of the American West* (New York: Oxford University Press, 1992).

Studies of European anti-Americanism include George Andreopoulos, *He chrese kai he katachrese tou antiamerikanismou sten Hellada: he periptose tou mnemonoiu Ford-Kissinger-Iakovou* (Athens: Polytypo, 1994); Volker Rolf Bergahn, *America and the Intellectual Cold Wars in Europe* (Princeton, N.J.: Princeton University Press, 2001); Dan Diner, *Feinbild Amerika: über die Beständigkeit eines Ressentiments* (Munich: Propyläen, 2002); Dan Diner and Sander L. Gilman, *America in the Eyes of the Germans: An Essay on Anti-Americanism,* trans. Allison Brown (Princeton, N.J.: MarkusWiener, 1996); David Ellwood, "Comparative Anti-Americanism in Western Europe," in Heide Fehrenbach and Uta G. Poiger, eds., *Transactions, Transgressions, Transformations: American Culture in Western Europe and Japan* (New York: Berghahn, 2000); David Ellwood and Rob Kroes, *Anti-Americanism in Europe* (Amsterdam: Free University Press, 1986); Philippe Grasset, *Le monde malade de l'Amérique: la doctrine américaine des origines à nos jours* (Lyon: Chronique sociale, 1999); Groupe de recherche et d'études nord-américaines (France), *L'Antiaméricanisme: Anti-Americanism at Home and Abroad* (Aix-en-Provence: Université de Provence, Service des Publications, 2000); Denis Lacorne, Jacques Rupnik, and Marie-France Toine, eds., *The Rise and Fall of Anti-Americanism: A Century of French Perception* (New York: Palgrave-MacMillan, 1990); Claus Leggewie, *Amerikas Welt: Die USA in unseren Köpfen* (Hamburg: Hoffmann und Campe, 2000); Noel Mamère, *Non merci, Oncle Sam* (Paris: Ramsay, 1999); Andrei S. Markovits, "On Anti-Americanism in West Germany," *New German Critique* 34 (winter 1985); Michela Nacci, *L'Antiamericanismo in Italia negli anni trenta* (Torino: Bollati Boringhieri, 1989); Jean-François Revel, *L'Obsession anti-américaine* (Paris: Plon, 2002); Philippe Roger, *L'Ennemi américain: généaologie de l'antiaméricanisme français* (Paris: Seuil, 2002); Mario Roy, *Pour en finir avec l'antiaméricanisme* (Montreal: Borâeal, 1993); Gesine Schwan, *Antikommunismus und Antiamerikanismus in Deutschland: Kontinuität und Wandel nach 1945* (Baden-Baden: Nomos Verlagsgesellschaft, 1999); Herbert J. Spiro, "Anti-Americanism in Western Europe," *Annals of the American Academy of Political Science* (May 1988); Emmanuel Todd, *Après l'empire: essai sur la décomposition du système américain* (Paris: Gallimard, 2002); and Frank Trommler and Joseph McVeigh, *America and the Germans: An Assessment of a Three-Hundred-Year History* (Philadelphia: University of Pennsylvania Press, 1985).

Other non-American studies of anti-Americanism include John L. Esposito, *Unholy War: Terror in the Name of Islam* (New York: Oxford University Press, 2002); J. L. Granatstein, *Yankee Go Home? Canadians and Anti-Americanism* (Toronto: HarperCollins, 1996); Byong-kuk Kim, *Counter-anti-Americanism in Korea: A Collection of Articles and Essays* (Seoul: Seoul Institute of International Economics, 1996); Leopold Krenston, *Anti-Americanism in the Middle East: Sudden War and the Problem of Oil* (Albuquerque, N.M.: American Classical College Press, 1985); Manwoo Lee, ed., *Current Issues in Korean-U.S. Relations* (Seoul: Institute for Far Eastern Studies, 1993); Alan L. McPherson, *Yankee No! Anti-Americanism in U.S.–Latin American Relations* (Cambridge, Mass.: Harvard University

Press, 2003); Alvin Z. Rubinstein, *Anti-Americanism in the Third World: Implications for U.S. Foreign Policy* (New York: Praeger, 1985); Peter Scowen, *Rogue Nation: The America the Rest of the World Knows* (Toronto: M&S, 2003); Eric Shiraev and Vladislav Zubok, *Anti-Americanism in Russia: From Stalin to Putin* (New York: Palgrave, 2000); Guanhua Wang, *In Search of Justice: The 1905–1906 Chinese Anti-American Boycott* (Cambridge, Mass.: Harvard University Press, 2001). and Hong Zhang, *America Perceived: The Making of Chinese Images of the United States, 1945–1953* (Westport, Conn.: Greenwood Press, 2002).

Studies of anti-Americanism written in the United States include Richard Crockatt, *America and Anti-Americanism* (New York: Taylor and Francis, 2002); Richard Crockatt, *America Embattled: 9/11, Anti-Americanism and the Global Order* (New York: Routledge, 2003); Edgar Friedenberg, ed., *The Anti-American Generation* (New York: Transaction, 1971); Oscar Handlin, *The Distortion of America* (New York: Transaction, 1996); Mark Hertsgaard, *The Eagle's Shadow: Why America Fascinates and Infuriates the World* (New York: Farrar, Straus and Giroux, 2002); Paul Hollander, *Anti-Americanism: Critiques at Home and Abroad, 1965–1990* (New York: Oxford University Press, 1992); Daniel C. Maguire, *The New Subversives: Anti-Americanism of the Religious Right* (New York: Continuum, 1982); Thomas Bruce Morgan, *Among the Anti-Americans* (New York: Holt, Rinehart and Winston, 1967); and Simon Schama, "The Unloved American," *New Yorker* (March 10, 2003).

About the Contributors

Vangelis Calotychos is Assistant Professor of Comparative Literature and Hellenic Studies at New York University. He has edited *Cyprus and Its People: Nation, Identity, and Experience in an Unimaginable Community, 1955–1997,* and co-edited a special issue of the *Journal of Mediterranean Studies* (1999) titled *Divisive Cities, Divided Cities: Nicosia.* His *Modern Greece: A Cultural Poetics* (Berg) appeared in 2003. He is currently writing a set of essays on narrative and film in the Balkans.

Patrick Deer is Assistant Professor of English at New York University. He is currently completing the manuscript of *Modernism in Camouflage: War Culture and British Literature.* His research interests include modernism, the twentieth-century novel and film, war culture, and cultural and postcolonial studies.

Ana María Dopico teaches in the Department of Comparative Literature and the Department of Spanish and Portuguese at New York University. She is currently writing about Cuba in a book titled *Cubanologies: Dialectics of National Culture.* She recently completed a forthcoming book on uneven development, visual culture, and the novel, titled *Houses Divided: Social Crisis and Genealogical Fictions in the Americas.*

Linda Gordon teaches history at New York University. Her most recent book, *The Great Arizona Orphan Abduction,* a story of Mexican-white racial conflict, won the Bancroft prize for best book in U.S. history and the Beveridge prize for best book on the Americas. She is currently writing about documentary photography and political culture.

Greg Grandin is the author of *The Blood of Guatemala: A History of Race and Nation,* which won the Latin American Studies Bryce Wood award. His new book, *The Last Colonial Massacre: Latin America in the Cold War,* was just published by the University of Chicago Press. He has written on revolutions, genocide, and human rights and teaches in the history department of New York University.

Harry Harootunian is Professor of History and chair of East Asian Studies at New York University. His recent books include *Overcome by Modernity* (Princeton, 2000) and *History's Disquiet* (Columbia, 2001).

Rebecca E. Karl teaches Modern Chinese History at New York University. She is the author of *Staging the World: Chinese Nationalism at the Turn of the Twentieth Century* (Duke, 2000) and co-editor (with P. Zarrow) of *Rethinking the 1898 Reforms: Political and Cultural Change in Modern China* (Harvard, CEAS Publications, 2002). She is also co-editor (with S. Makdisi and C. Casarino) of *Marxism beyond Marxism* (Routledge, 1996).

Rashid Khalidi is Director of the Middle East Institute and Edward Said Professor of Arab Studies at Columbia University. His publications include *Under Siege: PLO Decision-Making during the 1982 War* (Columbia, 1986) and *Palestinian Identity: The Construction of Modern National Consciousness* (Columbia, 1997). His new book, *Resurrecting Empire,* appeared this year from Beacon Press.

Timothy Mitchell is Professor of Politics at New York University. His books include *Colonising Egypt* (Cambridge, 1988), *Questions of Modernity* (Minnesota, 2000), and *Rule of Experts: Egypt, Techno-Politics, Modernity* (California, 2002).

Mary Nolan is Professor of History at New York University. She is the author of *Visions of Modernity: American Business and the Modernization of Germany* (Oxford, 1994) and co-editor, with Omer Bartov and Atina Grossmann, of *Crimes of War: Guilt and Denial in the Twentieth Century* (New Press, 2002).

Hyun Ok Park is Assistant Professor in the Department of East Asian Studies at New York University. She is the author of the forthcoming book *Two Dreams in One Bed: Manchuria and the Origin of the North Korean Revolution.* Her current research concerns neoliberalism, colonial memory, and Korean migrants in and from China, Japan, and North Korea.

Mary Louise Pratt is Silver Professor at New York University, where she teaches Latin American literature and culture and cultural theory. She has published extensively on gender in Latin American writing, globalization and mobility, and imperialism and modernity. Her book *Imperial Eyes: Travel Writing and Transculturation* (1992) has been translated into Spanish and Portuguese.

Moss Roberts is Professor of Chinese in the Department of East Asian Studies at New York University. He is the translator of *Three Kingdoms: A Historical Novel, Dao De Jing: The Book of the Way,* and *Chinese Fairy Tales and Fantasies.* He is also the author of the article "Bad Karma in Asia," published in *Learning Places,* edited by Masao Miyoshi and Harry Harootunian.

Andrew Ross is Professor of American Studies at New York University. He is the author of several books, including, most recently, *Low Pay, High Profile: The Global Push for Fair Labor, No-Collar: The Humane Workplace and Its Hidden Costs, The Celebration Chronicles: Life, Liberty, and the Pursuit of Property Value in Disney's New Town,* and *Real Love: In Pursuit of Cultural Justice* (NYU Press, 1998). He has also edited several books, including *No Sweat: Fashion, Free Trade, and the Rights of Garment Workers.*

Kristin Ross teaches Comparative Literature at New York University. She is the author of *The Emergence of Social Space: Rimbaud and the Paris Commune* (Minnesota, 1988), *Fast Cars, Clean Bodies: Decolonization and the Reordering of French Culture* (MIT, 1995), which won the Laurence Wylie award for French cultural studies, and *May '68 and Its Afterlives* (Chicago, 2002). Her last two books have been translated into French.

Ella Shohat is Professor of Cultural Studies at New York University. Her award-winning publications include *Israeli Cinema: East/West and the Politics of Representation, Unthinking Eurocentrism* (co-authored with R. Stam), *Dangerous Liaisons: Gender, Nation, and Postcolonial Perspectives* (co-edited), *Talking Visions: Multicultural Feminism in a Transnational Age, Forbidden Reminiscences,* and *Multiculturalism, Postcoloniality, and Transnational Media* (co-edited). *The Culture Wars: A Debate in Translation* (co-authored with R. Stam) will be published by New York University Press. Her writing has been translated into several languages, including

French, Spanish, Portuguese, Arabic, Hebrew, German, Polish, and Turkish.

John Kuo Wei Tchen is Associate Professor of History and Individualized Learning and Director of Asian/Pacific/American Studies at New York University. He is author of *New York before Chinatown: Orientalism and the Shaping of American Culture, 1776–1882,* and co-founder of the Museum of Chinese in the Americas. In 1991, he was awarded the National Medal of Humanities (Charles Frankel Prize).

George Yúdice is Professor of American Studies, Spanish and Portuguese, and directs the Center for Caribbean Studies at New York University. His current research is on trade, environment, and cultural policy in Central America. His most recent books are *Cultural Policy* (co-authored with Toby Miller; Sage Publications, 2002) and *The Expediency of Culture: Uses of Culture in the Global Era* (Duke, 2003).

Index

"A-bomb" scare (1950): Britain, 166–167
Abd al-Aziz Ibn Sa'ud: control of Arabian peninsula, 96
Abd al-Karim Qasim: assassination attempt, 91
Acheson, Dean: Bush administration, 263; "Narcissus psychosis," 25; recognition of Chinese government, 258
Afghanistan: Iran, 93; Japan, 228; mujahideen, 94; Pakistan, 93–94, 99–100; Soviets in, 93–94, 100; U.S. intervention, 33–34, 93–94, 99–100, 104n20; "What We're Fighting For" (manifesto), 198
Africa: American missionaries, 111; colonialism, 109; cotton farmers, 252; democratization, 109
Aguinaldo, Emilio: American annexation of Philippines, 262–263
Akihito, Crown Prince of Japan: marriage, 213
Al-Jazeera: Iraq War coverage, 6
Al-Qaida: attacks on U.S., 100; leaders, 96
Albright, Madeleine: Pew Research Center polling, 9; sanctions on Iraq, 103n17
Alexandria Why? (Chahine), 113
Alférez, Enrique: hunt for Villa, 34
Algeria: United States, 111; War of Independence (1954-1962), 147
Ali, Muhammad: propagandist for U.S., 73–74
Ali, Tariq: "anti-Americanism of fools," 292
Alivizatos, Nikos: 17N antidote, 186
Allen, George: American boastfulness, 23
Alliance for Progress, 25
"America" (the term): Martí, 47; meaning, 19, 21

"American": equated with "white," 277, 302; meaning, 301–304
American anti-Americanism. *See* United States, anti-Americanism in
American Empire: anti-Americanism, 139; Greeks in, 162–163; Hobsbawm on, 300n16; Ignatieff and, 5, 128, 269n19, 289; Macmillan on, 162–163; Manifest Destiny, 302
American exceptionalism: American anti-Americanism, 279; phrase typifying, 1; tenets, 9
"American Ideology, The" (Amin), 106–107, 112
American imperialism: acceptance by Americans, 8; Butler's role, 2–3; France, 146–147; Iraq War, 146, 154; Rice on, 159
American people: distinguished from Bush administration, 74–75; hostility to Bush administration, 74–75; hostility to U.S. cold war policies, 168
Americanism: Bush's definition, 301; recasting of, 307; victims of, 304
Americanismo: anti-Americanism, 37–43; defined, 35
Amerikakritik: anti-Americanism, 134, 138; defined, 134
Amin, Samir: collapse of U.S. economy, 153; "The American Ideology," 106–107, 112
Amino Toshihiko: anti-Americanism, 199
Anderson, Lindsey: *March to Aldermarston*, 168
Anglo-American Francophobia: Murdoch press, 145–146, 154n3
Al-Ani, Muwafak: refusal to relinquish his post, 235

Korea, 224, 225, 227; Opium Wars, 267; "philo-Americans," 243, 247, 250n20; post-Mao period, 240, 243; "postwar" in, 239; Qing dynasty, 236, 242; state power, 252, 267; Taiwan, 253–254; Tian'anmen Incident, 240; turn of the twentieth century, 241–242; United States, 237, 247, 252–254, 256–259, 260, 265–268, 309; war on terrorism, 253; xenophobia, 235–236

China Can Say No (Chinese publication), 244, 250n19

China War (1931-1941): lack of opposition to, 256

Chinese Americans: anti-Chinese movement, 303; case of Wen Ho Lee, 308–311

Chinese Exclusion Act: reversal, 309, 310

Chow, Rey: fascist longings, 248

Christianity: Islam, 118–119

Chrysanthemum and the Sword, The (Benedict), 204

Churchill, Winston: "iron curtain" speech, 161

CIA: House Committee on Un-American Activities, 284–285; McCarthyism, 284; National Intelligence Estimate (1958), 25

Civil rights movement: constituencies, 277

"Clash of civilizations," 101

Clash of Civilizations, The (Huntington), 88

Clinton, Bill: Blair and, 169–170

CNN International: Iraq War coverage, 6

Coca-Cola Company: in Guatemala, 26

Cohen, Jeff: King's legacy, 306

Cohen, William: Western Hemisphere, 18

Cohn-Bendit, Daniel: proposed changes to French social security (1995), 150–151

Cold war (1945-1991): as American foreign policy, 255; American victory, 251; anti-Americanism, 22–23, 237; Britain, 166–167; Campaign for Nuclear Disarmament (CND), 167, 168, 169; China, 241; combatants, 286; deaths during, 3; decolonization, 286; interpretations, 251; lamenting its passing, 251; non-aligned movement, 286; U.S.-Latin American relations, 20

Colombia: anti-Americanism, 20; United States, 283

Colonialism: Africa, 109; Du Bois on, 251; French anti-colonialism, 147; Latin America, 109; Middle East, 109–110; United States, 110–111

Columbia Teachers College: women's movements in Latin America, 41

Common Market of the South (Mercosur), 71; Latin American integration, 71

Communists: Communist Party, Chinese (CCP), 240; Communist Party-USA (CPUSA), 276, 277, 285–286; Greece, 194

Confédération Paysanne: support for, 152

Cooper, Robert: liberal imperialism, 7

Cordovez, Diego: Afghani conflict, 94

Cosmic Race, The (Vasconcelos), 70

Counterinsurgency: Central America, 3; Latin America, 24–25, 37

Craig, Ian: *Cyprus Conspiracy, The* (with O'Malley), 183

Crossman, Richard: Macmillan to, 162

Cuba, 47–68; American culture, 51, 64; American Left, 58, 61; American tourists, 51; anti-Americanism, 48–68; anti-capitalism, 49, 57; anti-imperialism, 48, 57, 60; anti-racism, 52–54; Bay of Pigs (Playa Girón), 54, 61, 63; black Cubans, 52; Black Panthers, 53; blacks, 52–54; Butler in, 2; *castrismo*, 48; *Comités de Defensa de la Revolución* (Committees for the Defense of the Revolution, CDRs), 55–56, 59–60, 67n7; corruption, 51; counterinsurgency, 24; Cuban Revolution, 23–24; decay, 58; economy, 64; "Elián event," 60–63; exiles (*see* Cuban exile community in Miami); foreign investment, 57, 64; foreign trade, 59, 67n6; ¡*Fuera imperialistas yanquis!* ("Yankee go home!"), 55; *generación de hierba mala* (weed generation), 65–66; *gusanos* and its derivatives, 55; Helms-Burton Bill (1995), 57, 59; *imperialismo yanqui*, 54–55; Iraq War, 58–59; landholders, 50; leaving for U.S., 64–65; Mariel exodus, 68n9; middle class, 50–51, 63; national impotence, 51; Platt Amendment, 49–50, 67n3; pro-Americanism, 54–56; revolution of 1959 (*la revolución*), 48–49, 50, 52, 54–56; rural population, 51–52;

125, 132–133; anti-Americanism, 11, 125–126, 183; British-European relations, 172n6; Echelon system, 164–165, 175n24; intelligentsia, 1; internationalism, 128; Iraq War, 157n22; *la caduca Europa*, 35; Latin American attitudes toward, 35; polling anti-American views, 9; rift between it and U.S., 10; ruling class, 1; Rumsfeld on, 35, 129; study of anti-Americanism, 11; United States, 157n22; U.S. compared to, 128, 138–139. *See also specific countries, such as* Britain; Germany

European Union (EU): Bosnian genocide, 169; decision makers, 227; East European countries, 153, 188; economic power, 138; genetically modified foods, 182; nationalism, 227; United States, 192

Euroweenies: American media, 129

Evangelism: American ties overseas, 118–119

Fabela, Isidro: U.S. power, 20

Falklands War (1982): British greatness, 169

Family Embrace (Kojima), 212–213

Fanon, Franz: idol of third world, 287

Fascism: in United States, 75, 81

Felipe, Liliana: September 11 attacks (2001), 76–77

Feminism: Latin America, 41

Ferguson, Niall: British imperial experience, 13n8

55 Days at Peking (film), 235–236

First National City Bank: Butler's support, 2

Florika: posters, 279

Fondation Saint-Simon: dissolution, 152; leader, 149; "modernizing project," 149–150

Ford Motor Company: in Argentina, 26

Foreign investment: in Cuba, 57, 64

Foreign trade: Cuba's, 59

Foucault, Michel: in China, 245

Fox, Vincente: Bush and, George W., 36; Mexico as back yard, 44n8

Fox News: Anglo-American Francophobia, 145–146, 154n3

France, 144–157; '68-ers ('68 *gauchistes*), 145, 148–149; 1960s in, 145–146; Algerian War of Independence, 147; American imperialism, 146–147; anti-Americanism, 125, 152, 154; anti-capitalism, 147; anti-colonialism, 147; anti-imperialism, 147; "Axis of Weasel," 129; conservatives, 145–146; countryside, 152; *Daily News* cover, 146; eclipse of politics by ethics, 148–149; failure to remember history, 23; French Revolution, 149; globalization, 145, 152; Indochina War (1946-1954), 259; Iraq, 93; Iraq War, 144; May '68 events, 147–148; media intellectuals, 148; neoliberalism, 145, 152; "philo-Américans," 145; political culture, 152–153; Powell's threat, 129; social policy, 151; social science, 150–153; strikes against proposed changes to social security system (1995), 150–153, 156n16; think tanks, 149–150; third-worldism, 148, 155n7; "totalitarianism" in, 149; trade with Cuba, 59; United States, 149; U.S. compared to, 146–147, 152–153; *Wall Street Journal* on, 144; Zoellick on, 144

Francophobia: Anglo-American, 145–146, 154n3

Free-market fundamentalism: anti-Americanism, 27

Friedman, Thomas: Iraq War, 17; McDonald's, 28

Fuentes, Carlos: *La Muerte de Artemio Cruz* (The Death of Artemio Cruz), 41–43

Fuentes, Claudio: militaries in Latin America, 80

¡Fuera imperialistas yanquis!: Cuba, 55, 73

Fuguet, Alberto: McOndo group, 45n26

Fujimori, Alberto: Americano, 303

Fujioka: *The History Textbooks Don't Teach*, 218; textbook revision in Japan, 215–217

Fukuyama, Francis: end of history, 130

Furet, François: anti-Americanism defined, 149; death, 152; Fondation Saint-Simon, 149

Gaitskell, Hugh: British nuclear weapons, 167

Gandin, Greg: anti-Americanism, 242

Healey, Denis: on Thatcher, 163
Hearst, William Randolph: Villa and, 32–33
Helms-Burton Bill (1995): anti-Americanism, 57; end runs around, 59
Heston, Charlton: *55 Days at Peking*, 235
Hirohito: MacArthur photo, 213
Hiroshima Nagasaki World Peace Mission: delegates from, 305
Hispanism: in Latin America, 70
History: failure to remember, 23; periodizing it, 238–241
History Textbooks Don't Teach, The (Fujioka), 218
Hitchens, Christopher: break with the Left, 288
Hitler's Willing Executioners (Goldhagen), 136
Ho Chi Minh: idol of third world, 287; United States, 259, 283
Hobsbawm, Eric: American Empire, 300n16
Hoffman, Stanley: European anti-Americanism, 125–126
Hoggart, Richard: American culture, 168
Hollander, Paul: American anti-Americanism, 245–246; *Anti-Americanism: Rational and Irrational*, 11–12, 245; hostility toward U.S., 26; types of anti-Americanism, 17–18
Homeland Security. *See* United States Department of Homeland Security
Honduras: Butler in, 2
Hoover, J. Edgar: counterintelligence programs, 306
House Committee on Un-American Activities: CIA, 284–285
Hoyo kazoku (Kojima), 212–213
Hughes, Langston: "Let America Be America Again," 312
Human, All Too Human (Nietzsche), 248
Huntington, Samuel: *The Clash of Civilizations*, 88
Hussein, King of Jordan: abrogation of democracy, 116
Hussein, Saddam: American support, 32, 113; nationalization policies, 91; reinstatement, 199; Rumsfeld and, 92, 102n15, 114; satrap, 264

Idealism: nationalism, 292
Ideas That Conquered the World: Peace, Democracy, and Free Markets (Mandelbaum), 26
Ignatieff, Michael: acceptance of imperialism, 8; American Empire, 5, 128, 269n19, 289
IMF (International Monetary Fund): Argentina, 71; Bush administration, 71; control by, 294; globalization, 251; Korea, 224; Krugman on, 71; policies, 4; state-breaking, 267; U.S. armed forces, 294; weak states, 267
Imperialism: British experience, 13n8; liberal imperialism, 7; new imperialism, 7–9; rivalry among imperial powers, 22; wars and, 146. *See also* American imperialism; Anti-imperialism
"In the Kingdom of Terrorism" (Ashcroft), 60
India: pro-Americanism, 110
Indochina War (1946-1954): United States, 259
Intelligence operations: British-American cooperation, 164–165; Carnivore, 165; Echelon system, 164–165, 175n24; Government Communications Headquarters (GCHQ), 164; National Security Agency (NSA), 164; SIGINT, 164; Total Information Awareness (TIA), 165
Internationalism: American anti-Americanism, 292–293; Europe, 128; the Left (in United States), 296–297; trend toward, 292; Washington Consensus, 289
Iran: Afghanistan, 93; anti-Americanism, 112; Islamic revolution, 91, 92, 112; Mossadegh government overthrow, 259; United States, 91–92, 111, 259; the West to, 110
Iran-Iraq War (1980-1988): Reagan administration, 113; United States, 89, 92
Iraq: Baath party, 111, 114, 116; economy, 120; etatism, 122; France, 93; Gulf War (1990-1991), 92, 169–171; Kurds, 114; no-fly zones, 93, 165; Operation Desert Fox, 165; regime violence, 95; Russia, 93; sanctions, 92–93, 103n17, 113; United States, 92–93, 95, 114, 116 (*see also* Iraq War (2003–); weapons inspections, 93;

Britain, 158–165, 169–171; Cambodia, 264; Canada, 37; China, 237, 247, 252–254, 256–259, 260, 265–268, 309; China War (1931-1941), 256; cold war as, 255; Colombia, 283; counterinsurgency, 3, 24–25, 37, 291; Cyprus coup attempt (1974), 183–184; democracy, 115–116, 255; Egypt, 91, 116; Empire, 139, 162–163, 269n19; essentialist view, 107, 112; estrangement from rest of the world, 137; European Union, 192; foundations, 106–107; France, 149; free-market fundamentalism, 27; Germany, 126–129; Good Neighbor Policy, 20, 51; Greece, 182, 183–184, 186, 188; Grosfoguel on, 76; Gulf War (1990-1991), 92; Haiti, 283; Helms-Burton Bill (1995), 57, 59; humanitarian interventions, 289; idealistic justifications, 22, 292; "imperial but not imperialist," 159; imperialism, 2–3, 8–9, 146–147, 154, 159; incoherence, 294; Indochina War (1946-1954), 259; "inexperienced colossus," 167; intelligence operations, 164–165; intervention, 2, 19, 33–34, 91–92, 93–94, 99–100, 104n20, 139, 200, 254; Iran, 91–92, 111, 259; Iran-Iraq War, 89, 92; Iraq, 92–93, 95, 114, 116; Israel, 91, 94–95; Israeli-Palestinian conflict, 94–95, 104n22, 128; Japan, 201–204, 208, 209–212, 219, 228, 239, 260, 262; Korea, 221, 224, 228–229, 252; Korean War (1950-1953), 259–261; Kyoto Accord, 128; Latin America, 2, 18, 19–22, 27, 35–37, 69, 71, 72–73, 79–80; leftist critics, 107; Libya, 111, 169; Mexico, 32–33, 72; Middle East, 90–96, 100, 115–116; military might, 139, 295; military spending, 138; Monroe Doctrine, 2, 3, 37, 110; North Korea, 223–224, 225–226, 227–228; overthrow of Guatemalan government (1954), 20; a paper tiger, 243; Pax Americana, 128, 158; Philippine War (1899-1902), 261–263; Point Four program, 25; post-cold war, 127; preemption, 8, 138, 254, 289; promotion of armed conflict, 91–95, 100, 257, 260, 264; Protestantism, 106–107; Puerto Rico, 22; Punitive Expedition against Mexico,

33–34; "red team," 253; "rogue states," 87–88, 289; satraps, 264; Saudi Arabia, 96–97, 116; Schurz's Law, 262; September 11 attacks (2001), 307–308; Suez Crisis, 90, 110–111; support for political Islam, 94, 96–97, 99, 100, 114–115; Taft-Katsuhara agreement, 262; Taiwan, 257–259; Truman Doctrine, 3, 184; Turkey, 182, 183–184, 188; United Nations, 128; Venezuela, 283; Vietnam, 259; Vietnam War (1960-1975), 265; war memories, 136; Wilson's idealism, 22. *See also* War on terrorism

Unlimited War (Chinese publication), 244, 250n19

Unsinkable Aircraft Carrier, The (Campbell), 169

Uzbekistan: attitudes toward U.S., 10

Vargas Vila, José María: U.S. power, 20

Vasconcelos, José: *The Cosmic Race*, 70

Venezuela: neoliberalism, 27, 45n27; populism, 267; United States, 283

Ventura, Jesse: in Cuba, 59

Veríssimo, José: Americans, 38

Vietnam: Cambodia, 264; state as moral actor, 267; United States, 259

Vietnam War (1960-1975): Britain, 167–168; casualties, 261; extent, 261; Japan, 207, 210, 221; Korea, 255; Korean War, 260; MacNamara on, 261; United States, 265; Vietnam syndrome, 260; world reaction, 3

Villa, Pancho: American support, 32; attack on U.S., 33; Division del Norte, 32; Griffith and, 33, 43n1; Hearst and, 33; hunt for, 33–34; Reed and, 33; uprising against Diaz, 32; Wilson and, 32–33, 43n1

Villepin, Dominique de: "well-groomed," 154n3

Viñas, David: September 11 attacks (2001), 76

Wall Street Journal: France, 144

Wallace, William: post-cold war U.S., 127

Wallerstein, Immanuel: Iraq War rationale, 157n22

Wang Yusheng: preemptive theory, 254

War crimes: Cambodia, 264